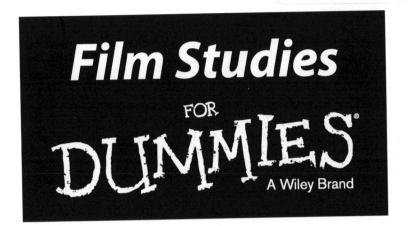

Film Studies

FOR

DUMMIES®

A Wiley Brand

by James Cateridge

FOR

DUMMIES®

A Wiley Brand

Film Studies For Dummies®

Published by: **John Wiley & Sons, Ltd.,** The Atrium, Southern Gate, Chichester, www.wiley.com

This edition first published 2015

© 2015 John Wiley & Sons, Ltd, Chichester, West Sussex.

Registered office

John Wiley & Sons Ltd, The Atrium, Southern Gate, Chichester, West Sussex, PO19 8SQ, United Kingdom

For details of our global editorial offices, for customer services and for information about how to apply for permission to reuse the copyright material in this book please see our website at www.wiley.com.

Wiley publishes in a variety of print and electronic formats and by print-on-demand. Some material included with standard print versions of this book may not be included in e-books or in print-on-demand. If this book refers to media such as a CD or DVD that is not included in the version you purchased, you may download this material at www.dummies.com. For more information about Wiley products, visit www.wiley.com.

Designations used by companies to distinguish their products are often claimed as trademarks. All brand names and product names used in this book are trade names, service marks, trademarks or registered trademarks of their respective owners. The publisher is not associated with any product or vendor mentioned in this book.

For general information on our other products and services, please contact our Customer Care Department within the U.S. at 877-762-2974, outside the U.S. at (001) 317-572-3993, or fax 317-572-4002. For technical support, please visit www.wiley.com/techsupport.

For technical support, please visit www.wiley.com/techsupport.

A catalogue record for this book is available from the British Library.

ISBN 978-1-118-88659-5 (paperback); ISBN 978-1-118-88653-3 (ebk);

ISBN 978-1-118-88656-4 (ebk)

Printed in Great Britain by TJ International, Padstow, Cornwall

10 9 8 7 6 5 4 3 2 1

Contents at a Glance

Table of Contents

Introduction

You may already consider yourself a film buff – or get called a film geek behind your back (absolutely nothing wrong with that, all the best film students and film scholars start out that way). If you have a passion for film of any kind, hold on to it. Wear your film-geek label with pride.

But if you want to become a successful film student, you need to add a few tools to your toolbox, which is where this book comes in. A good film student doesn't simply memorise film facts – who played who in what and whether they received Oscars that year. After all, the Internet now remembers all these details. Instead, a film student can take a movie to bits to see how it works, place it into its historical or social context, or use it to help explain and understand aspects such as politics and national identity. Film studies isn't about *what* and *who,* it's about *how* and most importantly *why.*

If you take a class in film studies – or choose to pursue a degree in it – I'm afraid that you're going to have to put up with lots of sniggering about 'Mickey Mouse studies'. Everybody watches films, don't they? Does that mean universities should hand out degrees with subscriptions to Netflix? Ignore these people. They're just jealous.

Unlike many other forms of art, films were and continue to be genuinely, staggeringly popular – and some people confuse popularity with stupidity. But that's the stupidest mistake of all. To be popular, films need to resonate deeply with great swathes of the world's population while also providing a direct emotional connection with every single ticket-buying audience member. And that, in my humble opinion, is rather clever.

To those who question the value of your chosen subject, remind them that studying novels or plays was considered frivolous and ridiculous as recently as 100 years ago. The world has changed, and cinema has reflected and sometimes contributed to these changes.

For those lucky enough to study or teach it, film studies isn't just a hobby – it's an academic discipline that stretches and tests your skills and knowledge. Unfortunately, when film became a discipline, it also acquired bucket loads of jargon. And nothing is more likely to make you feel like a dummy than a dense, unreadable book that presumes you already know a lot more than you do.

So this book is *Film Studies For Dummies* not because I think you're an idiot (on the contrary, you've already shown wise judgement in reading this far!)

but because I'm aware of the barriers that some (but not all) film studies books put up to readers. Don't worry, this book doesn't do barriers.

About This Book

Scholars have a few conventional ways of writing about films, which generally involve keeping things as clear and uncluttered as possible. So I use such conventions in this book to help you get accustomed to them.

I put film titles into *italics* to help separate them visually from the rest of the text. The first time I mention a film in a section, I include a year after it in brackets. This year is when the film was first released in cinemas, not when it was produced (which often takes several years anyway). The release date gives you an instant idea of historical context and avoids confusion between films with similar or identical titles.

When talking about film characters, knowing who plays them is important. So the first time I mention a character, the actor's name appear in brackets afterwards. Some film studies books also give the director's name in brackets after the film's first mention, but I don't follow that convention. Doing so tends to signal a reverence for directors over and above the other people who collaborate on a film, which is a matter of some debate in film studies (as you find out as you read on).

Films made in other countries around the world usually have two titles, one in the original language and an English translation. The one that I place first and use for subsequent mentions often comes down to familiarity. Some foreign films are very well known by their English titles and so I place that first, for example *The Seventh Seal* (*Det sjunde inseglet*) (1957). Whereas others tend to keep their original title and sometimes require no English translation, such as *La Dolce Vita* (1960).

When analysing and describing films, I introduce certain technical terms to you. Most are clear and easy enough to understand and use. However the terms used to describe *shots* (short sections of continuous action which are edited together into longer *sequences*) can cause confusion. To be clear from the word go, I have stuck to the following conventions when describing the amount of *time* that a shot takes or the *distance* of the camera from the shot:

- ✔ **Close-up:** The camera is close to the subject (such as an actor) and it therefore fills the frame.

- ✔ **Wide shot:** The camera is far away from the subject and it appears small in the frame, surrounded by its environment.

✔ **Short take:** The shot is over in a few seconds before it is replaced by another image through editing.

✔ **Long take:** The shot lasts for a long time, such as minutes or even (very occasionally) hours.

Finally, notice that I coop up some sections of text in grey boxes. Poor sidebars. They contain detailed information or specific examples that you don't strictly need to remember. You can ignore them if you want. But doing so makes make them sad.

Foolish Assumptions

You may have some assumptions about me as a film scholar. You probably think that I spend too much time watching films and need to get out more. You aren't far wrong. But enough about me, here's what I think about you:

✔ You already love films, have seen plenty of them and want to see more.

✔ You may well be coming to the end of your formal education and considering your options for further study. May I suggest doing film studies? This book can help you decide whether it's right for you and get you going in the correct direction.

✔ If you're already doing film studies, well done. Good decision. This book can serve as your handy reference guide to important topics – or as a way of finding new methods or theories to use.

✔ If you have no interest in doing film studies at university, but simply want to deepen your knowledge of one of life's great pleasures – watching movies – great. You're also in the right place.

If any or several of the preceding sound like you, read on.

Icons Used in This Book

If you like films, you're probably a visual person. So this book uses the zippy visual convention of icons to draw your eyes to important sections or help you scan through for the bits you want.

This icon indicates handy hints and small activities that you can do to help practise the big ideas.

Some bits of this book are more important than others. They may be key concepts or facts that you need to grasp in order to move forward. This icon highlights them so that you don't have to use a highlighter pen.

Examples make all ideas easier to get your head around, and so this book features plenty of mini case studies of films. To pick them out, follow the icon.

If you're scared of theory, this icon may not have the desired effect. But I hope that this book shows that you can understand the difficult concepts and cure your theory-phobia.

Film scholars love a good argument. This icon signals when two different ways of understanding a particular topic exist.

Beyond the Book

In addition to the amazing content that you hold in your hands, this book also includes companion digital content. Check out the free Cheat Sheet at www.dummies.com/cheatsheet/filmstudies for definitions of essential film studies terms, quick bite-sized chunks of meaty film theory and a handy overview of film history broken down into well-known movements.

Each part of this book features a link to an online article by yours truly. Check out each part page or go to www.dummies.com/extras/filmstudies to find articles that extend the content covered in the book.

Where to Go from Here

Film studies is big, and so is this book. If you have no idea where to begin, I recommend reading Chapter 1 first, because it serves as a kind of overview of the whole field. I hope that it starts those little light bulbs going off above your head. If this happens, look for more on that topic in the contents page and off you go.

Each part brings together chapters that look at films in similar ways. To explore different types of films, Part II is your place to start. Or if you want to get theoretical, head straight to Part IV. You can choose to read the book from beginning to end if you like, or you can jump around from section to section. The choice is yours. Enjoy the ride.

Part I
Getting Started with Film Studies

In this part . . .

- ✔ Appreciate the art of storytelling on film.
- ✔ Differentiate the contributions of film professionals, including screenwriters, directors, cinematographers, editors and many others.
- ✔ Gaze at film stars and go behind their glamorous images.
- ✔ Analyse film narratives, dissect shots and sequences, and understand the editing process.

Chapter 1

Becoming a Fantastic Film Student

In This Chapter

▶ Starting your film studies journey

▶ Analysing the building blocks of film

▶ Appreciating the importance of films to the world

Film studies is about appreciating, understanding and explaining the greatest art form of the 20th century, which despite repeated predictions to the contrary is still going strong. The discipline involves research into and analysis of films, first and foremost, but also film-makers, film cultures, the film industry and film audiences.

To fulfil its aims, film studies borrows the best methods and theories from other academic areas, notably literary (or other cultural) studies and philosophy, as well as political science, sociology and psychology. In addition, analysing films uses similar tools to analysing paintings and photographs, but with the essential addition of movement.

If you already love film and want to become a film student, you've come to the right place. In this chapter, I take you through the basics of studying film: from learning how to watch films critically, to understanding the different types of film writing that you can use for research, to justifying the meaning and importance of cinema for the wider world. Everyone knows that film is important, but as a film student you need to develop ways to say *why* and *how* it matters.

Upping Your Cinematic Game

To study films, you have to do more than simply watch them; you have to try to *understand* them, which doesn't just happen – studying films requires time and effort. And put on your leggings, like the kids from *Fame* (1980), cos right here's where you start paying. In sweat.

Going beyond merely watching films

Luckily, many (if not most) people love watching films. But many people decide that simply enjoying movies is enough for them, or even worry that studying films may destroy the pleasure they take from them.

You needn't worry about ruining the fun of watching films as you step into the world of film studies. Studying films not only helps you to understand why everyone needs a bit of escapism, but also offers entirely new ways to enjoy cinema:

- ✔ Understanding cinematic narrative structures can make even the dumbest action movie seem quite profound (check out Chapters 4 and 5).

- ✔ Knowing about film history can make a 100-year-old silent film as fresh and exciting as the day it was first screened (see Chapter 2 to read about early cinema).

- ✔ Appreciating the many techniques, skills and creative decisions that go into creating a successful picture can keep you interested even when the story sags.

- ✔ Viewing a wider range of films builds up your reference points and helps you understand how the classics influence contemporary cinema.

- ✔ Reading and appreciating film criticism means that you always have an opinion about what you just saw. Prepare yourself to start winning pub debates with ease.

Film studies is fun, yes, but that doesn't necessarily mean that it's easy. You've been watching films in your own particular way for most of your life, and making the effort to step back and analyse something so instinctive and pleasurable can be quite difficult. Like trying to explain why you love ice cream – or sausages!

To start doing this kind of analysis, I recommend starting with your favourite film of all time. I don't mean the film you use as your favourite to impress people (step forward, *Citizen Kane*). I mean your genuine favourite, the one you watch while you're ill in bed or after getting back from a late night out.

Ask yourself what you enjoy about this film: the familiar storyline or the rewarding pay-off when the protagonists complete their journeys? Do you relate to one particular character or does the film showcase your favourite star (the person you want to be like or be with)? Or does the music – or the gorgeous images – keep you coming back?

Whatever your main reason (and be honest), focus on that and watch your film again, by yourself with no interruptions. This time, take notes. Doing so is really important. Write down every thought that occurs to you about how the film works and why you find it enjoyable. Even draw pictures if you want to. Stick men shooting each other can be a surprisingly effective way to capture and recall what is happening on screen.

If you can manage to view and take notes successfully with your favourite film, congratulations, you've broken free from the chains of habitual watching and are now analysing, assessing and being critical. That's where you need to start.

Connecting film studies to other stuff you can study

Film studies is inherently *interdisciplinary,* which means that it steals the best theories and research methods from other fields of study and applies them to films. This aspect of film studies is useful, because even if you've never studied films before you may well have encountered a few film studies methods already.

I hope that the following experiences and related methods come flooding back to you as you read this book.

Studying stories

Analysing storytelling is a process that's very similar regardless of whether you find the story in a book, on the stage or on the silver screen. So if you spent any time grappling with literary classics at school, you have a basic understanding of concepts such as characterisation and narrative point of view, which you can apply to films.

Look a little deeper and you soon realise that some of the theories you use to understand books and those you use in film studies are strikingly similar. For example, you may be familiar with the notion that you can boil down all stories to seven (or even just three) basic universal plots, which have entertained humans throughout history.

This notion of *universal stories* or *myths* comes from a branch of literary theory called *structuralism,* which also happens to be useful when studying films. Even Hollywood producers use a type of shorthand all the time when describing movies:

- ✔ Boy meets girl. Boy hates girl. Boy falls for girl. Boy loses girl. Boy fights to get girl back. Girl gives in.

- ✔ Girl versus shark. Shark wins. Boy versus shark. Boy loses first round due to personality flaw. Boy tackles personality flaw. Boy beats shark.

- ✔ Cowboy rides into border town. Cowboy shoots bad people. Cowboy rides off into the sunset.

Breaking films down into basic plot elements – and implying that the same stories are repeated over and over with only minor changes – is pure structuralism. So you see, Hollywood isn't as stupid as it often seems. (For much more on structuralism, flip to Chapter 13.)

Studying people and places

Watching films is an enormously popular activity across the world, and like any large-scale human activity, you can use methods from the social sciences to analyse and explain the phenomenon. When you take a sociological approach to studying film, you're less interested in the films themselves and more interested in the people who consume or produce them.

Audience research is an important branch of film studies, which gathers data from its human subjects in many different ways. You can achieve broad surveys by using simple questionnaires, or gain more detailed and nuanced analysis through individual interviews or focus groups. The data provided can be *quantitative,* such as percentages or charts, or *qualitative,* like explanations of behaviour or emotional responses.

Cinema is a global phenomenon, and so analysing films in relation to places can be helpful. The long-standing and continued interest in studies of national cinemas is the most obvious spatial concern of film studies, as Part III of this book attests. But the national character of film has also been tested by film scholars driven by the concept of *transnationalism.* For example, studying the films of a population who are displaced or dispersed across many countries or even continents provides a transnational perspective on so-called migrant or *diasporic* cinema.

Studying the past

To understand how cinema works in a particular place, you also need to think about how it developed over time. Therefore another important area of film studies draws from historical theories and methods. Historical research relies on traces of evidence to help illuminate the past, and so archives of material (including film archives) are vital.

Of course films themselves are a kind of historical evidence, particularly the *actuality films* (short scenes taken from real life) that were popular in the early days of cinema (see Chapter 2). Just take a look at a few of the Lumière brothers' films or those of Mitchell and Kenyon in Britain (I delve into British cinema of all sorts in Chapter 10). You soon realise just how much you can discover from looking into the eyes of factory workers as they left to go home at the end of a regular working day, over a century ago.

Focusing on creativity, industry and technology

Film is such a rich, varied and important object of study because it exists at the intersection of three major forces of the modern era: creativity, industry and technology – each of which I explore in the following sections.

Considering creativity

Of course film is an art form, but stop for a moment to think about what that really means. What exactly are the creative decisions that make one film different from another? What makes films 'art'?

During the first few decades of film as it found its feet as a mass medium of entertainment, only crazy radicals thought of films as art. Back then everyone knew that art hung on gallery walls and had absolutely nothing to do with what entertained people on their evenings off.

But in the years following World War II, when popular cinema was at its zenith, a few French radicals came up with an argument that changed the way people think about film: *the auteur theory*. Borrowing from the literary Romantics, the auteur critics argued that films were the expression of a single creative force: the director.

According to auteur theorists, directors such as Alfred Hitchcock, Howard Hawks and John Ford weren't simply hacks for hire; they were *artists*. Their personal visions and imaginations were powerful enough to overcome any institutional barriers. The auteur theory is attractive but problematic, because unlike books and poems commercial Hollywood films are massive collaborative projects (I talk a lot more about Hollywood in Chapter 9).

Whether you agree with the auteur theory or not (and film studies encourages well-argued disagreements), at least it raises the possibility that films can be great works of art. (Dive into Chapter 14 and see how the auteur theory works – or doesn't work – for your film-viewing experience.)

Other theoretical frameworks that scholars later applied to film downplay the role of the artist/director and argue that film is an art form because it developed its own specific language and grammar (see Chapters 13 and 15).

Some film-makers like to think of themselves as more arty than others, such as radical types. *Avant-garde cinema* positions itself against the mainstream language of film, subverts its rules and conventions, and denies its audience easy explanations or simple pleasures. I know, that doesn't sound like much fun, but don't dismiss it. At its best, avant-garde film innovates and leads where mainstream film later follows. (I bravely attempt to decipher avant-garde cinema in Chapter 7.)

And, of course, some films are literally art in the sense of being made of paintings or drawings: animated ones. The craft and technique of the greatest animation is dazzling: from Walt Disney's ornate features to inventive Looney Tunes cartoons (see Chapter 6 for more on these), not to mention world-beating Japanese anime (see Chapter 12).

But the most important way in which films are art is that they mean something to their audiences. The greatest art is emotionally engaging and helps you to discover a little bit more about the world and your place in it. I'm sure that certain films have played that role in your life. If not, trust me, you're watching the wrong kind of films.

Investigating industrial perspectives

Films cost a lot of money to make and can generate a lot of money in return. This simple, obvious fact means that you can't ignore economic issues when studying the movies. Yes, cinema is an art form, but unlike starving poets or misunderstood painters, struggling directors have to make financial deals to get their visions onto the screen while still finding ways to pay the bills.

Hollywood invests a great deal of time and effort (and money) trying to convince audiences that 'there's no business like show business', but this mantra is basically baloney. The same basic economic principles guide the behaviour of individuals and companies in the film industry as in every other type of business:

✔ Movie producers invest in products, which compete in a marketplace to make back their costs and (investors hope) deliver a healthy profit.

✔ Entertainment companies have to pay a range of employees, from top star actors (who can be male or female – wander star-struck to Chapter 3 for more) to the people who clean out their trailers.

✔ Film companies can grow, be bought out by other bigger companies or go bust.

Making films is different, however, to producing other industrial products, such as cars or chocolate bars, in some key ways:

✔ Each individual product is unique, and therefore risky, because demand for it is uncertain – which is why summer blockbusters tend to be sequels or remakes to mitigate the risk.

✔ Successful films have a practically unlimited shelf life and can go on generating revenue for decades to come.

✔ Films are complex creative products that require a diverse range of skills from many different people all at the same time. Just as a chain is only as strong as its weakest link, one of its major players performing below par can ruin a film. And everyone knows how reliable and consistent movie stars are, right?

✔ Reputation is the most valuable commodity for any film executive, director or actor. If you're a studio boss deciding whether to invest in a big budget production and you hear that the writer-director has recently fallen off the wagon, why be a schmuck and invest?

✔ Bad behaviour, technological setbacks or simple weather issues can easily throw intricate shooting schedules into chaos, haemorrhaging cash all over the place like blood in a Tarantino movie.

Many people in Hollywood repeat that you're only as good as your last picture, and the industry certainly has a brutal turnover of stars, directors, producers and studio bosses. The stakes are high, but the potential rewards are great. If you want job security, go work in a bank. On second thoughts. . . .

Thinking through technology

Cinema is truly an art form of the Victorian age. At its birth, it required huge, heavy machinery to record, develop and project moving images. Take a look at the design and style of these early machines (preferably in a museum or at least online) and you may be reminded of other great technological legacies of the 19th century, such as telephones and steam trains.

The technology that delivers the moving-picture experience has changed almost beyond recognition over the decades. The simplest way to see these changes is as a series of inevitable developments driving towards some theoretically perfect future technology: early moving pictures were silent and black and white, and so naturally sound and colour were later added.

But this way of thinking about technological development (known as *determinism*) has drawbacks. It assumes that consumers of early versions of the technology were unsatisfied because of its primitive state. No evidence exists that this was the case, just as it isn't true today. Were you aware that you wanted a high-definition TV screen until you first saw one in action? No: much more sensible to see a combination of factors driving cinema's technological development, most obviously connected to economic issues.

What tends to happen in reality is that an egghead invents an amazing new bit of technology, which is too expensive or risky to take up straight away. Eventually, one industry crisis or another causes someone to take the plunge. If it works, everyone jumps on the bandwagon – as happened with sound, colour, widescreen and 3D in the film industry.

To understand technological change you need to think carefully about the reasons that a technology *becomes widespread* at a particular time, which is often many years after it's theoretically possible. Check out the nearby sidebar 'Why sound came along when it did' for a great example.

Why sound came along when it did

The arrival of synchronised sound to the film industry in 1927 is the perfect example that what's most important isn't only the technology but usually the money that goes with it. Adding sound to film was technologically possible much earlier than 1927, but when early cinemas were booming the demand for change simply didn't exist.

Only in the late 1920s, as audience numbers faltered due to a deteriorating economy, did Warner Bros. decide to risk the innovation with much-loved stage performer Al Jolson in *The*

Jazz Singer (1927). The film was such a smash hit that 'the movies' very quickly became 'the talkies'.

Interestingly, the expense of investment in new projectors and sound systems was offset by savings on labour costs. Who got fired? Well, nearly every cinema in the world had at least one musician on the payroll, and many had bands and even full orchestras. These folks simply weren't needed thanks to synchronised sound. Don't play it again, Sam.

Writing about films: Reviews, criticism and academic style

In today's digital age, film scholars and film lovers have more ways than ever to write about film and to get that writing published. Even if all you do is post a couple of reviews on Amazon, you're a kind of film critic.

But to be a successful film student, you need to be able to tell the difference between different levels of writing about film. And of course, you have to do a bit of writing yourself.

Reviewing film reviewers

I'd like you to look back, way back into the mists of time, to that unbearably primitive era before the Internet. Imagine that you have a hankering to go to the pictures, but IMDb, Rotten Tomatoes and Ain't It Cool News don't exist. How on earth do you find out what's playing at your local cinema? And what's more, how do you know whether the films are any good or not?

Whether you remember it or not, just a few years ago you had to stand up (like some sort of cave-dweller), go to the shops and buy a newspaper or a film magazine just to be able to make that decision. The basic purpose of film reviewing before the Internet was informative. Reviewers had to have opinions, and their reviews had to make judgements on various films' quality, but these reviewers were permitted to be as personal and subjective as they liked.

Movie fans were therefore expected to find a reviewer or magazine whose opinion most closely matched their own and to consult them regularly. Of course, entertaining, well-written and pithy reviews also helped. Entertaining reviews can be worth reading even if you don't agree with the reviewers' verdicts. The best-known film journalists such as Pauline Kael, Roger Ebert or Mark Kermode develop their own distinctive style and stick to it.

As a film student, you probably end up using film reviews as part of your research at one point or another. If you're looking into a very old film, reviews may be the only source of printed information available. Even for more recent movies, reviews can be useful as barometers of how the film was received on its original release.

You can make the case that film reviews are representative of audience taste during a particular period, because if the readers never agreed with the reviewers' opinions, those writers wouldn't last long in the job.

But you also have to use reviews with caution, because you can't assume that audiences always agreed with reviewers, or that films considered classics today were recognised as such on first release. (Read 'Some like it *not*' for particularly surprising initial reactions to a few beloved movies.) If possible, you need to be aware of the editorial or political bias of the sources you use. In the UK, for example, don't be surprised to find broadsheets such as *The Guardian* acclaiming art-house releases that tabloids simultaneously slate.

Being critical about film criticism

The differences between film journalism and film criticism are subtle but important. Whereas film journalism aims primarily to inform, film criticism attempts to discuss, argue and educate. Film criticism tends to be research-driven and present a case that the writer deems original and important. Criticism is also historical, whereas journalism tends to require a topical hook. Instead of the newspaper or popular magazine, film criticism's natural home is the film journal, a publication that may support a film club or society or have loftier intellectual ambitions.

Some like it *not*

Film history is littered with examples of films that reviewers mauled on original release but are now considered classics:

✔ ***The Wizard of Oz*** **(1939)**: 'Displays no trace of imagination, good taste or ingenuity . . . I say it's a stinkeroo.' *The New Yorker*, 1939.

✔ ***Sunset Boulevard*** **(1950)**: 'A pretentious slice of Roquefort.' *The New Yorker*, 1950.

✔ ***Bonnie and Clyde*** **(1967)**: 'Like Bonnie and Clyde themselves, the film rides off in all directions and ends up full of holes.' *Time*, 1967.

✔ ***Star Wars*** **(1977)**: 'The only way that *Star Wars* could have been exciting was through its visual imagination and special effects. Both are unexceptional.' *The New Republic*, 1977.

Key examples of film journals in Europe and the US include:

- ✔ ***Close Up* (1927–33):** Claimed on its launch to be 'the first to approach films from the angles of art, experiment and possibility'. It was vital in establishing an intellectual film culture in Europe and is associated with the London Film Society, which was the first to screen radical films such as *Battleship Potemkin* (1925) in the UK.

- ✔ ***Cahiers du Cinéma* (1951–today):** Founded by André Bazin, whose writing on realism made him an influential early film theorist. *Cahiers . . .* is a great example of how film culture (such as a journal stuffed with new ideas) can go on to influence cinema itself, because many of its writers became the film-makers of the French New Wave in the late 1950s (see Chapters 11 and 14).

- ✔ ***Film Culture* (1954–99):** Run by Adolfas and Jonas Mekas. This journal provided a space to define and debate American Underground cinema (see Chapter 7). It also acted as a sort of mini award panel, giving prizes each year to independent film-makers.

Early film criticism, such as the writing found in these journals, was the direct forefather of film studies as an academic discipline. These critics were doing many of the things that film studies now does: theorising about how films work, researching films and directors, and writing a history of film-making and film language. Except that they were doing this work without the support of the university system, which wasn't ready to accept film as an art form worthy of study until the 1970s.

Partly for this reason, film journals are an essential source for film studies research. For film history, they provide vital information and colour, and many of the founding texts of film theory originated on their pages. Since film studies was allowed into the hallowed halls of academia, other important journals have come along, and these publications feature much of the best and most cutting-edge research in the field. They're now usually available online through membership of university libraries, and so you have no excuse not to use them in your own research projects.

Writing like a film student

One of the most difficult skills for new students of film to develop is achieving the right tone and style in written assignments: too conversational and you read like someone making stuff up as you go along; try to emulate the dense, complex style of much film theory and you're likely to come across as pretentious, dry or confused. Film studies writing is a continual balancing act between readability and being authoritative, while ensuring that your own voice comes through loud and clear.

As someone who reads a lot of student work, I offer the following list of dos and don'ts in your own writing:

- ✔ **Do decide what you want to argue and stick to it.** An argument can grow out of your initial reaction to a film, but you must refine it and put your argument into context. For example, if you find yourself unavoidably dragged into enjoying a terrible rom-com or lousy action film, think about what the film is doing to you and why you're trying to resist. You can, perhaps, come up with a convincing argument about different levels of engagement with a film.

- ✔ **Don't be afraid to include yourself.** Writing in the first person, particularly in an introduction or conclusion, sounds more confident and precise than the weirdly passive alternative: 'I carry out a Marxist analysis of the films of Sharon Stone' sounds much better than 'This essay carries out a Marxist analysis of the films of Sharon Stone'. What, by itself?

- ✔ **Do make sure that you know your film studies vocabulary and use the terms correctly.** A good glossary can really help. Nothing undermines the reader's confidence in your ability like getting the basics wrong. You can start with the Cheat Sheet for this particular publication (available online at www.dummies.com/cheatsheet/filmstudies), but the full, updated glossary in the tenth edition of David Bordwell and Kristin Thompson's *Film Art* (McGraw-Hill, 2012) is pretty hard to beat.

- ✔ **Don't over-praise the film or film-maker that you're writing about.** This can be difficult if you're using a film that's really special to you, but please resist the temptation to tell your readers that you love it. They want to know *why* you think it's interesting or important.

- ✔ **Do demonstrate your passion for your subject by throwing yourself into it with conviction.** Do as much reading as you can and have confidence in your own ideas. You aren't going to get top marks for every essay, but who does? At least you can learn and improve from your mistakes.

Studying Pictures, Moving and Otherwise

As I hope the preceding sections show, a lot more goes on in a typical movie sequence than simply moving the plot forward. Trying to understand how all the different components of cinema work together at the same time is pretty difficult. To help, the following sections describe how to strip away the layers of film-making craft and think about film, one element at a time.

Reading a painting or drawing

Wait a minute, you may be thinking, I don't remember signing up for an art-appreciation class. You're right. I'm not trying to convince you that every single frame of film is as significant to the world as Di Vinci's *Mona Lisa* or Van Gogh's *Sunflowers*. But knowing how to talk about two-dimensional artwork is worthwhile, because many of the visual conventions of film appear even more clearly in the older art forms of painting and drawing. Here are just a few:

- ✔ **Aesthetics:** Deals with the concepts of contrast, such as the balance between light and shade, harmony or randomness of composition, and symmetry or asymmetry. Each of these elements can have effects upon the viewer's vision, as well as suggesting psychological states. Bright, symmetrical images are calming or celebratory, whereas darkness and chaotic compositions are unsettling or disturbing.

- ✔ **Colours:** Have strong emotional connotations, which come from a combination of science and aesthetics. For example, you're taught that red signals danger in nature, and psychological testing demonstrates that humans find red stimulating and arousing. But different cultures interpret this effect differently. Westerners may make the mental leap from red to danger and sex, but within Chinese culture the colour is associated with innocent happiness and joy.

- ✔ **Composition:** All objects have a position in space and a relationship to one another that the artist chooses carefully. A painting's composition affects how the viewer 'reads' it. Horizontal and vertical lines can structure the planes of the image and diagonals are associated with perspective and therefore depth.

- ✔ **Space:** Illusions of space and depth are central to how viewers perceive a flat image in two dimensions. Realistic perspective uses decreasing object size to suggest increased distance from the viewer, and landscape painting can employ atmospheric effects as space moves into the distance. *Perspective* also implies a viewpoint, which can be that of the viewer or of an implied other, affecting the meaning of the image.

To further demystify these terms from the art world, you could try getting hold of a copy of *Art For Dummies* (John Wiley & Sons, 1999) by Thomas Hoving or *Art History For Dummies* (John Wiley & Sons, 2007) by Jessie Bryant Wilder.

Remember that people from different cultures or historical periods attach different meanings to aesthetic qualities such as space, colour and composition. I'm not suggesting that you don't use these ideas when analysing film, simply that you don't become too prescriptive or culturally myopic as to assume that everyone sees in the same way.

Reading a photograph

Building on some of the basic aesthetic terms in the preceding section, you can take things a step further and think about photographs. The key difference between paintings and photographs is obvious: paintings are imaginative representations whereas photographs are mechanical reproductions of reality. This simple difference, however, has far-reaching implications for photography and film, including issues of realism.

You can look at a photograph and apply the same analytical tools you use for paintings. Photographers employ composition, space and (sometimes) colour in similar ways, with presumably equivalent physiological and emotional effects on the viewer, although again these responses may be culturally specific. Furthermore, photographers can manipulate depth and perspective via lens technology and adjust *focus* to provide 'flat' or 'deep-focus' images.

Viewers presume that a photograph is a chosen image from pre-existing reality, and so how the photographer *frames* the image is vital. A close-up, particularly of a human face, provides intense, stimulating detail, but omits the environment that provides emotional context. For example, a tight close-up of a child crying may provoke an anxious response because you don't know what's causing the child to cry. Wider-angle framing includes this context, in part, but all photographs still have an implied larger space, which is excluded from the image itself.

The ease with which people can produce and reproduce photographs (compared to paintings) means that these images have acquired vital roles in public and private lives. News reportage, paparazzi shots and undercover reporting all rely on photography's claim to 'truth' and its relationship with reality. Meanwhile snaps of your children playing, fondly remembered holidays and portraits of loved ones who are no longer living are a crucial part of the visual texture of your family life and history, and by extension of social media such as Facebook.

These everyday uses of photography provide frames of reference affecting how you 'read' photographs. Film-makers are extremely sensitive to these meanings and use still images in many different ways. For a good example, check out the opening sequence of period gangster flick *Bonnie and Clyde* (1967), which consists of a succession of antique snapshots and family portraits, some of which are of the real gangsters, and some of the actors (Warren Beatty and Faye Dunaway) playing them. Whether real or faked, these domestic, mundane images serve to humanise the legendary killers.

Capturing movement in film

Well, they ain't called 'the movies' for nothing. Movement is so vital to the experience of cinema that, for the first film spectators, it was practically all that mattered. The subjects of the earliest films screened in public were trains rolling into stations and people flooding out of factory gates – audiences were astounded and enraptured. Moving pictures brought deathly still images back to life and captured moments onto celluloid for posterity. Fast-forward over a century to digital cinema, and films are more kinetic and mobile than ever. (I discuss the changing face of 21st-century film in Chapter 16.)

So when analysing films, you need to be able to discuss composition, colour and framing as for a still image, while clearly not ignoring the fact that film images move. Not only do objects and people within the film frame move, the frame itself is often moving due to shifts in camera angle or placement.

Trying to capture, describe and analyse the different levels of movement in film can be rather challenging, and so consider them in turn:

✔ **Camera movement:** As well as staying still, cameras can move in different ways:

- *Pan* from side to side.

- *Tilt* up and down, keeping space uniform but reframing to allow character movement.

- *Track* (that is, move in space) alongside characters as they move horizontally.

Also, *crane shots* can create more spectacular vertical movements that often signal the beginning and end of films or sequences.

✔ **Lens movement:** A camera can stay completely still and simulate rapid movement into or away from an object using zoom lenses. Spotting this technique can be tricky, and so you need to look for the flattening of depth that occurs with zooming. Most difficult of all to describe is the simultaneous camera and lens movement known by cinematographers as a *dolly zoom*. This shot holds the actor in frame at a consistent size but the background appears to fall away. You can spot its disorientating effect in *Vertigo* (1958) and *Jaws* (1975).

✔ **Objects moving:** Cognitive research shows that your eyes are instantly drawn to moving objects, particularly if the rest of the frame is still. Film-makers use this fact to their advantage, such as in the clichéd horror-movie shot that holds on an empty room before something shifts almost imperceptibly in the corner. You may find the terminology from dance or performance studies useful when describing the motion of people.

✔ **Speed of film:** Optical (and now digital) effects can slow down time, speed it up or pause it completely, as you often see in action cinema. But independent film-makers such as Martin Scorsese and Quentin Tarantino also use these effects: think of the freeze-frames in *Goodfellas* (1990) or the slow-mo group walk in *Reservoir Dogs* (1992).

Expressing Why Film Matters to the World

If you're reading this book you're probably a bit of a film geek – nothing wrong with that, welcome to the club – and so obviously film means something to you. But does it matter to everyone else? The following sections tackle this question by focusing on some of the issues that film has explored in the past – and continues to do so in profound ways.

Probing into politics

Some films are openly political, in that they make an argument about some kind of social injustice:

- ✔ **Avant-garde film:** Many of the radical artists who make experimental, avant-garde films are politically motivated. The early Surrealists such as Luis Buñuel wanted to shock audiences out of their complacency by revealing how weird everyday life is. More recently, feminist film-makers such as Laura Mulvey experimented with new forms of film language that don't marginalise or objectify women.

- ✔ **Documentary film:** Has a long and (mostly) honourable tradition of trying to record the world as it is and bring important issues to wider public attention. Just think about the fuss that Michael Moore's *Fahrenheit 9/11* (2004) caused and you see that documentary film-makers continue to play a role in global political debate. I delve deeper into documentaries in Chapter 8.

- ✔ **Fiction film:** These movies are often about politics too. The hothouse atmosphere of the American capital is the perfect setting for satires, thrillers and biopics such as *Mr Smith Goes to Washington* (1939), *All the President's Men* (1976) or *Lincoln* (2012). But films don't have to be about the political process itself to have political agendas, as illustrated by the films of Sergei Eisenstein, Jean-Luc Godard and Ken Loach.

- ✔ **Propaganda film:** The persuasive power of the documentary also has a dark side, as the propaganda produced during World War II demonstrates. For example, Leni Riefenstahl's *Triumph of the Will* (*Triumph des Willens*) (1935) reached new artistic heights for the documentary form but is forever tarnished by the Nazi regime that commissioned it (for more on this film's difficult place in cinema history, see Chapter 8).

That's all very well, you may be thinking, but the majority of film audiences don't choose to watch 'political' films. They may occasionally stray into a well-made, Oscar-nominated biopic about a political or historical figure, but they're unlikely to sit through a hard-hitting documentary let alone an avant-garde experiment deconstructing their everyday lives. Doesn't this mean that the political impact of film is limited to a specialised, niche audience and that political film-makers are, in effect, preaching to the converted?

Actually, no, because one of the major lessons of film theory is that all film is political – even the silliest, most frivolous musical or the campest, trashiest sci-fi film. Yes, even the films of Michael Bay. Especially the films of Michael Bay, in fact, because so many people choose to watch and enjoy them. The key concept here is *ideology,* and it comes from the writings of Karl Marx and his followers. I explore ideology in depth in Chapter 13, but for now you just need to remember that all film is political, whether it's explicitly about politics or about enormous, shape-shifting robots bashing the hell out of each other.

Reviewing race and nationality

If all is political, as I suggest in the preceding section, you may be thinking in what ways? Well, start with the fairly obvious point that the majority of films represent human beings on screen, being themselves (or some version of themselves) in documentaries or playing characters in fiction films.

The word 'represent' is important here, and you may want to think of it with a hyphen: *re*-present. Film is never a straightforward capturing and relaying of reality, a simple presentation of people on screen. It's a *re*-presentation, because what appears on screen is inevitably altered in some way.

The idea of *re*-presentation is important because human societies consist of different social groups that are rarely equal to each other. In predominantly white Western societies, people from ethnic minorities often face prejudice and discrimination in their everyday lives. The portrayal of ethnic groups in popular culture, such as in novels, TV shows or films (mostly made by white middle-class people), embodies and repeats this prejudice. The discrimination may be unthinking or unintentional, but it's nonetheless hurtful and damaging.

Viewed from today's perspective, many *classical* Hollywood films (which aren't just 'classic' as in 'great', but also made during the period between 1930 and 1960 known as Classical Hollywood) perpetuate stereotypes or simplistic representations of people of colour. The civil-war epic *Gone with the Wind* (1939), set in the Deep South before slavery was abolished, feels uncomfortably racist for audiences today. The film is full of disturbing images, such as black slave children fanning their spoiled infant masters. Hattie McDaniel may have won an Oscar, but her role of Mammy was still a slave, albeit a spirited one.

Issues of representation are central within film studies, and scholars often set out to expose stereotypical portrayals of people from ethnic minorities. They argue that viewers need to be taught to notice the invisible crowd of black servants or musicians in the background. The Hollywood musical has received particular attention, because producers exploited talented black performers such as Paul Robeson and Lena Horne without ever granting them the recognition or stardom of their white contemporaries.

Representation also looms large in studies of cinema from other nations. The concept of *national cinema* presumes that films made within a particular country have something to say about the national identity of their characters. Political scientist Benedict Anderson's claim that nations are like 'imagined communities' is central to ideas of national cinema, because it creates a space for cinema to function as part of that imagination. Regionally popular genres, such as the Brazilian *chanchada* (musical comedy), use traditional folk art and music to keep a nostalgic sense of national identity alive – and dancing (I write more on Brazilian cinema in Chapter 12).

Exploring gender

In 1985, the American cartoonist Alison Bechdel drew a strip in which her female creation makes a striking claim: she'd only watch movies if they have at least two female characters – *and* they talk to each other about something other than men. Journalists picked up this small joke and turned it into *the Bechdel Test,* which aims to highlight the limited portrayal of women in popular media. Perhaps you wouldn't expect action films or westerns to pass this test, but, perhaps surprisingly, many rom-coms and melodramas also fail.

The public's interest in the Bechdel Test reflects a fascinating contradiction at the heart of popular cinema. On the one hand, cinema has always been marketed as a public entertainment suitable for, and often directly aimed at, women. You can think of many of the most successful films of all time as women's films: *Gone with the Wind* (1939), *Titanic* (1997) and *The Sound of Music* (1965) to name but a few. Yet the narrative structures of popular film often relegate female characters to the roles of girlfriend, wife and/or mother to active male heroes. Plus, of course, the number of female directors is still very small.

Feminist film scholars have played an important role in bringing the issue of women's representation to the fore, often in relation to sexuality and violence. But feminist film theory also highlights ways in which the visual language of cinema itself can be thought of as gendered, and as part of the system of *patriarchy* (male dominance). Scholar and film-maker Laura Mulvey notably argued that cinema was characterised by *a male gaze* that turns women on screen into objects to be looked at, by other characters and by male audience members (see Chapter 13).

You can't ignore that films also represent male characters on screen, and understanding how this works is important, not least for feminist film critics. For example, why do you think that male action heroes of the 1980s, such as Arnold Schwarzenegger, are so over-the-top and ridiculously masculine? Yes, it probably has something to do with the macho tone of political debate under President Reagan, but you can also see it as a kind of backlash against the gains feminism made in the public sphere.

While I'm talking action films, has it ever struck you as curious that for films aimed squarely at young men, they tend to spend a lot of screen time gazing not at women – but at muscular male physiques? This kind of question animates film scholars with a gay or *queer* perspective. Homosexuality was basically taboo for much of cinema history (and still is in parts of the world), and so queer film studies has developed oppositional ways of reading against the grain to find unspoken desires lurking within classic and contemporary movies (check out Chapter 15 for more).

Chapter 2

Putting Words and Pictures into Motion: The Film-Making Team

In This Chapter

▶ Thinking about film as a collaborative process

▶ Introducing the key creative players

▶ Valuing the technical wizards who make the magic happen

*I*f you ever stay in the cinema right to the end of the film, remaining seated as the credits roll and everyone else races to the exit, you probably gaze at the apparently endless list of names. Perhaps you wonder, 'What do all these people actually *do?*' I don't even attempt to describe every last job involved in making a movie, but in this chapter I do acquaint you with all the major contributors to a film – and more importantly show you how what they do affects what you watch on screen.

Helming a Film: Directors and Their Collaborators

Directors win the big awards, get invited to the best parties and often date the leading actors. But most of all directors get symbolic ownership over a film through the opening credits or title sequence, which often starts out with the label 'A film by XY' or 'An XY film' immediately after the studio and production company credits. After then listing the leading actors and other major contributors, the director's name typically appears last before the film begins.

If you ever visit a working film set, you notice quickly that directors are important, but they're far from the all-powerful creative gods that many people presume them to be. A director's key skill is, in fact, collaboration.

They need to build instant working relationships with a lot of different 'creative' people, they have to keep actors happy and they must bring every element together at the exact right time when they cry 'Action!'

The independent 'total film-maker' may be an appealing myth, but that's all it is. Look carefully at the credits of all the best directors, and you find that they prefer to work with the same people over and over again. Hitchcock movies sound so distinctive thanks to the composer Bernard Herrmann, and costume designer Edith Head dressed Hitchcock's ice maiden female leads to kill. But his most important collaborator was Alma Reville: screenwriter, editor, continuity person and occasional actress. Oh, and his wife.

Of course a few directors *may* have let their delusions of grandeur get the better of them. Charlie Chaplin was an amazingly talented man, but his credit list on *Limelight* (1952) raises an eyebrow. He was not only the star (alongside fellow veteran silent comedian Buster Keaton), but he also wrote the screenplay, produced, directed, wrote and arranged the music, and choreographed the dance routines. He probably made the sandwiches too.

But even Chaplin didn't do everything himself. Recent histories have uncovered the importance of his 'assistants'. For example, Charles Reisner was his (uncredited) assistant director and gag man on *The Gold Rush* (1925), before directing *The Three Stooges* and *Abbot and Costello* in his own right. (For a closer look at the idea of directors as the major creative force behind their films, turn to Chapter 14.)

Thickening the Plot: Screenwriters

Before every great film, there was a great screenplay. The beloved hero, the dastardly villain, the great car chase, the perfect witty put-down – they're all in that 120 pages or so of typed text. So, as I describe in this section, a great script is a powerful document indeed.

'Authoring' a film

Screenwriters occupy a peculiar position in the film-making hierarchy. Although they're absolutely essential to the creative process – without a strong central idea, interesting characters and believable dialogue, no film can succeed – after their beloved ideas go into production, they have little or no control over what happens next.

In Hollywood, the average script is redrafted many times, often by different writers brought in to tighten up particular aspects, such as bolstering a star's character or improving the gags. Blockbusters can be written by dozens of people, despite the fact that the Writers Guild of America limits the official number of collaborators to just three. Screenwriters must therefore watch their work being fundamentally changed before it even reaches an audience. Screenwriters need skins like rhinoceroses.

So can a screenwriter be considered the 'author' of a film? Well, yes, but only if you're able to see the concept of authorship as being multiple and collaborative. The problem, however, is where do you stop? For example, the character Indiana Jones (see the nearby sidebar 'Plunging into development hell') is derivative of 1930s and 40s serial fiction, so shouldn't those pulp writers and comic book authors also get a mention? And what about Indy's literary precedents such as H Rider Haggard's *King Solomon's Mines*?

 If you follow this logic to its conclusion, you may decide that the concept of cinematic authorship is basically irrelevant, because the inputs to a complex creative product such as a Hollywood movie are so fractured and dispersed. French literary theorist Roland Barthes made a similar argument in his 1967 post-structuralist essay when he loudly proclaimed 'the death of the author'. That's all very well, M. Barthes, but somebody still has to write the script, *non?* Turn to Chapter 15 for much more on film theory, including post-structuralism.

What's a good script worth?

In 1967, famed novelist and fledgling screenwriter William Goldman found himself without a studio commission, and so he decided to write his pet project about two American outlaws. The script for *Butch Cassidy and the Sundance Kid* (1969) generated so much excitement that a bidding war commenced between the Hollywood studios, with Warner Bros. eventually paying $400,000 ($2.7 million in today's money). Screenwriters have been chasing these lucrative paydays ever since.

Spending loads of cash on speculative scripts reached frenzied levels in the 1980s and 1990s, when *Lethal Weapon, Independence Day* and most famously *Basic Instinct* became must-have properties. The $3 million paid to Joe Eszterhas for *Basic Instinct* (1992) wasn't a bad investment given the film's sexy notoriety and healthy box-office success.

However, as Goldman himself famously argued, 'nobody knows anything' when it comes to predicting which films are going to become hits when they're released, and certainly not when they're at the script stage. Moneybags Joe Eszterhas was also paid $2 million for the financial disaster *Showgirls* (1995), which only goes to prove that a script is merely a blueprint, the foundations of a film. Plenty can go wrong after the cameras start rolling.

Plunging into development hell

Development is the name of the indefinite revision period that Hollywood executives apparently created for the express purpose of torturing screenwriters. In this murky realm, multiple stakeholders read original scripts and all offer 'notes' (corrections) that often conflict with each other. Redrafts after redrafts follow, almost interminably, leading to delays of years or even decades.

Screenwriter David Hughes has documented several of these tales of woe, including the story behind *Indiana Jones and the Kingdom of the Crystal Skull* (2008), which took 19 years to reach the screen. The list of top writers who produced drafts or were rumoured to be involved is staggering: from Frank Darabont (*The Shawshank Redemption*) to Tom Stoppard (*Shakespeare in Love*).

The film's eventual writing credit is fittingly complex, attributing the 'screenplay' to David Koepp (*Jurassic Park*), but the 'story' to producer George Lucas and Jeff Nathanson (*The Terminal*), and finally the 'characters' to Lucas and Philip Kaufman who developed the original Indiana Jones story with director Steven Spielberg. No wonder the process took so long.

Studying screenwriting

Knocking out a film or TV show feels like something that everyone with a laptop can try. If you're good at telling hilarious stories in the bar to your friends then maybe, just maybe, the next blockbuster comedy can have your name attached to it. Of course would-be writers soon discover that defeating the blank page (or screen) is nowhere near as easy as they hoped.

Screenwriting is an enticing career that requires basic skills that you must know and rules that you must follow. Many professional screenwriters, being naturally thoughtful and eloquent, have persuasive theories about what works and what doesn't. They're also often unemployed. This potent combination has resulted in a highly lucrative market for screenwriting teaching.

Thousands of books, blogs and taught courses are available, all offering the promise of screenwriting perfection. Therefore, picking the good advice from the bad can be difficult. But following are a few key texts that all aspiring screenwriters need to read:

- *Adventures in the Screen Trade* **by William Goldman:** A classic insider's account of Hollywood in the 1960s and 70s from one of its most successful screenwriters.

- johnaugust.com: A top popular Google-ranked blog from one of Tim Burton's favourite writers, including audio podcasts and downloadable scripts.

> ✔ *Screenplay* **by Syd Field:** A bestseller since 1979, *Screenplay* emphasises story structure as the key element of screenwriting craft.
>
> ✔ *The Hero with a Thousand Faces* **by Joseph Campbell:** An ambitious study of mythic storytelling in all forms, first published in 1949. It apparently inspired George Lucas to write *Star Wars* (1978).
>
> ✔ *The Screenwriter's Bible* **by David Trottier:** A practical 'how to' guide with a particularly useful section on formatting a script.

Industry logic dictates that the best courses for studying screenwriting are found near the major production centres of Los Angeles (University of Southern California) and New York (Columbia University), and to a lesser extent European capitals such as London (The National Film and Television School). But Cairo, Mumbai and Sao Paolo also have well-established and lively film schools.

Whatever you read and wherever you study, a guaranteed pathway into the film industry doesn't exist. Getting your work up on the screen depends on the same strange alchemy of talent, hard work and schmoozing as it does for everybody else.

Writing action

In essence, screenwriters can decide only what their characters say (see the next section) and what they do. Novelists can spend chapter after chapter exploring the inner worlds of their protagonists, but any script that tries to do the same is instantly dismissed. In screenwriting, to borrow from F Scott Fitzgerald (ironically, a novelist who struggled as a screenwriter), *action is character*.

For an example of how to create character through action alone, the opening 20 minutes of Pixar's *Wall-E* (2008) is pretty hard to beat. Andrew Stanton's script, available online through Disney Studios, has a full ten pages of wonderfully terse action directions that introduce the central figure, a waste-compacting robot (here known under his early name of Wally) alone on a completely trashed Earth:

> *Wally discovers a BRA in the garbage.*
> *Unsure what it's for.*
> *Tries placing it over his eyes, like glasses.*
> *Tosses it in his cooler.*

The movie's slapstick comedy is balanced against the pathos of Wall-E's careful stewardship of his only companion, a cockroach. His routines, the items he chooses to collect and disregard, and most of all his love of the show tune

'Put on Your Sunday Clothes' from an old VHS of *Hello Dolly!* (1969) tell so much about this little robot, so economically, that you don't need words – or even human facial expressions – to feel an instant affection for him.

Some movie aficionados refer to these powerful wordless segments as *pure cinema,* reflecting the notion that film developed much of its visual language before it had access to spoken dialogue through synchronised soundtracks. What makes film different from every other medium is its ability to capture movement through space: dancers, car chases, gun fights and all.

Although this passion for characterful action is particularly strong in Hollywood cinema, other traditions around the world have different rhythms and tempos. For example, the quiet stillness of classical Japanese cinema, exemplified by Yasujiro Ozu, stands in stark contrast to the crash, bang, wallop of Hollywood.

Writing dialogue

The idea of pure cinema is appealing, but a primary function of any script since the days of 'the talkies' is to capture, and therefore control, what actors say to each other. After all, scripts are also commonly known as screen*plays.* English playwright Terence Rattigan is sometimes quoted as saying that the screenplay is a child of its mother, the silent movie, and its father, the theatre drama. Clever chap, that Rattigan.

Describing what constitutes good dialogue is very difficult, but you know bad dialogue when you hear it. Some level of exposition is essential to locate events, characters and actions, but no one wants to hear a secondary character wheeled in purely to explain the background. Similarly, characterisation through dialogue can be appallingly clunky when characters try to tell the audience what they are. Viewers need to observe character in action to believe it.

It was the best of lines, it was the worst of lines

George Lucas may be the richest film-maker on the planet thanks to the *Star Wars* franchise, but industry consensus agrees that his dialogue generally stinks. Even his star Harrison Ford is on record as saying 'George, you can write this s**t, but you sure as hell can't say it!' Luckily, for the first three films at least, the cheesy dialogue is all part of the B-movie feel, and those ground-breaking visuals more than compensate. As for the recent pompous prequels however . . . .

Although the general rule is that if you notice dialogue it isn't working, certain writers excel in creating memorable, stand-out dialogue. Quentin Tarantino's scripts are action packed and incredibly talky, with long dialogues about nothing in particular, and yet they still sound incredibly *cool* coming out of his characters mouths. The 'Royale with cheese' discussion from *Pulp Fiction* (1994) basically resurrected John Travolta's career.

The best way to get to grips with what screenwriting brings to finished films is simply to read a lot of them. Many great screenplays are available to buy or borrow from your local library. Try reading scripts for films that you haven't seen yet, because then you can really let your imagination get to work purely based on the written word. Of course you can always watch the films afterwards to understand the connections between words on the page and images on the screen. This section gives you plenty of ideas, from *Wall-E* to *Butch Cassidy and the Sundance Kid*. So get reading those classic films!

Showing Them the Money: Film Producers

Producers have the most important and the least understood job in film-making. Many people think that they know what a director, editor or cinematographer does (if the latter's role is a mystery to you, read the later section 'Painting with Light: Cinematographers'), but a producer? Not so much.

As I discuss in this section, understanding the film producer's role is more of a challenge than the other key creative inputs because their influence is difficult to observe on screen. Their projects tend to be many and varied, in different styles and different genres, because they choose to make what they can sell.

Giving producers their due

The producer is often the only person who sees a film project through from the beginning to the end. The writer may originate the idea, the characters and the plot, the director has the vision and the collaborative skills to ensure that top-quality footage goes in the can, and the editor shapes and structures the finished product (check out the later section 'Cutting and reconnecting: Editors' for more details), but only the producer is responsible for overseeing the entire process.

For this reason, producers have as good a claim as anyone to be the overriding influence on or 'author' of a film.

Adding further weight to this claim is the thorny issue of *final cut,* or who decides when a film is ready to be released. The producer, standing in for the studio or financiers, generally holds this power rather than the editor or even the director. Commercial film-making is a business first and foremost, and great producers make the tough business decisions.

But a major flaw becomes apparent in this argument (that the producer is the sole, individual bearer of cinematic authorship) when you look at most major films' credits. Often loads of producers are attached, with different titles signifying slightly different roles. Here are some common ones, roughly from most to least important:

- ✔ **Producers:** Secure finance, oversee budgets and manage the production office.

- ✔ **Executive producers:** Represent the studio's interests on set, or provide a major source of finance themselves, or are sometimes prestigious 'consultants' on the production (often the case with major stars).

- ✔ **Associate producers:** Work under the main producer and are responsible for specific elements of the process, such as completing finance or overseeing post-production.

- ✔ **Line producers:** Directly responsible for the pre-production or planning phase of a project and attempt to ensure that shooting is completed on time and on budget.

- ✔ **Co-producers:** Line managers with some creative input during the development process, or producers from other companies that are co-producing the film.

Confused yet? Basically this multi-layered hierarchy attempts to share the huge responsibilities of the producer role among many individuals and ensure that each of the many stakeholders in a project feel properly valued and important. The bevy of titles certainly represents shared *ownership* of a project, but whether this can qualify as authorship or not is another question.

Fundamentally, producers in all their guises are businesspeople. They may make a hundred different decisions on a daily basis that affect the finished product, but effectively they farm out the more obviously creative elements of film-making to other people, notably the director.

The idea of producer as businessperson accounts for the unease auteur theorists (see Chapter 14) traditionally feel about producers. Many critics argue from political positions that are opposed to free-market economics, and as a result they often cast directors in the role of noble artists struggling against nefarious moneymen who want to stifle their visions. But who gets their sweaty hands on the ultimate accolade of industry esteem, the Best Picture Oscar? The producer, who doesn't give a darn at that moment whether he's an author or not.

Producing the studio goods

The producer's role and importance were largely defined by a system of film-making that no longer exists, at least not in the United States. The Hollywood studio system was an incredibly efficient, world-conquering way to make movies that relied on tight contractual controls. Writers, stars and directors were all employees of the major studios, and their bosses were the producers (for more on the studio system, see Chapter 9).

Among the first and greatest of the studio producers was Irving Thalberg, who, in 1925, rose from humble office assistant to head of production at MGM, aged just 26. In 12 short years before he died, he produced more than 400 films, discovered stars such as Clark Gable and Joan Crawford, and helped write Hollywood's voluntary code of moral conduct known as the Hays Code (in operation from 1930 to 1968). For an example of his work that has stood the test of time, try *Grand Hotel* (1932), a sumptuous, star-packed adaptation of a hit stage play.

Thalberg is credited with creating many of the film producer's basic strategies. He tended to choose pre-existing source material, such as Broadway plays or novels, and he worked on scripts collaboratively using meetings known as story conferences. Under his management MGM became renowned for high production values: the biggest and the best of everything. Even today, pre-sold properties from a range of different media (TV shows, comic books, video games and so on) made with high production values define the Hollywood blockbuster.

Thalberg was also notorious for firing the director Erich von Stroheim, whose extravagant ways regularly exceeded budgetary restrictions. This spat became an industry legend and the model for future tussles between, for example, producer David O Selznick and director Alfred Hitchcock.

As with all movie industry gossip, however, be careful of taking these stories at face value. They're part of the mythology that Hollywood is happy to maintain: art competes with finance to produce the best entertainment money can buy.

Of course, Hollywood wasn't the only town with a studio system and therefore studio producers. For as long as cinema audiences were large enough to support large-scale local production (basically pre-1960), Britain had the Rank Organisation, Italy had Cinecittà and Germany had UFA (see Chapters 10 and 11). The political turmoil of Europe during this period also meant that many of the most successful producers ended up working for Hollywood in exile, such as UFA's Erich Pommer.

In the modern film industry, the closest equivalent to the classical Hollywood studio system is in India. The Indian film industry is very large and very diverse, with major production centres in Mumbai, Chennai and Hyderabad (see Chapter 12). The biggest Indian film producers, such as Aditya Chopra, are celebrities in their own right, and many popular stars also become producers. This level of self-promotion may have horrified the quietly spoken Thalberg, but the chutzpah of these producers is infectious and undeniable.

When good producers go bad

Many producers in post-studio-system-era Hollywood wielded such power and became so wealthy that their falls from grace were truly spectacular. In the late 1960s, Robert Evans was a surprise appointment as head of production at Paramount given his previous reputation as a playboy actor. Despite his lack of track record, he turned out to be a natural producer, choosing to develop era-defining hits such as *The Godfather* (1972) and *Chinatown* (1974).

Come the 1980s Evans was an independent producer, a major cocaine user and a cuckold, having lost his wife Ali McGraw to heart-throb actor Steve McQueen. He was even implicated in a drug-related murder case. Although cleared, he was cast out of Hollywood for many years, but at least he survived to tell his scandalous tales himself in autobiography and documentary *The Kid Stays in the Picture* (2002).

Other producers who lived too fast weren't so lucky. Don Simpson was the epitome of 1980s Hollywood excess who spent his proceeds from films such as *Top Gun* (1986) on a lavish and amoral lifestyle. At one point he was spending $60,000 a month on prescription drugs just to keep himself going. Unsurprisingly his heart gave out in 1996.

Going it alone: Independent producers

These days, the dividing line between studio and independent producers is increasingly blurry. Most producers work as freelancers, while the people doing their former jobs within what's left of the Hollywood major studios are called *executives*. Even the clear separation between mainstream and independent film-making that existed in the 1970s and 80s has become difficult to maintain, with companies such as Miramax providing real marketing muscle for smaller, quirkier films.

So what was the difference between studio and independent producing, if it ever really existed? In the Golden Age of Hollywood, if Irving Thalberg of MGM represented studio professionalism and reliability then the risk-taking, no-holds-barred independent approach was defined by David O Selznick. Selznick started as a studio guy at RKO but soon ventured out on his own forming his own production company and striking a distribution deal with United Artists. His biggest success? Oh, only *Gone with the Wind* (1939), still the highest grossing film of all time after adjusting for inflation.

After the breakdown of the Hollywood studio system in the 1950s and 60s, the independent producer really came to the fore. With all creative talent freed from restrictive contracts, the producer's challenge was to pull together an attractive 'package' for the studios, which were now essentially financiers and distributors. This shift in roles gave increased power to talent agents, who began to assume duties previously assigned to producers. The rise of agencies also led to inflated production costs as star and director salaries rocketed.

Ever since Steven Soderbergh's microbudget *Sex, Lies and Videotape* (1989) crossed over from the niche independent market into the mainstream, Hollywood has increasingly courted leftfield, up-and-coming film-makers. Nobody was more central to this trend than Harvey Weinstein of Miramax, known for his tough approach to acquisitions (including cutting them if needed) and his incredible ability to garner Academy Award nominations for his films.

Film producers tend to be natural storytellers, and so you can read plenty of fantastic warts-and-all autobiographies. The documentary film about Robert Evans, *The Kid Stays in the Picture* (2002), is practically required viewing.

Bizarre coincidence alert! In James Cagney's biopic of horror actor Lon Chaney, *Man of a Thousand Faces* (1957), legendary studio producer Irving Thalberg is played by none other than Robert J Evans in his pre-head of Paramount Pictures days. Hollywood is a small town after all.

Painting with Light: Cinematographers

Yes, I'm shamelessly borrowing this section's heading from one of the best books ever written about film-making, by cinematographer John Alton. 'Painting with light' is a lovely phrase, and it expresses the visual artistry and ambition of many cinematographers. First published in 1949 and recently republished (University of California Press, 2013), Alton's book remains so useful because it's filled with diagrams and technical illustrations that still inform today's cinematography practice.

Directing the photography

No other role in film-making so perfectly balances creativity and technology as that of the *cinematographer,* whose importance within the film-making process is probably best signalled by the descriptive alternative title of *director of photography* (or DP). Being labelled as a 'director' elevates cinematographers above the other technicians, and indeed many directors rely heavily on their DPs to achieve the visuals that they desire. The label also reflects the managerial aspect of the role, however, because cinematographers generally oversee and lead a team of camera operators, electricians and lighting crew. (Check out 'Making it happen: Technical crew' later in this chapter for more details.)

The cinematographer is so vital to the success of a film that this professional is usually among the first to be hired, either by the producer or director, who may have their favourite DP. During the development or pre-production stages, the cinematographer and the director collaborate closely to find a shared visual style. This collaboration often involves research, such as searching out particular paintings, photographs or buildings that serve as inspiration. Cinematographers then make a series of technical decisions each of which has a significant effect upon the finished film.

During *principal photography* (the physical shooting of the film), cinematographers handle the following tasks:

- Checking and testing all camera equipment and lighting.
- Setting up each scene, placing the cameras and lights.
- *Blocking* the set, which involves marking out the movement of actors and any camera equipment.
- Working with actors to ensure that their performances are recorded accurately by the cameras.
- Watching and approving the *rushes* or *dailies,* the shots recorded each day in their raw, unedited state.

In addition, developments in *digital grading* and *image manipulation* (that is, changing the colours or other elements of the image via computer) mean that the cinematographer now even has a key role to play during post-production.

Although guiding the actors is still primarily the responsibility of the director, the cinematographer often makes them *look* so remarkable. For this reason, the most powerful stars often insist that the best available cinematographers light and shoot them.

In 1957, at the height of her success, Marilyn Monroe demanded that Jack Cardiff be hired as cinematographer on *The Prince and the Showgirl.* As the director was her co-star, the notorious control freak Laurence Olivier, you can imagine how well this request was received. In the end, Monroe was right, because the film's rich, saturated colours (provided by shooting in Technicolor, Cardiff's speciality) are perfect for the film's frothy fairy-tale tone.

Achieving 'the look'

When creating a specific visual style or *look* for a film, cinematographers can call on the long tradition of aesthetic practices inherited from other art forms, particularly painting and still photography (see Chapter 1). Many cinematographers are open and passionate about their chosen influences. For example, Jack Cardiff loved the Dutch old masters Rembrandt and Vermeer and often set up his lighting to emulate the highlights and shadows of their paintings.

Other vital influences on mainstream cinematography have come from national traditions. For instance, the early silent films known collectively as *German expressionism* cast a long shadow (often quite literally) over international cinema in general – and over film noir in particular (see Chapter 5). This influence is partly due to expressionism's striking use of diagonal lines and extreme light and shade, but also because many of the best German directors and cameramen ended up working in America due to the two world wars. Check out Fritz Lang's *The Big Heat* (1953) for a perfect example of how expressionism mingled with the American gangster film.

Avant-garde or experimental films have also been a rich source of visual inspiration for cinematography. For example, American artist and film-maker Stan Brakhage, known for scratching celluloid or sticking translucent items to it, is cited as a key influence by (among others) Jeff Cronenweth, who shot David Fincher's *Fight Club* (1999). This connection makes perfect sense when you watch Tyler Durden (Brad Pitt) cutting shots from pornographic films into Disney cartoons. (See Chapter 7 for more on Stan Brakhage's unusual vision.)

Of course influences extend well beyond intellectual and respectable art forms. The high-gloss, high-impact style of 1980s advertising found its way into films such as *Top Gun* (1986) through directors and cinematographers who worked across both media. The signature style of this and other so-called high-concept films is bold backlighting and high-contrast images reminiscent of posters or adverts. The sex scene between Tom Cruise and Kelly McGillis in *Top Gun* is a perfect example: their bodies become silhouettes against a strong blue backlight.

Comics and graphic novels have also had a significant influence over blockbuster cinematography in recent decades. The bright hyper-real colours of *Dick Tracy* (1990) and *Batman and Robin* (1997) may have been superceded by the darker, noir-ish style of *Sin City* (2005) and the Dark Knight franchise, but in both cases cinematographers get to strut their stuff. These cinematographers may not be Rembrandt, but the films certainly look impressive.

Harnessing technology

Cinematographers may consider themselves artists, but unlike painters and sculptors their medium is inherently technological. Even shooting on location using entirely natural light, their decisions about camera lenses, film stocks and screen ratios can completely change the quality of the final image. All these choices require advanced (and constantly advancing) technical know-how. Check out the nearby sidebar 'Shooting *Brokeback Mountain* (2005)' for a great example of how technical choices impact a final film.

Modern film audiences expect realism, which demands that exteriors are shot on location, or someplace that appears so. Most interior footage, however, can be achieved in a controlled studio setting, which allows the cinematographer full control over the lighting in ways that are impossible outside in daylight or confining real-world rooms. Multiple light sources are often combined to create a wide range of possible effects.

If you've seen *Casablanca* (1942) – and if you haven't, why not? – you likely noticed that its female star, Ingrid Bergman, often appears to glow from within. Of course, Bergman was extraordinarily beautiful, but expert lighting produces that glow. Classical studio lighting creates a bright, even image and favours the human figures in the frame. At least three lights are essential for this effect, but often many more were used to highlight clothing or eyes moist with romantic longing.

The origins of this style of *three-point lighting* are technological, having to do with cameras and film stocks of the period that required bright illumination. But the reasons for its continued dominance are more complex and interesting. The visual treatment of female stars was (and is) clearly an important issue for feminist film theory (see Chapter 13). But more broadly, the clarity and perfect focus of classical Hollywood implies a way of looking at the world that's controllable and contained.

Although a much broader palate of visual textures and technologies are available to the modern cinematographer, the choices go beyond artistic and venture into the ideological. Each new technological development leaves its mark on the cinematography of the era, particularly if it resonates with dominant themes of the day. For example, the extreme zoom in or out of a scene is characteristic of 1970s American cinema; it was a good fit for the paranoid political thrillers of that era and later.

Digital video has caused seismic changes in recent cinematographic practice, because many of the techniques required for shooting on celluloid film no longer apply. Although a high-gloss, perfect Hollywood look is still entirely possible, and indeed often used for romantic comedies and family films, digital video has shifted audience expectations of realism in fascinating ways. The lo-fi, handheld feel of the first films shot with digital video, such as Mike Figgis's *Timecode* (2000), have subsequently infiltrated mainstream action films thanks to documentary film-maker Paul Greengrass's *Bourne* trilogy (see Chapter 16).

Shooting *Brokeback Mountain* (2005)

Ang Lee's *Brokeback Mountain* (2005) tells an unconventional tale of forbidden love between two cowboys in 1960s America. It won Oscars for the director and the up-and-coming Mexican cinematographer Rodrigo Prieto. Prieto describes his approach to cinematography in broadly narrative terms: image as subservient to story.

Prieto originally planned to shoot the film's spectacular Rocky Mountain sequences in the widescreen format (or *ratio*) of 2.35:1 (which is over twice as wide as it is tall). In tests, however, he discovered that this wide frame struggled to represent the extreme vertical lines of the mountains. Changing the ratio to 1.85:1 allowed

him to produce more vertical compositions – as well as a closer attention to the actors' bodies in the frame. This decision enabled one of the film's most striking images: that of the cowboy lovers' standing embrace.

Prieto also chose to use different film stock for the film's early mountain sequences and the later domestic storyline. The mountain shots are pristine and crisp as a result, whereas the later interiors have a subtle grainy and nostalgic feel. The effects of these two relatively straightforward technological choices are fundamental to the film's position, which challenges the previously held perception of homosexual love as something unnatural and unromantic.

Courtesy Moviestore Collection/REX

Getting the Film in the Can: Production

Of all the phases of film-making, from initial pitching to the final post-production touches, the shooting or production stage is certainly the busiest, and probably the most documented and discussed. People pay attention to production because it often takes place in the public eye: either literally, if shot on location, or metaphorically, via extensive coverage in film magazines and DVD extras.

Despite all the attention that production receives, the coverage still tends to focus mainly on directors and stars, along with the occasional attention-grabbing special-effects technique (for example, the use of motion-capture technology in *The Lord of the Rings* trilogy). So in this section I draw your attention to a few unsung heroes of the film-making team.

Setting the scene: Art directors

The French phrase *mise-en-scène,* meaning literally 'put in the scene', holds an important place in film studies terminology and therefore theory (see Chapter 4). Fundamentally, the term brings attention to the physical material of film-making: the sets, the props, the costumes and so on. And the person in charge of finding, designing or making all this stuff is the art director.

Like the cinematographer (see the earlier section 'Directing the photography'), the art director leads a large team of specialists who work together to provide the perfect environment for the actors, vehicles for them to drive and objects for them to interact with. Unlike the cinematographer, however, the role of art director also exists in the theatre, and many art directors gain valuable experience behind the stage before moving behind the camera.

Art directors may need to be 'arty' in the sense of producing drawings, designs or even painting backdrops for use on set, but their art is better understood in the sense of craftsmanship and design. For films involving artificial sets, a thorough understanding of construction and architectural methods is required, as is a responsibility for the health and safety of the crew.

The art director has a key influence on a film's level of visual spectacle. Having long placed emphasis on storytelling and narrative, film studies now generally acknowledges that this spectacle is one of the key pleasures of cinema-going (for an example, see the section on Tom Gunning in Chapter 17). Audiences love the antique sets and ornate costumes of period drama, the outlandish and surreal environments of science fiction and the machinery of action cinema, particularly cars and guns, even when they don't especially connect with the story.

Partly for these reasons, the most spectacular art direction tends to receive the most attention and acclaim – including Oscars. In fact one of Hollywood's most prolific art directors, MGM's Cedric Gibbons, created the iconic golden statuette. Here's a little more about Gibbons and a few other legendary art directors:

- ✔ **Cedric Gibbons (1892–1960):** Won 11 Oscars and worked on more than 1,000 films during Hollywood's studio era. He was largely responsible for the MGM style of high production values and lavish spectacle. Take a look at *The Wizard of Oz* (1939) and *An American in Paris* (1951).

- ✔ **John Box (1920–2005):** Started out as an architect and stage designer before becoming the pre-eminent art director for epics such as *Lawrence of Arabia* (1962) and *Doctor Zhivago* (1965). He was renowned for his ability to recreate enormous exotic sets in unlikely locations, including building the Great Wall of China in Wales.

- ✔ **Richard Sylbert (1928–2002):** A master of creating heightened reality in films such as *Rosemary's Baby* (1968), *The Cotton Club* (1984) and particularly *Dick Tracy* (1990), Warren Beatty's heavily stylised comic-strip misfire. He even got to be head of production at Paramount briefly in the late 1970s.

As hard-working freelancers, art designers naturally need to sell their skills and experience in order to secure future contracts, which means that many upload promotional *showreels* to websites such as YouTube and Vimeo. Watch a couple and you quickly get a sense of the results that get them hired. Search for British art director Simon Bowles, whose showreel displays the lush period detail of *Hyde Park on Hudson* (2012) and impressive Roman interiors of *Centurion* (2010).

Turning the creative vision into a reality: Technical crew

Economists call films 'complex creative products', meaning that they require a great deal of effort, time and people to achieve. Nowhere are these characteristics more apparent than in the bustling catering areas on a large film set, where hundreds of burgers and cups of coffee are regularly doled out to the hungry workers. All good producers know that an army of film crew marches on its stomach.

A film's technical crew takes the artistic ideas and technological innovations of the senior creative players, such as the production designer, and makes them happen. You need a particular style of Bakelite telephone commonly used in 1920s Paris? Call the props guy. Fuse blown on that lighting rig? You need to speak to one of the grips. Star can't quite squeeze into that figure-hugging costume? That's a job for the *cutter* (or costume fitter).

The job titles of these vital members of staff can be rather obscure, and so here's a quick breakdown of the strangest:

- ✔ **Best boy:** First assistant to the gaffer or key grip – and, of course, is sometimes a woman.

- ✔ **Dolly grip:** Operates camera *dollies* (moveable rigs laid on tracks) and *cranes* (machines that lift the camera high into the air).

- ✔ **Gaffer:** Chief electrician on set with responsibility for keeping the lights on, laying cables and following safety regulations.

- ✔ **Key grip:** Works closely with the cinematographer to design and maintain the lighting set-ups.

Although many of these roles are by definition invisible on screen (no one's going to hire boom operators who allow their furry sound-recording equipment to fall into frame), others, such as costume designers, provide vital elements of visual spectacle for all the world to see. For this reason many of the world's top fashion names have dabbled in film, including Hubert de Givenchy (*Breakfast at Tiffany's,* 1961), Giorgio Armani (*American Gigolo,* 1980) and Jean Paul Gaultier (*The Fifth Element,* 1997).

Whether you're an internationally renowned fashion designer or an apprentice electrician who nobody has ever heard of, the nature of film production demands that all staff members pull their weight – or the whole edifice can crumble. A chain is only as strong as its weakest link, and one substandard element has let down many a film, negating the great work done elsewhere.

The 'weakest link' organisation of film-making, combined with the fact that everybody works on short-term contracts, means that word-of-mouth reputation (and gossip) is a vital force in the film industry. Why risk hiring the gaffer who, according to your sources, fell off the wagon last month and turned up on set stinking of booze and knocking rigs over? News of failures gets round fast, and job security is basically an illusion.

Putting the Footage on the Screen: Post-Production

Post-production is the bit after production (the clue's in the title!). This section focuses on the work that comes *after* the cameras stop rolling.

Cutting and constructing: Editors

Editing is vital for telling a story while using the conventions of film (see Chapter 4), but editors themselves are rarely dragged from their darkened edit suites and thrust into the spotlight.

The principal task of the editor is reducing the hours and hours of footage shot for a typical film down to something around typical feature film length. Selecting the best take from the many available is a key skill, as is varying the length of shot used to create the right rhythm of a scene and a sequence. Classical *continuity editing* relies on long-standing conventions to appear seamless, but editors can choose to stretch or break these rules to achieve particular effects.

Editing was one of the first areas of film-making to benefit from the digital revolution, because editing software, such as Final Cut Pro, is now industry standard. Cutting films on celluloid was a masterful skill but extremely labour-intensive and difficult to change after editors made decisions. Digital editing allows much greater flexibility, but some more experienced editors miss the discipline and precision of editing on film.

Good editing is often designed to go unnoticed, but training your brain to start noticing the cuts is relatively easy. Find a film renowned for its cutting, such as *Bonnie and Clyde* (1967) or *Saving Private Ryan* (1998), and watch sequences with the sound on mute. Without sound to act as a psychological bridge between shots, the transitions seem much more jarring. You may well be surprised at how many shots make up a typical sequence, even in slower-paced movies.

Sticking with a favourite editor

Some editors choose to work on footage 'sight unseen', with no input during production and limited interaction with the director, but many others strike up lasting creative relationships with top directors. For example, Thelma Schoonmaker has edited all of Martin Scorsese's films since *Raging Bull* (1980), and three have won Oscars for editing (but only one for direction). Schoonmaker was previously married to British director Michael Powell, who was a great inspiration for the young Scorsese.

Sally Menke was Quentin Tarantino's trusted editor from *Reservoir Dogs* (1992) onwards, and her cutting greatly contributes to the film's characteristic rhythms. Loose-limbed conversations are juxtaposed with shocks of extreme violence. Menke sadly died in 2010 aged 56.

These two examples amply demonstrate that editing is one area of film production where many women reach the top of the profession.

William Chang Suk-ping is a very unusual combination of production designer, costume designer and film editor, and his work in all three fields is vital for the acclaimed films directed by Wong Kar-wai. *In the Mood for Love* (2000) and *2046* (2004) demonstrate Chang's mysterious and subtle editing style and his fabulous frocks.

Of course these days you can also try a bit of editing yourself without much expense. iMovie (on all Mac computers and even iPhones) is a great, user-friendly mini version of Final Cut Pro.

Amplifying the images: Sound designers and composers

Cheap high-definition video cameras bring decent image quality within the reach of amateur film-makers, and editing is easy to do on a laptop. But watch a few homemade films, even student films on YouTube, and you quickly realise that they don't sound half as good as they look. Dialogue often drops in and out under over-prominent music, key sound effects are missing entirely and mumbling non-professional actors fluff key lines of dialogue. Good sound design is *difficult*.

Although some of the sound for films is recorded during principal photography, a surprising amount is added later, in post-production. Dialogue is a good example. Many of the words you hear in the final cut of a film are *overdubbed* onto the action through a process known as *automated dialogue replacement* (ADR). In addition, technicians known as *Foley artists* record sound effects, such as opening doors, crunching footsteps or fist punches, in studios. Even after all the required sounds and music are recorded, mixing and arranging layers of sound to fit into the modern surround-sound landscape is an extremely complex next step.

The great irony here is that everyone thinks of sound as a natural accompaniment to images, in that pre-sound or 'silent' cinema feels fundamentally lacking to modern audiences. However the reality is that film sound is much more artificial and unnatural than many cinematic images.

Similarly, film music only seems natural and 'right' because that's what you expect to hear (see Chapter 4). If you think about it, having an invisible orchestra strike up a mournful tune out of nowhere is a pretty bizarre way to enhance moving pictures. But it works.

Much of the work of film composers is by necessity done after the film is reaching completion, largely because they can't finalise their musical timings until the edit is nearly locked down. Therefore they have to compose very quickly, and often rely on a team of copyists and orchestras to speed things up. However some prominent composers prefer to get involved much earlier in the process, discussing themes with directors, and occasionally providing temporary music to play during shooting.

The great strength of film music lies in its magpie ability to combine a wide variety of styles, influences and instrumentation:

- The traditional orchestral film score, such as John Williams's soaring themes for *Superman* (1978) and *E.T. the Extra-Terrestrial* (1982), are by far the most popular and widely heard examples of contemporary 'classical music'.

- Many intellectual avant-garde composers produce strange, atonal scores for populist genre pictures, including horror and sci-fi. Just try listening to Leonard Rosenman's score for *Fantastic Voyage* (1966) or Elisabeth Lutyens's work on *The Skull* (1965) out of context. They're seriously weird.

- Film composers are also great innovators in electronic music, introducing an unsuspecting movie audience to instruments such as the eerie theremin in Miklos Rozsa's score for *Spellbound* (1945) and the robotic vocoder in Wendy (then Walter) Carlos's music for *A Clockwork Orange* (1971).

Visualising the impossible: Special-effects artists

Clever French critic Andre Bazin argued that cinema is inherently 'realistic' due to its status as a mechanical reproduction of reality (see Chapter 13). But ever since the earliest days of film, camera operators, directors and effects artists have been playing around with showing the impossible on screen. Georges Méliès, Buster Keaton and Fritz Lang were all special-effects supremos even before the coming of sound.

Optical effects, such as superimposing one image over another, exploit the photographic properties of celluloid, whereas *physical effects* (including simple painted backdrops) alter the filmed event to create fantastical images. Innovation in these areas (and more recently in digital effects) has always been a significant draw for audiences. Cinema began as a novelty fairground sideshow, and in many ways it continues to offer similar pleasures (see Chapter 17 on Tom Gunning's 'cinema of attractions').

This drive for innovation means that the jobs that make up a special-effects team have changed more radically than any other area of film-making. Following are a few credits that are rarely seen today:

- **Animatronics:** The art of creating mechanical creatures and aliens is perhaps most famously exhibited in Steven Spielberg's *Jaws* (1975). But Jim Henson's work in this field in the 1980s and 90s is unlikely to ever be surpassed: just check out the stunning creations in his bizarre children's fable *The Dark Crystal* (1982).

- ✔ **Matte artists:** Paint spectacular and elaborate backdrops onto glass that are combined with live action elements. The effect can be whimsical and cartoon-like, such as the emerald city in *The Wizard of Oz* (1939), or relatively low key and realistic, as with the enormous warehouse shot from the end of *Raiders of the Lost Ark* (1981).

- ✔ **Model builders:** Construct intricate miniature sets that appear huge on screen. See *Metropolis* (1927) and *Blade Runner* (1982) for two examples six decades apart but alike in spirit. Miniatures are still regularly combined with digital effects in today's blockbusters, for example the walled city of Minis Tirith in *The Return of the King* (2003).

Computer imagery was first used in the mid-1970s to enhance traditional special-effects work. Digital composition was an excellent solution for the problems of superimposing real actors over artificial environments. The technology really took off, however, when creating unreal creatures, animals and sets entirely out of computer data became possible, whether a huge lumbering diplodocus in *Jurassic Park* (1993) or the sinking ship of *Titanic* (1997).

The importance of *computer-generated imagery* (CGI) – which creates moving images from computer software – in modern blockbuster cinema means that a whole wave of technology experts have become unlikely movie moguls. John Lasseter of Pixar is the foremost example, overseeing the birth of the truly ground-breaking and entirely digital *Toy Story* (1995). Pixar in Silicon Valley, Northern California, also famously offers a working environment that minimises hierarchy and maximises play, which is the antithesis of the old Hollywood studio mentality. Truly, the geeks shall inherit the Earth, or at least the entertainment industry.

You can read all the scandalous biographies, watch every single minute of the DVD extras and scour the trade journals endlessly to get some idea of what film-making is kind of about. But nothing beats having a go at it yourself. Start small – a five-minute short is plenty – and don't overreach on the spectacle front. Develop an idea into a script, assemble a team of willing volunteers, assign them roles in front of and behind the camera, and get on with it. Before you know it you're feeling the bitterness of creative differences, the joy of the happy accident and most of all the absolute truth that film-making is collaboration, pure and simple.

Chapter 3

Watching the Stars Come Out: Film Stars, and Why We Love Them

*F*ilms tell stories, and stories are about people . . . or sometimes aliens . . . or talking dogs . . . but generally people. And because humans are social creatures, as a viewer you can't help but respond in some way to the enormous figures on the cinema screen. Yes, some of your responses to movies are about the characters – their noble victories and heart-breaking tragedies – but while these events are being played out you're basically spending two hours in the dark looking at people (which sounds creepier than it really is).

Although watching ordinary folk can be interesting for a bit, you really want to gaze at the most beautiful, charismatic and captivating people on Earth: film stars. But after a while, as I discuss in this chapter, even on-screen charisma isn't enough and you begin to want more. You want to reach out to these unearthly creatures, to understand them, or at least to buy the products they endorse in order to become a little bit more like them. As a result film stars hold enormous economic and social power.

Surveying Stars, in All Their Extraordinary Ordinariness

If film stars were completely different to (and better than) regular human beings in *every* way, audiences would soon tire of them. But they're not, and this flawed humanity is what keeps them interesting.

Just try and think of a major film star today who *hasn't* been through a personal, financial or drug-related crisis at some point in their life. Even super-wholesome Julia Roberts, the archetypal girl-next-door, had a disastrous marriage to a country music singer. Stars must constantly balance their extraordinary talent or beauty against flawed ordinariness to be compelling.

In this section, I delve into the alluring but complex world of the film star.

Distinguishing stars from actors

Of course not all the people you see up on screen are bona fide film stars. Many actors make a fine living taking less high-profile roles and not drawing attention to themselves. These people are known within the industry as *character actors,* which is a roundabout way of saying 'unconventional-looking', 'too old' or 'non-white'. Think Steve Buscemi, Olympia Dukakis and Danny Trejo: all very well-regarded actors, but not true movie stars.

Then there are acclaimed talents such as Philip Seymour Hoffman, who regularly played leading roles but in different types of films – often ensemble pieces or low-budget independent dramas. Hoffman's tragic, untimely death only served to emphasise that he was not an actor who was comfortable with the celebrity trappings of his career. Or, consider unknown actors who make a big impression in their first major role, like 9-year-old Quvenzhané Wallis in *Beasts of the Southern Wild* (2012). Wallis may have been Oscar-nominated, but whether hers was a truly 'star-making' debut remains to be seen.

So what separates stars from actors? It can't just be a question of the type of roles they receive or whether they receive top billing or appear farther down the list – and the distinction is almost certainly not based on perceived acting ability. For example, nobody thinks of casting Arnold Schwarzenegger in a role that requires a detailed, nuanced performance – or even an accent that isn't Austrian. But that didn't stop him from becoming a (literally) huge star.

Arnie's selling point to begin with was obviously his extreme, muscle-bound body, exploited to spectacular effect in sci-fi thrillers such as *The Terminator* (1984) and *Predator* (1987). Arnie became a star because he offered something unique (his body) in an era when body-consciousness was prevalent in Western society. But later in his acting career he also proved reasonably adept at comedy (or at least self-parody) in *Twins* (1988) and *Kindergarten Cop* (1990). Although his physical presence is always extraordinary, his comic roles present him in ordinary family situations.

The biggest film stars often come to stand for issues that are topical within their contemporary society. Arnie's image of indestructible masculinity also dovetailed neatly with the aggressive, hawkish politics of the Reagan administration in the US during the 1980s. Even his obvious foreignness spoke to the American dream: come to America and be rich beyond imagining.

The essential film-star quality: Relatability

Yes, *relatability* is a horrible, clumsy word, but it does a pretty good job of defining the intangible, special quality that makes for a great film star. It implies a connection or close association: a relatable star is someone with whom audiences can identify or empathise. But as an adjective, 'relatable' is suitably paradoxical; it ascribes a quality to someone that you can confirm or measure only in someone else. In other words, stars are relatable because people relate to them, full stop. (See the section 'Identifying with stars' to dig deeper into this idea.)

Relatability is a new word for a quality that has always been vital for film stars. Many of the earliest Hollywood stars, such as Mary Pickford and Charlie Chaplin were regular-looking people, and even the epitome of 1950s glamour, Marilyn Monroe, had a vulnerability that audiences loved.

Stars whom modern audiences deem particularly relatable are often female stars who appeal to women. In recent years the tag has often been applied to Jennifer Aniston and Cameron Diaz, both of whom have a flair for on-screen comedy and an ability to appear down-to-earth in interviews. Of course both are also exceptionally beautiful, which doesn't hurt.

But people who use this horrible word out loud always sound a bit silly. Director Zack Synder tried to claim that his 2013 reboot of *Superman* was 'more relatable, more human'. OK, so Henry Cavill may be a bit rougher around the edges than Christopher Reeve, but let's face facts: he's a flying alien in a red Lycra suit for heaven's sake!

Analysing star image

If part of stars' lustre extends beyond their on-screen performances, you need also to consider all the other material that circulates around them, including interviews, biographies, product endorsements and public appearances at award ceremonies. When you consider what particular stars mean to their audience, you have to take all these elements into account. Richard Dyer established this approach in his book *Stars* (2nd edition, 2008, British Film Institute), which combines *literary semiotics* (the study of signs in language, see Chapter 13) with sociology and cultural studies. *Stars* is one of a handful of books that set out the critical approach and methods for a new field of enquiry, in this case, *star studies*. As a film student, it is practically required reading. Dyer sets up the idea of a *star image,* which combines a star's performances on and off the screen, as an actor and as a celebrity (see 'Separating stardom from celebrity' later in this chapter).

Star images can work within or against the broader meanings of a film as a whole. For example, when you watch Tom Cruise battling invading aliens in *War of the Worlds* (2005), you're likely to think about his widely publicised status as a Scientologist and someone with a rather different relationship to extraterrestrial forces.

Star images accumulate meanings over time and mean different things to different audience members, just like films themselves. The star image is bigger than the star and operates within societies at the level of commonly held knowledge or even myth, so film stars can become symbolic of particular debates or points of conflict. Dyer's own example is that of Jane Fonda, an actress who combines elements of sex kitten, tomboy and political activist. Fonda's star image is therefore complex, even contradictory, multi-layered and rich in meanings for audiences and society at large.

Seeing stars as commodities

You don't have to stretch too far to think about film stars as living, breathing commodities. Stars sell their personalities and looks to make livings – their private lives belong to everyone, and everything that they touch from clothing to cars increases in value to their fans and the public at large. So unsurprisingly, the biggest film stars get seriously rich as a result.

The primary economic value of a film star comes from their apparent ability to mitigate risk for producers (check out Chapter 2 for more on producers' responsibilities). Cast a star, so the wisdom goes, and you have a much higher chance of making a profit from your movie. But stars also sell big ideas, such as the American dream, as well as mundane products such as coffee and aftershave.

Selling films

The economics of the film industry are structured around risk. Despite decades of market research, focus groups and test screenings, nobody can ever be certain whether a film is going to be a hit before it's released. So any means of moderating this risk is extremely valuable. Creating a movie based on pre-sold intellectual property, such as a bestselling novel, is one way to increase the possibility of success. Another is to cast the biggest stars.

In today's film industry, where studios and independents usually package each film as a one-off deal, stars have greater negotiating power than they had during the studio era, when they worked under contract. Their extravagant remuneration packages reflect their clout. Will Smith and Leonardo DiCaprio can command upfront fees of around $20 million per movie, and profit-share deals can be even more lucrative: Cameron Diaz reportedly made $42 million from the proceeds of *Bad Teacher* (2011).

That being said, anecdotal evidence points to a litany of failed films featuring well-paid actors, and *Forbes* even publishes an annual list of the 'worst value' stars. (Drew Barrymore and Adam Sandler have topped this list in recent years.) At the other end of the spectrum, few of the top-grossing films of all time are genuinely star-driven. *Star Wars* (1977), *Titanic* (1997) and *Avatar* (2009) all featured actors who were relative unknowns when the films were initially released.

An increasing weight of research suggests that stars' real economic value is not as high as their pay suggests. Studies carried out across extended periods reveal that the presence of stars has an inconsistent effect on profitability. Other factors, such as quality (based on reviews and awards), release date and whether the film is a sequel or part of a franchise, are much more reliable in predicting success. Of course, stars (and their agents) are well aware of the power of the franchise, which makes the latest comic book hero role a very attractive (and lucrative) proposition.

So why do stars continue to command such obscene salaries? For investors, the answer may be simply that they *appear* to be so valuable, regardless of whether this value turns into actual profit. For this reason, stars are often the first elements attached to a project because they provide credibility at this vital stage. Stars are also very useful when promoting films upon release. A rare interview from a big star can provide acres of column inches and visibility for forthcoming projects. Stars do sell films; they just don't always sell tickets.

One good way to discover which stars really pull in the dosh for their studios is to sign up for an online Fantasy Film League game. Several are available (try www.fantasyfilmleague.com or www.summermovieleague.com), and each works on a similar model to that of fantasy sports leagues. Buy a few stars, and keep an eye on their profitability while engaging in healthy competition with online friends. It's a win-win!

Contracting star labour

Star systems have developed in many nations across the international film industry (see the later section 'Exploring a world of stars'), but they tend to work best under tight contractual controls. In 1930s and 40s Hollywood, stars worked almost exclusively for their respective studios, which carefully stage-managed their images and personas across a range of films and publicity activities.

Under studio contracts, actors names were changed, noses fixed and biographies creatively embellished to create perfect figureheads for the competing studios. Stars 'manufactured' in this way included wartime pin-up Rita Hayworth (born Margarita Cansino), whom studio executives considered too Latin to succeed until she dyed her hair red and underwent painful hairline electrolysis and skin-lightening.

The contract system was clearly open for abuse, with moguls such as Jack Warner disciplining stars by casting them in obviously unsuitable roles that then led to decline, resulting in their suspension. One of Warner's most troublesome stars was James Cagney, who was typecast as a tough guy despite ambitions to be a song and dance man. Cagney sued Warner for breach of contract in 1935 and was influential in the early years of the Screen Actors Guild (see Chapter 9 for more on the rise of the Hollywood agents). When you gotta dance, you gotta dance. . . .

Selling other stuff

The adjective most frequently used in conjunction with film stars is definitely 'glamorous'. Stars are glamorous because they look fabulous at award ceremonies wearing the latest couture, or they're photographed holidaying in exclusive beach and ski resorts, or they can get tables at the best restaurants in the world. They ooze style, sophistication and class.

People tend to forget that in order to be film-star glamorous, you also must be ambitious, influential and just plain rich. But most non-film stars prefer focusing on the idea of glamour, probably because doing so allows people to feel less uncomfortable about wanting the lifestyles that many stars conspicuously flaunt. The image of desirable success that film stars project lies at the heart of Western consumer society, which makes stars the perfect vehicles for advertising.

The vital connection between film stars and advertising is nothing new. In the early years of the Hollywood film industry, female stars such as Mary Pickford advertised diverse products including Pompeian Night Cream ('Brings Beauty While You Sleep!'). By 1950, even man's man John Wayne was endorsing cigarettes alongside the dubious claim that 'Camels agree with your throat'.

Although the benefits of movie star endorsements for products and their advertisers are obvious, these deals can also extend stars' visibility and reach. But the principal benefit for stars is clearly financial. With fees from acting roles proving unpredictable for all but the biggest names, canny stars diversify their activities to ensure profitability and steady income. Over the past fifteen years, Jennifer Lopez has transformed herself from up-and-coming actress in *Out of Sight* (1998) to a global brand encompassing pop music, fashion, perfumes and TV production.

But dangers exist alongside opportunities. Products can fall out of public favour – no Hollywood star today advertises cigarettes, for example. Or conversely a star's image can suddenly be deemed incompatible with that of an endorsed product. Advertisers of Florida Orange Juice famously dropped Burt Reynolds after a messy divorce. Seems that OJ and infidelity just don't mix.

But more broadly, some stars are uncomfortable with having their economic power so obviously demonstrated and exploited. During the New Hollywood era of the late 1960s and 70s, when anti-establishment politics were the fashion, doing commercials just wasn't cool. This stigma led to a spate of big American stars going overseas to shoot commercials, particularly in Japan where the embarrassing images were presumed less likely to show up in the States.

In the age of the Internet, however, regionally exclusive media is clearly impossible, and yet still George Clooney's coffee ads can be seen everywhere except American television. Count yourself lucky, America, they're truly awful. But also incredibly lucrative; Clooney is widely reported to have banked $40 million from the endorsement deal. Now *that's* smooth and rich.

Identifying with stars

Desire defines the relationship between film stars and their audiences. You want stars to succeed in their on-screen quests for love or success. You want to look like them or be more like them and, of course, you sometimes want to do naughty things with/to them. These 'wants' are all different levels of desire, and their great power is that you can never truly satisfy these desires, no matter how much you try. Even if, by some incredible turn of events, you end up dating a movie star, you'll soon find out that they're regular people, like everyone else.

Do you have a favourite film star – someone who always convinces you to get out of the house and catch her latest film on the big screen? Do you follow someone obsessively on Twitter – or even attempt to see the object of your desire in the flesh at film premieres? Don't worry, you're not a total geek. Well, maybe a bit of geek, but that's practically essential in film studies circles.

Think seriously about why a particular actor appeals to you. Is it purely a physical thing? Probably not if the person is that important to you. As you dig deeper, you may well find an emotional connection to the star; you identify with that person in some way. Perhaps aspects of her star image (flip to the earlier section 'Analysing star image' for more details) that you gleaned through publicity interviews or on social media resonate with you – or maybe you respond to one or more of her key performances. Either way, your favourite stars make you feel like them in some way or other.

Identification in film studies is a slippery concept, because scholars use the term in different ways:

- ✔ In a commonsense way, identification describes an audience's connection with a character while watching a film. If you identify with the protagonist, you can imagine yourself in that person's place, therefore heightening feelings of tension, suspense and relief. You don't necessarily feel a deep connection with the actor or the character; just that the film is efficient in helping you suspend disbelief, or buy into the reality of the story world.

✔ At a more complex level, some film theorists argue that identifying with a character on screen is comparable to the fundamental psychological processes of *identity formation,* such as French psychoanalyst Jacques Lacan's 'mirror stage' (see Chapter 13). Put very simply, when a baby recognises herself in a mirror, she understands that her body and mind are united, but she also misunderstands by thinking that she's everywhere and everything. If you lose yourself in a film, you're like that baby!

You may find these and other theories of identification convincing – or not. But simply asking people how they relate to stars, through audience research, shows that fans really care about their idols. In the early 1990s, film scholar Jackie Stacey posted an advert in a women's magazine asking readers to share fan letters about favourite female stars from the 1940s and 50s. Stacey received more than 300 submissions, and from these accounts, she identified the following elements of female-star fandom (from most to least extreme responses):

✔ **Devotion and worship:** Seeing stars as 'goddesses', unattainably perfect creatures.

✔ **Desire to become:** Modelling yourself on what a star represents, such as the confidence of Marlene Dietrich, even if the goal is impossible.

✔ **Imitation and copying:** Trying to act like and look like the star, such as through clothing or hairstyles.

✔ **Pleasure in feminine power:** Enjoying strong women, such as Katharine Hepburn or Bette Davis, who get things done in their own ways and on their own terms.

✔ **Escapism:** Forgetting yourself and becoming lost in the film's moment.

Although Stacey was exploring women's relationship to female stars, similar studies reveal comparable responses from male fans to male stars. In fact, these relationships can be just as intense and commercially exploitable.

Sexing up the screen

Many people think of unbridled sexuality in films as a recent phenomenon, because the norms of what's acceptable to present on screen have generally become more relaxed in recent decades. But in fact early cinema featured extravagantly sexy performers, such as 'the Latin Lover' Rudolph Valentino and 'It Girl' Clara Bow. Valentino was renowned for his ability to drive female audiences of the 1920s wild with desire.

Partly thanks to the responses that sex symbols such as Valentino provoked, America's moral guardians put increasing pressure on the Hollywood studios until they came up with a system of self-regulation known as the *Hays Code,*

after Will Hays, head of the industry's professional body, the Motion Picture Producers and Distributors of America. 'The Code' was established in 1930 but only fully enforced four years later.

Under the Hays Code, the Hollywood studios agreed never to represent certain elements and to treat others with extreme caution. These limits had an immediate impact on the sexiest film stars because nudity of any kind was outlawed and on-screen sexual activity severely curtailed. Men and women were forbidden from appearing in bed together and kissing had a strict time limit. However, some historians argue that the Code actually *increased* the erotic appeal of stars by constructing psychologically rich signals for sexual activity, such as fetishes of clothing or cigarettes, and by implying rather than displaying sex.

To understand the eroticism under the Code, watch Rita Hayworth's dazzlingly sexy performance in *Gilda* (1946). Hayworth launches onto the screen in close-up with naked shoulders, luxurious hair bouncing. She later conducts an electrifying strip tease, which involves removing just a pair of long satin gloves. The trashy plot implies impotence, homosexuality and infidelity without falling foul of the letter of the Code. Although Gilda is punished for her bad behaviour, Hayworth is irrepressible.

Of course the sexualised visual treatment of female film stars is a sticky subject for film studies, which typically incorporates a feminist perspective. Laura Mulvey's groundbreaking work on visual pleasure and narrative cinema set up the notion of the *male gaze,* whereby female stars exist so that male characters (and a largely male audience) can look at them. As a result, watching a film echoes and reinforces sexist behaviour in society at large (see Chapter 13).

Since its publication in 1975, Mulvey's work has been extremely influential, but many other scholars have questioned and modified it. For example, the male gaze allows little space for the complexities of female spectatorship, notably how female audiences enjoy watching sexualised male stars such as Valentino as well as watching powerful or beautiful women.

The enormous success of the *Twilight* franchise (2008–12) is notable in this light. The five films are built around two contrasting male sex symbols: the ethereal and smouldering Robert Pattinson and the gym-built body of macho Taylor Lautner. This dynamic proved wildly successful with younger female audiences, inviting comparisons with boy-band stars from the pop-music industry. So are the *Twilight* films cynical financial exploitation of hormonal teenagers, or a safe and even empowering space for girls to explore their sexuality? The answer is probably both, and that's why star studies is so fascinating.

Queering stardom

Film stars are intoxicating objects of desire, including desire that extends beyond what's sometimes socially or culturally acceptable. As a result, many film stars have become important symbols or icons within gay and lesbian culture. Just as with heterosexual audiences, stars are valuable to gay audiences as role models and sex symbols, but the importance of certain stars to gay men and women often reaches further due to the lack of alternative reference points in 20th-century culture. This increasingly popular area of film study is part of the wider academic field of *queer studies.*

During the Golden Age of Hollywood, homosexuality was strictly taboo *and* an important element of gossip culture. The repressed sexuality of stars such as Rock Hudson (the truth of which was revealed upon his death in the 1980s) only fuelled the flames of speculation. And, as Vito Russo argues in his documentary *The Celluloid Closet* (1995), gay characters by any other name did appear on screen throughout this period. Can anyone possibly mistake Mrs Danvers's romantic attachment for her former boss, the eponymous *Rebecca* (1940)?

The most famous Hollywood icon for gay men is undoubtedly Judy Garland. Her combination of stunning vocal talent and tragic personal life has struck a chord within gay culture for decades. As Richard Dyer and others describe, female stars such as Garland carry a strong element of *camp,* in terms of their knowing theatricality, and their ability to render the trivial important (and vice versa). And those ruby slippers!

Working like a star: Acting, performing, inhabiting

When assessing the quality of a film, even in the most informal way, many people pass judgement on the actors' performances before any other element, often even before the story itself. For some reason, everyone feels qualified to dismiss particular actors as wooden or unconvincing, or to acclaim others as masters of their craft. But explaining *why* you're so impressed by a performance – or picking out what actors precisely *do* to make their work convincing – is much more difficult.

This challenge is partly because, as with other elements of the classical filmmaking style such as editing (see Chapter 4), movie acting is often meant to go unnoticed. *Naturalistic* actors aim to make you forget that they're people pretending to be other people, and the best ones often do just that. Then again, actors can also employ highly noticeable acting techniques, such as altering their physical appearance or adopting a different accent or voice, which can be equally impressive.

Dissecting performances

As a film student, try to develop the ability to take notice of understated acting and see past showy tics to help you understand how screen acting works (or indeed doesn't work).

Avoid the following pitfalls when critiquing actors:

- **Don't confuse performance with character.** For example, you may be tempted to credit Ingrid Bergman for Ilsa's core emotional dilemma in *Casablanca:* the tension between romantic love and pragmatism in the face of adversity. But this powerful struggle was already in the script before the actress joined the film. Bergman did, however, beautifully embody the dilemma in unspoken ways, through her wonderfully specific gestures and body language.

- **Don't assume that stars are just playing themselves.** Even for stars whose performances across many films are similar and consistent, such as action heroes or slapstick comedians, actors still do a great deal of work to make their films emotionally coherent.

- **Try not to react negatively to performance styles from different historical periods or cultural contexts.** The extravagant miming and gesturing of many actors in early cinema was carried over from popular theatre where oversized performances were required just to be understood. Similarly performances in Bollywood films can seem cartoonish and camp to Western audiences who're used to a far more restrained acting style.

Do examine carefully how actors use their bodies to construct performances. Some film genres place heavy physical demands on an actor, particularly action films, musicals and certain types of comedy (anything starring Jim Carrey). The way actors run, fight or dance is choreographed to some extent, but still their specific physical qualities create different meanings and emphases.

An actor's facial expressions and gestures in close-up often create intense moments of conflict or drama in film. For a great example, watch the very end of *The Graduate* (1967). Not the thrilling race against time and interrupted wedding, but the final scene with Dustin Hoffman's Ben and Katharine Ross's Elaine escaping on the bus. Hoffman's face shifts from exhilaration and triumph, through doubt, to disillusionment all in one long take. These gestures completely change the tone of the film's conclusion.

Actors' voices are just as important as their bodies, and getting an accent right is crucial. For example, perhaps you were as mystified as everyone else by Keanu Reeves's notorious accent in *Dracula* (1992). But accents are just one part of an overall package of vocal performance. Actors can also alter the *quality* of their voices – pitch and resonances – through effort or coaching to produce different effects for different roles. Compare the gruff authority of Jon Hamm's Don Draper in TV's *Mad Men* to his more vocally melodious comic turn in *Bridesmaids* (2011).

A useful way of separating performance from character is to compare two different actors playing the same role. Remakes can be great for this game, but you also need to bear in mind that acting styles change over time and across national boundaries. Gus Van Sant's 'shot for shot' remake of Hitchcock's *Psycho* (1960 and 1998) is a particularly interesting example. Many critics questioned why Van Sant even needed to make his film, but students of film acting will at least be forever grateful.

Meeting 'the method'

Being a hybrid, interdisciplinary field of study, film studies borrows its language for talking about performance from other areas, particularly theatre studies and aspects of psychology. For this reason, several key terms and frames of reference from these fields are important to understand when you're analysing film acting.

Crucial to these discussions is the idea of *naturalistic acting*, in which actors depict realistic, believable human characters. The term *naturalism* developed from 19th-century drama, when putting real life on to the stage was a deeply radical strategy. Actors in naturalistic plays, such as August Strindberg's *Miss Julie* (1888), were encouraged to find their characters by understanding their environments and circumstances.

Naturalism was a major influence on the Russian theatre director Constantin Stanislavski, who as a young actor was notorious for disguising himself as a tramp or a gypsy to understand his roles. Stanislavski hated the then dominant style of 'mechanical' theatre acting, which used stylised gestures and clichés to present stock characters to the audience. He advocated a holistic emotional and physical approach that blends the actor into the scripted character. Failing that, get drunk and sleep on the streets.

Through his leadership of the New York Actors' Studio from 1951, Lee Strasberg brought Stanslavski's theories into American drama and film, and popularised the *method* school of acting. Strasberg's method centres on the idea of *affective memory,* which asks actors to build up stores of emotive responses that they can then use when playing roles. Under Strasberg, training affective memory was a process often akin to psychotherapy, which other disciples of Stanislavski such as Stella Adler saw as irresponsible and dangerous.

Although elements of Stanislavski's training had been employed by actors such as Marlene Dietrich in the 1930s, method acting shot into the public consciousness with Marlon Brando's scorching performances in *A Streetcar*

Named Desire (1951) and *On The Waterfront* (1954). Brando's intense gaze, sudden outpourings of fury or despair, and ability to lose himself in his roles were widely attributed to Strasberg, although ironically he trained with Adler. Either way, film acting had a new champion.

The method spread rapidly through Strasberg's Actors Studio, which attracted students as diverse as James Dean, Paul Newman and Marilyn Monroe. But the approach wasn't without its detractors. The typical method performance is showy and shouty and doesn't suit every type of role. Also, method actors can also be notoriously difficult on set. Working on *Marathon Man* (1976) with method-trained Dustin Hoffman, Laurence Olivier famously quipped 'Try *acting,* dear boy . . . it's much easier!'

Exploring a World of Stars

The Hollywood star system was so culturally and financially significant throughout the 20th century that it has tended to dominate film-studies work on stardom. This bias towards Hollywood often excludes consideration of the rich variety of stars and star systems in different cultural contexts. Sometimes stars can be exceptionally famous with local audiences and all but unknown elsewhere, such as Fan Bingbing, the beautiful Chinese actress and singer, whereas others, for example Brigitte Bardot, burst out of a national context onto the international scene.

As a result, film stars have a particular importance to the circulation of ideas around national identity, something I discuss in this section in connection with European stars. I also take a look here at the most significant star-making film industry in the world today, the Bollywood system in India, which has invited comparisons with Hollywood in its heyday.

Pondering European stardom

The long-running, well-established film industries and the different languages and cultures of Europe have produced a wide range of film stars, sometimes echoing or imitating American 'types' and other times generating distinctive and culturally specific icons. The study of European film stars has a great deal in common with the study of national identities. What's the most useful approach: defining European stars by what's special about them or saying that 'they're not like Hollywood stars'?

Chapter 11 examines the film industry throughout continental Europe.

Britain

The stars of British cinema often trained in the theatre, either the classical tradition of Laurence Olivier and Kenneth Branagh or the earthy music halls of Gracie Fields. During the 1940s and 1950s the well-established Rank Organisation imitated Hollywood by developing its stars under contract, producing Dirk Bogarde and Diana Dors as British sex symbols. Nonetheless, the biggest British stars have always been tempted away to Hollywood: Cary Grant, Julie Andrews and more recently Andrew Garfield and Carey Mulligan to name but a few. Chapter 10 explores British film-making in greater detail.

France

French cinema has tended to be far more separate (in financial and cultural terms) from Hollywood than the British, and so the French star system developed in more idiosyncratic directions. Scholar Ginette Vincendeau identifies the following defining characteristics of French film stardom:

- ✔ Stars have more control over their images than their American equivalents. For example, Juliette Binoche refused to participate in promotion for *Wuthering Heights* (1992) over a disagreement with the film's producers.

- ✔ Stars have the ability to straddle mainstream and art cinema, as Gerard Depardieu's varied back catalogue amply demonstrates.

- ✔ The French New Wave movement of the 1960s produced a significant and long-lasting grouping of stars, led by Jean-Paul Belmondo and Jeanne Moreau.

Italy

Italian cinema also had a famous post-war renaissance in the form of Neorealism, but typically Neorealist films were less glamorous (and therefore less star-driven) than those of the French New Wave. Anna Magnani is an icon of this period due to her powerful, earthy performances in films such as *Rome, Open City* (1945). Italian comedic stars, such as the clownish Toto, travelled little outside the country, but sex symbol Sophia Loren was the quintessential international glamour icon. See Chapter 11 for a closer look at Italy's beloved Toto.

Germany

The tragic intervention of World War II meant that the national identity of German actors and stars was a particular focus for international public opinion. Stars such as Conrad Veidt and Marlene Dietrich were able to work in Britain and Hollywood only by becoming naturalised citizens.

The Nazis were well aware of the propaganda potential of film stars, and Hitler and Goebbels surrounded themselves with glamorous women such as Zarah Leander. The actor Gustaf Gründgens was criticised for collaboration with the Nazi regime in the novel *Mephisto* (1936) by Klaus Mann (later adapted into a film).

Of course German actors today are just as able to cross over from national to transnational cinema stardom as those from other countries, as Daniel Brühl has demonstrated. (For a description of the term *transnational,* check out the later sidebar 'Whatever happened to international stardom?')

Spain

Spanish and Latin American film stars have always had a greater chance of international success due to the large Hispanic population in the United States and Latin America. Ramon Novarro, Dolores Del Rio and more recently Penélope Cruz and Javier Bardem have all made it big in Hollywood.

Seeing the new Hollywood in Bollywood

The term *Bollywood* refers to a subsection of the Indian film industry, which as a whole is huge and features many different languages (see Chapter 12). Bollywood is popular cinema, usually made in Hindi and based on the production centre of Mumbai (formerly Bombay). But what's interesting about this label is that it contains an obvious echo of the American film industry at its height and yet has also come to stand for the whole of Indian cinema in the Western imagination.

Whatever happened to international stardom?

The phenomenon of film stardom is a useful way to understand the difference between the terms *international* and *transnational,* with the latter largely replacing the former in contemporary film studies.

The word *international* suggests collaboration between nation states that are clearly defined and of roughly equal power and value. So describing film production and stars as international only makes sense when many countries around the world have significant competing film industries.

In recent decades, the globalisation of the film industry has led to companies with bases across the world making many films filled by casts of actors who have homes in different countries. Of course an enhanced ability to travel across borders, or to work *transnationally,* tends to benefit Hollywood actors more than those from other nations. The era of transnational cinema sees beyond borders, but often to the advantage of the biggest and the best.

You can interpret the common comparisons between the Hindi film indus-try and Hollywood as a patronising post-colonial critique (implying that Bollywood films are a poor imitation of Hollywood) or more positively as a well-intentioned (if sometimes poorly informed) compliment. Western journal-ists often look to Mumbai for a nostalgic hit of old-fashioned Hollywood glam-our, and this glamour is embodied in Bollywood film stars. The comparison tends to work as follows:

- ✔ Bollywood stars retain a powerful hold over the Indian public imagina-tion in a way that may have been lost in the West.

- ✔ The press and publicity around Bollywood film stars celebrates conspic-uous consumption, fashion and Western-style consumerism.

- ✔ Bollywood films often appear to be designed as obvious star vehicles to showcase the appeal of their lead actor or actress, just as with many classical Hollywood movies.

For some good examples of star-packed Bollywood films, check out the sec-tion on Indian cinemas in Chapter 12.

As an example, consider the career of Aishwarya Rai, former Miss World and current queen of the Bollywood box office. With her honeyed complexion, green eyes and raven locks, Rai's beauty is beyond doubt: even Julia Roberts called her 'the most beautiful woman in the world'. Her earning potential is equally impressive, because she makes as much as Roberts per film. But due to the flexible contracts typical in Bollywood, she has a much more prolific output: 44 starring roles since 1997 compared to Roberts's mere 20 or so.

Rai's most famous films are *Devdas* (2002), a glossy romantic drama filled with spectacular dance routines, *Pride and Prejudice* (2004), which provided her first English-speaking role, and *Enthiran* (2010), an ambitious sci-fi epic star-ring the biggest star of Tamil cinema, Rajinikanth.

Rai's celebrity status was further enhanced in 2007 when she married fellow actor Abhishek Bachchan, son of legendary star Amitabh and Jaya Bachchan, making her essentially Bollywood royalty. Her early career as a model means that she's an advertiser's dream, and her endorsements include top global brands such as Pepsi, L'Oreal and De Beers diamonds. Her image in India is that of a clean-living, religious woman with strong humanitarian concerns. The story of her rise to fame has difficult elements – such as an allegedly abusive relationship with fellow actor Salman Kahn – but these only seem to endear her further to her Bollywood fans.

Rai certainly has the demeanour and poise of Hollywood stars such as Grace Kelly and Elizabeth Taylor, the celebrity status and family connections of Douglas Fairbanks and Mary Pickford, and the marketability of Audrey Hepburn. But in truth her fan base is already on the way to eclipsing that of Hollywood in its prime. Before long American actresses will be aspiring to be like Rai, instead of the other way around.

Separating Stardom and Celebrity

Ask people to say what they think the difference is between a star and celebrity, and you're likely to get an answer along the lines of 'Stars are famous for having a talent, whereas celebrities are just famous for being famous'. This commonly held opinion involves a wealth of assumptions and value judgements. Most obviously, it implies that real stars are better than mere celebrities, who are debased fame-seekers.

In fact very few, if any, pure celebrities exist according to this definition. Even Paris Hilton, often cited as a talentless celebrity, became famous due to family connections and has proved extremely talented at self-promotion. The vast majority of celebrities are also actors, TV stars or sportspeople whose personalities have somehow come to eclipse what made them famous in the first place.

In this section I reveal that the boundaries between star and celeb were always blurry, and that the Internet is increasingly making such distinctions murkier than the streets of Victorian London in a Jack the Ripper flick.

Living private lives in the public gaze

Many people believe that celebrities have sold their souls to the devil. They have fame, influence, riches beyond their wildest dreams – but at what cost? Their privacy. Time and again you hear celebrities complaining about not being able to walk down the street or go shopping or eat a doughnut or whatever. Yes, that must be horrible. But they sort of knew what they were getting into, didn't they?

Being a star isn't just about being talented, it's also about constructing an image that appeals to the public in some way. And if you do that really, really well, you become a celebrity. Then all bets are off: your life is open season on past lovers, career mistakes and wardrobe malfunctions. Although technically celebrities have the same legal right to privacy as everyone else, in reality they can't sustain their careers without allowing the public access to themselves in one way or another.

People's insatiable thirst for celebrity gossip seems to be a fact of modern life. The interesting question is: why do they care so much about the private lives of people they've never met? Film (and media) studies has several possible explanations for this phenomenon:

> ✔ **In Western culture, celebrity worship has replaced religion as a means of publicly discussing ethics, beauty and morality.** How people talk about ethical issues such as adultery is often shaped by celebrity examples. In this sense, film stars truly are like gods (Morgan Freeman) or perhaps fallen angels (Robert Downey Jr).

✔ **Celebrity culture provides a valuable form of common ground or social glue within an increasingly fragmented society.** Whereas people used to gossip about the neighbours over the garden fence, they now chat about Lindsay Lohan on social media.

✔ **Celebrities distract people from how awful their daily lives are by reminding everyone to keep spending money.** Film stars are particularly good at encouraging escapism, while making you want to buy stuff to be more like them.

All these theories rely on a dissolving of the public/private divide, which still exists in everyday social life. You don't stare at a stranger's imperfect body on a beach and loudly discuss her cellulite with your friends, or broadcast the marital problems of your best friend on the Internet, do you? At least I hope not. But you've probably engaged in these types of interaction in connection with celebrities. Go on, admit it.

Stars have always engaged in official publicity, in which they appear on talk shows or give interviews to magazines, and these activities are valuable to their fans. But the gossip industry prizes a different type of information: the 'kiss and tell' exposé, the unflattering paparazzi shot or the naughty video leaked online. The appeal of these products is that they're 'authentic'; they appear to offer access to the real, flawed person behind the glowing professional facade.

But then, these days people are so accustomed to the way that celebrity works that they're even cynical about such apparently uncontrolled leaks. They know full well that celebrities have huge teams of spin doctors and publicists in their entourages. And the old adage that 'there's no such thing as bad publicity' is probably true in the majority of cases. Even Charlie Sheen, who had a very public mental breakdown on YouTube and Twitter in 2011, is still working.

Star-making in the 21st century

Andy Warhol's much-quoted prediction that 'in the future, everyone will be world-famous for 15 minutes' has come to stand for the proliferation of routes to fame in the 21st century, and in particular for the rise of Internet stardom. Direct public access to media channels has vastly increased the possibility of becoming famous in some way. People can upload videos of themselves to YouTube and achieve thousands of views and 'likes'.

But Warhol's outlandish idea has a caveat: this new, universal fame is temporary and fleeting. Public attention isn't infinite, and when the next big thing happens, you're toast. Also the cultural value of democratised stardom is different in that anything that's easy to achieve is seen as less worthwhile. The old-fashioned Hollywood stars that Warhol worshipped were like rare, precious gems, plucked from obscurity and polished like diamonds. If everyone wore diamonds, they'd be worth nothing.

The international phenomenon of *Big Brother* led to the explosion of so-called reality TV programming in the early 2000s. Originally conceived as a social experiment to explore human interaction under closely controlled circumstances, the show quickly morphed into a shortcut contestants could take to become famous, by proving how 'genuine' or 'authentic' they seemed while being broadcast live on national television. As every viewer knows, the worst crime for a *Big Brother* contestant is to be 'fake'.

One of the remarkable features about reality TV stars is that they don't travel internationally. Each country has its own version of the biggest franchises, and although winners from one country occasionally appear on another nation's show, they're rarely popular with the locals.

By contrast, YouTube is the very definition of transnational (see the earlier sidebar 'Whatever happened to international stardom?'). The video streaming site has produced several music stars, such as Lana del Rey, and globalised others such as South Korean pop star Psy ('Gangnam Style').

But is YouTube any use for aspiring film stars? Several have made promising starts. Caustic comedian and songwriter Bo Burnham successfully made his reputation by posting homemade videos online, before launching sell-out international stand-up tours. He's reportedly signed a deal to write a musical for comedy producer Judd Apatow. However his first 'old media' venture, a sitcom for MTV, was cancelled after just one season. Are his 15 minutes now up? Only time will tell.

Chapter 4

Building Movie Stories

*W*hen you take a look at the very earliest films that still survive (which today you can do very easily online), you can be forgiven for thinking that cinema didn't begin by telling stories. Films made before the turn of the 20th century by the Lumière brothers include a train entering a station, workers leaving the factory gates and a baby eating breakfast. They aren't exactly packed with dramatic incidents.

Yet movement and dynamism are present in all these brief snapshots of (apparently) real life. And, perhaps inevitably, when you watch these earliest films, you can't help but think of them as snippets from some much larger chain of events. Where has the train come from and who are those passengers streaming off it into a brand-new location? What will all those factory workers do now that they've finished their labours? Is the baby going to behave and eat his breakfast?!

The point is that humans can't help but create stories – even when they have limited information. Storytelling is how you make sense of the world, understand the past, think through possibilities and plan ahead. In evolutionary terms, biologists believe that the ability to tell stories enabled early humans to pass down information from generation to generation and thereby gradually become cleverer and cleverer. Sorry, more clever. So human civilisation is composed of stories, and this chapter explores the techniques and approaches that filmmakers use to create the greatest stories ever told.

Uncovering Mise-en-Scène

Time for a French cinematic term. *Mise-en-scène* literally means 'put on the stage' and fittingly originates from the theatrical tradition that long predates cinema. If you think about everything that's put on a stage for a play, you begin to understand basic mise-en-scène: props, sets, actors, costumes and so on. Fundamentally, mise-en-scène is stuff. But it's also concerned with much more, including the following:

- ✔ How the stuff is lit, where it's placed and how it sits in relation to other stuff. In other words, mise-en-scène is what the stuff means and what it's doing to tell the story.

- ✔ Why the stuff is present – whether purely for *verisimilitude* (the appearance of reality) or for more interesting, symbolic reasons.

- ✔ As a signal of a film's genre, in which case this stuff is iconography (see Chapter 5 for more on this subject).

- ✔ Being fundamental to a director's toolkit to create a film (if you believe in the director as all-powerful; see Chapter 14).

The best way to appreciate mise-en-scène is to practise looking at it and for it. In this section I analyse one moment from a classical Hollywood movie as illustration. I also discuss mise-en-scène in terms of the notoriously complex issue of realism in film, as well as its use in one genre – melodrama.

Analysing a scene

Figure 4-1 is a film still from *Letter from an Unknown Woman* (1948), Max Ophüls's meticulously constructed romantic melodrama. A note of caution: *film stills* are usually shot by a photographer on set and so aren't quite the same thing as frames from the finished film. This example, however, clearly shows all the stuff in the scene and how it's presented to the audience, and so for the purposes of mise-en-scène analysis it works just fine.

So what can you see in this one image of one scene from this film? At first glance, it appears to be a romantic image of a young couple taking an exciting train journey together. The train carriage is comfortable and plush, with grand touches such as the elaborate curtain tie. The male character, Stefan (Louis Jourdan), is smoothly handsome and well dressed and has a confident demeanour. His female companion Lisa (Joan Fontaine) is pretty in a girlish manner, her uplifted gaze and submissive pose suggesting her youth. She's also dressed in white, the colour of innocence.

Figure 4-1:
Mise-en-scène in *Letter from an Unknown Woman* (1948).

If you watch the scene from the film, however, you know that everything here is a fake. The train journey is an elaborate fairground ride that the characters are enjoying. The carriage is static while an old man shifts painted scenery by means of a bicycle and gears. The impression of movement works because it's similar to rear-projection effects used in the cinema (flip to the later sidebar 'Drive-in movies' for more on this technique). So the mise-en-scène signals its own fabricated artificiality, while you watch an innocent girl being seduced by a lothario who has used the same trick on many other women. This scene becomes a fascinating example of how mise-en-scène can function as ironic commentary upon the action taking place on screen.

Looking deeply at all that stuff

Mise-en-scène is the basis of film style. Used in its broadest sense, the term can also mean not only what's 'put onto' the screen, but also everything that viewers see, such as colour, shot composition and the framing of space, both on and off screen. Of course, you can't literally see anything that is off screen, but nearly all films construct a space that is larger than the frame, often by showing characters looking or gesturing out of it.

In order to go deeper into appreciating *Letter from an Unknown Woman,* you need to watch the film to see everything in action – which is no bad thing because it's one of the masterpieces of classic mise-en-scène analysis. At the very least, watch the train ride scene online, which should hopefully whet your appetite for the whole movie.

The fake train-ride scene contains an example of director Ophüls's careful framing of space to make the characters look as if they're on a theatrical stage. Before they move together to embrace, Lisa and Stefan sit opposite one another with the scenery trundling past, framed by heavy velvet curtains. This set-up mirrors an earlier scene in a restaurant booth, which also frames the pair through curtains, emphatically drawn across the edges of the screen by a waiter. This repeated use of curtains to frame the image reinforces the sense that both the actors and the characters are playing roles.

Lighting is another key element of mise-en-scène because it influences the way you perceive all the other elements. In the train scene, the lighting is low, signalling night-time with romantic and sexual possibilities. The relative darkness of the scene also makes Lisa stand out all the more clearly with her pale skin and white blouse. In the following close-ups, Fontaine is lit in the *high-key style* often used for Hollywood stars, so that she appears to glow from within. This lighting choice illustrates her girlish happiness, as well as further suggesting an element of fantasy, of an impossible romantic ideal.

Actors themselves are partly just objects in the frame, and so you can also discuss their performances as an element of mise-en-scène in action. In this instance, the train scene is vital for Fontaine's performance as Lisa; she must convince the audience that she's a young girl trying to seem more sophisticated and older than she is. She accomplishes this through nervous gestures, such as turning a rose in her fingers, as well as her excitable speech patterns when she recounts a memory from childhood. Jourdan has less to do here, but his strutting walk over to pay for another ride says it all.

All these elements – the sets, costumes, actors, lighting, framing and performance – work together in complex ways to produce meaning for the audience. *Letter from an Unknown Woman* may be an unusually rich film for this type of analysis, but you can apply the same method to any film that you watch.

Presenting the world as you know it (sort of)

In fiction film, mise-en-scène is generally used in a relatively realistic kind of way. My vague phrasing is deliberate, because few things are more slippery than the concept of so-called realism in film studies. In this section I use *realism* to mean the ways in which filmmakers attempt to create a visual impression of real life within their fictional worlds. So try and hold onto this idea of realism as I explore it purely in relation to mise-en-scène.

To begin with, audiences have a commonsense notion of what looks realistic within a given film or scene. You can probably think of films ruined when you noticed a prop, a set or a hairstyle that just wasn't realistic or was from the wrong historical period. Try mentioning Mel Gibson and kilts to any Scottish friends and then stand back (kilts weren't invented until 200 years after the events of *Braveheart* (1995)).

But of course, strictly speaking, nothing is remotely realistic about any fictional scene arranged for the camera. Most films use carefully constructed sets as environments, and even when films are shot in real locations the space is carefully managed. When you accept that a film looks realistic, you're choosing to believe in a carefully constructed lie. In addition, the rules and conventions surrounding what's acceptably realistic and what isn't are culturally and historically specific.

A sequence (or an entire film) can use extremely stylised, unrealistic mise-en-scène in the service of *psychological realism* (by which I mean presenting reality as seen or experienced by a particular character). Dream sequences, for example, are often heavily stylised, with the most famous one being the surreal sets and props designed by Salvador Dalí for Alfred Hitchcock's *Spellbound* (1945). Curtains covered in eyes are snipped by enormous scissors, and later a man stands on the roof of an impossible building with a melted wheel in his hand. Both elements represent memories that have been repressed by the film's amnesiac hero. Take a look, it's seriously weird.

Drive-in movies

You can find a good example of how conventions of what looks realistic on screen change over time by watching driving sequences in movies. Prior to about 1965, actors typically sat in a car on a sound stage and a process called *rear projection* gave the appearance of moving images seen through the car windows. Rear projection involves projecting a second moving image onto a screen outside the car to create the illusion that the car is moving through space.

If you watch the car chases in James Bond's first outing, *Dr. No* (1962), today, they look amusingly quaint due to this technique. Sean Connery does a good job of matching all his glances to the vehicles attempting to ram his Aston Martin off the road, but the movement of the car doesn't sync with the moving images of the road behind. Plus, other issues with focus and depth clearly indicate that the car was in a studio, being rocked back and forth.

Despite Connery being shaken, not stirred, audiences of the film in 1962 were well used to this convention. They were able to suspend their disbelief and enjoy the thrill of the chase.

Mise-en-scène also places a film in its historical moment. Just watch any film made more than about 15 years ago and try not to be distracted by the outlandish hairstyles or outdated costumes, elements which of course went unnoticed at the time of its release. Similarly, mise-en-scène marks a film as being set in a specific place and culture. Put simply, when stuff appears 20-feet high on a cinema screen, it starts to tell its own stories.

Creating emotional pictures: Melodramatic mise-en-scène

Melodrama is an awkward term (not the first in film studies), which is somewhere between a genre and a broader category of film-making. The film industry uses it to refer to any exciting or emotional film, such as crime thrillers or biopics. But film-studies scholars tend to use the term to refer to a smaller group of films, usually domestic dramas based around female characters. These movies are also known as *women's pictures* due to their intended audience appeal.

German émigré Douglas Sirk directed many of the best-loved melodramas in Hollywood during the 1950s. In these films, such as *All That Heaven Allows* (1955) and *Imitation of Life* (1959), wives and mothers go through emotional turmoil while attempting to maintain the illusion of a perfect American middle-class existence. Take a look at a clip from one of Sirk's films (plenty are available on YouTube) and you get a sense of their distinctive elements: heightened emotion and gorgeous soft furnishings.

Feminist scholars including Laura Mulvey and Christine Gledhill argue that emotion and setting are fundamentally connected through melodramatic mise-en-scène. In certain film genres, notably the musical and the action film, characters have obvious ways to express excessive emotion, such as bursting into song or blowing stuff up. By contrast, in these domestic melodramas characters are restrained by social expectations, which means the visuals and sound have to express what the characters can't.

For example, in *All That Heaven Allows* Jane Wyman plays Cary, wealthy widow with two grown-up children. When she falls in love with the much younger Ron (Rock Hudson), her children emotionally blackmail her into giving him up to maintain appearances. Ron and Cary's developing relationship is literally embodied in the film's mise-en-scène, as Ron buys a dilapidated farmhouse and renovates it. When it's complete, he invites Cary over to admire his handiwork.

Cary is suitably impressed by the friendly fireplace and the idyllic country view from the spectacular picture window. Ron finally admits what has been clear to the audience for some time – he's been creating not just a house but a family home for them to live in together. After he proposes, Cary walks wordlessly to the window, where the couple stand silhouetted against the snow outside. Mournful music grows as Cary is forced to choose between Ron's burning fireplace and the freezing storm outside.

Speaking the Language and Grammar of Film

In many ways, film is like a language of its own. Using film you can argue a case, pass on information and tell a great story. But just imagine for a minute that you're an alien passing as human on the Earth (bear with me). You decide to watch a movie. Perhaps you can recognise people, gestures or words, but can you make any sense of space, character and story? Of course not, because you don't understand the *grammar* of film – the rules and conventions built up over time, which audiences understand as tools in the service of the story.

Studying the grammar of a foreign language can be difficult and dull, but the good news is that you're already a fluent speaker of cinema. So this section's discussion of scenes, sequences and shots isn't going to leave you feeling as if you're from another planet.

Making a scene (and a sequence)

As with mise-en-scène (see the preceding section), the idea of breaking a story down into *scenes,* which are presented to the audience in larger *sequences* or *acts,* predates cinema itself. In the theatre, each scene requires an element of visible work – a scene changing – which clearly marks the boundaries between each element. In film, this work is largely invisible, and so audiences require different signals or cues to orient themselves to otherwise jarring shifts in space or time.

Here's how these signals work traditionally to build up an understandable flow of information:

- ✔ A scene often takes place in a single location, which is usually clearly marked by an *establishing shot* (often an exterior or a wide shot of an entire room) before the action commences.

- ✔ After the scene gets going, it usually unfolds in real time until it reaches a conclusion. No disorienting gaps appear in the time line during the course of the scene.

✔ A scene can be a single shot, but usually it's composed of a series of shots (see 'Selecting shots' later in this chapter for details). Shots are then edited skilfully together to create coherent space and time. Check out the later section 'Solving the Puzzle: Editing Film' for editing insights.

✔ Actions, *eye-lines* (where the actors are looking) and sound are matched across editing transitions to create a feeling of unity. Film-makers also add music to hold a scene together.

✔ All shots that are edited together have some sort of *transition* from the first to the next, the most common being the simple cut. Film-makers sometimes signal boundaries between scenes or longer sequences with more unusual transitions, such as the wipe or the fade to black. (You can find illustrations and examples of these techniques online – try the support websites for major editing software, such as Final Cut Pro, for example.)

Of course all these rules can be bent or broken. Space is frequently manipulated so that a scene includes multiple locations – through careful editing between the two locations or by using split-screen effects. For example, many of the telephone conversations in *When Harry Met Sally . . .* (1989) are presented with characters in bed on either side of the phone and the screen. Flashbacks are a means of incorporating brief temporal disruptions to a scene's continuity without confusing the audience too much.

Sequences are larger sections of story built up from several smaller scenes. Many genres (see Chapter 5 for details) have conventional structures made of recognisable sequences. Consider horror films of the 'teen slasher' sub-genre. They typically have an opening sequence recounting one unexplained gory murder, followed by a sequence establishing a community of young nubile victims. The victims are dispatched in their own dedicated sequences before the final character (usually a girl) defeats the killer and/or escapes.

Selecting shots

As well as tennis players and bourbon drinkers, film-makers also need to think carefully about their shot selection. For film-makers, the shot is the basic building block which makes up scenes, sequences and films. This is illustrated by the common practice of turning a screenplay into a detailed *shot list*, which helps the production team to plan their resources. Film-making practice can create an infinite variety of types of shots, but for the purposes of this section I focus upon those that have well-established meanings within film grammar.

All the uses of close-ups or wide shots that I discuss in this section, and the elements that signal the transitions between scenes and sequences in the preceding section, are fundamentally *conventions.* Therefore, the elements' meanings develop over time and require various degrees of audience knowledge to be recognised. They also work differently in other cultural contexts, for example in early Russian cinema the close-ups of Sergei Eisenstein's films are to illustrate types of people rather than provide psychological depth (for more on Eisenstein's cinematic style and theory, flip to the later section 'Considering alternatives to the classical model').

The wide shot

Fiction films tell stories about people, and so any shot that favours the landscape over the human figure is unusual and is used to create specific effects.

Wide shots step back from the action to include the whole length of the human body (and often all of the characters in a scene) and *extreme wide shots* can be shot from miles away. Both are most commonly used as *establishing shots,* which give an overview of space at the beginning of a scene or sequence, but film-makers also use wide shots to create other grand gestures. (Flip to the later sidebar 'How wide is wide' for the technical details of wide shots.)

Wide shots are often required to capture the full impact of elaborate fight sequences, such as those between Neo (Keanu Reeves) and his cloned electronic enemies in *The Matrix* (1999), or dance sequences, as in *StreetDance 3D* (2010). Meanwhile extreme wide shots are often used to allow the audience to appreciate and wonder at grand, expensive set design or spectacular natural environments.

In *The Lord of the Rings* trilogy (2001–2003), the frequent extreme wide shots of the New Zealand setting filled with enormous armies show off the film's technical wizardry and reinforce the epic scale of the story. Conversely, an extreme wide shot featuring a solitary human figure can create a sense of vulnerability or loneliness. This approach is taken to extremes in *Gravity* (2013) when Sandra Bullock floats off into nothingness.

And finally . . . the extreme wide shot can also signal the ending to a story. For classic examples, check out the static, formal conclusion of *The Third Man* (1949) as the love interest Anna walks directly towards, and then past, the protagonist Holly. Or most famously of all, *The Searchers* (1956), which frames John Wayne through a front door overlooking Monument Valley. These endings are visually striking and provide a satisfying sense of closure, but they are also ambiguous and intriguing. The characters return to the world, but the world goes on, largely unconcerned.

How wide is wide?

The width of a wide shot depends partly upon the shape of the film frame itself. If directors and cinematographers choose to shoot in the squarish *academy ratio* (1.3:1, which means that the frame is 1.3 units in width for every 1 unit of height), not much space is available on either side of the human characters. This width maintains the focus on the humans in the frame, which works just fine for most narrative-driven classical Hollywood films. Nowadays academy ratio has a nostalgic feel, as in the Oscar-winning 'silent film' *The Artist* (2011).

The widescreen formats of 1.85:1 and 2.35:1 tend to achieve the opposite effect, supplying more and more environment relative to the characters. The widescreen formats were developed in the 1950s and 60s to emphasise the spectacle of the cinematic image compared to television, and their first use was for epics, westerns and musicals. But widescreen frames can also be intimate, because they allow two characters to be held in close-up on screen together.

The close-up

The close-up shot of the human face has special emotional power. For many early film-makers, the close-up was what made cinema magical and entirely different from any other medium. Unlike the wide shot, with its associations of spectacle and abundance partly drawn from the theatre, the close-up offered a new and thrilling intimacy. Within the emergent film grammar of early cinema, the close-up was reserved for moments of emotional intensity.

In Hollywood, director DW Griffith was famed for his ability to get right up close to his characters. For his long-suffering heroines, such as Lillian Gish in *The Mothering Heart* (1913), the close-up is a means to generate audience empathy, while his villains' faces fill the screen in terrifying manner. This convention was so well established by the 1920s that Buster Keaton was able to subvert it for comedic effect, his famously impassive features giving away nothing even in close-up.

Close-ups can create other effects, such as:

✔ Drawing the audience's attention to a crucial detail that other characters may miss. In *The Hobbit: An Unexpected Journey* (2012), the ring falls out of Gollum's pocket and into Bilbo's grasp in a slow-motion close-up.

✔ Suggesting that audiences are entering a character's memory or dream space after a close-up of a face dissolves to another scene. A good example here comes in *Casablanca* (1942), when Rick (Humphrey Bogart) hears music that triggers the memory of his Parisian love affair with Ilsa (Ingrid Bergman).

✔ Unsettling and disorienting audiences with extreme close-ups, such as the abstract, mysterious shots of eyes and mouths during the opening of the arty sci-fi film *Under the Skin* (2013).

Film acting in close-up

The introduction of the close-up as a common feature of film grammar had an important effect on styles of acting in cinema. The wide shots of spectacular fantasies made by George Méliès demanded broad gestures from the actors, which audiences were able to pick out from the busy mise-en-scène and understand without the help of dialogue. For example, when the scientists of *La Voyage dans la Lune* (1902) reach their destination, they're tired. How do you know? Because they stretch their arms and rub their eyes!

By contrast the close-ups of DW Griffith or Charlie Chaplin films allow subtle facial gestures to tell the story or make you laugh or cry. Chaplin even had an interesting (and much quoted) philosophy about shot distances and life: 'Life is a tragedy when seen in close-up, but a comedy in long-shot.'

Solving the Puzzle: Editing Film

Try sequence these into putting words the correct. Thanks, now you're an editor. Read on to find out how film editors bring similar coherence to a collection of individual clips of film.

Getting the story moving

Early films borrowed from narrative structures with which audiences were already familiar:

- ✔ **Theatrical:** From plays, film-makers took the idea of scenes, in which the action is broken down into meaningful moments that all take place at one location. Early cameras were enormous and difficult to move around, and so the static viewpoint of the theatrical scene was also easy to achieve on film.

- ✔ **Literary:** From novels, film-makers took chapter titles and dialogue inserts, which were useful ways to cover editing transitions and orient audiences.

For certain types of early film, particularly literary adaptations, these techniques were all the editing required. But these films clearly didn't make the most of cinema's two biggest advantages as a storytelling medium: the excitement of movement and the ability to capture the vivid real world up on a screen.

The most cinematic story elements in this light are chase sequences, and early examples are central to the development of film editing.

The small British studio run by Cecil Hepworth produced several interesting chase films, including *Rescued by Rover* (1905), in which the hero of the day is a dog. Rover is racing against time to find his master's kidnapped baby. He charges out of the house and then is seen running obliquely towards the camera in a similar direction across four separate locations, including crossing a river. This sequence builds a sense that the action takes place over a large area. Keeping the direction of Rover's movement similar here is vital to the effect and the logic of the story.

This coherence of movement across several shots is an example of the *180-degree rule*, a film-making convention designed to ensure that audiences understand where characters are located in space even if the camera moves or the action cuts. Similarly, two characters facing each other (in a gun fight, perhaps) should always be shot from the same side of an imaginary line that runs horizontally between the two figures. This keeps the same character on the same side of the screen to avoid confusing the audience. Of course you can find exceptions to this rule, but the fact that it exists at all reveals a key emphasis of narrative cinema: to create a coherent sense of space and time.

Piecing together a film: Continuity editing

When you hear people talk about a 'classical Hollywood' film style, they often mean a system of editing that aims to create a consistent flow of space and time in the service of telling a story. This system is known as *continuity editing*, because it tries to ensure this consistency. Continuity editing is built out of elements that developed at different times and in different countries, but it became the dominant style of editing in the late 1920s, and it arguably still is today.

The best way to understand continuity editing is to take an example of a scene from pretty much any Hollywood film of the studio era. Ideally, the scene you choose isn't a particularly memorable or exciting one, just one that quietly advances the story. Watch the scene again and again until you've made a list of all the individual shots that build up the scene. Drawing little sketches can help, like creating a storyboard for the shot after the fact. Note the take length (in time), the distance (wide or close) and any unusual transitions.

You almost certainly find that a typical scene from a typical Hollywood film is constructed as follows:

✔ The scene is likely to start with an establishing shot, which identifies the space in which the action takes place; it's usually a wide shot (see the earlier 'Selecting shots' section).

✔ The space is analysed into its components as the scene progresses, principally the characters and their relation to each other in space, normally without violating the 180-degree rule (which I define in the preceding section).

✔ Two characters interacting with each other follow the *shot/reverse shot* pattern, which repeats shots from two opposing points of view.

✔ The entry of a new character will be signalled by an *eye-line match,* in which one character looks off-screen in the direction of the new character and the next shot shows exactly what the character sees.

✔ If a character gets up and walks away, a *match on action* connects any required cuts together. For example, a shot on one side of a door will match up to one from the other side as a character exits the room.

This pattern is remarkably consistent throughout much of classical Hollywood cinema, and indeed remains the most familiar editing structure today. Influential film scholar David Bordwell has called the dominant editing style of contemporary cinema *intensified continuity,* because the overall system remains in place while certain elements have become more pronounced. Most notably, the average length of take is now much shorter than in the classical period, resulting in a more restless camera and a greater range of viewpoints upon the story space.

Considering alternatives to the classical model

When you think about it, film editing isn't smooth or continuous in any way. Your eyes just get used to one space and set of objects and then, suddenly, everything changes. The use of the word *cutting* as a synonym for editing comes from the practice of chopping up the film to reorder scenes, but it's a suitably violent metaphor for what can be a jarring assault on your senses.

Russian film-makers of the 1910s and 20s, such as Sergei Eisenstein, lived in tumultuous political times and understood the violence of the cut. Eisenstein argued that art was about conflict and that what matters in editing is the clash of meaning between two shots joined together. This clash creates *montage,* which presents complex ideas by cutting unconnected images together. The often abrasive and politically motivated results of Eisenstein's editing aren't likely to win over the popular audiences of Hollywood, although a technique similar to montage is used in children's cartoons whenever visual elements are inserted as jokes. Here's an essay title idea for you: 'Discuss Eisenstein's influence on the work of Daffy Duck'!

Other editing strategies that contrast with the classical model use different techniques to enhance the so-called realism of their films. The French critic Andre Bazin was an advocate of realism in the sense of removing artificial elements from the film-making process. Rather than the breaking down of space and time that happens with the continuity system, Bazin argued that takes should last as long as possible, and that deep focus (where both the foreground and background are sharp) should be used to present characters within their environment. Bazin's key example of this technique was *Citizen Kane* (1941), with his arguments helping to create the formidable critical reputation of Orson Welles's film.

Taken to an extreme, the long take favoured by Bazin can result in very few cuts, or even none at all. Hitchcock's *Rope* (1948) takes place in real time in one apartment space and appears to be all one take (actually it's several long takes edited together but the cuts are carefully concealed). In 2002, director Alexander Sokurov completed an ambitious project to create a full-length film from just one take. The result, *Russian Ark* (2002), is a magnificent achievement that's barely concerned with realism, because it spans multiple time-frames in a dream-like manner.

The opposite strategy to the long take is to cut quickly and disregard gaps in space and time. This technique is the *jump cut* often found in French New Wave films such as *À Bout de Souffle* (1960). Although these cuts can be jarring, they do not incorporate elements from outside of the story world in the manner of Eisenstein's montage. Instead they're intended to represent psychological realism, in that your lived experience of events (and especially your memory of them) is often fractured in such a manner. Sorry, what was that? Drifted off for a second there. . . .

The Kuleshov effect

Lev Kuleshov, one of Sergei Eisenstein's fellow radicals, designed an experiment to test the power of film editing. Kuleshov cut a shot of the actor Ivan Mosjoukine's face, preceded by three different images: a bowl of soup, a girl in a coffin or a sultry woman. Showing the different versions to audiences, Kuleshov claimed that they read different emotions into the actor's face depending on which shot preceded it.

Cheeky Alfred Hitchcock had his own version of the Kuleshov effect. Hitchcock cut together a shot of himself looking intently out of a window and then smiling, followed by two different shots. In the first, he's looking at a baby, and Hitch seems warm and fatherly. In the second, it's a sexy young lady. He always was a dirty old man, that one.

Charting the Roles of Characters in Narrative

Despite the almost endless possibilities of film form and structure, the vast majority of films that audiences consume tell similar stories in very similar ways. Things start out mostly okay, with a central character (or *protagonist*), and then Something Bad Happens. That character decides to sort it out, and after a bit succeeds. The end. These narrative patterns are so familiar because they've surrounded you since you were a small child. But this familiarity makes trying to understand them all the more important.

Causing an effect with an event

What makes a good story? Consider these two events:

- Poor girl loses slipper
- Poor girl marries handsome prince

This description doesn't yet qualify as a story because you have no idea what connects the two events. You need more information: specifically that the poor girl met her fairy godmother who transformed her into a beautiful princess, that she went to the ball, danced with the prince and they fell in love, and that she left behind a glass slipper that enabled him to track her down. Now you can see that the first event *causes* the second – and you have the story of Cinderella.

Nearly all stories, including movies, rely upon this chain of cause and effect – or *causality,* to use a clever word. Causality creates momentum and pace, and keeps stories moving forward with a minimum of audience confusion. Causality is what answers the questions that hook you into the drama. How will Cinderella ever get to the ball? With the help of her fairy godmother. How will the prince find his true love again? With the slipper.

The slipper plot point is a crucial one in all versions of *Cinderella* (including the Disney movie of 1950), because the protagonist doesn't know that she left it behind. As a result, the audience has more information than the protagonist, which creates dramatic tension. Sometimes the opposite can occur, and a character knows something crucial about a story before the audience does, such as the killer knowing exactly whodunnit long before we do in an Agatha Christie murder mystery.

The classic whodunnit plot starts with an *effect* (a murdered body) and then plays a game with the audience to establish the *cause* (whodunnit, how and why). The figure of the investigator or detective is crucial in revealing these causes or uncovering red herrings to distract the audience's attention. The detective builds relationships with the suspects in order to understand their characters, which may be the motive for the murder. Character traits such as jealousy, greed or lustiness are the ultimate causes of the killing and therefore the plot.

All these examples revolve around three key and distinct terms:

- **Story:** Everything that happens in the fictional world between the beginning and the end, including events that viewers infer or presume to have happened.

- **Plot:** What viewers see on screen and hear on the soundtrack to allow them to construct a story in their heads. Plots can begin anywhere on the chain of story events and can leap backwards and forwards in time and space.

- **Narrative:** Flow of story information constructed by the plot at any given moment. Narrative implies a point of view, which may be that of one of the characters or of an *omniscient* (all-seeing) narrator.

Characterising heroes and villains

When a film's protagonist acts heroically and is on the side of 'good' that character becomes your principal point of identification within a story. The use of the term *hero* (who can be male or female) in this context is a specific one and partly a hangover from older traditions of mythic or epic storytelling, but it's also appropriate for most narratives of popular cinema, because the hero is expected to display (and often acquire) positive, active character traits in order to achieve his goals. For example, in *Star Wars* (1977) Luke Skywalker needs to develop self-discipline, control and leadership to defeat Darth Vader. Oh, and a bit of magic (the Force).

Even in more complex, character-driven narratives the hero is usually called upon to display admirable heroic qualities at some level. In *Amélie* (2001) the lonely protagonist lives in a fantasy world. Her goal is simply to talk to the man she loves, proving that you don't have to save the world to be heroic. Amélie's shyness is an example of a character trait that puts *internal obstacles* in the way of her goals, in the absence of a recognisable *external antagonist* or *villain*.

Drama is about conflict, be it internal, as with *Amélie*, or external, as in *Star Wars*. Therefore the function of the villain in narrative terms is to provide a goal (his defeat by the hero) but also to complicate the plot by creating obstacles for the hero to overcome. Another common function of the great movie villains is to disrupt the happy balance of everyday life and cause a state of imbalance that has to be corrected. In *Batman* (1989), the Joker incites the action by killing Bruce Wayne's parents, thereby creating his winged nemesis.

This circular model of narrative (balance, disruption, return to balance) was established by literary theorist Tzvetan Todorov through the study of Russian folk tales. The implication of this theory, along with others by Claude Lévi-Strauss (see Chapter 13), is that mythic storytelling is universal throughout human culture and history. Such ideas have been influential among Hollywood screenwriters. Check out *The Writer's Journey: Mythic Structures for Writers* by Christopher Vogler (3rd edition, 2007, Michael Wiese). But be aware that turning film stories into universal myths has its dangers, principally because to do so excludes historical context and the elements that make film special: moving images and sound.

Meeting sidekicks and helpers

Vladimir Propp (another smart Russian theorist) analysed 100 Russian folk tales and found that certain character types recurred in many of them if not all. You can boil down these stock characters as follows:

- **The hero:** Who goes on a quest.
- **The villain:** Who tries to defeat the hero.
- **The dispatcher, helper or donor:** Who sends off, assists or gives the hero some kind of magical object (such as a potion).
- **The princess:** Who's also the prize for the hero. In folk tales and many types of film, the gender balance remains traditional. But, clearly, film genres exist where the hero is usually female and the 'prize' is a handsome prince of some variety – most obviously the romantic comedy.

Sidekicks and helpers exist to add interest to the plot, to create or resolve subplots, or to generate other emotional effects. The first film in *The Lord of the Rings* trilogy is subtitled *The Fellowship of the Ring* (2001) and is almost entirely about constructing a motley crew of sidekicks and helpers for the hero, Frodo (Elijah Wood). The wizard Gandalf (Ian McKellen), the warrior Aragorn (Viggo Mortensen) and the faithful friend Sam (Sean Astin) are essential for Frodo to reach his goal of destroying the ring. But they also all have their own goals and journeys to complete, providing contrast and counterpoint, as well as constructing a huge world of characters and stories.

Sidekicks are also vital outside the realm of fairy tales and fantasy:

- ✔ **Action adventure:** Such as *Indiana Jones and the Temple of Doom* (1984) and the *Pirates of the Caribbean* franchise. In the latter, the sidekick Jack Sparrow (Johnny Depp) proved more popular with audiences than the soggy romantic leads.

- ✔ **Cop 'buddy' comedy:** Such as *Lethal Weapon* (1987) or *Rush Hour* (1998) and sequels. These films force a mismatched pair to work together, generating laughs and possibilities for personal growth.

- ✔ **Family animation:** Such as Dory in *Finding Nemo* (2003) or Donkey in *Shrek* (2001). Again these pairings often start with animosity and then grow into mutual respect.

The fact that sidekicks are often mismatched with the hero adds further weight to the ideas of Claude Lévi-Strauss, who argued that all narrative is built around *binary oppositions* (check out Chapter 13 for details). In *Lethal Weapon*, Murtaugh (Danny Glover) is black and a veteran family man who likes to do things by the book. His partner Riggs (Mel Gibson) is young, white and crazily irresponsible. This set-up allows the film to play with binary oppositions on race, age and masculinity to comedic or dramatic effect.

Listening and Understanding Film Sound

Film sound, which includes dialogue, sound effects and music, can be a tricky area for some film students (and scholars for that matter). Although the visual elements of film are relatively easy to describe, students often feel at a loss when discussing sound. How do you capture in words the quality of an actor's voice? What type of music is playing and which instruments create it? How does sound design create or reinforce cinematic space?

Playing with emotions

To begin to understand what film sound does, just get rid of it for a moment. Try watching a section from your favourite blockbuster with the sound on mute. You quickly realise that the sound is doing a lot more than you realised. Apart from the obvious lack of dialogue and music, many layers of sound in a modern film are carefully designed to produce a response from the audience.

The functions of film sound include:

- ✔ **Environmental context:** Is the action in a busy street or a quiet park? What's the weather doing? Are any sounds associated with specific locations (perhaps church bells, animal noises or the sea)?

✔ **Establishing space:** Modern multichannel surround-sound systems allow sound designers to create complex *soundscapes* in which particular sounds envelop the audience.

✔ **Holding a sequence together:** When a scene cuts rapidly but the sound remains constant, an audience feels less disoriented. Psychologists have a name for this feeling of being drawn into a coherent world: *suture*.

✔ **Vocal performance:** Not just what's said, but *how* it's said. Volume, rhythm of speech, accent and timbre (low and smoky or high and squeaky) all affect the meaning of a line or an entire scene.

All these elements are working on your brain while you watch a film, some consciously – for example when you notice a character's accent and wonder where he's from – and some on a deeper level. Neuroscientists argue that sound is fundamental to human consciousness because hearing develops very early, even before you're born. Sound provides vital information about the world, and your hearing is always working directly with your emotional state to ensure that you respond.

Certain sounds seem to be hard-wired to provoke a response, particularly those that signal danger for loved ones. Few people can bear to hear a baby screaming without wanting to take action, for example. Other associations seem more likely to vary from person to person and culture to culture. Rain on a roof can make you feel restful or anxious depending on the context. You almost certainly have to learn to find wind chimes soothing. Or irritating!

Gladiator. As *heard* on screen

Gladiator (2000) is a good example of modern blockbuster sound design. It consolidates the position of Hans Zimmer as Hollywood's leading film composer, as well as winning an Oscar for Best Sound. For example, listen to the moment when Maximus (Russell Crowe) completes his training and enters the great arena of the Coliseum for the first time.

As Maximus puts on his armour in the dungeons, he's surrounded by metallic clanks, roaring torches and echoing footsteps. He and his fellow gladiators are silent, rendered powerless by the barking orders: 'When the emperor enters, raise your weapons, salute him.' The orchestral music is placed low in the sound mix, but it builds slowly in volume and pitch. All these elements work to produce tension and excitement in an audience.

As the gladiators climb the stairs and step out into the arena, the music reaches a crescendo in time with an enormous roar from the crowd. The camera then begins to circle around the men in the middle of the arena, displaying the entire circuit of the stadium. The sound also appears to circle with this movement, locating the audience with Maximus and his men. The danger and the thrill of the entire scene are palpable. In this case the spectacle isn't just visual; it's also aural.

Lack of sound can have just as profound an effect upon your emotions. In war films such as *Saving Private Ryan* (1998), silence is used as a counterpoint to the oppressive noise of battle. This choice can be expressive (as when an explosion temporarily 'deafens' the audience) or symbolic, silence having a deathly feel about it. In sci-fi films that aim at realism, such as *Gravity* (2013), the lack of air in space translates into long sequences of silence. After all, in space, no one can hear you scream.

Distinguishing between diegetic and non-diegetic sound

What's this, a film-studies term that isn't French? *Sacre bleu!*

Diegetic sound comes from the Greek *diegesis*, which means 'a story that's spoken to an audience'. Within the study of literature, the term describes the world of the story. So if something is diegetic it belongs within the story world. Think about this in relation to a novel for a moment. Many novels have a *narrator*, a voice telling the story that's outside the world of the characters. So not everything in many books is diegetic.

The same principle extends to filmed stories. Although films go to great lengths to create engaging and believable worlds, be they realistic or wildly imaginary, some elements of a film don't strictly belong to this world – the opening credits for example. Although rare, non-diegetic shots can also be inserted into films. One example is the opening of Charlie Chaplin's *Modern Times* (1936), when a herd of sheep dissolves into factory workers as they rush out of the gates.

The situation with sound is, however, completely different. Audiences are conditioned to accept elements of the soundtrack that are outside the story world, particularly the musical score, but also voice-over narration. These elements are commonly called *non-diegetic* sound. By contrast, *diegetic* sound is located within the world of the story, such as most dialogue and sound effects. This distinction sounds simple enough to understand and maintain. But as sound theorist Michel Chion describes, films are full of examples that don't quite fit in either category, or deliberately play with the categories to create particular effects:

- ✔ Music often starts in one category and then shifts into another. For example, Bernard Herrmann's famous saxophone theme for *Taxi Driver* (1976) is used as score throughout, but it also plays on a record when Iris (Jodie Foster) dances with her pimp.

- ✔ Voices can be heard on screen without viewers seeing their source, such as relayed voices from radios or televisions. Are these properly from within the story world or not?

✔ Internal dialogue or voices can also sometimes be overlaid as the character's thoughts. For example, *Look Who's Talking* (1989) features Bruce Willis as the voice of an on-screen baby.

✔ General background sounds (birds singing, wind in trees) aren't always tied to a visual source. Are they still diegetic? After all, most ambient sounds are added in post-production, just like a musical score.

Listening to unheard melodies: Film music

Some people believe that to notice and study film music is to destroy its effects. According to this viewpoint, film scoring is designed to work at a level somewhere beneath conscious thought, on the emotional rather than the rational plane. The music is therefore encouraging the dreamlike state of losing yourself within a film. Asking how film music works disrupts this effect, making it impossible to study.

That's all very well, but you know from your own experience of watching films that your level of attention upon the musical elements of a film naturally fluctuates. You experience certain points when you forget that the music exists, but equally you have moments when you do notice it, whether for positive or negative reasons. In addition, when you hear music that you recognise in films, be it pop or classical, your own memories of that music are bound to affect how you respond to the story.

This model of *unheard melodies* – to use film scholar Claudia Gorbman's term – has a strong connection to the other elements of classical Hollywood storytelling. Just as with editors who employ continuity editing (for a definition, check out the earlier section 'Piecing together a film: Continuity editing'), the theory is that if you notice it, it isn't working.

Like continuity editing, film scoring has developed its own set of codes and conventions that audiences recognise:

✔ Music needs to be subordinate to narrative form and dialogue. Scores are written to fit the length of the scene, not the other way round. Furthermore, the voices of the actors must be louder in the sound mix.

✔ Music has to be familiar and tonally appropriate to the scene, which is why romantic, orchestral scoring dominates classical Hollywood: audiences were already comfortable with that style.

✔ Music can signal the beginning and end of a film, particular historical periods or locations, or even narrative point of view by associating musical motifs with major characters.

✔ Music provides a smooth, continuous experience for audiences by 'plugging the gaps' between dialogue scenes, and adds interesting patterns of repetition and variation through musical themes.

Above all, music means emotion. Films that create powerful emotional responses often have memorable soundtracks. The creeping undertow of fear in *Jaws* (1975), the dreamlike film noir atmosphere of *Blade Runner* (1982) or the nostalgic romance of *Drive* (2011) would be very different without their accompanying music. Although research demonstrates that some elements of music have a measurable effect on physiological states, particularly pitch and tempo, many more of these associations are learned, cultural and vary from individual to individual.

On a completely different note, film music has an important economic function for the film industry. Scores from popular films have always generated extra income for producers, whether through sales of piano sheet music, vinyl LPs, CDs or digital downloads. Many of the biggest selling albums of all time are soundtracks, including those for *Saturday Night Fever* (1977), *The Bodyguard* (1992) and *Titanic* (1997). Hit songs are valuable promotional tools for films, particularly since the advent of the music video.

Buying a soundtrack of your favourite film is a strange decision when you think about it. You don't pay for a silent DVD, and so why purchase the film without the moving images? The fact that millions of film fans do suggests that the music is performing an interesting set of functions, including acting as an emotional trigger to remember the film itself. But it also provides the music itself with a life separate to its movie origins. For many people the only classical, jazz or world music albums that they own are film soundtracks. Soundtracks seem to be able to open people's ears to musical diversity.

Pop lyrics in *The Graduate* (1967)

During the title sequence of *The Graduate* (1967), Benjamin (Dustin Hoffman) is carried along a moving walkway in an airport. His face is blank. He's held to the far right of the widescreen frame as people rush past from left to right. Benjamin picks up his suitcase and walks away into the crowds and then out of the airport. He continues to display no discernable emotion. Yet by the time this sequence is over, you already feel his sense of dislocation, his angst. How is this possible? You've seen very little visual information up to this point and heard no dialogue apart from the voice of the captain as Benjamin's plane lands. The answer, of course, is in the music:

throughout this sequence Simon and Garfunkel's 'The Sound of Silence' is played in its entirety.

This dark, dramatic song has complex lyrics: 'People talking without speaking / People hearing without listening'. On a thematic level, the lyrics speak of Benjamin's alienation from the world and his own difficulties in communicating. But some contemporary reviews felt that the film was 'cheating' by borrowing these insights from the song's lyrics and transferring them to its inarticulate protagonist. This example therefore demonstrates some of the possibilities and the dangers of using pop songs in cinema.

Part II

Taking All Types: Genres, Modes and Style

Courtesy Sony/Everett/REX

In this part . . .

- ✔ Sort out film genres and styles.
- ✔ Draw deeper meaning from animated films and cartoons.
- ✔ Endeavour to explain avant-garde films.
- ✔ Get closer to truth and reality with documentaries.

Chapter 5

Distinguishing Films by Type: Genres and Style

. . . .

In This Chapter

▶ Classifying movies into genres, modes and cycles

▶ Understanding why genres exist and how they function in society

▶ Analysing well-known genres from musicals to horror films

. . . .

*G*enre is just French for 'type' (in this case, type of film). All film audiences have an instinctive understanding of genre, whether they speak French or not. You know that if you're watching a movie and everyone's wearing Stetsons and shooting at Native Americans, it's a western. If the cast is wearing space helmets and shooting at aliens, it's science fiction (sci-fi). And if everybody suddenly stops shooting and bursts into song, it's a musical. Or you really need to lay off the flu medication.

You can recognise genres from the specific films themselves because genres use conventions or *codes,* which become deeply ingrained in audiences over time and through repetition. If you watch enough horror movies, rom-coms or musicals, you know what to expect after about the first five minutes or so. But crucially, this familiarity doesn't mean that genre films are boring – quite the opposite. As I describe in this chapter, which also guides you through some of the most popular genres, the play between repetition and variation is what keeps genres alive and kicking.

 Every individual audience member (yes, even you) comes to genre with their own set of built-in responses, likes and dislikes, and even prejudices. For example, film fans today sometimes struggle with individual examples of genres which are no longer in common circulation, such as the western or the musical. They might then use this initial experience as an excuse to dismiss *all* westerns or *all* musicals. If you have a prejudice against a particular genre, try really hard to get through it. Watch some of the examples suggested in this chapter, and think about their conventions and contexts. And you just might find that you are a musicals fan after all.

Defining Genre

Like many major film studies terms, *genre* is a simple idea that gets extremely complicated as soon as you start to think about it. Although the French word is a fancy intellectual add-on, the concept of genre has been central to film-making ever since Hollywood stepped up a gear into an industrial mode of production. Producers and the industry use genre as a way of categorising and differentiating their products. Think of the physical shelves in a DVD store or a sub-menu on Netflix.

Consumer categories and genres aren't necessarily the same thing. Is animation a genre? What about documentary? Film scholars sometimes call these overarching styles of film-making *modes* in order to separate them from the genres of fiction film. A mode such as documentary, however, can work just like a genre for audiences, because documentaries also use conventions built up over time by generations of film-makers. Chapters 6 and 8 dive deeper into animation and documentary, respectively.

Like all systems of categorisation, genre has benefits and drawbacks. On the positive side, producers and cinema managers can use genre to make their products quickly attractive to the right kinds of audiences. They can precisely target marketing materials, such as posters and trailers, towards the fans of a specific genre. Just take a look at a few horror film posters of recent years and you see the same images recurring: masks, blood, saws, screaming girls and so on. I discuss these key images, or *iconography,* in 'Seeing why westerns are westerns' later in this chapter.

Another angle on genre: Cycles

You can also think about genres by grouping films within production *cycles.* After one production company has a surprise success with one type of film, the rest of the industry quickly jumps on the bandwagon to try and emulate the initial success. The market eventually becomes saturated, and the cycle then dies out.

For example, *The Blackboard Jungle* (1955) and *Dangerous Minds* (1995) are about white teachers sent into struggling schools containing pupils from many racial backgrounds. You can describe both films as part of the so-called social-problem genre. Alternatively, you can consider *Blackboard Jungle* as part of a 'teenage rebellion' cycle of the 1950s, most famously represented by *Rebel Without a Cause* (1955), and *Dangerous Minds* alongside other ghetto action films such as *Boyz n the Hood* (1991). Locating these films within cycles enables you to explore much more precisely their respective historical contexts and understand their popularity with contemporary audiences.

The major downside of genre as a classification system is that films are complex. Placing a film in one neat category or the next is often challenging. Try it yourself. Spend a rainy afternoon reorganising your DVD collection into genre categories. You're sure to encounter many crossover cases, for example:

✔ Do you file *Crouching Tiger, Hidden Dragon* (2000) under 'World Cinema', 'Action Films' or 'Historical Romance'?

✔ Is *Pulp Fiction* (1994) a comedy or a crime thriller?

✔ Does the fact that Marilyn Monroe sings several numbers in *Some Like It Hot* (1959) make it a musical?

The problem here is two-fold:

✔ The elements that qualify a film for one genre or another aren't clearly defined or set in stone. Audience members have their own viewing history and therefore different sets of expectations around genre.

✔ Many (if not all) films use elements from different *generic conventions* (that is, established or agreed-upon aspects specific to a particular genre): most action films have a romantic subplot, for instance, and many comedies use elements of melodrama to provide light and shade. So decisions about where to place a particular film are essentially subjective and personal.

Banking on genre: The Hollywood Machine

Popular films need to be different enough from what has gone before to stand out as new and exciting for audiences – but not *too* different. They also need to be similar to previously successful films in order to minimise the risk of their expensive production costs. These contradictory economic imperatives are suitably reconciled within the idea of genre film-making.

The financial logic is undeniable. Genre film-making allows studios to produce films as cheaply as possible while ensuring that they make more hits than misses. Many histories of studio-era Hollywood (the period between 1930 and 1950 or so) stress the generic output of the major studios:

✔ MGM specialised in glossy musicals such as *The Wizard of Oz* (1939) and *Meet Me in St Louis* (1944).

✔ Warner Bros. made gritty gangster films such as *Little Caesar* (1931) and *The Public Enemy* (1931).

✔ Universal made its reputation with the horror movies *Dracula* (1931) and *Frankenstein* (also 1931, which was clearly a great year for genre films!).

But even these brief examples expose problems with a generic view of Hollywood history:

- ✔ Warner Bros. certainly enjoyed success with crime films, but it also produced the ground-breaking musical *The Jazz Singer* (1927), as well as films in many other genres.

- ✔ MGM's high production values mattered more to it than the generic content. In 1939 they released both the fantasy musical *The Wizard of Oz* and the epic melodrama *Gone with the Wind*.

- ✔ Universal won Best Picture Oscar for the war movie *All Quiet on the Western Front* (1930) only a year before its successful horror cycle commenced.

Clearly no major studio could afford to specialise in only one genre and put all its eggs in one basket.

Don't forget the differences between the biggest and the best films a studio releases – their 'A-pictures' – and their cheaper, less challenging 'B-movies'. Studios produced B-movies quickly with a great deal of stylistic cost-saving, such as recycling sets, and these films were often generic. Meanwhile A-pictures needed broad appeal across several genres. For example, *The Wizard of Oz* is a fantasy adventure, a family film and a musical partly because it cost so much to produce.

Enjoying repetition – up to a point

Repetition is a key feature of genre. Did I mention that repetition was a key feature of genre? Good, because repetition is a key feature of genre.

As all children know, if a story is good first time round, it's even better second, third and fiftieth time around. Yes, audiences like suspense and surprises, but they also love the cosy familiarity of knowing exactly what to expect. Time and time again.

During the early 20th century, literary theorists noticed the strong similarities between the types of stories that people have told each other over time. They began to wonder whether certain fundamental elements, or *myths,* exist across human civilisation. This notion is the basis of *structuralism,* which argues that essential (and irresolvable) human conflicts cause these similarities (see Chapter 13 for more on structuralism).

Thomas Schatz extends structuralism from literature to film by suggesting that film genres work in one of two ways: leading towards social order (westerns, crime films) or social integration (musicals, comedies). Genres humanise opposing value systems and conflicts between good guys and bad guys, and romantic couplings signify temporary resolutions. Therefore film genres are like modern-day rituals, performed to help people make sense of society.

Structuralists may offer attractive explanations for the power of genre, but by emphasising universality their methods obviously have to downplay historical context and change over time. In response, several contrasting theories about the development of genres have emerged, including the *evolutionary model,* which sets out the following stages:

1. **Artistic innovation creates a genre, which finds favour from audiences who happily soak up its conventions through repetition.**

2. **Over-familiarity eventually causes audiences to tire of the conventions, and genres become *self-referential* (about themselves) or parodies of themselves.**

3. **Self-referentiality diverts audiences only for so long before they demand wholesale renewal of conventions or dismiss the genre altogether.**

The teen-slasher film offers a good example of evolutionary development, because it's a sub-genre of the horror film (flip nervously to 'Lurking in the Shadows: Horror' later for more on this genre). After the success of *Halloween* (1978) and *Friday the 13th* (1980) came endless sequels and imitations, until the heavily self-conscious *Scream* (1996) franchise renewed the genre, albeit temporarily. Teen-slasher films have since (arguably) been replaced by supernatural horror and so-called torture porn films such as *Saw* (2004) and its sequels.

Bending genres

Other ways of thinking about the way genres develop and change tend to stress their amazing adaptability and ability to absorb ideas from different film-making traditions or national cinemas. Most film industries around the world have developed their own distinctive variations on Hollywood genres. Some of the better-known examples include:

- ✔ So-called spaghetti westerns made largely in Italy and Spain, such as *A Fistful of Dollars* (1964).

- ✔ *Yakuza films,* crime thrillers about the Japanese mafia, such as *Sonatine* (1993).

- ✔ The literate, period-drama-style Hammer Horror films produced in Britain in the 1950s and 60s, including *The Curse of Frankenstein* (1957).

Mixing up genres

You can observe this generic blending (or *hybridity* if you want to show off) in many 1980s blockbusters. *Back to the Future* (1985) starts out as a high-school comedy, as Marty McFly (Michael J Fox) skips school with his girlfriend and plays his guitar too loud. It then shifts gear quite abruptly into a sci-fi thriller, with terrorists shooting at the mad professor as he sends Marty back in time.

Then the bulk of the film is back in high-school comedy mode but filtered through a vision of the 1950s, which owes as much to musicals such as *Grease* (1978) and TV shows like *Happy Days* as it does to any kind of historical reality. The time-travel plot has Marty accidentally dating his own mother, leading to moments reminiscent of a so-called body-swap comedy such as *Freaky Friday* (1976). Plus, don't forget a musical number for good measure.

Then again, you can argue that the film comedy form has always been open to generic mingling of this kind. Just watch a few Laurel and Hardy movies; they happily use settings and iconography from westerns, war films and horror movies.

Genres are never static: in fact the best way to think of them is as a *process* rather than as a noun. For example, genre films that travel internationally often go on to influence Hollywood in return. Probably the most obvious example of this cross-fertilisation is Quentin Tarantino's two *Kill Bill* films which borrow/steal from many international genres, including Hong Kong martial arts films.

For more high-brow film critics, genre cinema and art cinema are considered polar opposites: the former is seen as mindless repetitive pap and the other is clever, individual and ground-breaking. But this view is overly simplistic, because many European art-film directors have worked within genres, including Rainer Werner Fassbinder whose *Ali: Fear Eats the Soul* (1974) is a reworking of Hollywood melodrama *Imitation of Life* (1959). And Jacques Demy's *Les Parapluies de Cherbourg* (1964) is as romantic and joyful as the greatest Hollywood musicals.

Some commentators believe that such formal experimentation and exchange has led to the collapsing of all generic boundaries to the extent that categories are now meaningless. The blending and mixing of genres is a key feature of postmodernism. (This period is *post* (or after) because the modernist period was about experimentation and playing with categories, whereas postmodernism appears to dissolve them completely. Check out Chapter 15 for many more deep thoughts.)

Right, now you know about the idea of genre itself you can move on to look at some examples. Too many genres and sub-genres exist to cover here in detail, so I've chosen examples which are useful for illustrating particular points about the look, meanings and feel of genre filmmaking as a whole. Each is also a type of film that has attracted a good deal of critical and scholarly attention. (I focus mainly on Hollywood genre films, so if you want to know more about Italian comedies or Japanese horror films, turn to Chapters 11 and 12.)

Appreciating What a Man's Got to Do: Westerns

Surely no other genre is as instantly recognisable and as distinctly American as the western. Westerns have iconic scenery (such as the eerie landscape of Monument Valley), familiar costumes (Stetson hats, low-slung holsters and dust-covered boots) and defining themes (particularly civilisation versus the wilderness).

To understand the place of the western in contemporary American culture, take a look at *Toy Story 2* (1999). In the second episode of Pixar's poignant childhood fable, the central dilemma faces cowboy toy Woody (Tom Hanks), who must choose between everlasting life as a preserved classic toy – or temporary fun with his owner, Andy, and friends.

A pivotal moment comes when Woody discovers his origins as merchandise for a black-and-white TV show called *Woody's Roundup*. Watching the show, Woody's face is in awe, somewhat comically given the cheaply produced puppets on screen. No matter: the jolly fiddle music, cardboard cacti and swinging saloon doors instantly evoke the western genre, with its sense of adventure and legendary imaginative hold over boys and girls of all ages.

Linking westerns and the birth of Hollywood

Westerns have a special place in the hearts of many film studies scholars:

- They were the first genre of popular cinema, along with gangster films, that important film critics such as Andre Bazin took seriously, beginning in the 1950s.

- They have possibly the most obvious visual identity of all film genres and have been vital in establishing ideas of iconography (turn to the later section 'Seeing why westerns are westerns').

- Their essential relationship with American history and myth provide rich source material for ideological analysis.

Westerns before cinema

Hollywood didn't invent the mythology of the American west for itself. Cowboy stories were already a staple of popular culture with adventure novels (such as *The Last of the Mohicans* by James Fenimore Cooper, published in 1826 and set in the 1750s), the so-called dime novels of the late 19th century, and pulp magazines, all of which preceded 20th-century cowboy comics.

In addition, the huge open spaces of the western landscape were a favourite subject of 19th-century American painters such as Albert Bierstadt, whose huge canvases attracted great public attention when exhibited publically.

Finally, audiences were already familiar with western-themed melodramas from their popularity on the stage. Short scenes or plays (such as *The Great Train Robbery* (1896) by Scott Marble) played large and small venues from the early 1800s through the Victorian era and featured stock villains, heroes and damsels – plus vocal audience participation.

The popularity of westerns throughout much of early Hollywood history has led some film historians to conclude that the genre is somehow fundamental to the development of American cinema. Most obviously, the relocation of the American film industry from its birth in New York to Southern California in the 1910s provided mythical echoes of the wild frontier, along with fantastic exterior locations in the desert.

The film most historians see as the first film western came very early, in 1903. *The Great Train Robbery* was an adaptation of a popular stage play and has bandits, guns and spectacular scenery captured through location shooting. Its sophisticated editing (something I discuss in Chapter 4) depicts events happening at the same time in different locales to create tension.

When it was first shown in cinemas, *The Great Train Robbery* came with an accompanying additional scene, which could be shown either at the beginning or at the end. As Figure 5-1 shows, this prologue/epilogue is a close-up of one of the bandits, who calmly raises a pistol, aims it at the screen and fires. Twice. Legend has it that audience members seeing the film for the first time ducked – or even fired back at the screen in self-defence.

This startling moment feels more like an avant-garde film than a crowd-pleasing thriller. It's a vivid reminder of what film scholar Tom Gunning called 'the cinema of attractions' (see Chapter 4). Many early films are like the fairgrounds in which they were often shown – confrontational, sensational and designed to provoke an immediate sensual response in viewers. Later westerns may have more sophisticated stories than *The Great Train Robbery*, but at their best they retain its thrill of immediacy.

Figure 5-1:
Stick 'em
up! The final
moment
of *The
Great Train
Robbery*
(1903).

Courtesy Everett Collection/REX

Seeing why westerns are westerns

Although a musical or a comedy can be set just about anywhere, in any time period and with *mise-en-scène* in any style (check out Chapter 4 where I define this term), a western just isn't a western without most of these key ingredients:

- ✔ **Cowboys:** Preferably wearing chaps, spurs and Stetson hats.

- ✔ **Desert setting:** Complete with cacti, canyons and log cabins.

- ✔ **Horses:** Pulling stagecoaches, galloping and tipping their riders to the ground when shot at.

- ✔ **Pistols and rifles:** For cowboys to shoot each other and Native Americans.

- ✔ **Wild-west saloon:** Don't forget the frequent fist-fights.

Film studies groups together these remarkably consistent images, settings and props as *iconography*. This idea stems from visual arts criticism, where certain objects depicted in paintings are invested with special symbolic meaning. For example, in religious art, doves are sometimes used to represent the Holy Spirit. When applied to films, iconography is useful to describe generic conventions in visual, rather than narrative, terms.

As an example, consider the iconography of the pistol within film westerns. As indicated by the closing shot of *The Great Train Robbery* in the preceding section, the display of weaponry is a key feature of the genre. Notably:

✔ Guns are explosive, providing visual spectacle in and of themselves. The firing of a gun was – and sometimes still is – a potent special effect.

✔ The cowboy's pistol often contrasts with the spear or bow of the Native Americans, symbolising the pioneers' pursuit of progress and mastery of the environment through technology.

✔ Guns are (how to put this politely?) *intimate* symbols of masculinity. A guy can measure his status and his power by the size of his pistol.

Thus, in the wild uncivilised west, the gun is the rule of law, a physical symbol of *patriarchal* (that is, male-dominated) authority. The famous gun shootouts of *High Noon* (1952) and many other westerns offer loving close-ups of polished pistols that fetishise the weapons, lending them supernatural and sexual power. Put it away, Mr Wayne; you'll have someone's eye out.

Pitting two sides against each other

In a famous breakdown of the western genre in 1969, film scholar Jim Kitses proposes that cowboy films function on the basis of *binary oppositions* including:

✔ Civilisation versus the wilderness

✔ Community versus individualism

✔ Freedom versus responsibility

✔ Settling versus nomadic wandering

✔ Tradition versus change

The list can go on and on. The western continues to resonate because these conflicts are common human experiences across history and cultures.

Take another look at this list of binary oppositions, and consider it in relation to two common gender stereotypes of the western: the restless wandering hero and the domesticated, stay-at-home wife/girlfriend/sister. It's not difficult to read each pair of conflicting values as gendered in some way, with the hero standing for freedom, individualism and change, and the wife for responsibility, community and tradition. In this sense, binary oppositions such as those identified by Kitses always have implications for readings of genre in terms of political or social issues of gender, class and race.

This analysis becomes all the more interesting when you consider the position of Native Americans. In the major opposition between civilisation and the wilderness, Native Americans are clearly allied with the wild, untamed country. They're represented as deeply traditional and resistant to change, often violently so. Plus, they're a very strong community, usually appearing on screen as a tribe rather than as individual characters within the drama. In some ways, although they're traditionally the 'bad guys' within the western narrative, they're less like the wandering, individualistic cowboy and more like an inversion of the townsfolk whom the cowboy rides in to protect.

In John Ford's (and John Wayne's) *Stagecoach* (1939), one of the first westerns to be released as an A-picture, the representation of Native Americans is a notable blind spot of Ford's otherwise humanist approach. The Apaches who attack the isolated stagecoach of the title are clearly savages, and as they appear to be winning the battle, one of the white male passengers threatens to shoot a woman travelling with them to save her from a fate worse than death at their hands.

They Died with Their Boots On (1941) takes a problematic historical incident – the Battle of Little Bighorn and a famous defeat for General Custer and his Yankee army – as its subject. The film falls in line with history (as ever, written by the victors) by treating Custer's defeat as a noble victory for his values. The film does, however, include signs of a more progressive approach to Native Americans, with Custer's widow Libby arguing that the Indians must be protected 'in their own country'.

By 1990, few westerns were being released. One notable exception was Kevin Costner's directorial debut, *Dances With Wolves,* which tells the story of John Dunbar (Costner), an exiled Civil War soldier who 'goes native' and lives within a Sioux tribe for several years. Going against the Hollywood tradition of casting actors from other ethnic groups (notably Latinos) as 'Indians', Costner cast Native American actors (and non-actors) and featured dialogue in the Lakota language, translated in subtitles. Costner was rewarded for his liberal approach with several Oscars.

Letting Yourself Go: Musicals

Music and cinema have always been great together. Even though pre-recorded synchronised sound on film wasn't widespread until the late 1920s, the early days of cinema were never truly 'silent'. The first films shown in fairgrounds or popular theatre venues generally had musical accompaniment of some kind, and when purpose-built cinemas appeared they had space in front of the screen for at least a piano and sometimes full orchestras.

So put on a CD of show tunes as accompaniment, as I take you on a tour of the musical's origins, its defining attributes and the reasons for its popularity.

Showcasing fantastic performers

The close association between popular theatre and early cinema meant that many performers moved between the two media. The great novelty of moving pictures was their motion, and so dancing was a natural fit for the new medium. In addition, films featuring dance stars were a useful way for mass audiences to access the greatest contemporary performers such as prima ballerina Anna Pavlova or jazz star Josephine Baker.

The route into film for singing stars of the stage was blown wide open by the release of *The Jazz Singer* in 1927. Al Jolson's exuberant singing style and lively ragtime piano playing had already made him a huge star on Broadway and across the US. Experiments with film sound occurred throughout the 1920s, but not until Warner Bros. took a risk with the Vitaphone sound-on-disc system and brought Jolson on board did the format – and the screen musical – really take off.

The film musical quickly became the perfect vehicle to bring musical performance to the widest possible audience:

- Many theatrical singers followed Jolson's lead, notably Judy Garland, Barbra Streisand and John Travolta (seriously).

- Dancers Fred Astaire and Ginger Rogers, Gene Kelly and Cyd Charisse were all theatre trained before becoming Hollywood legends.

- Elvis Presley starred in a staggering 31 musical films in 13 years, 19 of which had bestselling soundtrack albums. Thankyouverymuch!

- Pop musicians since the 1970s have had limited success in the musical genre. David Bowie flopped in *Absolute Beginners* (1986); Madonna's only acclaimed vocal performance was in *Evita* (1996); Mariah Carey's *Glitter* (2001) is awful. The nearby sidebar 'Video killed the musical star?' ponders this trend.

Video killed the musical star?

Probably the main reason that pop stars of recent decades have not tended to make the transition to movies is that they simply don't need the format to showcase their talents. Instead they have MTV and more recently YouTube. The music-video format has a great deal in common with musical numbers within musical films, and many well-known videos pay homage to Hollywood (for example, Madonna's 'Material Girl', Michael Jackson's 'Thriller' and Björk's 'It's Oh So Quiet').

Two of the most talked about film musicals of recent years, *Moulin Rouge!* (2001) and *Mamma Mia!* (2008) both have exclamation marks after their names – as if nobody can quite believe they were serious! Neither film showcases stars with notable musical talent (step forward Pierce Brosnan). Instead their appeal seems to be largely down to their use of pre-existing pop tunes instead of original scores. They're as much karaoke as Broadway.

Integrating numbers with plot

The presence of musical performances defines the musical genre as a whole, and so you can further classify musicals depending on the relationship between those numbers and the rest of the film.

Backstage musicals

A large section of musicals qualify as the so-called backstage variety, whereby the musical numbers are justified because the entire film is set in a theatre or similar performance space. (The nearby sidebar 'But nobody bursts into song in real life!' seeks to explain all that singing and dancing.)

For a great example of an early backstage musical, try *42nd Street* (1933), a film that sets out many conventions of the genre. It has a slight but diverting plot, largely about the financial shenanigans behind a Broadway show, but its most significant narrative device is the rags-to-riches plot – the sudden rise to stardom of the understudy when the star falls ill.

The numbers in *42nd Street* may be 'realistically' motivated in that they're part of the stage show, but they also take on an increasingly excessive and spectacular nature to the point where space and time begin to stretch in impossible ways. The rendition of the title tune begins with Ruby Keeler alone on stage against a painted backdrop, and then cuts to a much larger soundstage filled with dozens of people, cars and even a police horse.

But nobody bursts into song in real life!

Although few Hollywood films are 'realistic' in the sense of being like a documentary (see Chapter 8), most at least adhere to the principle that characters act vaguely like real people do in real life. But not musicals, which is partly why they can be an acquired taste. If you're not used to the 'breaking into song' moment then it can feel entirely weird. However, get used to it and a great musical number is like no other experience in cinema.

If they're not performing on stage (as I describe in the nearby 'Backstage musicals' section), how can you accept characters in musicals singing and dancing in such a clearly unrealistic fashion? One possible explanation is the special status of music in culture. Music has a deep affective power. Think of how a song can express your emotional state in ways that are impossible through words alone.

So when characters feel a moment of intense, overwhelming emotion, why not belt it out in song, or release all that energy with some flamboyant dance moves? Wouldn't you love to be able to do that in your everyday life? Don't worry, I'm not suggesting you try it (however great you sound when crooning in the shower).

A much more recent, but surprisingly faithful example of the backstage genre, is *8 Mile* (2002), starring abrasive rapper Eminem. This film may be a gritty portrayal of life on the streets of Detroit, but at its heart it's also a rags-to-riches tale about a talented performer overcoming the odds to make it in show business. Its numbers are semi-improvised rap battles rather than show tunes, but they're as vocally impressive as many Judy Garland standards. If you're still not convinced, you could also count the scandalously sexy *Cabaret* (1972) or the gritty disco classic *Saturday Night Fever* (1977) as backstage musicals.

Integrated musicals

Musicals set in other environments where the stars nonetheless burst into song at the drop of a hat are sometimes called *integrated musicals,* in that the songs are in some way integral to the plot and help move the story along. The songs also tend to help define or expand the characters on screen, and certainly heighten audience identification with them. Here are a few classic integrated musicals:

- ✔ *Easter Parade* (1948) stars film's greatest dancer, Fred Astaire, with probably its greatest singer, Judy Garland. Garland's character professes her love by singing 'It Only Happens when I Dance with You'. Indeed, Fred's got the moves.

- ✔ *The Sound of Music* (1965), the megahit musical starring Julie Andrews, includes numerous songs that are life-lessons for its characters. In 'Sixteen Going on Seventeen' and 'I Have Confidence', characters sing and dance as a natural extension to their emotions.

- ✔ *Grease* (1978) revived the high-school movie with added rock and roll songs that express the vigour of youth and its heightened emotional states. The 'Summer Nights' number does essential narrative work by setting up the central love story, and Stockard Channing's rendition of 'There Are Worse Things I Could Do' adds a surprisingly adult note.

Feeling better through musicals

All right, in this section things are about to get heady in happy-go-lucky musical land. Because the numbers in integrated musicals often happen in everyday settings, such as schools or convents, the films' choreographers and set designers have to be creative in terms of dance steps and props. These inventive moments led to the convention of *bricolage,* whereby characters grab whatever is around them and dance or create music with it. Think Gene Kelly dancing with his trusty umbrella in *Singin' in the Rain* (1952).

You can think of using bricolage to integrate the environment into entertainment as a nostalgic reminder of folk-art traditions within a carefully constructed industrial product.

Critic Richard Dyer points to elements of musicals as offering utopian visions of society that are pleasurable for audiences.

Utopia is a vision of an ideal world where all the typical problems of society are solved. Although musicals don't tend to offer fully realised imaginative worlds (unlike sci-fi, for example), they're very good at creating the *sensation* of utopia, what it may *feel* like.

Musicals offer utopian solutions to all sorts of everyday problems:

- Energy and exuberance through exceptional performances counters the exhaustion and blandness of everyday life.

- Abundance and sensual spectacle in the form of fine costumes, rich orchestrations and luxurious settings corrects poverty and wealth inequality.

- Intense emotions conveyed in song and dance contrasts with dreary, predictable jobs and relationships.

- Emotionally transparent and spontaneous characters combat feelings that media, advertising, corporations or governments are manipulating modern life.

- Being part of a strong community via group singing or dancing alleviates contemporary feelings of fragmentation and loneliness.

The post-musical? *Moulin Rouge!*

No one can accuse director Baz Luhrman of being subtle. *Moulin Rouge!* (2001) is hyperkinetic, saturated in vivid colours and full of stylised, manic performances. Energy and abundance nearly overflows: the introduction of Satine has Nicole Kidman swinging across hundreds of dancing extras. The rich community of the nightclub and bohemian Paris is overwhelming. The film also has no problem with intense emotion: the rooftop duet between Satine and Ewan McGregor's Christian piles up love song after love song to hysterical effect.

The one element of Richard Dyer's utopian sensibility (see the nearby section 'Feeling better through musicals') that's seriously lacking in *Moulin Rouge!*, however, is that of transparency and spontaneity. The use of pre-existing pop music and the constant referencing of other film musicals means that emotion is diluted by being filtered through all sorts of other texts. The result is a distancing effect, as if all feeling is placed within metaphorical quotation marks.

Musicals like *Moulin Rouge!* still offer a great deal of pleasure to audiences, but half a century after the peak of the Hollywood musical, audiences no longer seem to mind having their emotions *knowingly* manipulated. For example, several numbers in the Oscar-winning *Chicago* (2002) take place in a fantasy space that clearly signals the artificiality of the genre.

Admittedly, Dyer's analysis works best within the period known as Hollywood's *Golden Age* (that is, the 1930s to the 1950s), when movies were the dominant form of popular entertainment, and audiences were by and large working class. But certain pleasures of the musical genre – such as the transcendent performances of Judy Garland or Fred Astaire – are as powerful for audiences now as they have ever been.

Lurking in the Shadows: Horror

One of the most satisfying and logical ways of classifying genre is to group films according to how they make you feel: comedies are 'feel-good films', melodramas are 'weepies' and suspense films are 'thrillers'. But of the widely accepted and discussed film genres, only one is exclusively defined in emotional terms: horror.

Given this core emotional purpose – to induce fear and disgust in the audience – the horror genre has proved particularly fertile for psychological analysis. Issues of gender representation are also vital, because threats to life are often mixed up with sexuality in fascinating and disturbing ways. These universal human responses mean that horror is a truly international genre, with lively traditions in many different cultural contexts.

Read this section through the gaps between your fingers as I cover the history of horror's granddaddy, Dracula, the psychology of being terrified and why cinematic horror is so popular across the globe.

Drawing first blood

The history of the horror film can be traced through the movies featuring its most famous monster: the vampire, and in particular the Lord of the Undead, Count Dracula himself. The modern vampire legend has its roots in fiction, with *Dracula* (1897) by Bram Stoker appearing almost simultaneously with the invention of cinema. Crucially, this timing meant the novel was still in copyright for the first few decades of the film industry.

Stoker's estate refused to grant FW Murnau the rights to adapt the novel, but few audiences are fooled by the simple change of name from Dracula to Count Orlok in *Nosferatu* (1922). As part of the movement later called German Expressionism, *Nosferatu* benefits from truly weird visuals and extraordinary make-up and sets (see 'Sharing the nightmares from Elm Street and elsewhere' later for more on Expressionism). Max Schreck's vampire is completely unlike the suave gentleman of later adaptations, being deformed and bestial – kind of like a really evil mole.

A few years later, Universal Studios acquired the rights to the Dracula character by adapting a 1924 stage play that had been endorsed by Stoker's estate. Originally planned as a grand epic on the scale of hits such as *The Phantom of the Opera* (1925), the film was scaled down as the Great Depression hit. The eventual result is a claustrophobic, if rather stagey, version of the novel.

On stage the Count had been played by unknown Hungarian actor Bela Lugosi, who (being cheap to hire) reprised the role on film despite the producer's misgivings. Lugosi's distinctive Eastern European accent is now forever associated with the role. Audiences were terrified of his performance, with newspaper reports of people fainting from fear providing useful publicity. Universal's *Dracula* (1931) was a gamble, but it repaid its modest investment handsomely, instigating a profitable cycle of horror films at the studio.

The next major reincarnation of the Count came from the unlikely source of the British film industry. Hammer Horror's 1958 version starring Christopher Lee was more literary, with careful period detail, and much more bloody, with colour photography ably enhancing the disgusting gore.

After Hammer bled the Count dry, more recent adaptations have attempted to render a more sympathetic version of the character. In Francis Ford Coppola's *Bram Stoker's Dracula* (1992) Gary Oldman's performance provokes pathos as well as fear. Dracula is recast as a tragic figure, doomed to unrequited love for all eternity. The recent *Twilight* franchise capitalised upon this romantic potential of the vampire to hugely profitable effect.

Of course, Dracula is by no means the only recurring nightmare in the history of horror on screen. That other great invention of Gothic literature, Frankenstein's monster comes back to life again and again, most recently as an unlikely action hero in *I, Frankenstein* (2014). And the rotting, decomposed figure of the zombie is currently more popular than ever, thanks to the straight-forwardly terrifying *28 Days Later* (2002) and the tongue-in-blistered-cheek *Shaun of the Dead* (2004).

Facing your inner demons

Horror films regularly present unpleasant, disgusting or deeply disturbing images or ideas, and yet audiences can't help but *ignore* the warning embodied in the title of Nicolas Roeg's horror film *Don't Look Now* (1973). Even if you're peeking from behind a cushion, you have to watch.

So why do people enjoy being scared? Answering this and similar questions is what psychoanalytical film theory was made for. Sigmund Freud, the grandfather of modern psychoanalysis, had plenty of ideas about fear and pleasure, and scholars have applied many of these to the cinema, especially to horror films.

Crucially, Freud considered the human psyche to be split into a relatively small *conscious* mind, over which you have control, and a much larger, darker *subconscious* containing your primitive urges, including violence and sexual desire. The conscious mind must constantly keep the subconscious in check in order to maintain the facade of civilisation. *Repression* is the key idea here; people have to bottle up things in order to try and avoid becoming raving lunatics. But what you repress always returns in one form or another.

In the earlier 'Enjoying repetition – up to a point' section, I discuss the theory that genre films act as rituals that serve a social purpose. In this light, horror films are a safe way in which the repressed can return from your subconscious, be faced by your conscious mind and be temporarily neutralised. Movie monsters therefore symbolise things that society chooses to repress – but can't properly keep a lid on.

In the contemporary Western context, these threats extend beyond the safety of the soul and the body to anything that threatens heterosexual marriage and the family. This reason is why so many classic horror films have monsters that are children, for example *The Omen* (1976) and *The Exorcist* (1973), or childlike in some way, such as Michael Myers from the *Halloween* films. These characters terrify because deep down you know that all humans were monstrous creatures of unregulated desire as infants, and had to go through the painful process of becoming adults by repressing those desires. Bet you never look at the knife-wielding Chucky doll from the *Child's Play* films in quite the same way again!

Having nightmares on Elm Street and elsewhere

Horror films travel surprisingly well. Think about it. In Bram Stoker's novel and several film versions, Count Dracula starts as a distant foreign threat and then spreads, like a sickness, until he's uncomfortably close to home. Similarly, horror films produced across the world slip much more easily across national and linguistic boundaries than films made in other genres.

Girls and gore

Female sexuality is often a focus for horror films, as is violence against women. The first rule of the slasher film, self-consciously expressed in *Scream* (1996) and its sequels, is that only the female virgins survive. All the teen-agers signified as being sexually active are bru-tally killed, one by one. Film scholar Robin Wood claims that the killing of women represents the repression of the feminine side of men, which is necessary to being a functioning (heterosexual) adult and father.

Alternatively, Barbara Creed argues that the horror film's focus on female sexuality is about the failure of sexual repression to con-trol women. Creed's analysis focuses upon films such as *Carrie* (1976) whose monster is unleashed at the point when Carrie becomes menstrual and is then publically drenched in blood.

Several factors help horror films to cross cultures:

- ✔ **Flexibility:** The horror genre is incredibly broad in terms of subject matter and style, unlike, say, the western. Horror has dozens of sub-genres and has gone through numerous production cycles. The genre responds well to new ideas from other cultures.

- ✔ **Primarily visual:** Horror films rely on visual elements to achieve their emotional impact. Therefore, unlike for example comedies, their power is less likely to be lost in translation.

- ✔ **Strength of the 'other' to terrify:** Despite the apparent similarities between what scares people across the world, cultural differences do exist in how horror is manifest. As a result, various culture-specific incarnations can seem even stranger to international audiences.

The films collectively known as *German Expressionism* emerged from a dis-tinctive cultural moment in 1920s Weimar Germany (flip to Chapter 11 for details). Their legacy for horror film aesthetics lies in their use of *chiaroscuro* lighting techniques, which create extreme contrast between bright pools of light and deep black shade. These films also use skewed camera angles to suggest fear and madness, a technique that has returned to the forefront with the recent wave of handheld 'found footage' horror (*The Blair Witch Project* (1999)).

Italian *giallo* (yellow) films of the 1960s and beyond were potboiler thrillers, which cover several sub-genres including murder mysteries. Their name comes from the yellow covers of pulp novels published by Mondadori. Later *gialli* developed into experimental horror films courtesy of directors Mario Bava and Dario Argento, who poured buckets of gore and stylised visuals into the generic mix. These films are often discussed as influences upon the American slasher film of the late 1970s and 80s.

The continued strength of the horror genre lies in its ability to refresh itself by absorbing offshoots such as *giallo* films back into the mainstream. The most obvious incarnation of this phenomenon is Hollywood's habit of remaking successful horror films from other national contexts. The Japanese ghost story *Ringu* (1998), the Nordic vampire film *Let the Right One In* (2008) and even South Korean 'extreme cinema' such as *Oldboy* (2003) have all recently received the Hollywood treatment.

Voyaging Beyond: Sci-Fi

The very term *science fiction* (sci-fi) is a fascinating contradiction. On the one hand, science suggests objectivity, truth and evidence; on the other hand, fiction is pure imagination with no rational basis. But bring the two together and you start to realise that maybe they're not so different. Fundamentally, both are means to satisfy human curiosity about the world and people themselves.

Science fiction is often about the relationship between humans and technology, which makes it a perfect genre for the mechanical, chemical and now digital medium of film. Whether you believe that technology is bringing society to a higher, enlightened state, or that it will lead ultimately to destruction, sci-fi allows audiences to play out both these eventualities, and to imagine worlds on other planets or other moments in time.

In this section, I travel to the planet Sci-Fi to discuss the past of a genre so often concerned with the future, as well as imaginary worlds and what it means to be human in the face of technological progress.

Rocketing to the moon

As the nearest and most easily observable extra-terrestrial object, the moon has always been the subject of speculation, myth and legend. During the 20th century the satellite was brought tantalisingly within human reach thanks to the international space race, triggering fantasies of space exploration in the young (and not so young) the world over. In this sense, the astro/cosmonaut of sci-fi isn't so different from the pioneering cowboy of the western genre (check out the earlier section 'Appreciating What a Man's Got to Do: Westerns' for more about life on the range).

Fittingly the subject of the first significant science fiction film was a trip to the moon. Georges Méliès *Le Voyage dans la Lune* (1902) is one of the most enduringly popular films of early cinema due to its striking and playful images and its technical prowess. Méliès used lavish, moveable sets, extravagant costumes and visual effects such as the *stop trick,* where shooting pauses for a moment, making objects seem to disappear. The celluloid was also hand-painted for added visual spectacle.

By the time of *Destination Moon* (1950), the US was about to engage in a space race with Cold War rival the Soviet Union. A propaganda agenda was certainly operating here, with scientists educating and persuading doubters in the best way they knew how – with a Woody Woodpecker cartoon! Just fire up YouTube to watch Woody learn about jet propulsion and gravitational fields; you too may begin to believe the authoritative narrator who states that 'the moon is a great deal easier to reach than you realise'.

Although released just a few months before the US actually reached the moon, Stanley Kubrick's *2001: A Space Odyssey* (1968) has a loftier agenda. This is epic sci-fi that aims to explore the place of humans in the universe. The moon features here as a mere stop-off point on the way to farther destinations, including an enigmatic lesson for humanity in the shape of a huge black monolith. Kubrick's meticulous direction brought a new realism to the special effects, introducing *front projection* (a sophisticated way to combine actors with moving backdrops) and detailed miniature work.

By the 1990s the Cold War had thawed and the huge cost of the space programme was becoming unsustainable. The Challenger disaster of 1986, in which seven astronauts died on take-off, was a horrific demonstration of the dangers of space travel. In this context, *Apollo 13* (1995) retells the events of the near disastrous space mission of 1970 as a tense thriller starring Tom Hanks. Zero-gravity scenes were shot inside the freefalling aeroplanes used to train astronauts, known as 'vomit comets'. Houston, we have a problem.

Exploring imaginary worlds

Film scholar Vivian Sobchack argues that science fiction relies upon the collision of real and imaginary worlds to create its impact. The much-discussed ending of *The Planet of the Apes* (1968) is the perfect example, as Charlton Heston's astronaut realises that the planet run by apes upon which he thought he was 'shipwrecked' is, in fact, Earth. 'You maniacs!' he cries. 'You blew it up! Damn you all to hell.'

You can make the distinction between *science fiction,* which presents events that may be possible given current scientific knowledge, and *science fantasy,* in which you stop caring about the story's basis in reality and simply suspend disbelief. But this separation is difficult to sustain in the face of films that are realistic in tone but set in the future (such as *2001: A Space Odyssey*), resulting in fun but ultimately pointless arguments about whether sci-fi gurus such as Arthur C Clarke accurately predicted the future.

All cinematic imaginary worlds, whether scientifically plausible or not, must contain familiar reference points to allow audiences to engage with the stories. This necessity leads to the widely accepted convention that aliens in the far reaches of the universe are often 'humanoid' and speak English with an American accent. The pre-eminent example here is, of course, *Star Wars* (1977) and its sequels and prequels. And pre-sequels. Or something.

The universe of *Star Wars* is so familiar to audiences the world over, and so heavily invested with fan debate, that stepping back and thinking about its significance can be tricky. But its huge popularity and influence are exactly why you need to try to understand this phenomenon. Here are a few frameworks you can use to explore the *Star Wars* universe (Chapters 13 and 14 contain more on these approaches):

- **Psychoanalysis:** The Oedipal conflict between father (Darth Vader) and son (Luke Skywalker) is almost too obvious. What about seeing the relationship between the droids R2-D2 and C-3PO as one that mirrors the human psyche? R2-D2 is instinctive id and C-3PO rational superego.

- **Representation:** Many aliens are given traits (and even accents) associated with ethnic minorities on Earth. Jar Jar Binks is the most discussed (and disliked) example of creating a borderline racist 'other' figure.

- **Semiotics:** You can break down the conflicts between characters into oppositions, such as human/alien, order/chaos, democracy/dictatorship and so on. This approach strips away the imaginary world and exposes the symbolic tensions behind all those rubber alien masks.

All of these different approaches are reminders that – despite its somewhat geeky reputation – sci-fi does deserve to be taken seriously. You just need to look beyond the spectacular special effects and thrilling zero-gravity fight sequences. After all, imaginary worlds are effectively just different ways of looking at our own.

Dreaming of electric sheep and mechanical men

If a key question of the western (mosey along to the earlier 'Appreciating What a Man's Got to Do: Westerns' section) is what it means to be a man, sci-fi likes to go one better and think about what it means to be human. Of course that's mainly because it's the only film genre that regularly features non-human characters. Well, that and children's animated features, weirdly enough.

Science fiction fan cultures

Of all film and television genres, sci-fi seems to produce the most devoted and organised fan communities. To name but a few examples, *Star Wars, Star Trek* and *Dr Who* all have legions of fans who develop their own distinctive sub-cultures within the broader sci-fi universe. In the last decade, much of this activity has moved online, and the potential to build huge transnational communities is in evidence.

Conferences and festivals are still vital though, with the biggest such as San Diego's Comic Con now regularly attracting A-list film stars and big-name directors. At conferences, fans often dress up as their favourite characters, an activity recently termed *cosplay*.

Fan communities are fascinating examples of the circulation of *sub-cultural capital*. Fans value themselves and others not according to their material wealth, but according to their knowledge – or their ability to speak Klingon without a human accent.

Forget about aliens for a moment and focus on the figures that best represent the intersection of technology and humanity: robots, androids, or even better, *cyborgs* who're literally combinations of (wo)man and machine.

The idea of a mechanical person, or at least one constructed by another person (rather than by God), is what animates Frankenstein's monster. The terrifying potential in this character crosses the boundaries between sci-fi and horror. Mary Shelley's novel *Frankenstein* is often read as symptomatic of popular fears around the advances of science in the 19th century, and you can also apply this concept to the more obviously fabricated robots of 20th century sci-fi cinema.

A Frankenstein-style mad professor also features in one of the earliest sci-fi films: Fritz Lang's extravagant and spectacular *Metropolis* (1927). For various complicated and not entirely clear reasons, the scientist is called upon to create a robot double of an innocent female character, Maria. Brigitte Helm's performance in the dual role is truly something to behold: as Maria she simpers and cowers, as her mechanical double she's a hyper animated floozy. The disturbing sexuality of female robots is also an idea explored in many later films such as *Blade Runner* (1982).

The 1980s and 1990s produced a distinctive cycle of sci-fi films featuring robots, androids and cyborgs. They're often violent action films such as *The Terminator* (1984) and *Robocop* (1987), where mechanical killers hunt remarkably squishy humans. Both these films clearly play with computer-age anxieties about technology replacing humanity, particularly in *The Terminator*'s apocalyptic vision of sentient, war-mongering machines.

The notion of so-called virtual reality, which became common currency in the early 1990s, provoked fictions that did away with the human altogether. One early example, *The Lawnmower Man* (1992), tells the story of a mentally disabled gardener who becomes an all-powerful superhero online and turns into a monster. *The Matrix* (1999) and its sequels took this one step further and imagined an entire universe created by computer, fed by energy from battery-farmed humans. At least you can someday learn kung fu by download. Or perhaps even film studies. . . .

Peering Through the Darkness: Film Noir

The scene is a darkened, smoky bar at midnight. A detective sits alone, shooting back bourbon. Raindrops sparkle on the window like diamonds and a neon sign blinks on and off. A woman dressed in black satin slinks over and sits next to him. He doesn't blink. 'Mind if I smoke?' she purrs. She's already smoking. 'Mind if I drink?' he replies, finishing the bottle.

The iconography of film noir is so instantly recognisable that evoking or parodying it is all too easy. But try to discuss film noir as a genre with consistent conventions and meanings and you soon find that it's as slippery as its devious female characters. What makes film noir so interesting as a category is that, according to some film scholars, it doesn't really qualify as a genre at all. And yet, you know film noir when you feel it.

So peer with me through the shadowy gloom as I attempt to shine a revealing spotlight on this most complex of genres, including its visual style and its protagonists.

Testing the limits of genre

Here's a tricky question. If westerns and sci-fi are defined by their narrative setting and iconography, horror by its emotional effect and musicals by the fact that everyone suddenly bursts into song, what defines film noir? Its name, using yet another French word (meaning 'black') implies darkness, evil and despair. You can, indeed, find these tonal qualities in many of the films generally considered to be noirs, but of course such qualities aren't exclusive to film noir.

Neither can you define which films count as noirs by looking at how the film industry or audiences discussed them at the time of release. During the 1940s and 50s, for example, the films that scholars consider to be classic film noirs were generally referred to as 'crime thrillers', 'gangster films' and 'psychological dramas'. Their source material is sometimes drawn from 'hardboiled' detective writers such as Dashiell Hammett and Raymond Chandler, but sometimes not.

The truth is that French film critics created *film noir* as a category by looking at a set of American movies several years after their initial releases. Few films were released in Europe during World War II, leaving a large backlog of American movies that hit after peace was restored. These films struck the French critics as being markedly different to what had come before. They looked and felt, how you say? *Darker,* non?

So historical coincidence caused a somewhat general impression that film critics solidified into a *canon,* or key group, of films. This group varies in size and scope but nearly always includes the following films:

- *The Maltese Falcon* **(1941):** A bafflingly complex detective yarn adapted from Dashiell Hammett and starring world-weary Humphrey Bogart.
- *Double Indemnity* **(1944):** A sordid tale of infidelity and double-crossing directed by Billy Wilder.
- *Laura* **(1944):** A murder mystery where the detective falls in love with the dead victim, discovers she's still alive and then tries to kill her.

By defining a genre and then choosing a canon of films that qualify as belonging to it, critics are clearly in danger of *tautology,* or what's sometimes called 'the empiricist's dilemma'. Tautology is a chicken-and-egg situation. What defines the category? The films. How do you choose the films? By those that fit into the category. See what I mean? Doesn't really make sense does it?

Although the same logic can apply to all attempts to categorise genres, film noir suffers particularly from the empiricist's dilemma because outside critics originally imposed the category, instead of industry insiders developing it. In a further twist to the tale, the more recent self-conscious incarnation – *neo-noir* – is an example of the film industry listening to critics and then making movies that fit the category (walk over to the mean streets of the nearby sidebar 'From noir to neo-noir'). Confused yet?

Seeing noir as a style

If film noir struggles to qualify as a genre, perhaps it's more a style of film-making or an aesthetic approach to a range of different subject matters. Obviously 'noir-ish' crime thrillers certainly exist, but can you equally imagine a noir-ish western, musical or comedy?

In order to answer this question, you need first to establish which stylistic elements make up a noir-ish approach. The films described as noir tend to be:

✔ **Dark:** Obviously. More specifically, most scenes take place at night and are lit with high contrast between dark and light.

✔ **Narrated through voice-over:** This convention can take you deeper into the protagonist's inner psychology – or add further levels of deceit through the use of unreliable narration.

✔ **Structured around oblique, diagonal lines:** The classic example is angled lighting through venetian blinds, which casts oblique lines over characters faces, as if they're behind prison bars.

✔ **Wet:** It's usually raining, and when it's not, the streets glisten nonetheless. Riverbanks and beaches at night provide additional inky backdrops.

These stylistic elements can appear in different types of films, and indeed they often are. You find them in productions as diverse as Hitchcock's gothic women's picture *Rebecca* (1940) and *Letter From an Unknown Woman* (1948), a lavish romantic melodrama.

One of the best-known cinematographers of the noir period was John Alton, whose book *Painting with Light* (1949) remains a classic guide to the craft. Alton describes the techniques used in these films as 'mystery lighting' or 'criminal lighting', suggesting that they were already well-established conventions of genre film-making well before World War II. For example, the original version of *Scarface* from 1932 has several noir-ish sequences.

From noir to neo-noir

The elements of style thought of as noir-ish predate the key movies of the initial group of film noir movies, but they were also resurrected several decades later for a cycle of films known as neo-noir. The nostalgic period detail of *Chinatown* (1974) leads this set of films, although *Chinatown* notably defies noir conventions by being mostly shot during the day in sun-drenched Los Angeles.

These self-reflexive neo-noir films cover multiple genres. *Blade Runner* (1982) is sci-fi-noir, *Basic Instinct* (1992) is erotic-thriller-noir and the snow-bound comedy *Fargo* (1996) has even been described as 'film blanc'.

If the extensive and growing list of neo-noir films (such as *Drive* (2011)) is anything to go by, film noir does indeed seem to make more sense as a loosely-defined style than as a tight genre. But the question is whether the use of neo-noir style actually means anything, or is it just empty quotation or 'pastiche'? (In film studies circles, 'pastiche' is different from 'parody', which mocks conventions. By contrast, pastiche just quotes different styles with no apparent agenda.) Frederick Jameson's influential definition of postmodernism was based upon an analysis of neo-noir *Body Heat* (1981), which he described as stylistically rich but lacking in emotional impact.

Detecting spider women and their prey

Whether film noir is a genre or a style, undeniably the films associated with the term present a highly pessimistic view of male–female relations. Basically, romance isn't to be trusted, and love leads to disaster or even death. The male characters, often detectives or criminals, are either cynical and bitter or naive and stupid.

The source of this danger? Women, or more specifically (yet another French term) the *femmes fatales*. These 'deadly women' are beautiful and sexy and use their sexuality to nefarious ends:

- ✔ In *Double Indemnity* (1944), Phyllis Dietrichson (Barbara Stanwyck) lures insurance salesman Walter Neff (Fred MacMurray) into a plot to kill her husband and claim on his life policy. She then seduces her daughter's boyfriend in an attempt to get him to kill Neff. Naughty, naughty girl.

- ✔ In *Out of the Past* (1947), Kathie Moffat (Jane Greer) abruptly settles a fist fight between two of her lovers by shooting one of them in the head.

- ✔ In *The Postman Always Rings Twice* (1946), Cora Smith (Lana Turner) bewitches her older husband's young employee to the extent that murder is practically foreplay.

As this short selection indicates, the femme fatale is often literally deadly for her husband or lover (or sometimes both). She's positioned clearly as an object of physical desire for her male prey, with the camera lingering over her legs or lips as she smokes cigarettes or puts on lipstick. She wants money or power rather than romantic fulfilment. And she usually dies before the film's climax, having nonetheless destroyed the life of the male protagonist.

Critical differences of opinion abound with regard to the femme fatale and her relationship to feminist film theory. In *psychoanalytic theory* (which explores the subconscious processes of cinema spectatorship – see Chapter 13), she's the prime example of an objectified female who exists only to be looked at by other male characters and the audience. Her place in the narrative can be seen as a punishment of female transgression: the femme fatale who kills her husband invariably winds up dead herself, neutralising her threat to the nuclear family.

Although the femme fatale rarely goes unpunished in the films, her on-screen presence is often so potent as to render her ultimate fate irrelevant. American audiences during these films' original releases were well used to the convention of last-minute moral readjustment, a requirement of the Hays Code (check out Chapter 9), and didn't always take these endings seriously. Bearing this in mind, these women's transgressions resonate as powerful stands against unhappy marriages and even against patriarchy as a whole.

For example, do audiences really buy the unconvincing ending of *Gilda* (1946), when Rita Hayworth's eponymous femme fatale makes up with gangster Johnny (Glenn Ford)? No, they remember Hayworth's incandescence, her outfits and hair, and the way she runs rings round the pathetic men in her orbit. And audience research, such as Jackie Stacy's, has confirmed that female film fans often find portrayals of powerful women on screen liberating and pleasurable (as I describe in Chapter 3).

Watching Boy Meet Girl, Time and Again: Romantic Comedy

Scholars generally consider the romantic comedy to be a sub-genre of the larger field of comedy. But early definitions of comedy, such as those used to describe Shakespearean plays, stressed narrative elements related to male–female relationships (love and romance, marriage as conclusion) instead of humour or lightness of tone. In this sense, all comedies are romantic to a greater or lesser degree.

In the contemporary film industry, the romantic comedy (or rom-com) is a well-established genre. Familiar narrative patterns generally define these films: boy meets girl, boy hates girl, boy changes mind and wins girl, boy loses girl, boy wins girl back. These films are also commonly aimed at and marketed to female audiences. Hence another commonly used but less complimentary moniker: the 'chick flick'.

In this section you get the chance, if you so desire, to go all gooey as the path of true love refuses to run smooth and gender roles are put through the wringer, but all's well in the end.

Romancing the same old story

The rom-com relies on romance. Sounds obvious doesn't it? But stop for a minute to think about what romance means. In contemporary usage, *romance* refers to a love story or courtship, generally between a man and a woman. It involves codes of behaviour (monogamy, for instance) and rituals (the first date, proposing marriage) that are specific to different cultures and different time periods.

Put simply, being romantic or behaving in a romantic way isn't instinctive behaviour: you need to learn it. And you acquire and learn to navigate these codes through friends, family and popular culture – which is where rom-coms come in. In the 20th century, Hollywood movies became the perfect purveyors of 'true love' and 'happy ever after' romances.

Here are some examples of the movies that made audiences believe in Hollywood romance:

- *Why Change Your Wife?* (1920), an example of Cecil B. DeMille's witty, society comedies of marriage, which were successful on both stage and screen.

- *It Happened One Night* (1934), directed by Frank Capra, was a big hit and it set off a cycle of fast-talking, battle-of-the-sexes films or 'screwball comedies' such as *The Philadelphia Story* (1940).

- *Pillow Talk* (1959) is one of a series of films starring wholesome Doris Day and Rock Hudson that hinted towards sex without ever being explicit.

- *Annie Hall* (1977) is Woody Allen's deconstruction of the romantic comedy genre that led to other so-called nervous romances of the 1970s.

- *Pretty Woman* (1990) represents a return to the genre's traditional values. The film made a megastar of Julia Roberts.

Of course, Hollywood didn't create the idea of romance. Many of its signs and codes were already well established, and so here the idea of discourse can be particularly useful. French philosopher Michel Foucault used the term *discourse* to describe the complex web of ideas, knowledge and communication that circulate around culture and together comprise 'common knowledge' on a particular subject (see Chapter 13).

Thinking of romance as a discourse highlights its nature as something society constructs, instead of it being seen as an essential human truth that simply exists. This construction is constantly evolving and balancing opposing ideas, known as *dialectics*. Crucially, discourses can evolve through the stories that society tells itself, such as film genres. In this sense, the romance narrative of the rom-com isn't just a reflection of a discourse, it's the discourse itself, living and breathing and full of contradictions.

Interestingly, one of the key elements of the romantic discourse in Hollywood rom-coms, which has been present from the earliest examples of the genre, is the explicit discussion of romance itself. Often one or both parts of the romantic coupling claim not to believe in true love or Hollywood clichés. For example:

- ***Friends With Benefits* (2011):** Jamie (Mila Kunis) and Dylan (Justin Timberlake) attempt to avoid romance by staying as friends who have sex. Of course this doesn't work. At one point Jamie kicks a poster advertising another rom-com and screams 'Shut up, Katherine Heigl! You stupid liar!'

> ✔ ***Sleepless in Seattle* (1993):** Sam (Tom Hanks) listens to his friend's wife describe the plot of *An Affair to Remember* (1957) and become emotional to the point of tears, before smirking to his friend: 'That's a *chick*'s movie!' Later he recreates the 'chick's movie' climax with himself in the lead role.

These films attempt to be knowingly cynical about romance and overarchingly romantic at the same time, a desire that mirrors many reactions from audience members who often treat these films as 'guilty pleasures', wanting the kick of true love but being fully aware of the films' artifice.

Digging deeper into chick flicks

The term *chick flick* is the cause of some debate in film studies. Some scholars see it as a patronising term that devalues female audiences and the pleasures they derive from cinema. If critics or commentators use 'chick flick' as a means of dismissing a film, then they are helping to maintain a long tradition of cultural distinctions that are gendered. Intellectual high art is masculine and important, while emotive popular culture is feminine and therefore less worthy. However some younger female audiences have *co-opted,* or taken back, the term, and now use it in an ironic or celebratory fashion.

Chick flicks aren't necessarily frivolous rom-coms, however, they can also be:

> ✔ **Buddy films:** Such as *Thelma and Louise* (1991) or *Ghost World* (2001)
>
> ✔ **Musicals or dance films:** Such as *Dirty Dancing* (1987) or *Mamma Mia!* (2008)
>
> ✔ **Period films:** Such as *Pride and Prejudice* (2005) or *Marie Antoinette* (2006)
>
> ✔ **Weepies:** Such as the notorious tear-jerkers *Beaches* (1988) or *The Notebook* (2004)

This list features an incredibly diverse range of films. Of course, if you attempt to define a genre by the gender of those who enjoy it, don't be surprised to find a wide variety of preferences and styles.

Feeling bromantic

Some scholars notice a significant gender shift going on in rom-com land. The recent films made by producer Judd Apatow (and imitators) have been described as male-centred romantic comedies. *The 40-Year-Old Virgin* (2005), *Knocked Up* (2007) and *I Love You, Man* (2009) all feature heterosexual romance in their plots, but each places equal (if not higher) value upon close male friendships. For this reason they've also been termed *bromance* movies.

In bromance movies, decidedly un-alpha males (played by 'regular guy' actors such as Seth Rogen and Jason Segel) form close friendships with other men to discuss their relationships with women. These discussions are often open and explicit, suggesting sexual confidence, but nonetheless anxious about sexual performance and other issues. Although the male friends are clearly presented as straight and involved in heterosexual pregnancies and marriages, they also become extremely close and often employ comic homoeroticism.

The bromance cycle can be read as a symptom of a crisis in modern heterosexual masculinity, triggered by factors such as the increased acceptance of homosexuality. Alternatively, some viewers have taken seriously the sexist values expressed ironically by the male characters, creating an unpleasant backlash against feminism and women's increased power in society. Either way, this unexpected turn in the romantic comedy is evidence that genre remains significant and has plenty to say about gender relations, whether you like what's said or not.

Why genres never (completely) die

Genre has been essential within the history of film and is very likely to remain so. Every genre goes through cyclical patterns of decline and renewal, which can presumably continue for as long as films are being made.

The romantic comedy, for example, has been through several different phases during its life as a cinematic genre. It began with screen adaptations of plays or novels about marriage, and really found its feet during the social upheavals of the 1930s and 40s. The genre fell out of favour in the sexually liberated 1960s, but was reconfigured by the nervous romances of the 1970s and came back strong in the 1990s, launching stars such as Julia Roberts and Meg Ryan. It continues to be a popular genre within today's film industry and shows little sign of passing into respectful old age.

But what about those genres that, unlike romcoms, have genuinely fallen out of favour with the public and declined in numbers to the point of practical extinction? You can count the musical and the western among these apparently extinct genres, because both were mainstays of the film industry for decades before almost disappearing from production slates.

Although few musical films are made these days, stage musicals remain popular, and television and the Internet have taken on the role of bringing musical performers to the widest possible audiences. As for the western, I return to the example I use to open this chapter: a film's genre depends on what or whom the characters are shooting. Westerns and sci-fi are different incarnations of 'adventure films', just with different settings and iconography. Isn't Han Solo basically a cowboy in space?

Chapter 6

Getting Animated about Animation

In This Chapter
▶ Analysing the appeal of cartoons for children and grown-ups
▶ Understanding the workings of the greatest animation studios
▶ Encountering animation from all over the world

*T*hose poor misguided people who think that studying films is a waste of time sometimes use the term 'Mickey Mouse Studies' as an insult. But what's so wrong about studying Mickey Mouse anyway?

Mickey Mouse was a vital pioneer in the world of character animation and went on to become one of the most recognisable fictional characters ever created. If that wasn't enough, he's also a formidable brand representing the enormous power of one of the world's biggest producers of entertainment, Walt Disney. Surely that's worth taking seriously.

But there's so much more to animation than just lovable Disney characters. In this chapter you encounter a wide range of styles and techniques aimed at kids and adults alike, as well as taking a tour around a world filled with cartoons.

Considering Much More than Kids' Stuff

Yes, most short cartoons and longer animated films are aimed at children, but that's no reason to write them off as irrelevant. Animation instantly fascinates young children who don't glance twice at a live-action film. Why is that? Is it most animation's graphic boldness and rich colours? Or because the boundless magic of animated worlds – where animals can burst into song or smack each other with frying pans – is closer to the way kids see life? Whatever the reason, animation and childhood (and therefore nostalgia) are closely linked.

But of course not *all* animation is kids' stuff. Classic Hollywood cartoons, such as *Merry Melodies* and *Looney Tunes,* were screened in cinemas as part of a varied programme of entertainment aimed at the entire family. The evidence suggests that such cartoons were (and remain) just as popular with grown-ups as with their kids. Plus, animation's potential for creating abstract images or wild flights of fantasy is also appealing to artists and film-makers outside of the mainstream. Finally, the boundaries between live-action cinema and animation are increasingly blurred in the digital age.

Bringing images to life

The noun *animation* comes from the verb 'to animate', which essentially means 'to bring to life'. Thinking of animation in this way brings into focus the close relationship between animation and cinema as a whole. After all, film is essentially animation that uses photographs rather than drawings (flip to the nearby sidebar 'Drawing real life?' for details). The well-known toys that prefigured cinema, such as the spinning zoetrope or even the simple flick book, used drawings not photographs to tell stories. So in a way, animation gave birth to cinema rather than the other way around.

In this book, I use the term animation to mean any type of moving image that doesn't require photographs as a source, and it includes a wide variety of techniques (roughly from the oldest to the most recent):

- ✔ **Cel animation:** Traditional animation using hand-drawn images traced one on top of the other (using clear celluloid sheets or 'cels') and then photographed. This type of animation can be basic, where only sketched characters appear on screen, or complex, with rich, multilayered backgrounds.

- ✔ **Rotoscoping:** A process that traces photographic moving image stills, turning them into animation that moves realistically. Rotoscoping was widely used in early cartoons to increase the speed of production, but also provides the eerie quality of Disney's human protagonists such as Snow White. It has also been revived in digital form, for example in Richard Linklater's *Waking Life* (2001).

- ✔ **Stop-motion animation:** Uses physical objects that are manipulated between frames to produce the illusion of movement. Variants abound, including *claymation* that uses modelling clay (such as Wallace and Gromit), models combined with live-action photography (Ray Harryhausen's special effects monsters) or paper-style cut-outs (early *South Park* (1997 to present day)).

- **Computer animation:** Involves digitally created images. This technique has developed rapidly from simple lines and vectors in the 1970s to the complex, photorealistic 3D environments of today's Pixar films. *Motion capture* allows animators to record realistic movements from actors and apply them to digital characters (Gollum in the *Lord of the Rings* trilogy).

- **DIY animation:** Has grown exponentially during the digital age, with fans developing their own hybrid forms of animation such as *machinima,* which creates stories using videogame engines and characters, or *Lego films,* using the popular children's building toys. Distributed on YouTube, these films can gain millions of fans around the world.

Drawing real life?

Animation is a reminder that the movement of cinema images is a magical illusion. This illusion depends on several physiological processes including *persistence of vision,* which means that still images projected quickly enough — around 16 (or more) frames per second — blur seamlessly into each other. Viewers accept this movement as natural or realistic when it uses photographic images, but animation works in the same way and nobody demands 'realism' from cartoons. Some styles are deemed more 'realistic' than others, such as Disney's early animated films, but this is clearly a relative comparison. The principal joy of animation is its freedom from the bounds of reality, which makes cartoons perfect for kids and avant-garde film-makers alike.

Everybody walk the dinosaur

Early animated short films, such as *Gertie the Dinosaur* (1914), moved towards being cartoons by developing engaging characters for their animated creations. Gertie also demonstrated that animals behaving like people (being *anthropomorphised*) is inherently funny. She makes eye contact with the audience like a vaudeville comedian, expresses human emotional responses such as crying, and dances or does tricks on command.

This film was originally exhibited on stage alongside its creator, showman Winsor McCay, who appeared to interact with his comedy creation. Gertie doesn't always play ball, however, setting up an unruly and amusing relationship between animated character and off-screen animator, which is echoed in many later *Looney Tunes* cartoons (notably *Duck Amuck* (1953) starring Daffy Duck).

Making kids (and grown-ups) laugh

The connection between cartoons and comedy is as fundamental as the link between animation and childhood. Drawings or other types of animated objects disrupt the fabric of reality, encouraging absurd, impossible characters, environments and events that are often extremely funny. The term *cartoon* was first used for artists' sketches, and then in the 19th-century print media it became associated with grotesque caricatures of well-known figures. London's *Punch* magazine was loved by the public and hated by politicians in equal measure. The ability of cartoons to puncture the egos of the powerful is still evident today in TV shows such as *South Park*.

The visual gags in early cartoon shorts developed into the complex set of visual codes found in the series produced by Warner Bros. and MGM, such as *Looney Tunes*. As described by animation scholar Paul Wells and distilled in Table 6-1, this comedy shorthand established a world in which everyday expectations are turned on their head or exaggerated to an absurd degree.

Table 6-1	Common Visual Gags in Cartoon Comedy
Funny Event or Object	*Comic Possibility or Expectation*
Anvils	Perch over heads, ready to topple; often flatten whatever they fall on
Tongues stuck out	Dying of thirst or overtaken by lust
Blurred, spinning lines and/or smoke	Characters fighting
Black bombs with lit fuses	Melodramatic suspense; explosions rarely do lasting damage
Head surrounded by birds or stars	Confusion after a blow to the head
Eyelids	Can be operated like rollerblinds
Corn on the cob	Fast food, eaten as if mechanised

These visual gags or puns are working with language in complex ways. The literary theory of *semiotics* says that language is a code that uses symbols (or *signifiers*) to produce meanings (the *signified*). Animation plays with these codes to comic effect. To consider an example from Table 6-1, the idea that eyelids are like rollerblinds is a simple visual rhyme and a figure of speech, in that you can consider windows to be the 'eyes of a house'. In animation, the figurative (eyelids are like rollerblinds) can become the literal (eyelids *are* rollerblinds!). The reverse is also possible: the figurative birds circling a character's head after being whacked can become literal birds and fly away.

Many more cartoon gags centre around the body or bodily processes such as eating, snoring and so on. Bodies in cartoons are also often subject to horrendous violence. In *Tom and Jerry* the beleaguered Tom is regularly burnt, drowned, decapitated or flattened. Why is this funny? Sigmund Freud claimed that jokes give pleasure because they relieve the pressure of behaving normally in a civilised society. When you watch cartoons, you can enjoy the embarrassing, uncontrollable nature of your own body, as well as indulging in a spot of *schadenfreude,* the pleasure taken in other's misfortunes.

Animating counterculture

Although every society has its protest movements, the counterculture of the late 1960s gained significant momentum in part due to the large number of teenagers and young adults born during the post-World War II baby boom. This generation's radical ideas around war, race relationships and gender were already driving contemporary art, literature and music, and this exploration was soon extended to animation.

To understand how quickly countercultural music, style and art spread into the mainstream of Western culture during this decade, just compare The Beatles of 1963 with their late 1960s reinvention. They went from the 'Fab Four' pop band playing cheerful 1950's rock and roll, to long-haired hippies releasing experimental concept albums in just a few short years. Their first two hit films, *A Hard Day's Night* (1964) and *Help!* (1965), are cheeky and irreverent performance pieces, with the band members playing zany, cartoonish versions of themselves. In 1968, The Beatles *became* cartoon characters in the British animated film *Yellow Submarine* (1968), with even their on-screen voices being supplied by actors.

Yellow Submarine was directed by George Dunning, a Canadian and a former colleague of influential avant-garde animator Norman McLaren. It's a perfect distillation of the countercultural psychedelic movement in animated form:

- ✔ Visuals are flat but complex and richly coloured, with motifs including rainbows, flowers and the word 'LOVE' in bold capitals.

- ✔ Narrative logic is surreal and dreamlike. During the sequence accompanying the song 'When I'm Sixty-Four', time flows backwards and forwards, and at one point the Yellow Submarine carrying the band members meets itself coming back in time.

- ✔ Characters are stylised incarnations of countercultural ideas. The bad guys (the 'blue meanies') are music-haters who steal colour out of the world, and John Lennon is introduced as a chemically altered Frankenstein's monster.

> ✔ Several sequences are designed to resemble the hallucinations prompted by the drug LSD, particularly 'Lucy in the Sky with Diamonds', which rotoscopes (see above section 'Bringing Images to Life') a chorus girl into abstract forms with realistic movement and also uses rapid flashing effects.

Yellow Submarine was an international hit and paved the way for other animated films aimed at adults. Few were more 'adult' (as in 'rude') than *Fritz the Cat* (1972). Based on underground comic book artist Robert Crumb's character, *Fritz the Cat* was animated by former Paramount cel artist Ralph Bakshi. It showcases cartoon nudity, group sex, prolific drug use and violence, all within a stylised urban environment filled with anthropomorphic characters. Although the film's anarchic spirit and free-love ethos are true to hippy counterculture, its representation of female and black characters attracted criticism, particularly after it became a surprise smash hit.

Although mass cinema audiences for radical animation proved a short-lived phenomenon, these films had an impact on generations of animators to come. On TV, Terry Gilliam's animated segments for *Monty Python's Flying Circus* (1969–74) are very similar to the cut-out, Pop Art college sections of *Yellow Submarine*. And the 1980's 'ban the bomb' movement, which protested against nuclear weapons, found expression in Jimmy Murakami's film adaptation of Raymond Briggs's *When the Wind Blows* (1986). This movie looks like Murakami's gentle Christmas classic *The Snowman* (1982), but don't be fooled: it's a devastating tale of a loveable old couple dying in a nuclear holocaust. Fun!

Going full circle: Cinema gets animated

At the birth of moving pictures, cinema and animation were one and the same thing. The zoetrope and the magic-lantern technology that preceded cinema used drawings, not photographs. Even after the Lumière brothers startled audiences with their photographic *actuality films* (scenes taken from real life), early film-makers continued to experiment with different techniques for creating moving images, often blending animation as defined today with live-action film. For a good example, check out J Stuart Blackton's *Humorous Phases of Funny Faces* (1906): it shows a hand drawing faces on a blackboard, which then magically come to life.

Between the 1920s and 1940s, when audiences consumed cinema as a continuous stream of mixed programming (see Chapter 9), animation was separated off into cartoon *shorts,* while the features (Disney excepted) were *films* that used photographic moving images. Then TV arrived, and even animated shorts were lost to cinemas. Only a few films, such as Disney's live-action extravaganza *Mary Poppins* (1964), continued to use animated segments as a kind of added production value. The main element of mainstream cinema that remained open to animation was the title sequence (such as in *Grease* (1978)).

Who Framed Roger Rabbit (1988) was, at the time, a landmark achievement in special effects. Its story of 'toons' who live among (or at least alongside) humans required complex animation and *compositing* techniques (that is, overlaying photographic images with animated ones) to blend the two elements together. The toon characters, including the sexy femme fatale Jessica Rabbit, are carefully lit and shaded to appear 3D. They also interact with props, which were suspended on robot arms or cables during filming. All very impressive, but viewed from today's perspective, *Who Framed Roger Rabbit* feels like the end of an era, the pinnacle of the combination between traditional cel animation and live-action cinema.

In the 1990s, computers took over animation:

- *Beauty and the Beast* (1991), Disney's return to form, uses cel animation laid on top of computer-generated backgrounds, allowing spectacular camera movements around the Beast's castle.

- *Terminator 2: Judgment Day* (1991) and *Jurassic Park* (1993) blew audiences' minds with digital morphing and photorealistic dinosaurs.

- *Toy Story* (1995) was the first feature-length digital animation film, a form that all but replaced traditional animation in mainstream cinema within a couple of years.

- *Star Wars Episode 1: The Phantom Menace* (1999) uses computer-generated images (CGI) extensively for backgrounds, vehicles, weather and even supporting characters (though Jar Jar Binks is probably best forgotten).

Developments since the 1990s have only served to bring the status of big-budget cinema as 'live action' further into question. The use of motion capture to create realistic movement for digitally animated characters blurs the boundaries between performance and technology. (When will Andy Serkis, renowned as the king of motion capture acting after Gollum, King Kong, and the chimpanzee Caeser from *Rise of the Planet of the Apes* (2011), finally get an Oscar nomination?)

In a sense, CGI has returned cinema to its animated roots. Digital stand-ins for real actors are also used extensively in fight sequences or action shots. Just watch any of the big superhero movies of the last five years and try to spot where reality ends and animation begins.

Touring the Great Cartoon Factories

John Lasseter, Pixar supremo, often speaks of his fond memories of going to the pictures in his childhood, when cartoons still had a place in cinema schedules. Children and adults alike loved those brief, seven or eight minutes of brightly coloured chaos. True to his words, Lasseter ensures that every time you pay to see a Pixar feature film in the cinema you get a little animated surprise beforehand, as a playful reminder of the Golden Age of Hollywood cartoons.

In the following sections we track Disney's unstoppable rise from small animation studio to global entertainment giants, noting their collaboration with the kings of digital animation, Pixar. We will also pay overdue attention to innovators and pioneers the Fleischer brothers – creators of iconic characters Betty Boop and Popeye – and take a dangerous leap into the anarchic world of Warner's Looney Tunes stable.

Disney: The mouse shall inherit the Earth

Charles Pathé of Pathé Frères – the first internationally successful film production company – said 'I did not invent the cinema, but I *industrialised* it'. Walt Disney could legitimately make the same claim in the field of animated films.

Before Disney, other animators invented techniques, streamlined the animation process and created popular characters, but none had the long-lasting cultural and economic impact of Mickey Mouse. Other animation studios came and went, and though Disney's journey from fledgling cartoon producer to global entertainment juggernaut was hardly smooth sailing, Walt's combination of business sense and storytelling ability continues to animate the company nearly 50 years after his death.

Walt's success didn't arrive overnight. Together with his first business partner and fellow cartoonist Ub Iwerks, Disney tried and failed to break into the animation business for around ten years before the company struck gold with a certain loveable anthropomorphised rodent. Mickey's debut short, *Steamboat Willie* (1928), caused a sensation due to its strong visual characterisations and innovative use of synchronised music and sound effects (see the nearby sidebar 'Mickey Mousing'). Mickey's curvy design was comforting to the eye, his falsetto voice was childlike and innocent, and his adventures were nonthreatening enough to reassure even the most anxious of parents.

Recognising the immense value of his creation as not just a cartoon star but also a visual brand, Disney began merchandising in earnest, producing clothes, toys and most famously watches featuring Mickey. Meanwhile his studio produced a popular series of music-driven shorts known as *Silly Symphonies* including the following:

✔ *The Skeleton Dance* (1929) demonstrates the darker, spookier style of Walt's business partner and animator Iwerks. Skeletons in a graveyard dance to specially composed music, without a cute animal in sight.

✔ *Three Little Pigs* (1933), a bright Technicolor confection with detailed character animation of its piggy trio, was a huge success. It won an Oscar and spawned the hit song 'Who's Afraid of the Big Bad Wolf?' But the sequels failed, fuelling Walt's antipathy towards repeating himself, or as the great man said: 'You can't top pigs with pigs!'

✔ *The Old Mill* (1937) showcased Disney's development of the *multiplane camera,* which automatically moves several layers of background artwork in front of the lens, creating a deeper image. See *The Old Mill*'s opening scene: a spider's web superimposed over a mill at sunrise. This short represented a shift towards a more 'realistic' animation style (check out the earlier sidebar 'Drawing real life?') with spectacular atmospheric effects such as lighting and reflective water.

Above all the *Silly Symphonies* allowed Disney to experiment with techniques and refine style in pursuit of Walt's ultimate goal, a feature-length animated film. *Snow White and the Seven Dwarfs* (1937) was a hugely expensive gamble, taking around 1,000 artists three years to produce and going six times over budget. Walt was forced to remortgage his house to pay for its completion. Luckily for his wife and kids, the film was a huge hit all over the world, and thanks to its many re-releases it remains one of the most profitable films ever released. Disney was awarded an honorary Oscar for innovation: one full-size statuette and seven small ones.

The Disney house style that was established by the early animated features (and barely changed over the coming decades) is one of lush, multilayered landscapes, detailed character animation and dense orchestral scoring. It's so recognisable that other film-makers can easily parody it. In *Shrek* (2001), Princess Fiona waltzes through a Disney-esque forest before engaging in a duet with a bluebird. When Fiona's warbling gets too high pitched, the bird explodes, representing DreamWorks Animation's confidence about dispatching the Disney legacy. The recent phenomenal success of *Enchanted* (2007) and especially *Frozen* (2013), however, demonstrates that the Disney animated feature is alive and kicking. And warbling . . . Let it go! Let it go!

The Fleischer brothers: Betty pops out of the inkwell

Unlike Walt Disney (see the preceding section), Max and Dave Fleischer are barely remembered today, which is a shame, because not only did they create enduring cartoon characters, but also they advanced the art of animation through technical innovation.

Mickey Mousing

Disney's early sound cartoons are notable for their clever synchronisation of music and movement. In *Steamboat Willie* (1928), when Minnie Mouse runs alongside the boat trying to climb aboard, a frantic woodwind theme climbs rapidly up and down, illustrating her panic. When Mickey's adversary Pegleg Pete spits tobacco, it circles back around with a high-pitched whistling sound.

This close association between music and on-screen movement is known in the industry as 'Mickey Mousing' thanks to Disney's popularisation of the technique, but it's also used in live-action films. For example, during the opening sequence of Howard Hawk's film noir *The Big Sleep* (1946), flirty, spoiled Carmen Sternwood (Martha Vickers) falls into the arms of Philip Marlowe (Humphrey Bogart) to the accompaniment of a rapid downward scale on a harp. This technique amplifies the comic artificiality of the gesture – because Carmen sure ain't no angel.

Their first invention came to Max in 1915 while he worked as a strip cartoonist for a popular science magazine. His invention, the rotoscope, offered the first mechanical method for creating animated images. Single frames of a series of moving photographic images were projected onto a light box where an artist traced them. In this way realistic movement, and hence character performance, were more easily created.

Ambitious studio Paramount hired Max to contribute short animations to its entertainment programming, resulting in the *Out of the Inkwell* series, a popular blend of live action and rotoscoped characters. In these shorts, the character Koko the Clown grows out of the inkwell and interacts with the animator and the physical environment around him. The effect remains striking and it formed the basis of later live-action-animation mash-ups from *Mary Poppins* to *Who Framed Roger Rabbit*.

After setting up their own studio in 1921, the Fleischers were bursting with new ideas, including:

- ✔ The 'bouncing ball' leaping from word to word in song lyrics printed as subtitles, for their *Song Car-Tune* shorts made from 1924, which helped audiences to sing along with a live musical accompaniment. The brothers even developed their own sound-on-film system, but this innovation didn't catch on.

- ✔ The method known as *in-betweening*, where the best animators draw the key action frames and leave juniors to fill in the gaps. Delegating labour improved efficiency of the notoriously intensive animation process.

- ✔ Using 3D model backgrounds instead of flat drawings to help create the illusion of depth. Disney later modified this technique with its multiplane camera (check out the preceding section for details).

But none of these inventions were enough to sustain the studio without engaging characters. Fortunately, the Fleischer Studios' first star Betty Boop was capable of provoking strong audience reactions. Betty was a sexy flapper, with short hair and even shorter hemlines. Her antics included being chased by men who tried to steal her 'boop-oop-a-doop'. Not surprisingly, Betty provoked disapproval from moral guardians, and after the Hays Code restrictions were imposed in 1934 (as I describe in Chapter 9), she was redrawn as a career girl with a full-length skirt and an aging sidekick, Grampy. Not surprisingly, audiences missed the racy party girl Betty.

The Fleischer brothers' next star was Popeye the Sailor, whose popularity eventually rivalled that of Mickey Mouse. Popeye started out as a comic strip character in 1929 and made his animated debut in a Betty Boop short in 1933. His trademarks were his unintelligible accent, his oversized, tattooed forearms and his love of canned spinach – which resulted in soaring sales for the leafy vegetable in the US. His appeal to serviceman kept him relevant during World War II and beyond, and his character was revived several times on television. (A live-action *Popeye* starring Robin Williams was a notable flop of 1980. Its visuals are weird, but even weirder is the fact that New Hollywood auteur Robert Altman directed it.)

Warner Bros.: Daffy Duck, Porky Pig and related anarchists

If the classic Disney style featured sweet, innocent characters in beautiful, realistic settings, its main competition in the field of cartoon shorts, Warner Bros., was quite the opposite. These 'toons are literally loony: crazed, manic characters with speech impediments, raging against a brutal world filled with Acme bombs and falling grand pianos. Warner Bros. established a dream team of animators in the mid-1930s made up of Tex Avery, Chuck Jones and Bob Clampett. Audiences then and now love their combined whacky and irreverent style.

The impressive roster of Warner Bros. cartoon characters includes:

- **Bugs Bunny:** The smart-mouthed, wise-cracking trickster who easily outwits his rivals including big-game hunter Elmer Fudd. His catchphrase 'What's up, Doc?' is an amusingly calm enquiry into whatever ridiculous situation unfolds in front of him.

- **Daffy Duck:** The zaniest, most screwball of all the *Looney Tunes* characters: prone to manic laughter, furious anger and frantic dance routines. *Duck Amuck* (1953) is the closest Hollywood animation ever got to producing an avant-garde animated film.

- **Porky Pig:** A slow-witted, stammering straight 'man' who's often the foil for the crazier characters. Bob Clampett's *Porky in Wackyland* (1938) is a black-and-white short that rivals *Yellow Submarine* (1968) for surrealist inventiveness.

Warner's visual trademarks reject the realism of Disney animation for a bolder, comic-strip style. Colours are bright but flat and unshaded, outlines heavy and black, and backgrounds simplified, sometimes to the point of becoming abstract geometric shapes. Music is completely subordinate to the movement on screen, echoing or illustrating the characters' movements, or a backdrop to big production numbers – most famously in *What's Opera, Doc?* (1957), in which Bugs and Elmer parody Wagnerian opera, modern ballet and even Disney's *Fantasia* (1940).

Despite high points such as *What's Opera Doc?*, by the late 1950s Warner's animation wing was about to become another victim of the breakdown of the studio system, and specifically the outlawing of block-booking that had ensured high exhibition fees for packages of entertainment (see Chapter 9). As cartoon shorts left the cinema, they found a natural home on television where they became a staple of children's programming.

Warner's more recent experiments with feature-length animation, such as Brad Bird's *The Iron Giant* (1999), have won acclaim but not big box office success. But don't forget that Warner Bros. is responsible for the heavily digitally animated *Matrix* and *Harry Potter* franchises, so the company is still doing very nicely indeed out of animation.

Toons are people, too: Animating race and gender

Just because they're made with drawings (or computers) rather than photographs doesn't make cartoons exempt from issues of representation: animation has a relationship to reality, which is why it can move you, scare you or make you laugh. The necessary economy of cartoons means that they often invoke stereotypes as narrative shortcuts or as the focus of comedy. Either approach can be a problem when you consider that kids consume cartoons like lollipops.

Over time, society's ideas of what's acceptable change and develop, which has led to some older cartoons being withheld from circulation due to what viewers now consider to be racist imagery. Warner's *Jungle Jitters* (1938) depicts African tribesmen as savage cannibals and hasn't been shown on TV since the late 1960s. In the wartime cartoon *Bugs Bunny Nips the Nips* (1944) the all-American rabbit greets Japanese soldiers as 'slant eyes' and 'monkey face'.

Feminists have long been critical of Disney's female characters, who are generally princesses who require rescuing by handsome princes. Recent Disney heroines appear designed to address these concerns, but often in confusing, contradictory ways. For example, Rapunzel in *Tangled* (2010) is a comparatively active heroine who often has to rescue her handsome (but vain) love interest, Flynn. Yet the film also provides a devious female villain whose desire to stay young and beautiful instigates the plot. And of course, Rapunzel does fall for Flynn in the end.

And finally, although no openly gay major cartoon characters exist yet, Bugs Bunny has always raised a few eyebrows due to his penchant for donning women's clothing to distract Elmer Fudd.

Pixar: Not just a Toy Story

The apparently unstoppable rise of Pixar Animation Studios demonstrates that the key to producing successful animation is to marry new technology with old-fashioned, character-driven storytelling. Pixar's remarkable run of critically acclaimed and commercially successful films has taken the studio from small offshoot of George Lucas's Lucasfilm to Hollywood major via its partnership with the Walt Disney Corporation. Although (geographically speaking) it's not a Hollywood company at all, being based instead in Northern California near the high-tech hub of Silicon Valley.

The company's technological innovator was Ed Catmull, a computer scientist who recognised the cinematic potential of CGI. But Catmull's ambition to create entirely computer-generated movies required a lot more than technological know-how. Pixar needed an animator to inject warmth, humour and personality, and appropriately enough this came in the form of a staff animator fired from Disney: John Lasseter. Lasseter's short films, especially *Luxo Jr.* (1986), created endearing characters out of inanimate objects such as *Luxo Jr.*'s desk lamp, which became the company's corporate logo.

Lasseter's CGI shorts created a big impression, but they weren't financially viable in themselves. Pixar kept afloat by working in commercials as it entered the four-year long production process for its first feature. *Toy Story* (1995) was a big financial risk, even with the backing of Disney. But it succeeded, not only because it was the first film of its kind, but also because of a central idea with a strong pull for kids – many children imagine their toys coming to life when they aren't around – coupled with a smart script filled with pop culture references that made parents laugh as much as their children.

Almost 20 years later, several Pixar titles (*Finding Nemo* (2003) and *Toy Story 3* (2010)) rank among the highest grossing films of all time, and the company has won 27 Academy Awards. Although several competitors have joined Pixar in the market of feature-length CGI animation, particularly DreamWorks Animation with the successful *Shrek* franchise, Pixar films receive greater critical adoration than other studios' output. For example, after the release of *Up!* (2009) and *Toy Story 3* (2010), a rash of cynical film critics admitted that Pixar films made them blub like babies.

What accounts for these films' tear-jerking power? Pixar films reassure adult audiences with clever, knowing humour before delivering their emotional kicks in the guts. In *Up!*, the montage sequence depicting Carl's life with his true love Ellie is made even more poignant by its prefiguring comedic childhood scenes. Many of these films also contain a strong element of nostalgia. The *Toy Story* films present multiple layers of nostalgia for adult viewers: the loss of their own childhood, combined with parental anxiety about kids growing up and becoming useless burdens in old age. And you thought it was just about toys?

Spanning the Globe: A World of Cartoons

As a primarily visual medium, animation has always travelled well internationally, and it's easily dubbed into different languages. Its close connection with the visual arts means that different styles of animation have developed all over the world, benefitting greatly from distinctive local visual traditions. Compared to live-action film-making, much smaller teams can produce animation with much lower budgets, provided the artists are devoted enough to work very long hours with little guaranteed financial return. These factors make producing high-quality, distinctive animation outside of the mainstream and without the backing of Hollywood possible.

In this section, I provide you with some examples of lesser-known animation traditions from around the Europe and the Middle East. Probably the best-known examples of animated world cinema are Japanese anime, but these films are so central to Japanese film culture that you can read about them in context in Chapter 12.

However, remember that Hollywood is also a global producer of animation, which can lead to some sticky situations – as I describe in the next section.

Taking over, one toon at a time

The Walt Disney Corporation is a truly global enterprise. Led by the worldwide popularity of Mickey Mouse, its short cartoons and then its animated features have been shown successfully all over the world. *Snow White and the Seven Dwarfs* (1937) was (for a few years) the biggest box office hit of all time and was screened in places as far flung as Shanghai in China. Although the company originally relied on RKO and United Artists for international distribution, Disney set up its own global distribution wing, Buena Vista, in 1953. Disney now has offices in over 40 countries and employs around 150,000 people worldwide.

This success has made the Disney brand synonymous with the process of *globalisation,* the international spread of big business. This issue is controversial, because local economies and cultures often suffer when big multinationals move in. Some critics use another, more loaded term to describe this process: *cultural imperialism,* which suggests that cultural products such as films, fashion and pop music invade other cultures around the world, replacing diversity with bland similarity. The introduction of Disney's international resorts, first in Tokyo in 1983, and then near Paris in 1992, provoked widespread concern that local cultural traditions were being replaced or 'Disney-fied'.

Disney animation also borrows (or steals, depending on your perspective) stories and characters from around the world. Just think about it, and you soon realise that very few of the company's feature length films have a specifically American source and setting. Instead they're generally imported from the following:

- **British novels:** Walt was a well-known *anglophile* (lover of England), and the studio's output from the 1950s and 1960s has a strong British flavour, including *Peter Pan* (1953), *One Hundred and One Dalmatians* (1961) and *Mary Poppins* (1964).

- **European fairy tales:** Notable sources include the works of Hans Christian Andersen (*The Little Mermaid* (1989)), the Brothers Grimm (*Tangled* (2010)) and Charles Perrault (*Sleeping Beauty* (1959)).

- **Global myths and legends:** Films include the Arabic *Aladdin* (1992), the Chinese *Mulan* (1998) and the Greek *Hercules* (1997).

But Disney doesn't just grab the best children's stories from around the world – it also sells them back in glorious Disney-fied form. Consider the depictions of Eastern cultures in *Aladdin* and *Mulan*. In both films, the East is a place of magic and mysticism, which is implicitly contrasted with American rationalism and science and found wanting. Characters are either simple racial stereotypes (Aladdin's love interest Jasmine is overtly sensual like a belly dancer) or just plain unrealistic, such as Mulan, who criticises ancient Chinese society with the moral compass of a modern American teenager.

Aladdin and *Mulan* are examples of how people in the West enjoy simplistic fantasies of the East, a process that cultural theorist Edward Said defined as *orientalism*. Orientalism makes Westerners feel better about themselves by defining the East as inferior, opposite or 'other'. Orientalism in art and literature dates from the period when several Western cultures had extensive colonies abroad and therefore had a direct political stake in portraying colonised cultures as inferior. In today's largely post-colonial era, these images and ideas survive in media including animated films.

Playing it straight? European animation

Compared to the large-scale industrialisation of cartoons in the US, animation in Western and Eastern Europe flourishes in small pockets of talent and innovation, but it has rarely gathered enough critical mass to become self-sustaining financially. Nonetheless this small-scale, handmade approach has consistently generated outstanding animators, new ideas and techniques, particularly given the close association between avant-garde film-making (see Chapter 7) and animation within European film culture. Although Europe produces relatively few full-length animated features, those that do get made and released internationally stand out as distinctive alternatives to the mainstream.

Western Europe

The following countries have produced notable animation:

- **Britain:** London provided a home for animators displaced by two world wars, and some government subsidy for experimental animation, such as Len Lye's *A Colour Box* (1935) – check out Chapter 7 for more. Revenues from advertising allowed the animation company of Halas and Batchelor to produce a few features such as *Animal Farm* (1954). Channel Four Television has supported experimental animation for 30 years, and recently the Aardman company became a world leader in stop-motion animation thanks to much-loved characters Wallace and Gromit.

- **France:** As with live-action cinema, France produced animation pioneers, including Charles-Émile Reynaud and Émile Cohl, and has a tradition of quality animation. The series of films based on the French comic book *Asterix the Gaul* (starting with *Asterix the Gaul* in 1967) are made in Belgium but add Gallic flavour to European popular animation. In recent years Sylvain Chomet's distinctive comedic style – notably *Les Triplettes de Belleville* (*Belleville Rendez-vous* in the UK (2003)) – found favour with international festival and art house audiences.

- **Germany:** The artistic hotspot of Weimar Berlin produced experimental animation by Hans Richter and Walther Ruttmann as well as Lotte Reiniger's delicate cut-out *Die Abenteuer des Prinzen Achmed* (*The Adventures of Prince Achmed*) (1926), probably the world's first animated feature film. During World War II animation was produced as propaganda. In recent years Germany has attempted to enter the CGI animated movie market with films such as *Tarzan* (2013).

- **Italy:** Arnaldo Ginna and Bruno Corra's futurist films (1910–14), created by painting directly onto celluloid, are among the first abstract animations. Italy's tradition of popular adult comic books translated into a few feature films, but most animation has been related to advertising and television. In the 1960s, Gamma Film in Milan produced animation auteur Bruno Bozzetto, whose best-known film, *Allegro Non Troppo* (1976), is a parody of Disney's *Fantasia* (1940).

Eastern Europe

Throughout most of the 20th century, Eastern European and Russian animators worked in a very different political and artistic context to their colleagues in Western Europe.

In the early years of the Soviet Union, state-sponsored animation was literally rolled out to the provinces on trains, which used carriages as theatres. Russia's major animation studio Soyuzmultfilm had only limited freedom from strict state requirements that imposed so-called socialist realism. Only occasionally did animated films find international release, with one notable exception being Aleksandr Ptushko's *Novyy Gulliver* (*The New Gulliver*) (1935).

The rest of Eastern Europe suffered a similar fate, with the Communist state providing funding at the expense of local cultural diversity. However animation has also proved a subversive tool of expression in these countries. In Croatia, Zagreb Film produced minimal, modernist animation that won international awards (Dušan Vukotić's *Surogat* (*The Substitute*) (1961)). The Czech surrealist Jan Švankmajer was banned from making films for ten years after his *Leonardův deník* (*Leonardo's Diary*) (1972). As the Cold War thawed during the 1980s, Estonian Pritt Pärn's rough and ready animated films shed new light on life behind the Iron Curtain. His colleague Igor Kovalyov moved to the US to make Nickelodeon's hit children's television series *Rugrats* (1991–2004).

Drawing a history of violence: Animation from the Middle East

Prior to 2007, even the most committed cinephile struggled to name a major animated film to come out of the Middle East: and then, like buses, two came along simultaneously. *Persepolis* (2007) is a French–American co-production adapted from Marjane Satrapi's autobiographical graphic novel and tells the story of the Islamic Revolution through young Marji's eyes. *Waltz with Bashir* (2008) is also an international co-production made by Israeli director Ari Folman; it's also autobiographical in tone and looks back at traumatic political events – the 1982 Lebanon War – from a current perspective. Both films won widespread acclaim including major awards and enjoying widespread theatrical distribution.

Persepolis and *Waltz with Bashir* make creative use of animation to explore the intersection between memory, narrative and history against the backdrop of events beyond individual control. *Persepolis* places the audience inside young Marji's mind, with the stylised (mostly) black-and-white animation allowing equal reality to her dreams, fantasies and childhood memories. The history of modern Iran is told in fragments of gossip and family encounters, as well as grander segments of official history, rendered in a cut-out silhouette style reminiscent of ancient Islamic art. In *Waltz with Bashir*, Ari must reconstruct events that he has wiped from his memory by visiting fellow soldiers and asking them to tell him what they can remember. The film suggests that Israeli culture has a kind of collective amnesia about atrocities committed within living memory.

The style and purpose of animation within the two films creates an interesting contrast. As Figure 6-1 shows, *Persepolis* has the feel of hand-drawn ink illustrations, with deep solid blacks, bright whites and not much grey in between. The style reinforces the sense that the film is a personal, subjective account of events remembered and then drawn by Marji. On the other hand, *Waltz with Bashir* is an animated documentary, which takes audio footage of Folman's interview and overlays bold and vivid images created from a mixture of digital rotoscoping and traditional cel animation. The documentary's claim for truth clashes with animation's wild imagination in uncomfortable ways.

Figure 6-1:
Animation as childhood memory in *Persepolis* (2007).

Courtesy Sony/Everett/REX

At one point, Folman asks whether he can sketch one of his interviewees playing with his son. Wanting to remain anonymous, the interviewee states: 'That's okay, if you draw it, it isn't real'. This small comment feels like a rationale for the film's use of animation as a distancing device and as an impressionistic tool to come closer to the confusing and disorientating experience of being caught in a war zone.

Chapter 7

Leading from the Front: Avant-Garde Film

*W*hat colour is grass? The sky? Green and blue, right? Everyone knows that. But go outside and sit on a lawn or a patch of parkland and have a proper long look at the grass. Is it really just green – that vivid crayon green that you used to colour it in as a kid? Or is it a whole range of colours from grey to brown to yellow? While you're there, lie on your back for five minutes and stare at the sky. Not just blue, is it? You see whites and greys and sometimes oranges and greens. Stare at the sky for long enough and you may also see those weird floaty things that are part of your eyeballs.

My point here, borrowed from American avant-garde film-maker Stan Brakhage, is that the way you talk about vision is quite different from what you actually see. The situation is the same with film. Film students and fans talk about character, narrative, theme and genre, when what they really see and hear are a series of moving photographs of people they don't know, doing inexplicable, exciting things to each other, accompanied by unrealistic sound effects and loud music with no obvious source.

The concern of avant-garde film, which I attempt valiantly to describe in this chapter, is to break down the accepted conventions that allow you to make sense of your film-watching experience, because avant-garde film-makers believe that the concealed artificiality of mainstream film is inherently dishonest. The avant-garde films I discuss can be challenging and even occasionally unpleasant, but if you can give yourself up to the experience, you gain access to millions of different and fascinating perspectives on what cinema can do.

Advance! Attempting to Pin Down the Avant-Garde

Of all the types of film I discuss in this book, avant-garde film is the least known and understood. If you dip even a toe into these films, you're likely to encounter a great deal of complex theory and jargon-heavy discussion, which can be off-putting for the average movie fan.

Additionally, until just a few years ago, avant-garde film was difficult to get to see due to the fact that it isn't often screened in mainstream cinemas and the fact that a lot of it falls foul of censorship restrictions. But since the DVD format brought practically everything into the home arena and the Internet revolutionised distribution (see Chapter 16), finding and watching these films has never been easier.

Try and watch as many of the films I discuss in this chapter as possible, in any way you can. Reasonable quality versions of many of them circulate on YouTube, although clearly DVD and Blu-ray offer higher definition. Either way, the particular viewing experiences they provide are often impossible to recreate in written text.

Standing against the mainstream

So, here's another French word. *Avant-garde* was originally a military term for a group of soldiers who forge ahead into battle. When artists adopted it in the 19th or early 20th centuries, the term came to mean creative types with radical, innovative views or techniques, who were separate from – and generally opposed to – the mainstream. The implication is that avant-garde art is somehow ahead of its time, and is leading the way towards greater enlightenment for all. Of course this claim is very grand, and history hasn't always worked out the way that the avant-garde radicals expected. But you have to admire their ambition nonetheless.

Avant-garde film is also sometimes called *experimental film,* which is a broader, more inclusive term, or *artists' film,* which is somewhat more elitist. Whatever you call it, the avant-garde always exists in opposition to popular mainstream cinema, as Table 7-1 shows.

You may well be thinking: wait a minute here. I'm quite happy with mainstream cinema, thank you very much. I like my blockbusters and even the occasional foreign language film, but that's as far as it goes. This avant-garde stuff just sounds way too . . . pretentious.

If so, don't worry. Certainly this mindset exists and is probably characteristic of the vast majority of film fans. For the time being, however, I can only say to keep an open mind. A film student who refuses any type of film without even trying it is seriously limiting their own options.

Table 7-1   Comparing the Characteristics of Mainstream and Avant-Garde Films

Mainstream Cinema	Avant-Garde Film
Expensive, therefore produced by big multinational businesses for profit	Cheaper, often made in a workshop or educational environment, or with state support
Feature-length films using actors, sets and props to tell stories about people	Any-length films (from seconds to days) that are usually non-narrative (check out the later section 'Not worrying about the story')
Built around *causality* (characters act to achieve goals) and *closure* (conflicts are resolved)	Breaks causal links and opens up films to multiple interpretations
Aims to entertain an audience with pleasurable narrative or spectacle	Aims to shock an audience out of complacent pleasures
Conceals the processes of its own construction through techniques such as continuity editing (see Chapter 2)	Displays the processes of its own construction (as in *structural film*, defined in the following section)
Watched in cinemas or at home by very wide audiences	Viewed in clubs, film societies or in art galleries (and now at home) by a small but committed audience

Sampling the many facets of the avant-garde

The blanket term *avant-garde film* covers an incredibly diverse range of film-making practices, which often overlap with areas of animation (see Chapter 6), documentary (Chapter 8) and art cinema (check out the later sidebar 'The best of both worlds: Art cinema'). The nature of avant-garde film-making, however, which often flourishes in a workshop community of like-minded artists, means that art and film historians typically identify significant movements or clusters of activity within specific historical moments or locations.

In order to get to grips with the avant-garde, familiarise yourself with a few of the following movements, film-makers and films. The huge variety of practices I describe here means that you should be able to find something here that you at least appreciate, and perhaps even enjoy. So, roughly in order from oldest to most recent, here they are:

✔ **European Avant-Garde:** When the word *Avant-Garde* is capitalised, it tends to refer to 1920s Paris and Berlin, when artists from other media began to embrace cinema. The results were abstract animations (see the later 'Determining when a cartoon isn't just a cartoon' section) or cubist films such as Fernand Legér's *Ballet Mécanique* (1924).

✔ **Surrealism:** The surrealists took elements recognisable from conventional films (plot, character, locations) and then mixed them all around until nothing made conventional sense. René Clair's *Entr'acte* (1924) attacks art and the middle-class bourgeoisie. Luis Buñuel and Salvador Dalí's *Un Chien Andalou* (1929) is filled with disturbing imagery linking sex and death (check out the later section 'Dissecting cows and priests in chains' for much more on this avant-garde classic).

✔ **Underground film:** Associated particularly with New York in the 1950s and 1960s, underground film is largely unconcerned with 'art' but instead offers a voice to alternative lifestyles and philosophies. These films gleefully ignore taboos around sexuality and gender. Kenneth Anger's *Scorpio Rising* (1964) blends innocent pop music with gay sado-masochistic bikers. Andy Warhol's *Couch* (1964) features various Beat Generation artists and poets getting it on, on a couch.

✔ **Structural film:** A movement of the 1960s and 1970s that was stripped back and minimalist. Films are structured by the basic qualities of cinema such as time and space. Michael Snow's *Wavelength* (1967) is a 45-minute slow zoom into an empty room. Plus a murder! Malcolm le Grice's *Berlin Horse* (1970) superimposes short looping sections of negative and positive film featuring – you guessed it – a horse.

✔ **Found footage film:** These collages are made out of bits of other films recovered from archives or other storage media. For *Rose Hobart* (1936), artist Joseph Cornell re-edited the Universal film *East of Borneo* (1931) to focus on its leading lady, thus predating the fad for re-cutting movies and trailers on YouTube by around 70 years. Now that's avant-garde.

✔ **Young British Artists (YBAs):** Since the 1990s, video art has become increasingly significant within the art gallery world, particularly in the UK. Sam Taylor-Wood develops Andy Warhol's obsession with celebrity into video portraits such as *David* (Beckham, sleeping, in 2004). Steve McQueen won the art world's prestigious Turner Prize in 1999 for his video art and more recently a Best Picture Oscar for *12 Years a Slave* (2013). The fact that many YBAs now make feature films illustrates that hostility to commercial film-making is no longer a prerequisite for video artists.

How to watch avant-garde films

If you find avant-garde film difficult to get hold of – or to sit through after you have – here are some practical tips to help you get the most out of the experience:

✔ **Knowledge is power**: Read up about the film-makers before you watch their films. Interviews where they discuss their ideas at length can be especially helpful. Although you may have different opinions about their work, at least you have somewhere to start.

✔ **Watch in context**: Although the Internet is great for easy access to obscure films, you almost certainly get more out of watching avant-garde films along with a like-minded cinema audience. Film festivals are great places to sample unusual material. Most contemporary video art is intended to be seen in a gallery or in a particular location, and so get out and about.

✔ **Don't worry if you don't get it**: Difficult I know, but try to stay calm when you don't understand what's going on or when you feel confused or disorientated. That's probably how the artist meant you to feel. Right and wrong answers often don't exist. Just go with the flow.

Determining when a cartoon isn't just a cartoon

The most familiar examples of animation are undoubtedly cartoons in cinemas and on television for children (and adult) audiences, but the field of animation has much more to offer beyond Walt Disney and Tex Avery (check out Chapter 6 for all about traditional animation). Look at animation another way, and it becomes moving art. Right from the early days of cinema, animation has been a favourite form for experimental and avant-garde film-makers because of its handmade nature, its relationship with drawing and sculpture, and its freedom from the constraints placed on conventional film-making, particularly regarding storytelling and realism.

Following are some key examples of avant-garde animation:

✔ Viking Eggeling's abstract film *Diagonal-Symphonie* (1924) was made using paper cut-outs painstakingly manipulated and then photographed one frame at a time. These shapes grow and move, becoming more complex and resembling musical forms: staves, piano cables, perhaps a harp. It's a bold, striking and hypnotic film.

Experimental animation meets rock and roll

Before YouTube, the animated films made by avant-garde film-makers weren't often seen outside of experimental film festivals or late-night TV slots. However, these films' reach and influence goes further than you may think, partly because mainstream film-makers often borrow the innovative ideas and techniques.

Music videos in particular have proved to be a natural home for more abstract animated forms. Just take a look at Peter Gabriel's dazzling pixelated *Sledgehammer* (1986), where frozen chickens dance like Busby Berkeley showgirls around the singer's head. Michel Gondry's music videos often borrow from experimental animation, such as Björk's 'Human Behaviour' (1993), which is clearly influenced by Yuriy Norshteyn, or his Lego film for 'Fell in Love with a Girl' (2002) by the White Stripes.

- ✔ Len Lye's *A Colour Box* (1935) was created entirely without a camera: its colourful patterns and shapes were painted directly onto the celluloid. This technique creates an entirely different impression of movement from regular animation. The shapes often appear to dance along with the upbeat jazzy score.

- ✔ Norman McLaren's *Neighbours* (1952) is a black comedy short that won an Oscar. It uses a technique known as *pixilation* in which actors are used as stop-motion puppets, enabling them to glide around or even fly through the air. Its abstract soundtrack was created by scratching the edge of the celluloid print, which the projector then reads as sound.

- ✔ Stan Vanderbeek was an innovator in the field of computer animation. Together with Kenneth Knowlton he created a series of text-based animations called *Poem Field* in the late 1960s. These films challenge the spectator with harsh gaudy colours and jazz-noise sound.

- ✔ Yuriy Norshteyn's *Hedgehog in the Fog* (1975) builds on the tradition of Russian animators using folk tales as source material. It's a delightful and odd little film that explores a misty wood from the perspective of a terrified hedgehog.

Exploring Three Important Avant-Garde Ideas

Avant-garde film-makers have their own particular set of ideas, themes and aesthetic strategies that they employ in their work. However, a few over-reaching big ideas link many of these films. In this section I discuss three of the most important.

Playing around with time

The key difference between film and the other visual arts – painting, sculpture and photography – is time. Film has duration, movement and change. All films use time in one way or another, from short *actualities*, early slice-of-life films that occupy the length of time necessary for a train to enter a station, to the complex structures of conventional narrative cinema. Fiction films generally manage time through continuity editing (see Chapter 2), which provides a flow of story events from beginning to end. Time can speed up (in *montage sequences,* which compress many hours or even days of action into a few seconds) or slow down (in long takes which make use of real time), but it generally moves relentlessly forward. Exceptions – such as Christopher Nolan's *Memento* (2000) – only serve to reinforce the general rule.

Of course forward-moving is only one way to represent how human beings experience time, and it's a pretty artificial approach at that. Describing cinema as life with all the boring bits cut out may be a bit clichéd, but it's a cliché for good reason.

Avant-garde films often offer alternative structures and viewpoints to expose the artificial ways in which mainstream films handle time when telling their stories. The early European Avant-Garde was influenced by cubism in the visual arts, notably the idea that time and space can collapse in on each other within a single image. So when you look at a cubist painting by Pablo Picasso, such as *The Accordionist* (1911), you're looking at its subject from different angles and even moments in time.

Maya Deren and Alexander Hammid's *Meshes of the Afternoon* (1943) is one of the founding films of the American avant-garde and, as its name suggests, it's a fascinating study in the subjective experience of time. In this carefully composed black and white film, Deren repeatedly enters a house by climbing up stairs, sometimes pursuing a faceless figure or encountering herself apparently asleep in a chair. Film historian and experimental film archivist P Adams Sitney compares the film's structure to a spiral shape, because events are repeated but also overlap or intertwine with each other. The woozy effect of the film is like trying to remember a strange dream while you're still half asleep.

Although it treats time in an unusual way, *Meshes of the Afternoon* is filled with movement and a story of sorts: it certainly isn't boring. By contrast, Andy Warhol's most extreme non-narrative films simply gaze at their subject for interminable lengths of time, testing the patience of even the most committed avant-garde audiences:

✔ *Sleep* (1963) is almost five and a half hours of his friend John Giorno asleep in bed. Not a single-take film as many people assume, it uses edits, repeated sections and freeze-frames.

- ✔ *Eat* (1964) watches the painter Robert Indiana eating a mushroom in close-up for 45 minutes. It was shot on four-minute reels, which end with *flare-ups* (the bright light of the projector through the blank celluloid at the end of the reels) and are simply replaced with the same shot after reels have been changed.

- ✔ *Empire* (1964) is one single take of the Empire State Building in New York. Overnight shooting lasted for six and a half hours, but to extend the experience still further, Warhol insisted the film was projected in slow motion, resulting in more than eight hours of nothing happening, apart from natural light changes and floodlights turning on.

Warhol rightly described these works as 'anti-films', because their complete lack of artifice and artistic intervention is almost as shocking as their extreme running times. Of course hardly anyone is capable of watching the whole of *Empire* in one sitting in a cinema, which is entirely the point. Warhol's static films force his audience to confront the passing of time head on with no distractions. And that's quite an experience in itself.

Not worrying about the story

In literature, making the distinction between prose and poetry is important. Prose often tells a story and relies upon events occurring in sequence. Poetry can have a story, but it doesn't need one. It can just as easily be about meaning that exists in one moment of time, about exploring psychological states or about impressions of beauty. Poetry is also about language itself – the rhythms, constructions and possibilities. Of course this distinction isn't absolute, most prose has poetic elements and poetry can tell stories. But the fundamental purpose of each practice is different.

Just as literature has prose and poetry, cinema has narrative and avant-garde film. Avant-garde film is similar to poetry in its diversity of forms, its attention to artistic methods and techniques and its use of metaphor (comparisons or clashes between images) rather than continuity. Indeed these similarities are not lost on avant-garde film-makers who have often compared themselves to poets or taken poetry as their subject. Jean Cocteau was a Parisian and a Bohemian who produced art across a range of media. His 1930 *Le Sang d'un Poète* (*The Blood of a Poet*) is an early sound film that begins with an intertitle manifesto: 'Every poem is a coat of arms. It must be deciphered.'

Le Sang d'un Poète does have a story of sorts, but unlike conventional narrative cinema the motivations of its characters are mysterious and events don't link together in a clear cause-and-event chain. It begins with an artist sketching a face on a canvas. The mouth of the painting comes to life and begins to speak, and so the artist rubs it out with his hand, to where it transfers. The mouth ends up on a female statue, who advises the poet to leap into a mirror. Through the looking glass, the poet finds himself in a hotel where he peers into different rooms. The film then cuts to an outdoor scene where children are playing snowballs. One child (presumably the poet himself) is hit by a chunk of marble and dies, as does the poet. The ending is an image of the female statue with a lyre.

Not exactly a taut plotline filled with narrative tension is it? But think of the film as a poem instead of a story and you can use different bits of your brain (and analytical tools) to make sense of it – or 'decipher it' in Cocteau's terms. Coats of arms use visual symbols to represent the history of a family, and *Le Sang d'un Poète* is also full of distinctive images that reach back to Ancient Greece: the statue, figures wearing masks posed as tableau images, the laurels placed upon the dying poet's head. Additionally, hints of the myth of Orpheus, the poet who travelled to the underworld to regain his lost love, crop up in the film. But it's no staid retelling of a Greek myth. It shocks and scandalises with its sexual references and female impersonators. Don't worry about the story, just enjoy the lovely poetic imagery.

The problem with narrative

A defining characteristic of avant-garde film is that it doesn't concern itself with telling stories in the same way as the majority of commercial cinema. It may contain elements of narrative and even draw on the narrative techniques of mainstream film (editing, using actors and so on), but it often does so to subvert these conventions and expose them as artificial.

So what exactly is the problem with narrative? Surely enjoying a good story doesn't do any harm. Well, perhaps it does, because of the inherent but hidden social and even political messages that such films contain (of what's sometimes called the *dominant ideology*).

Just think about your standard romantic comedy for example. These days, most characters in rom-coms are postmodern and self-aware enough to say that they hate the clichéd notion of romantic love. But still they go after it all the same. And although current Hollywood action men often quip, they're basically enacting violent fantasies, often against foreigners and in the service of the American dream.

Feminist film-makers and critics claim that narrative cinema does a particular disservice to women, because it objectifies female characters and marginalises female audiences. Academic and film-maker Laura Mulvey argues that narrative cinema must be replaced with a radical alternative. She also made a few examples of what she hoped this cinema can look like, such as *Riddles of the Sphinx* (1977) with Peter Wollen. It isn't much fun, but that's entirely the point.

Embracing abstract images

When avant-garde film chooses to do away with narrative altogether, the result is often abstract work that explores the elements of time, movement and sound. Consider again the idea I introduce at the beginning of this chapter: is grass really green? Or do you just think of it as green because that's how people described it to you as a child?

The gap between how you discuss images and what you actually see was a central theme of the American avant-garde film-maker Stan Brakhage. Brakhage was an artist, writer and teacher who was part of the New York underground film movement of the 1950s and 1960s, but his films are more personal and idiosyncratic than those of his contemporaries, including Andy Warhol and Maya Deren (whom I discuss in the earlier section 'Playing around with time').

Brakhage used the film camera as a tool to represent how he perceived and understood the world in visual terms. His films therefore contain elements of documentary, abstract animation and even home movies. Here are some key examples in chronological order:

- *Window Water Baby Moving* **(1959):** A document of the birth of Brakhage's first child. Shots of his wife Jane happy and relaxed in bathwater are intercut with a highly detailed birth sequence. Beautiful, but not for the squeamish.

- *Dog Man Star* **(1961–4):** A cycle of five silent films that all together run to around 75 minutes. Each segment uses a bewildering array of techniques including close-up shots of bodies or other organic forms, painting directly onto the celluloid, or scratches that remove parts of the image revealing bright light beneath.

- *Mothlight* **(1963):** A handmade film created without a camera. Instead Brakhage trapped a series of transparent or translucent objects – including moth wings, blades of grass and flower petals – between two strips of tape and printed the result onto celluloid to be projected. The resulting images dance and flicker around the screen.

You can see Brakhage's *Mothlight* as part of the structural film movement of the 1960s and 1970s (see 'Sampling the many facets of the avant-garde' earlier in this chapter), which produced such examples of abstract imagery as *Room Film* (1973), in which Peter Gidal's camera tracks incessantly around a room in extreme close-up.

More recently video and computer artists have deployed new media to create abstract moving images. But probably the most extreme example of abstract film remains Tony Conrad's *The Flicker* (1965), which contains only black and white frames that alternate with an increasing speed until they produce stroboscopic effects. The film must be seen in a darkened cinema, but beware – it has been known to cause seizures in unsuspecting audience members!

Drifting Off into a World of Dreams

The cinema-going experience – darkness, comfort, escaping from everyday life – has inspired many film theorists to compare it to dreaming. The metaphor of cinema as dream is particularly powerful for avant-garde film-makers who often count surrealism among their formative influences. The surrealist aesthetic is heavily symbolic and sexualised, drawing on ideas from psychoanalysis, which in fact are important within film theory more generally (see Chapter 13). But within avant-garde film dream logic, symbolism and imagery certainly find their fullest expression. But be careful, they may just give you some bad dreams of your own.

Dissecting cows and priests in chains

If you watch only one avant-garde film as a result of reading this chapter, make it *Un Chien Andalou* (1929). In fact, if you haven't seen it yet, go and watch it right now. You can find it on YouTube. I can wait 15 minutes.

Okay, so how was it? Shocking, confusing, hilarious? I concur with all these responses. Of the many, many films that I've watched with students, this film is the only one guaranteed to make everyone in the room gasp at the same time. After seeing it, you know exactly which point I mean, I'm sure. I can reassure you by saying that the eyeball wasn't really the actress's; it belonged to an unfortunate cow. But that doesn't lessen the visceral horror of that shot, coming so early in the film, which, until that point, feels fairly conventional. That moment is literally an attack on cinema's primary sense – sight – from which you struggle to recover during the rest for the film. The film starts you reeling right from the word go and gets only weirder from then on.

Un Chien Andalou has impeccable surrealist credentials because it was created through a partnership between film-maker Luis Buñuel and the painter Salvador Dalí. Unpacking the film's mythology is difficult, but Buñuel spoke of the script being sparked by images from their own dreams and then developed via a process akin to *automatic writing* (both contributors brainstormed a series of images that had no rational connection to each other). This process led the film-maker to argue that nothing in the film can be read as symbolic of anything else, and that the only possible way to interpret it was through the lens of psychoanalysis – which is exactly what film theorists later did (I cover film theory in Chapter 13).

If *Un Chien Andalou* is about anything, it's probably sex. And death. And rotting donkeys. At the core of the film is the deeply bizarre relationship between its male and female protagonists who love and attack each other in equal measure. She's introduced waiting for him in a room, reading a book. She rushes to the window to see him collapsed on the street. She descends to kiss him passionately, although he's inert.

Later, back in her room, he reciprocates with lascivious desire, touching her and imaging her naked breasts and bottom. His eyes roll back in a grotesque seizure accompanied by bloody drool falling down his chin. Intense and disturbing emotional states like this one come and go without explanation or motivation.

Figure 7-1:
Psycho-
sexual
baggage in
*Un Chien
Andalou*
(1929).

Courtesy Everett Collection/REX

As you may expect from a film with Salvador Dalí's involvement, *Un Chien Andalou* contains some unforgettable imagery. One example comes as the man attempts to seduce the woman and she resists. He then picks up two ropes and tries to pull them towards her. He turns out to be attempting to drag nothing less that two grand pianos topped by rotting donkeys and two priests in chains (see Figure 7-1).

One of the priests is Dalí himself wearing a sly expression. This image appears to be literal embodiment of the psychological notion of *baggage* – the mental stuff that you carry around that prevents you from behaving as you'd like to. In this case, his baggage includes religion (the priests), culture (the pianos) and fear of death (the donkeys). The entire film is insane and inspired.

Yet *Un Chien Andalou* is far from the collection of random images you may expect Buñuel's methodology to produce. For a start, it's a well-made film, using techniques drawn from narrative cinema to establish place and character. For example, the man's cycle ride through the streets is represented using establishing long shots, and then tracking close-ups and point-of-view shots that move in the opposite direction but similar velocity.

This entirely conventional editing pattern (as I discuss in Chapter 4) was as familiar to audiences in 1929 as it is today. Similarly, that shocking opening scene relies for its effect upon another convention, that of *match on action*. The movement of the man's hand with the razor is mirrored by the intervening shot of the clouds slicing the moon, and then comes the eyeball. The unsettling balance between conventional film-making technique and moments of radical breakdown give *Un Chien Andalou* its enduring power.

Going into a cinematic trance

The dream state is such a common subject across a broad swath of avant-garde films that archivist P Adams Sitney created a subcategory of experimental works, which he dubbed *trance films*. Sitney's key characteristics of trance films include:

- Sleeping protagonists who remain isolated from what they encounter during the dream state. The prototype here is the sleepwalking Cesare in *The Cabinet of Dr Caligari* (1920).

- Simple narratives, usually a physical journey through space, toward a climax of self-realisation or death. Stages along the way are marked by what is seen by the protagonist rather than by what is done. Cocteau's *Le Sang d'un Poète* is a prime example of this structure (see the earlier section 'Not worrying about the story').

- Dream landscapes (natural or architectural) that aren't bound by realistic notions of space, and which become an element of the film's symbolism. For example, in *At Land* (1944) the film-maker Maya Deren is washed up out of the sea and eventually disappears back into the sand dunes.

Kenneth Anger made *Fireworks* (1947) when he was just 20 years old. It features a protagonist (played by Anger) who begins the film asleep in bed, before (apparently) waking and leaving his apartment through a door marked 'Gents'. He then has a series of homoerotic and increasingly violent encounters with men dressed in military uniforms. His chest is opened with a broken bottle, and his heart is revealed to be a twitching compass. A sailor unzips his fly to reveal a sparkling Roman candle. Made when homosexuality was still criminalised in the US, Anger faced obscenity charges when the film was first screened. Despite its sleepy protagonist, *Fireworks* demonstrates that the trance film can be a suitable vehicle for incendiary sexual politics.

Although the trance film provided a fertile model for many avant-garde film-makers, it's clearly not the only way to represent dreams in celluloid form. *Gently Down the Stream* (1981) by Su Friedrich uses extracts from the film-maker's dream journal, hand-scratched into the film as text. These personal memories are intercut with fragments of religious icons or watery imagery, women swimming and rowing. The dream fragments range from the banal to the sexualised, but Friedrich offers no discernible structure among the flow of images and text.

Similarly, Peter Tscherkassky's *Dream Work* (2001) uses found footage (see 'Sampling the many facets of the avant-garde' earlier in this chapter) that stutters and leaps, creating a nightmarish intensity to the overlapping images and sounds.

Whether with gentle dreams or horrific nightmares, avant-garde film offers a slightly grubby window onto our shared wishes and desires. Dreams break all the cinematic rules of realism with regard to time and space, which is why dream sequences are often the place where mainstream narrative films come over all avant-garde. Just think about Buster Keaton dozing off and then leaping from a cinema auditorium into the screen in *Sherlock, Jr.* (1924) or the Salvador Dalí designed dream sequence in Alfred Hitchcock's *Spellbound* (1945). Or practically the whole of *Inception* (2010) – which brings me neatly to the next section.

Mixing with the Mainstream: Avant-garde Everywhere

If the early avant-garde film-makers saw themselves as radical soldiers, going into battle for their creative beliefs and aiming to revolutionise cinema as a whole, looking back on more than a century of film history you may be tempted to conclude that they lost. Avant-garde movements and ideas still flourish under certain circumstances, but they seem unlikely ever to rise up and replace mainstream cinema. Given a choice between challenging and complex films which mess with their minds and stories about recognisable characters told in a familiar style, audiences go for the latter almost every time. Surely the evidence suggests that the avant-garde has had a negligible effect upon what the masses choose to see in the multiplexes.

But when you look for them, you can find plenty of points of crossover between the avant-garde and the mainstream. For a start, remember that, no matter how 'mainstream' their work may appear to be, the vast majority of film-makers are creative, open-minded people. Even successful Hollywood directors are interested in their chosen art form and keen to experience as wide a range of aesthetic strategies as possible. For example, John Ford, the blustering, macho director of classic Westerns starring John Wayne (see Chapter 14), was a huge fan of German Expressionist film-makers such as FW Murnau and Fritz Lang, and Walt Disney brought in abstract animator Oskar Fischinger to work on his great pet project *Fantasia* (1940).

You can choose to interpret these artistic influences positively, as a creative dialogue, or negatively, as simple plagiarism. But however you perceive this exchange of techniques and ideas, you can't stop it happening. And why would you want to, given that many of the most interesting 'mainstream' films show some avant-garde influences. Here are just a few examples:

- ✔ *Psycho* **(1960):** The famous shower sequence uses rapid, disorientating editing techniques directly influenced by the montage of Soviet film-maker Sergei Eisenstein (see Chapter 4).

- ✔ *Mean Streets* **(1973):** Martin Scorsese's use of pop music as a score is innovative, but he almost certainly borrowed the idea from Kenneth Anger's *Scorpio Rising* (1964).

- ✔ *Se7en* **(1995):** The grimy handmade look of the opening credits sequence, with its scratched lettering and exposed celluloid sprockets, feels like a compendium of avant-garde techniques from Stan Brakhage to Andy Warhol.

Film-makers also cross from the avant-garde to the mainstream. David Lynch is a textbook example of an avant-garde film-maker whose off-kilter sensibility somehow meshed with the mainstream for *The Elephant Man* (1980) and the television series *Twin Peaks* (1990–1). Several emerging British directors of the past few years started out as video artists showing work in art galleries. Steve McQueen is the best-known example, with his *12 Years a Slave* (2012) becoming an Oscar-winning commercial success, but also worth noting are Clio Barnard for *The Selfish Giant* (2013) and Sam Taylor-Wood, who took on the challenge of adapting the controversial publishing phenomenon of the decade, *Fifty Shades of Grey* (due for release in 2015).

But this pattern of aesthetic influence is no one-way street. Despite the antagonism displayed towards mainstream cinema by early avant-gardists, more recently Hollywood film has become a subject for experimental film-makers. For example, the first feature by British director Sally Potter was inspired by her love of Hollywood musicals, but recast with a feminist perspective. *The Gold Diggers* (1983) also features a genuine star, Julie Christie. In the gallery space, Douglas Gordon's *24 Hour Psycho* (1993) projects Hitchcock's famous thriller at just two frames a second, meaning that it takes a full day and night to unspool. This film allows the viewer to see each individual frame as it gradually clicks by.

The best of both worlds: Art cinema

Another way to think about the place where the avant-garde and the mainstream meet is to give it a name and a set of practices in its own right: *art cinema*. Art cinema is the fertile middle ground where stories are told (as in mainstream cinema) but not in the way you expect. Stars can be hired, as long as they play against type, and aesthetic experimentation is prized rather than feared.

Film historian David Bordwell defines art cinema as a 'mode of film practice', like a genre (see Chapter 5), with its own set of codes and conventions. The primary narrative convention of art cinema is ambiguity, particularly endings. Meanwhile film scholar Steve Neale notes that art cinema is a viable economic niche of the film industry as a whole, with its own funding streams and exhibition venues, including film festivals and independent cinemas. Similarly art cinema thrives on DVD and Blu-ray releases by companies such as Criterion in the US and Artificial Eye in the UK.

The history of European cinema is characterised by art cinema movements such as German Expressionism, Italian Neorealism and New German Cinema (see Chapter 11). Similarly, much of what we call world cinema also qualifies as art cinema (for example, see the discussions of Brazilian Cinema Novo or Bengali Parallel Cinema in Chapter 12). Finally, for some examples of underrated art cinema directors such as Lynne Ramsey, Andrei Tarkovsky and Abbas Kiarostami, head straight to Chapter 19.

All these examples of artistic exchange, collaboration, homage or stealing suggest that the hostile connotations of the term *avant-garde* may no longer be appropriate for this type of film-making practice. The avant-garde didn't defeat the mainstream, and many of today's experimental film-makers no longer count that as their ultimate goal. Instead of thinking about the avant-garde and the mainstream as opposing sides in an endless aesthetic war, perhaps a more fitting analogy is to see them as two sides of the same cinematic coin.

Chapter 8

Getting Real: The Truth about Documentary

. . . .

In This Chapter

▶ Analysing documentaries, including their ethical dilemmas

▶ Considering the development of documentary film

▶ Untangling the real from the unreal in documentaries

. . . .

Documentary theorist Bill Nichols has claimed that, in a sense, all films are documentaries. Even the most fantastical fiction film provides information about the culture that produces it, as well as representing the actors and any physical locations used. With this thought in mind, he divides 'documentaries' into two categories: wish fulfilment (fiction films) and social representation (what people normally call documentaries).

Nichols is deliberately overstating his case in order to emphasise the similarities and crossovers between the two forms of film-making. In particular, he wants to overturn the notion that only fiction films tell stories. Documentaries are often as exciting and dramatic as narrative films, and generally less predictable, because they draw their subject matter from real life. Of course, the boundaries between the two forms are notoriously flexible, with many documentaries using techniques from fiction film to recreate events – and fiction borrowing heavily from documentary for its enhanced 'truth value' (that is, the implied authority of the documentary image).

You can accept Nichols's argument for its own merits, while also noting the clear and significant differences between fiction and documentary films, specifically the elements that make each genuinely powerful. Documentary films are also notable for the ethical questions they raise by filming real people in their own environments, the decisions film-makers take to intervene and change events or to stand back and observe, and the relationship of the film image to a pre-existing reality. So read on; things are about to get real.

Shaping Reality with Documentary Films

Scottish director and producer John Grierson provided the most famous definition of documentary film. He may not have coined the term, but he certainly made it his own in a newspaper review of Robert Flaherty's film about Polynesian culture, *Moana,* in 1926. A few years later he defined the documentary as 'the creative treatment of actuality'. This definition is so influential because it acknowledges a surprisingly modern view of the documentary – viewers aren't watching pure, simple reality on the screen, but a 'creative treatment' of it.

In other words, documentary film-makers take reality as their raw material and then shape it according to their creative wishes – which results in different types of documentary and can create a number of ethical issues.

Comparing the documentary to fiction and to real life

The principal point of comparison for documentary film has always been its apparent opposite – the fictional narrative film. Early advocates of the documentary, including John Grierson and especially artist and film-maker Dziga Vertov, saw narrative cinema as a waste of the medium's potential to show viewers the truth.

This analysis sees fictional films as problematic, because they obscure the deeper truths of society: in turn, the documentary is the solution to this problem. This argument has aesthetic and political implications. It places a set of public responsibilities upon the documentary, including the requirement to educate, inform and empower the viewing public by putting real life up on the cinema screen.

Realism is the slipperiest of slippery terms, particularly when applied to fiction and documentary films, as I show in Table 8-1.

Table 8-1	Comparing Realism in Fiction and Documentary Film
Fiction Film	**Documentary**
Mise-en-scène (locations, props, costumes, though see Chapter 4 for a full discussion of the term) can be real (shot on location) or 'faked' in a studio.	*Mise-en-scène* is found in real life.
Even if the characters are real people, they're played by actors, often stars.	The characters are real people apparently being themselves.

Fiction Film	Documentary
The camera, lights and other film-making apparatus remain unseen.	The film-making apparatus can sometimes be seen within the film.
The film-maker is an off-screen creative presence.	The film-maker can appear in the film and may even be the star.
Screenwriters create a narrative structure and dialogue.	The story events unfold with their own logic, and dialogue is natural speech.
Audiences accept the illusion of reality according to codes and conventions.	Audiences expect a degree of truthfulness and transparency.

Of course the boundary between documentary and fiction film is often far more blurred than the simple analysis in Table 8-1 suggests. Grierson and Flaherty's notion of the documentary allowed film-makers to reconstruct or even stage moments, as well as give participants explicit directions. In Flaherty's *Nanook of the North* (1922), his Inuit subject reacts with amazement and confusion at a phonograph, biting the record between his teeth. Flaherty admitted that Nanook was actually well accustomed to such technology and that the moment was a contrivance. (Flip to the later section 'Exploring the world and its people' for more on Flaherty and Nanook.) Reconstructions, whether subtle or spectacular – such as the thrilling climbing re-enactments in *Touching the Void* (2003) – are an essential element of the documentary film-maker's toolkit.

Film-makers make documentaries that are more than simply reality captured on camera. The decisions they make before, during and after shooting alter that reality into something else, like Grierson's notion of a 'creative treatment'. But what about the status of the individual image or shot in relation to real life? How real is real? Time to go deeper for a moment. Stick with me:

- ✔ The relationship of the image to reality was a central question of philosophy well before film studies. Ancient Greek philosopher Plato described a cave with shadow images projected onto the wall. If you were a prisoner chained to the wall in that cave for your whole life, you'd perceive the shadows as reality, at least until you were released. The implication is that images are representation, not reality, but they nonetheless have to power to feel real under certain circumstances.

- ✔ Film can be thought of as a language that uses signs and symbols, and for this reason it has often been studied using methods borrowed from linguistics. *Film semiotics* thinks of images or shots as 'signs' or 'indexes' of a pre-existing reality. Semiotics stresses that the way humans think is through language, and that therefore reality only exists for humans as signs and indexes. (Flip to Chapter 11 for more on semiotics.)

✔ Postmodern theorists such as Jean Baudrillard argue that modern mass media have saturated people with images to the extent that these images have replaced reality. As an example, think about the terrorist attacks of 9/11: what do you see in your mind? I bet that your head is replaying the images broadcast in constant rotation on television: the plane hitting the second tower, the dust avalanche in the Manhattan streets. These images, to all intents and purposes, *are* 9/11.

You don't need to go quite as far as Baudrillard – by disputing the existence of reality outside of images – to recognise that the truth value of the image is a crucial issue for producers and consumers of documentaries. An unspoken trust between film-maker and audience states that what you're seeing on the screen is a close approximation of a real (or *pro-filmic*) event. Television news and reportage wouldn't exist without this contract, which is constantly under renegotiation in the face of new recording technologies. For example, in recent years poor-quality digital video of news events recorded on bystanders' mobile phones has taken on greater truth value than professionally captured images.

Sorting documentaries: Six modes

When attempting to define the documentary film, you realise quickly that many different styles of such film-making exist, each with its own formal structure and aesthetic strategies. Responding to this diversity, Bill Nichols came up with a set of six subcategories, or *modes,* of the documentary:

✔ **Expository documentaries:** The traditional form, which uses an authoritative voice-over or presenter to address viewers directly and argue a case about history, nature or politics. A good recent example is Al Gore's passionate plea for action against global warming, *An Inconvenient Truth* (2006).

✔ **Observational documentaries:** Aim to show everyday life as it is, with minimal intrusion by the film-maker or film-making process. Also known as 'fly on the wall' films, they're most commonly found on television, but influential film examples include Frederick Wiseman's *Titicut Follies* (1967), an exposé of the treatment of mental-health patients.

✔ **Participatory documentaries:** Feature the film-maker as an on- or off-screen presence, who nonetheless retains an objective stance on events. Participants are interviewed as witnesses who testify for or against a particular case, and these films may also use archive footage or reconstructions. The Oscar-winning *Man on Wire* (2008) demonstrates a creative use of this mode.

✔ **Performative documentaries:** Share similarity with participatory documentaries, but the film-maker appears on-screen and also intervenes directly in events. Interviews are staged and encounters are often dramatic and surprising. The documentary becomes as much about the film-maker as the subject. Michael Moore's films (such as *Bowling for Columbine* (2002)) are great recent examples.

✔ **Poetic documentaries:** May be based on any of the six modes but have strong aesthetic or sensual forms that bring them closer to the feeling of poetry than prose. This mode includes many early documentaries, such as *Night Mail* (1936) with its rhythmic commentary written by poet WH Auden, or avant-garde films such as Stan Brakhage's *Window Water Baby Moving* (1959) (see Chapter 7).

✔ **Reflexive documentaries:** Explicitly comment on their own status as documentaries, through stylistic means (for example, by disrupting conventions such as the voice-over) or by featuring conversations about the nature of documentary truth. See Nick Broomfield's *Driving Me Crazy* (1988), which is about the film-maker's failed attempts to make a documentary.

In order to decide whether a documentary fits into one of Nichols's six modes, compare the use of one particular element across different films – the interview. The interview is a formal device common to almost all documentaries, but film-makers can employ it to very different ends. In expository or observational films, the film-maker gives interviewees visual preference and allows them to speak for themselves with little intervention or prompting. Participatory, reflexive and performative documentaries include dialogue between film-maker and interviewee, but the differences lie in the levels of intervention and insertion of the film-maker's personality. Poetic treatments may focus on the interviewee's voice or body language rather than the content of what the person says.

The trouble with the six modes

Although Nichols's set of subcategories is a useful way of thinking through the differences present in particular documentary films, it suffers the same problems as all such lists (or *taxonomies* to use a clever word). The boundaries between the categories are blurry and distinguishing between participatory, reflexive and performative films can be especially difficult. As with attempts to define genre categories of fiction film (see Chapter 5), the categorisation is only clear through examples, which raises the question of who chooses which examples fit where.

If you're wondering why people bother to categorise films at all, you make a good point. Reading between the lines, Nichols's categories seem to imply that early expository documentaries are somewhat primitive and naïve in relation to the issues around truth when compared to the more reflexive style of recent decades. Which isn't really fair to the pioneers, such as John Grierson, because they couldn't possibly know which type of documentaries would emerge in the future.

Weighing documentary ethics

A long-standing story in Western culture claims that when members of primitive tribes are faced with a camera for the first time they cower, fearing that the technology is going to steal their souls. Whether based on truth or not, this story is a useful analogy of a dilemma that documentary film-makers encounter. How can you capture the truth about your subjects when your presence and your equipment inevitably change your subjects' behaviour? And in ethical terms: how should you treat the human subjects of documentary? Even if the camera doesn't steal subjects' souls, it may damage their lives after the film is released.

Film-makers have to make countless ethical decisions to maintain a balance between observation and intervention. Where this balance lies is a fundamental measurement of the different philosophies of documentary making, from classic works of cinéma vérité (check out the later section 'Reclaiming objectivity: Direct cinema and cinéma vérité') to today's omnipresent reality TV.

Documentaries tend to be about real people living their own lives, which means that documentary film-makers have a responsibility towards their human subjects. The audience expects that film-makers treat people with respect and represent them honestly on camera. Particular difficulties can occur around films that depict vulnerable participants, such as young children or the mentally ill. This problem is partly due to the obvious difficulties of obtaining informed consent to film, but more broadly ethical or moral questions about exploiting such subjects in the name of entertainment pervade. These issues are even more fraught when they conflict with documentary film-makers' primary responsibility: to show the truth as they see it.

Frederick Wiseman's *Titicut Follies,* which observes life inside a home for the criminally insane in Massachusetts, was a controversial film for many reasons. It displays practices of which the American public were generally unaware, including patients being force-fed, bullied or forced to wander round naked. Although Wiseman was careful to obtain permissions from all participants (or their legal guardians), after the film was completed in 1967 the state government of Massachusetts banned it, giving the reason that it violated the privacy of patients. Despite Wiseman's continued appeals on the grounds of infringement of civil liberties, the film remained off-limits to all audiences except health professionals until 1991.

The observational style of *Titicut Follies* appears to show the real world without intervention. But of course this impression is a carefully crafted illusion. Wiseman's methodology of spending several weeks within an institution in order to shoot his material results in a huge amount of footage, and so every editing choice becomes an ethical decision on what to show and what to leave out. Documentary film-makers often see part of their role as confronting society's taboos, the things that people are too scared to talk about, but they must do so sensitively.

A grizzly dilemma

In *Grizzly Man* (2005), Werner Herzog faces many ethical dilemmas as he pieces together the story of Timothy Treadwell, an eccentric environmentalist who tried to live with bears in the wild. As you can imagine, this quest didn't end well, for Treadwell or, tragically, his girlfriend. Treadwell shot a video journal throughout his final weeks, and this footage makes up the bulk of the film, accompanied by Herzog's distinctive deadpan voice-over, but the film-maker himself also features on screen as he travels round interviewing witnesses.

When Herzog comes across an audio recording of the moment of the bear attack, an enormous ethical dilemma presents itself. The entire film is coloured by the fact of Treadwell and his girlfriend's death, but should viewers hear it? Herzog decides they shouldn't but he must, which he does on-screen wearing headphones. The result is an extraordinary moment that confronts *and* respects the ultimate human taboo: death.

Capturing the 20th Century on Camera

The term *documentary* relies upon the notion of the *document*, a piece of evidence in all senses, for lawyers, scientists and historians. For future historians looking back on the 20th century, documentary films are likely to be among the richest documents. Covering the entire 100-year span, from the earliest so-called actualities produced by the Lumière brothers in France to the digital experiments of 1999 such as the BBC's *Walking with Dinosaurs*, film-makers used a bewildering array of styles, techniques and methodologies to document the world on screen.

Faced with this rich history and diversity, knowing where to start can be difficult. So this section focuses on a few specific moments and places where documentary flourished.

Meeting plain-speaking Russians

Cinephiles may regard John Grierson (whom you can meet in the earlier section 'Shaping Reality with Documentary Films') as the father of the documentary movement in Britain and the West, but he was by no means the only pioneer in the field.

Chronologically speaking, Grierson was pipped to the post by a group of radical Russians. Post-Revolutionary Russia (basically from around 1918 onwards) was a hotbed of strident politics and artistic avant-gardes, such as Sergei Eisenstein's montage theory of narrative cinema (see Chapter 4). Meanwhile

Dziga Vertov, a film editor working on Soviet newsreels, set out his own ambitious manifesto in 1922. Vertov loved to write passionate diatribes using capital letters, so in his honour, here are the key elements of his revolutionary cinema:

- ✔ Narrative film, with its reliance on devices from other art forms such as literature and theatre, is ABSURD and DANGEROUS.

- ✔ The camera and the camera operator MUST join together as one organism to observe TRUTH through the KINO EYE ('kino' is Russian for 'cinema').

- ✔ KINO-PRAVDA ('cinema truth') OPENS up the film-making process to the audience and BREAKS THE SPELL of the cinema.

As good as his word, Vertov formed a group known as Kino Eye, made up of his editor wife, Elizaveta Svilova, and his cameraman brother, Mikhail Kaufman, to produce newsreels under the banner Kino-Pravda. The results are rather different to the static newsreel style with which you may be familiar, and they feel more like avant-garde experiments than pieces of journalism. Vertov filmed everyday life (schools, factories and so on), without the permission of his subjects, and used cinematic tricks in order to reveal deeper truths about society. For example, in a sequence designed to illustrate how bread is made, the bread pops out of the oven first and is then visually rewound into a field of corn. INGENIOUS.

Undeterred by the general confusion that greeted his increasingly odd newsreels, Vertov planned a full-length film to represent industrial and urban life in the Soviet Union: the exhilarating *Man with a Movie Camera* (1929). The film's breathtaking pace – it contains around four times the average number of shots of a typical film of the period – and complex editing style were bewildering to audiences in 1929, although these characteristics help it feel modern for today's viewers. Vertov's pledge to open up the film-making process is also evident: shots often contain his brother operating the camera or his wife editing the film. *Man with a Movie Camera* is in many ways an early example of a self-reflexive documentary (read the earlier 'Sorting documentaries: Six modes' for more on the different types of documentary film).

Like many a mad genius, his contemporaries at home or abroad didn't widely appreciate Vertov. Eisenstein critiqued his attack on fiction film and called him a 'film hooligan' – a label that probably pleased Vertov. For Grierson, whose very different vision of the documentary was to become the dominant expository mode, Vertov's tricks and self-reflexivity were 'ridiculous' and 'too clever by half'. Yet Vertov later influenced *cinéma vérité,* a movement that agreed that the film-maker should be in the film (see 'Reclaiming objectivity: Direct cinema and cinéma vérité' later in his chapter). Additionally, the critical status of *Man with a Movie Camera* has grown and grown, evidenced by an eighth place in highbrow British film magazine *Sight and Sound*'s greatest films poll in 2012.

Curioser and curioser . . .

Why do audiences enjoy documentaries? The form, like fiction film, offers many different pleasures, such as visual spectacle and emotional engagement with characters. But other enjoyments are specific to the documentary, such as being able to satisfy your curiosity about the world and its people.

In early cinema, this curiosity was evidenced by strong demand for *actualities,* such as footage of sporting events or royal coronations, and *travelogues* that brought the thrill of exotic places within the reach of the general public. These twin popular diversions became key forerunners for documentary film.

Exploring the world and its people

During the first half of the 20th century the British Empire still covered a quarter of the globe, but even the Brits hadn't reached a few bits of the world. Explorers gripped the public imagination with reports of high-profile expeditions to the North or South Poles and even the 'top of the world', Mount Everest. But obvious logistical challenges blocked these pioneers from capturing their adventures on film.

Camera operators needed to be explorers in their own right, and famous examples from the 1910s included the Australian Robert Hurley (whose *South* (1919) documents Herbert Shackleton's Antarctic expeditions) and the British Herbert Ponting. Ponting accompanied the ill-fated Terra Nova expedition to the South Pole from 1910 to 1913 in which Robert Scott and his four comrades lost their lives.

Ponting's *The Great White Silence* (shot in 1910–3 but not released as a film until 1924) documents Scott's sea journey to the Antarctic and his preparations for the attempt on the South Pole itself. It contains many of the first moving images of the region committed to film, including its whales and penguins, along with charming, incongruous scenes such as Scott's men playing football on the ice. Ponting's cinematography captures the awesome scale of the continent's spaces through extreme long shots of icebergs or sculpted canyons. The film is inevitably compromised by what it can't show, namely the expedition itself and its tragic aftermath, but Ponting did develop innovative storytelling techniques to recreate these events using maps, still images and the explorers' own words captured in journals.

The travelogue form proved open to detailed studies of places or people, with explorers providing footage for scientific or economic reasons. Robert Flaherty saw himself as an explorer first and film-maker second. He was the son of a prospector who searched large areas of the Canadian wilderness on behalf of steel companies, and as an adult he entered the profession establishing routes for railroads. During these expeditions Flaherty built close relationships with a tribe of Inuit people and began to take short films of them. The resulting footage was accidentally destroyed, and so he set out again, this time specifically to make a film about an Inuit family with whom he was well acquainted. The resulting film, *Nanook of the North* (1922), was one of the first feature-length films to resemble today's documentaries.

Nanook of the North is a warm, affectionate portrait of its subjects in their struggle against the harsh Arctic environment. The family interact with the camera, often meeting the audience's gaze with a playful smile. Controversially, Flaherty intervened with the family's way of life in order to shoot the scenes he wanted, for example asking them to hunt with traditional harpoons instead of their rifles. Many people interpret the most notorious orchestrated moment, Nanook's biting of a phonograph record to find out what it is, as patronising the Inuit. But Flaherty was being true to his own moral compass, and the respect that he feels for these people is clear, even if this level of intervention now feels misguided.

Filming poetry or propaganda? World War II on film

World War II wasn't the first conflict to be committed to celluloid. Extensive newsreels of World War I survive, as well as some longer propaganda films, such as the partly re-enacted *Battle of the Somme* (1916). Even the Boer war of 1899 to 1902 leaves a few cinematic traces. But World War II arrived at the peak of film's popularity as an art form, and the circumstances of war triggered record cinema audiences. Before television was the primary news medium, cinema newsreels were the only way for people to see the war for themselves. Unsurprisingly governments on both sides waged war on public hearts and minds with propaganda films.

In 1930s Britain, the film-maker and critic John Grierson carved out a space for state-sponsored documentary film-making. Working for the Empire Marketing Board, a government agency charged with protecting the interests of the British Empire, and later for the General Post Office (GPO), he brought together an international team of film-makers including Basil Wright, Paul Rotha and Humphrey Jennings to help produce his 'creative treatments of actuality'. By the time war broke out in 1939, Grierson had moved on to the Canadian Film Commission, but his team at the GPO formed the basis of the Crown Film Unit, which produced documentaries for the British government throughout the wartime period.

The best-known films of the Crown Film Unit include:

✔ ***Target for Tonight* (1941):** Director Harry Watt used dramatic reconstructions to create an effective and exciting recreation of an RAF bombing raid over Germany; audiences loved it.

✔ ***Listen to Britain* (1942):** Humphrey Jennings's impressionistic account of the sounds of wartime Britain included spitfire engines and heavy industry but also birdsong and classical and popular music.

✔ ***Western Approaches* (1944):** An ambitious Technicolor film shot by the master of colour cinematography, Jack Cardiff, which blends documentary footage with dramatic reconstruction using real members of the Merchant Navy.

These films raise important issues around the responsibilities and formal qualities of documentaries as official propaganda. Clearly the neutral objective stance of the documentary film-maker can't be maintained because the films have an explicit political and social purpose: to keep up British morale and therefore ensure continued public support for the war effort. However, and perhaps counter-intuitively, many film-makers produced creatively adventurous work within this strange moral framework. For example, Humphrey Jennings's wartime films are vital works of poetic documentary due to their striking camerawork and careful image–sound juxtapositions.

Propaganda is a difficult term to define, but you can think about it simply as documentaries that your enemies make. From the Nazi perspective, the films of Humphrey Jennings were hardly poetry – after all, one scene in *Listen to Britain* depicts a recital by the Jewish pianist Myra Hess being attended by Queen Elizabeth II. Similarly, the films produced under the Nazi regime, most famously Leni Riefenstahl's *Triumph des Willens* (*Triumph of the Will*) (1935), can never escape the circumstances of their production. Riefenstahl remains a divisive figure within cinema history because her obvious talents as a film-maker are weighed against her terrible ideological compromises.

Triumph of the Will is undoubtedly spectacular to look at. Riefenstahl's staging and shooting of the Congress at Nuremberg in 1934 highlights the full splendour of Nazi pomp and ceremony, including famous long shots of precise lines of troops that create abstract symmetrical images in deep focus (see Figure 8-1). This film is a good example of the extreme formalism of Nazi imagery, which supports film theorist Siegfried Kracauer's controversial claim that the cinema of the Weimar period, such as the Expressionist horror film *The Cabinet of Dr Caligari* (1920), displays a fear of chaos and disorder that the fearful symmetry of Nazi propaganda resolved (enter the crazy world of German Expressionism in Chapter 11).

Above all, the documentaries that both sides produced during World War II demonstrate that 'truth' is a relative concept, inescapably tied to politics and historical context.

Figure 8-1:
The fearful
symmetry
of Leni
Riefenstahl's
*Triumph
of the Will*
(1935).

Reclaiming objectivity: Direct cinema and cinéma vérité

After World War II demonstrated the heroic and horrific consequences of claiming cinematic truth for political ends (see the preceding section), the documentary form seemed inevitably compromised. After wartime propaganda revealed the manipulative nature of apparently objective documentaries, how do you put that genie back in the bottle? Restoring the truth value of the documentary took some time, as well as a radical technological shift.

The technology required to record images and sound is particularly important for documentary film-makers who most often work on location (as opposed to on a sound stage):

- ✔ In the days before sound on film, the silent, hand-cranked camera was relatively portable, although hardly unobtrusive. Watch *Man with a Movie Camera* for examples of how this type of camera looked in action on the streets.

✔ During the 1930s and 1940s, the requirement to shoot lip-synced dialogue on 35-millimetre film meant that cameras and recorders became much larger and heavier, reducing portability and the ability to record spontaneous action.

✔ By the end of the 1950s, several technological advances came together, including better 16-millimetre film stock, lenses for shooting with natural light and especially smaller, lighter (and sometimes integrated) sound recorders.

✔ By 1962, camera operators were able to hand-hold or rest on their shoulders the Nagra IIIB camera, allowing mobile shooting with minimal interference.

These new cameras and recorders enabled an entirely different style of shooting documentary film. For the first time, film-makers were able simply to follow their subjects around as they went about their business – or to take cameras into public spaces without causing huge disruption. The resulting images felt fresh, natural and spontaneous; these tools revitalised the documentary form in the 1960s and 1970s.

Although the new portable film-making technology reinforced the truth value of the recorded images and sounds, the ethical problem of the film-maker's own presence didn't go away (see the earlier section 'Weighing documentary ethics'). In fact in some ways it became heightened, because the possibility of entirely secret, unauthorised shooting opened up new ethical issues.

The continued problem of objectivity prompted two separate documentary movements during the early 1960s: direct cinema and cinéma vérité. These terms can be easily confused with each other, but closer examination reveals that they have important differences in terms of ethos and visual style, as Table 8-2 summarises.

Table 8-2	Differences between Direct Cinema and Cinéma Vérité
Direct Cinema	*Cinéma Vérité*
To obtain truth from the subject, the film-maker should be as unobtrusive as possible.	To obtain truth from the subject, the presence of the film-maker must be acknowledged or even discussed.
The principal method is observation of subjects behaving within their environment.	The principal method is participation between film-maker and subject, often through interviews.
Commentary is minimal or absent so that subjects can speak for themselves.	Commentary is vital, whether in voice-over or through on-screen presence.

(continued)

Table 8-2 *(continued)*

Direct Cinema	*Cinéma Vérité*
The audience members should forget the film-makers and feel as if they're in the room with the subjects.	The audience is free to identify with the film-maker's or the subject's position and point of view.
The film-maker is a 'fly on the wall', watching but practically invisible.	The film-maker is a 'fly in the soup', intervening to get a response.

As ever, the best way to understand these differences is to compare examples. *Primary* (1960) is a great example of American direct cinema, as well as a fascinating look behind the scenes of American politics. Film-maker Robert Drew accompanies John F Kennedy and Hubert Humphrey as they compete in the Democratic primaries. Drew gets in with the crowd or follows the candidates through corridors and up onto the public stage. By contrast, *Chronique d'un Eté* (*Chronicle of a Summer*) (1961) is pure Parisian verité: talky, intellectual and reflexive. The film even includes an example of its own reception as the film-makers screen it to an audience and gauge their responses. Both these films feel raw, truthful and honest, but in quite different ways.

Blending the Real and the Unreal: Documentary Today

Surprisingly, a significant number of feature-length documentaries have achieved financial success in cinemas in the 21st century, most notably the political films of Michael Moore and the nature documentary *March of the Penguins* (2005). But popularity has led to an increased level of concern about the depictions of 'reality' in these films. Similar concerns apply to documentaries in today's digital world: if documentaries are real human stories on film, what happens to the form in the age of social media, when many people's stories, if not their very identities, are constructed online?

In today's multiplexes, the real and the unreal seem increasingly intertwined.

Questioning America the beautiful

The American independent film-making sector has produced a recent spate of hit cinematic documentaries, characterised by a left-wing political agenda that launches attacks on big business and government policy. But these films are a world away from didactic history lessons or even the cool detachment of direct cinema (see 'Reclaiming objectivity: Direct cinema and cinéma vérité' earlier in this chapter). On the contrary, they feature big personalities, passionate rhetoric and emotional as well as political engagement.

The key figure of this style of documentary is an apparently unassuming regular Joe in baseball cap and jeans: Michael Moore. His first film, *Roger & Me* (1989), is an account of the damage done by General Motors to his hometown of Flint, Michigan, and his later films build upon this highly personalised, subjective approach.

Moore's breakthrough success was his emotive argument in favour of US gun control, *Bowling for Columbine* (2002). The film blends an array of techniques including:

- **Personal biography:** Moore starts the film in his hometown where he attempts to open a bank account that includes a free gun.

- **Interviews:** Moore interviews witnesses to the 1999 Columbine school shootings, as well as representatives from organisations such as weapons manufacturers Lockheed Martin and celebrities including Marilyn Manson.

- **Animation:** Moore parodies the animation style used in children's educational films to illustrate the history of America's relationship with firearms.

- **Archive footage:** Moore assembles a montage sequence of US foreign policy from 1953, which claims that the CIA trained Osama Bin Laden against the Soviet Union some 30 years before 9/11. It's set to the ironic counterpoint music of 'Wonderful World' sung by Louis Armstrong.

Moore's grand claim concerns America's addiction to fear, which politicians, the media and big business peddle to further their own interests.

His rhetoric and personality are very persuasive, but not everyone is convinced by his evidence. The film attracted particular criticism for Moore's 'ambush' of the elderly actor Charlton Heston, president of the National Rifle Association at the time. Moore clearly believes that ethical issues around interviewing participants are subordinate to the public interest in his case, but making people look ridiculous may also weaken his argument.

Bowling for Columbine paved the way not only for Moore's even more controversial and financially successful *Fahrenheit 9/11* (2004), but also for other documentary film-makers using maverick techniques, such as Morgan Spurlock. Spurlock put his own health in jeopardy to make *Super Size Me* (2004) by eating only McDonald's food for a month. Although he offers clear and indisputable evidence that doing so isn't good for human health, his experiment raises interesting questions about a documentary film-maker's right to damage his own body to make a point. His doctors and his mother advise him to stop, but he goes on with his 'challenge' regardless. In this case, the ends did justify the means, because McDonald's officially withdrew Supersize meals soon after the film's release.

An inconvenient exception to the trend

Some people see Michael Moore's emotive grandstanding and Morgan Spurlock's attention-grabbing experiments as symptoms of a crisis of the documentary form and its perceived truth. But in that case, what do you make of the success of a very traditional style of documentary, narrated by a former politician, Al Gore? *An Inconvenient Truth* (2006) uses many unfashionable devices, including filming a public lecture and on-screen bar charts to illustrate points.

This stripped-back approach pays off partly because Gore's argument feels rigorous in scientific terms, but also because of his extremely charismatic delivery. Gore whips his audience into a frenzy, and viewers are easily swept along. The film's box office success illustrates that audiences can still enjoy being lectured, provided the message and the speaker are compelling enough.

Marching with penguins and other creatures

Eadweard Muybridge, pioneer of the series photography that made cinema possible, invented his proto-projector zoopraxiscope device (in 1879) in order to settle an argument: namely, when horses run do all four legs ever leave the ground at one time? Turns out, they do. This event is the earliest example of the potential of cinema to help people understand the natural world. Cinema audiences have shown a keen interest in wildlife films ever since:

- ✔ Robert Flaherty and Herbert Ponting's exploratory films of the 1920s contain many scenes of animals in their natural habitat.

- ✔ Walt Disney produced a popular series of 'True Life Adventure' films in the 1950s, such as the Oscar-winning *The Living Desert* (1953); Disney recently re-entered the market with films such as *African Cats* (2011).

- ✔ The ultra-large IMAX format, which grew in popularity during the 1990s and 2000s, reinforced the spectacular nature of wildlife films (*Alaska: Spirit of the Wild* (1997), for instance).

- ✔ On television, the BBC's flagship nature documentaries narrated by David Attenborough are popular with audiences across the world, with some being adapted for cinema release (notably *The Blue Planet* (2001)).

The fact that the revival of the cinema documentary in the 2000s was partly led by waddling penguins therefore seems appropriate. *March of the Penguins* (2005) started life as a French independent production. Warner Bros. picked it up, gave it a new score and a Morgan Freeman voice-over, and heavily marketed it at family audiences. The campaign clearly worked; the film's gross of $77 million in the US alone makes it the second most successful documentary of all time (behind Michael Moore's *Fahrenheit 9/11*).

Posters for *March of the Penguins* feature the tagline 'In the harshest place on Earth, love finds a way', highlighting the film's key narrative strategy: anthropomorphism. The film's emotive voice-over consistently ascribes human emotions such as grief and love to its feathered protagonists. You may think, well what's so wrong with that? The penguins are behaving in ways that suggest that they love their partner and chicks, so what? And they're just so cute! Yes, they are, but do they share humans' emotional responses? Scientists don't believe so, which is why anthropomorphism is generally avoided by more serious wildlife documentaries.

Questions of scientific objectivity aside, the bizarre reception that greeted *March of the Penguins* in the US demonstrates that thinking about penguins as small feathered people has implications for human politics, especially with regard to gender relations. Some Christian groups and conservative commentators praised the film as being a parable of 'moral parenting' that championed monogamy, faithfulness and self-sacrifice for one's children, turning a remarkable story of nature's ingenuity into a tool to criticise 'aberrant' human behaviour such as single parenting or homosexuality. However, you can counter this argument with just two words: gay penguins. It happens, get over it.

Looking amazing: Documentary spectacle

If wildlife documentaries are so well established on television, and indeed David Attenborough's *Life in the Freezer* series had already covered the story of the emperor penguins' struggle to reproduce, why were so many millions of people willing to pay to see *March of the Penguins* in the cinema? Because it looks spectacular, especially on the big screen.

Film students often discuss spectacle as a cinema-going pleasure that exists in tension with narrative. Action films, musicals and horror films often 'pause' the story to impress viewers with incredible images, whether they're beautiful or violent (the images, that is, not the viewers!). Documentaries do the same, even though they draw their stories from real life.

The different truth value of a documentary image, however, means that spectacle here isn't quite the same as in narrative films. More traditional documentary film-makers tend to distrust spectacle as being a distraction from the flow of information, but if the point of the documentary is to satisfy your curiosity about what the world looks like, surely the bigger and more spectacular the better?

Documenting digitally

New technology has reinvigorated documentary film in the 21st century. The digital revolution puts cameras into people's pockets, and the Internet allows them to create and share instantly video of their lives with millions of users around the globe. In such a world, as a film student you have a responsibility to question how real these stories (and indeed these people) are. (Chapter 16 explores the digital revolution in greater detail.)

The surprise hit *Catfish* (2010) is built around the narrative possibilities of unstable digital identities. Nev, a young photographer and the film-maker's brother, is contacted through the Internet by an apparently prodigious 8-year-old painter called Abby. Nev becomes involved with her family and develops a romantic relationship with her older sister. When doubts creep in about the information passed online, the brothers set off on a quest to find the truth. The film then shifts gear into the tone of a thriller as disturbing possibilities begin to present themselves. Indeed the film was largely marketed as a thriller rather than a documentary, with its enigmatic title and provocative tagline: 'Don't let anyone tell you what it is'.

Perhaps more interesting than the thriller plot are the issues that the film opens up about the authenticity of documentary authorship in the digital age. Some critics simply refused to accept that the whole thing wasn't a set-up. Why were the film-makers filming in the first place? Were they indulging Nev's fairly obvious narcissism or just waiting for something interesting to happen? An initial conversation suggests that they're primarily interested in Abby as a subject, but this answer isn't entirely convincing. What the film-makers discover is a case of online identity theft motivated by honourable reasons. Their own motivations in making the film are far less clear-cut. Whether the film was set up or not, it struck a chord with young audiences and became a reality show for MTV.

You can also view the sharing of identities online in a far more positive, utopian fashion. *Crowd-sourcing* via the Internet has become a possible source of finance for film-makers and also presents opportunities for ambitious collaborative projects such as *Life in a Day* (2011). Instigated by Ridley Scott and Kevin Macdonald, the team chose a date (24 July 2010) at random and asked volunteers to film what they were doing, answer a few specific questions (such as 'What is in your pocket?') and upload the results. Nobody on the team was sure that they'd receive enough high-quality footage to produce a feature-length film. In the end the team were sent more than 81,000 submissions from 192 countries, totalling more than 4,500 hours of video.

Even in the digital age, however, the spread of technology is far from universal, and the team resorted to sending digital cameras to the developing world in order to guarantee global coverage. Macdonald later conceded that better training would have resulted in more of this footage being used, because even the concept of 'documentary' was foreign to many in the most far-flung regions. Despite this unwelcome puncturing of New-Age Internet universality with old-world problems, the team worked hard to assemble a coherent film from the many hours of material, using the temporal structure of a single day to unite people across the world doing mundane or life-changing things. It is this clarity of purpose brought by impressive editorial control that makes the film truly memorable.

Is YouTube the new home of documentary?

The rapid spread of cheap digital film-making equipment combined with the sharing technologies of the Internet have finally democratised the documentary. No longer is the form reserved for those with the financial or cultural capital required to make films. But can you really think of the clips uploaded to YouTube as documentaries in the traditional sense?

Certainly the service offers plenty of archive documentaries and student documentary films. But the most popular clips on the site are brief snapshots of people's lives, usually amusing in tone and often featuring family pets or children. These videos seem to confirm the utopian idealism of the Internet: that it builds communities and maintains families separated by large distances.

But remember that millions of people spend hours alone watching videos of other people completing videogames. These films are closer to simple instructional videos than any kind of documentary form that previously existed. They also reinforce the great paradox of the Internet: yes it can create or maintain enormous communities, but the types of interaction it encourages can socially isolate individual users even further.

Part III
Travelling a World of Wonders: Global Cinema

Courtesy Moviestore Collection/REX

In this part . . .

- ✔ Assess Hollywood's place in cinema's past, present and future.
- ✔ Sample British films from Brit-grit to frock flicks.
- ✔ Trek across Europe, comparing cinematic creations.
- ✔ Venture around the globe for fresh takes on film.

Chapter 9

Bringing Hollywood into Focus

*W*hat is 'Hollywood'? Clearly, it's not just a district of Los Angeles in Southern California. Hollywood is the American film industry, which for most of the 20th century was the largest and most influential in the world. Wherever Hollywood exported its movies, audiences adopted them as the bigger, brasher brothers of local films.

Hollywood has also come to stand for something even larger: its studios are now part of multinational corporations producing all kinds of films, TV shows, games and associated merchandising. Hollywood is entertainment made for audiences all over the globe.

Running the Dream Factory

The secret of Hollywood's success is simple: it creates lots of movies that lots of people want to see. Of course this goal is much easier said than done. Hollywood is an efficient industrial system and a powerful creative force. Hollywood films have an apparently universal appeal, but they're very carefully designed to be enjoyed by different audience sectors, and many millions of dollars are spent on marketing them, just to make sure. Hollywood's product isn't just the movies – it's the American dream. This section dissects the economic processes that make this dream a rich reality.

Mass producing movies

Most written accounts of how Hollywood works (both in a popular and more academic styles) are about film production, which is perfectly understandable; everyone wants to know what happens behind the closed doors of the mysterious movie studios, including how stars cope with their latest roles, the clashes of creative egos and the on-set triumphs and disasters. But film production is only a small element of what makes Hollywood successful: all the money is located in film distribution and exhibition.

Movies were (and probably still are) the best incentives to sell cinema tickets, and so if you want to sell lots and lots of tickets, you need a constant supply of appealing films to get audiences out of their homes time and time again. Hollywood's masterstroke was to make production as quick and efficient as possible, saving money through economies of scale while maintaining the aura of desirable expensiveness through high production values, big stars and so on.

For the most successful decades of the movie business, 1930 up until about 1950, this recipe was the basis of the *studio system*. In order to produce movies in house as quickly as possible, the studios needed permanent contracted staff at all levels. The Hollywood studio system included:

- ✔ **Directors:** Under the studio system directors rarely had influence on anything other than shooting scenes from a script, but they were required to co-ordinate technicians and coax good performances from actors.

- ✔ **Producers:** Each major studio had a head of production delegating to between five and ten producers, who were required to oversee at least three movies at a time, often specialising in particular genres.

- ✔ **Stars:** Studios often hired new actors on contract as bit-part players and then remodelled them (often physically) into glamorous movie stars. Stars' unpredictable behaviour was a major problem for studio heads.

- ✔ **Technicians:** Art directors led pre-production and cinematographers were vital during shooting, but studios also employed carpenters, electricians and cleaners to keep production moving. (Chapter 2 digs deeper into the original and current roles of technicians.)

- ✔ **Writers:** Studios employed a bank of writers who often contributed specific elements to a range of scripts, including gags, romantic subplots and so on.

The way audiences consumed films in the cinema was extremely different during the heyday of the Hollywood studios. Instead of going to see a single feature film as you do today, audiences attended cinemas regularly and habitually, watching a mixed programme of films that ran continuously. This programme included newsreels, cartoons, serials and trailers as well as the longer feature presentations.

The movies at 5 cents a pop

The future moguls of the Hollywood film industry started not as producers but as exhibitors, running cheap improvised movie houses known as *nickelodeons* (after the 5 cents admission cost). Shopfronts all over the US were converted into nickelodeons between 1905 and 1915, and they were extremely popular and profitable. The screened films lasted around five to ten minutes and were often simple *actualities* (forerunners of newsreels) or *scenics* (shots of landscapes taken from moving vehicles). Adolph Zukor (later chairman of Paramount), the Warner brothers, William Fox and Marcus Loew (creator of MGM) all began their businesses in the nickelodeons.

As a result, the studio system wasn't just a single production line making feature films. It was a series of separate lines, each with its own calibre of staff members. The biggest stars and best technical staff worked on expensive *A-pictures,* which made up only a small proportion of the total output but were able to generate a large percentage of profits. At the other end of the scale were the cheap *programmers,* with no stars, shorter running times and much lower budgets. This group of films receives almost no critical attention, but it made up more than half of the films that Hollywood released in the 1930s.

Controlling the supply chain

For the companies that made up Hollywood's studio system, film production was, in some ways, a necessary evil to ensure a constant supply of product in cinemas, because the major studios weren't primarily production houses. They were distribution firms that also had significant interests in physical cinemas and theatres. The powerful structure of the studio system is known as *vertical integration,* because the studios controlled the supply chain from top (production) to bottom (exhibition), via distribution channels in the middle.

The embryonic entertainment empires grew into a set of companies known as 'the big five' major studios:

- **MGM:** Formed after Loew's, a chain of upmarket movie theatres in New York, purchased Metro, Goldwyn and Mayer Pictures around 1920, bringing in Louis B Mayer to run the new company. Producer Irving Thalberg led the Hollywood production line, investing heavily in stars and literary properties to create quality pictures.

- **Paramount:** Resulted from New York entrepreneur Adolph Zukor setting up Famous Players to acquire films for his thriving nickelodeons (check out the nearby sidebar 'The movies at 5 cents a pop'). He struck a deal to create the first national distribution company with Paramount and proceeded to acquire aggressively other producers, eventually taking over Paramount itself. In the 1920s Paramount acquired more than 1,000 cinemas in the US.

- **RKO:** Formed by the Radio Corporation of America in 1928 to create a market for its proprietary sound system. Buying up a production studio and distribution firm, the company began to produce sound films and built its name on glossy musicals in the 1930s. RKO is the only one of the majors that did not survive beyond the studio era, after Howard Hughes stripped its assets in the 1950s.

- **Twentieth Century Fox:** Began with a merger between small distribution and production businesses in New York. Fox also invested in sound technology but over-expanded the company with expensive real estate. It became a major when it merged with Twentieth Century Pictures in 1935.

- **Warner Bros.:** Originally a family business with interests in exhibition and production, and a late entry into the studio system. The company took a risk with recorded sound technology that paid off handsomely. When it acquired cinema chain First National in 1929, it joined MGM and Paramount as a vertically integrated major.

By 1930, the Hollywood industry was effectively locked down by the five vertically integrated majors. This structure of several large firms controlling a market is known as an *oligopoly*. Of course other firms existed during the studio era, notably the 'little three' Columbia, Universal and United Artists, and independents such as Disney, but these companies had no cinema chains and therefore were unable to match the majors' power and influence.

Dominating international markets

Adolph Zukor led the way for the Hollywood studio system in the 1910s, but his Paramount wasn't the first company to dominate the international film business. That particular honour goes to the French. As early as 1905, Pathé Frères was already churning out a new film every day. Within a few years, its global distribution wing dominated the emerging film markets in Europe and the colonies in Asia, South America and Africa. Even in the highly competitive US market, Pathé had a majority market share by 1906.

Sorry, I don't speak Hollywood

Hollywood conquered world film markets during the 1920s, a time during which no one had to worry about spoken dialogue. Converting pre-sound films for foreign language territories was a relatively simple job of replacing the title insert screens. After *The Jazz Singer* (1927) brought a talking and singing Al Jolson to the world, however, Hollywood clearly had a problem on its hands. It could no longer argue that its films spoke the international language of cinema.

Some studios attempted to solve this problem by shooting multiple-language versions of their films, usually in Spanish, French and German. This approach proved to be unwieldy and expensive. Aware that some countries (notably France and Germany) would try to use arguments about protecting their linguistic heritage to restrict American imports, the MPPDA recommended the development of dubbing technologies. Most international audiences grew to accept dubbed films, but the arguments about protecting European languages from American media continue to this day.

So why isn't the centre of the international film business in Paris? The simple answer is political instability, and specifically two world wars. World War I destroyed the French economy and shut down all cinemas for a period of several years, by which time Pathé had lost its control over world markets. Zukor's Paramount and others obligingly stepped in to fill the gap. By 1920, Paramount had offices not only in the Anglophone markets of Britain, Canada and Australia, but also across the world. New York became the international hub for film distribution, a position it occupies to this day.

Paramount and the other emerging majors consolidated their power within the US and internationally through the establishment of a trade body, the Motion Picture Producers and Distribution Association (MPPDA), in 1922. This body had several vital functions:

- ✔ To neutralise the increasing moral panic over the disreputable nature of the movies with a voluntary production code (you can read more in the following section).

- ✔ To encourage co-operation between the major studios, effectively barring entry to new competitors and restricting international access to the huge and profitable US market.

- ✔ To work with the US State Department to lobby overseas governments who threatened to introduce restrictions on Hollywood imports.

This three-pronged approach was hugely successful. The large size of the domestic American market also meant that studios were able to recoup their costs at home and then sell their films cheaper overseas. Despite external shocks, including the Great Depression and World War II, and the problematic introduction of sound, by the end of the 1940s over two-thirds of Hollywood's revenue came from overseas and Hollywood films made up around half of the global film trade.

Appealing to everyone, offending no one

The biggest and most expensive films made by Hollywood past and present only make money by maintaining a wide audience appeal. As a result, blockbusters typically balance spectacular action against romantic subplots and often blend elements from different genres: comedy, sci-fi and so on.

The emphasis on action over dialogue and movement over stillness also enables many Hollywood films to travel well overseas. In all these ways, Hollywood can argue that its films succeed internationally because they have 'universal appeal' (not to mention the support of an aggressive and powerful trade body).

In the late 1920s, while the MPPDA was deftly spreading Hollywood films around the world, the trade body also had a significant problem at home to deal with. Movies were profitable and enormously popular, but they still weren't respectable. Social and religious groups argued that the movies were degrading moral standards. A series of scandals that rocked Hollywood during the jazz era – most famously the trial of apparently cuddly comedy star Fatty Arbuckle for the rape and murder of a young starlet – only strengthened these complaints.

The more risqué stars and films, such as Josephine Baker's saucy *Parisian Pleasures (La Revue des Revues)* (1927), had been attracting the attention of censors at a state-by-state level throughout the decade. Instead of letting the situation get to the level of national regulation, the MPPDA hired Will Hays to put in place a self-regulatory code of practice. The Motion Picture Production Code of 1930, known informally as the 'Hays Code', established a set of subjects that films simply couldn't depict, alongside topics that films had to treat with extreme caution. It remained in place until the late 1960s. The most important taboos, naturally enough, were sex and criminal behaviour, as Table 9-1 details in the style of the Code itself:

Table 9-1	The Hays Code Regulates Sex and Criminality
Sex	***Crimes against the Law***
The institution of marriage must be upheld over all other forms of sexuality.	Audience sympathy must remain with the law, and crimes must not inspire imitation.
Adultery must not be explicit or made to seem attractive.	Murder must not be presented in detail, and revenge in modern times is outlawed.
Scenes of passion must be essential to the plot and not stimulating or arousing.	Theft, robbery and safe-cracking must not be detailed enough to teach methods.
Seduction, rape or perversion of any kind is forbidden.	Firearms must be restricted to essentials.
Miscegenation (relationships between different races) is forbidden.	Illegal drugs and liquor (which was prohibited between 1920 and 1933) should not be shown.
Scenes of childbirth are not acceptable, even if depicted in silhouette.	Hangings or electrocutions as legal punishments for a crime are acceptable.

Producers had to work with the Hays office from early drafts of their scripts in order to ensure that their films met the Code, which often required difficult negotiations or compromises. Many film historians have noted that the review process created a system of *plausible deniability,* in which adult content was still present but had to be alluded to in coded form.

For example, in *Casablanca* (1942), Humphrey Bogart's Rick and Ingrid Bergman's Ilsa get a second chance at love in the midst of wartime chaos. The moral problem? Ilsa thinks that her freedom fighter husband is dead but soon discovers that he's very much alive. The scene when Ilsa threatens Rick with a gun before falling into his arms is therefore open to charges of portraying adultery, but the producers got round the Hays Code by dissolving from the couple's embrace to an establishing shot and then back to Rick enjoying a cigarette. Was it postcoital? You decide. . . .

Re-viewing Hollywood History

Hollywood plays such an important role in cinema around the world that understanding the story of American film is essential for film studies. What happens in Southern California reverberates around the globe. The story features big money, along with all its associated glamour (and bad behaviour), and colourful characters on and off the screen.

Getting a grasp on how films used to be made and consumed gives you vital context for viewing the great classics, as well as a deeper understanding of how cinema arrived where it is today.

Laying foundations for the Golden Age

Although Hollywood isn't *just* a suburb of Los Angeles, clearly it started out that way. Which begs the question: why here? What about this location led to the grouping and apparently unstoppable growth of some of the world's most powerful companies? A few reasons why film-making went west include:

✔ **To escape regulation:** Thomas Edison held patents for camera equipment and tried for decades to enforce his claim. Films shot around New York without Edison's approval sometimes had their equipment seized.

✔ **To join the boom town:** Between 1890 and 1915 the population of Los Angeles grew six-fold, aided by cheap rail travel and stories of unlimited opportunity.

✔ **To enjoy the light, climate and landscape:** Sunshine and warmth enabled year-round location shooting in California's varied settings – coast, desert and valley.

All these factors combined to shift the film-making balance of power quickly from New York to Los Angeles. The first Hollywood studios were built in 1911, and just four years later the LA Chamber of Commerce claimed that 80 per cent of all American movies were being made in its city. However, that famous visual claim of ownership – the HOLLYWOODLAND sign – wasn't built until 1923.

The growth of cinema-going in the US during the 1920s was remarkable, creating an enormous profit bubble for the new vertically integrated major studios (for an explanation of this term, flip to the earlier section 'Controlling the supply chain'). In 1922, the year that the MPPDA was formed, the average weekly attendance in cinemas was estimated at 40 million. By 1930 that figure had doubled to 80 million, and interestingly the majority of this audience – around 75 per cent – was female. This statistic confirms that cinema-going was now considered a safe pastime for all members of society. It also helps to explain the handsome major stars of this period, including Douglas Fairbanks and Rudolph Valentino.

Just three years later, the situation was rather different. The Great Depression began to hit cinemas and attendances dropped back to 55 million a week. Paramount, Universal and RKO were so badly hit that they went into receivership for several years. The costs of converting cinemas to sound equipment were also a major burden at this point, although eventually the change enabled cinemas to reduce costs. (Sound systems were cheaper to run than orchestras or even single musicians.)

The biggest film of all time

No, it wasn't directed by James Cameron. *Gone with the Wind* (1939) was such an enormous hit that it remains the biggest grossing film ever released when figures are adjusted for inflation. It took nearly $200 million in US cinemas alone, which equals a staggering $1.6 billion in 2014. Perhaps fittingly, it was also (at that time) the most expensive film ever made, costing $4 million, and it had the longest running time of 222 minutes.

If you can't imagine sitting still for almost four hours in a cinema, you're right: the film was generally screened in two parts with an intermission halfway through. That sounds like a night at the theatre, doesn't it? In fact this and other major films of the 1930s and 40s were treated more like major theatrical events than films. *Gone with the Wind* had a *roadshow* release, which meant that the best cinemas played it twice a day with reserved seating. But unlike other roadshows, it played in several cinemas in each city concurrently, getting the best of both worlds.

Audiences recovered during the late 1930s, and a series of mergers and take-overs rescued the studios. And then came 1939, Hollywood's *annus mirabilis* (year of wonders):

- $187 million was spent on producing 388 pictures, providing work for more than 33,000 production staff.

- Average weekly attendance was 85 million and continued at this peak throughout World War II.

- Films released included *Mr Smith Goes to Washington*, *Stagecoach* and *The Wizard of Oz*. But even these films were dwarfed by the unprecedented (and never to be bettered) success of *Gone with the Wind*.

Breaking up the studio system: The United States versus Paramount Pictures

The power of the big five major studios (Paramount, MGM, Warner Bros. Fox and RKO) was due to their status as vertically integrated operations. As I discuss earlier in 'Controlling the supply chain', these entities owned every aspect of cinema from production through distribution to exhibition. But how did this structure work in practice and why was it such an advantage in the marketplace?

Some keys to the major studios' success include:

✔ **They had their own cinemas, which guaranteed a market for the majors' films.** Locked-in exhibition venues reduced the risk of sinking money into production, as well as restricting the space for independent producers to enter the market.

✔ **They developed a *clearance* system, in which they classified each cinema as first-, second- or third-run.** The biggest films were restricted to first-run cinemas for the first few weeks, and then second-run and so on. First-run cinemas charged more and were generally owned by the majors, keeping the lion's share of box-office receipts within the studios.

✔ **They practised *block-booking*, in which as distributors the studies only rented their movies in blocks of five or six (or sometimes as many as 50) at a time.** Block-booking ensured that less attractive, low-budget films were still screened alongside the most desirable expensive features.

On the other hand, although these tactics were highly beneficial for the majors, they were seriously aggravating for the many small independent cinemas that still existed across the US. The independents weren't allowed to book the biggest films in the first few weeks of their release, and they had to put up with renting films they didn't want due to block-booking. Although this portion of the market only brought in around 20 per cent of the studios' income, the local 'Mom and Pop' theatres were important for the industry's image with the general public, and by extension with politicians.

Starting in the 1920s, the local cinemas rallied together to launch *anti-trust* legal challenges to the studios. By 1938 the studios were forced to concede that block-booking was unfair. But their business practices remained largely unchanged, and so complaints persisted. In 1944 the US Justice Department took action against the big five and the little three studios. Years of intense legal wrangling followed until the case reached the US Supreme Court in 1948. The studios lost and had to agree to sell off their cinema chains as a result.

This process of *divorcement* had a profound impact on Hollywood and was effectively the end of the old studio system. With no guaranteed market, film production became riskier. Studios produced fewer films, slashed payrolls of contracted staff and concentrated on distribution and leasing their valuable studio space to independent producers. All these changes, however, served to make the studios better suited to the new environment of falling audiences and competition from television. Ironically the small independent cinemas were the biggest losers, with many closing over the coming decades.

Monopoly, not just a board game

The legal challenges that broke up the studio system grew out of a liberal, free-market model of government, which places value upon economic competition. For an industry to be competitive, it should have no significant barriers to entry, resulting in a large number of sellers who compete against each other with similar products. Imagine a food market where sellers can set up stalls selling vegetables. All other things being equal, you buy the vegetables from the cheapest seller. As a result, quality is high and prices low.

However, if one seller becomes so big that it dominates the market, that's a *monopoly* – or an *oligopoly* when a small group controls the market. In a monopoly or oligopoly, uncompetitive practices can take hold, such as collusion, price-fixing and preventing new competitors from entering the market. If you can buy vegetables only from one stall, you have to accept its higher prices and lower quality controls. And nobody wants expensive, mouldy carrots.

Rolling with the changes: New Hollywood

In the period following divorcement, fewer Hollywood films were released, but production costs grew higher and higher. Cinema-going habits changed rapidly too. Instead of going two or three times a week to see whatever film was showing, audiences now went less often to see the biggest event movies. Colour and widescreen technologies were used for blockbusters to reinforce the spectacle of cinema relative to TV screens at home (3D became briefly popular for similar reasons).

The big hits of this period were biblical epics such as *The Ten Commandments* (1956) and *Ben-Hur* (1959) or musicals such as *West Side Story* (1961), *Mary Poppins* (1964) and especially *The Sound of Music* (1965). All were family-friendly, good old-fashioned Hollywood entertainment. Most were *roadshow* releases, which meant that they were screened exclusively at the best cinemas charging higher ticket prices for pre-booked seats and a grander theatrical experience. Roadshow engagements often lasted for months or even years with the most popular blockbusters.

The roadshows made respectable money, but Hollywood faced a long-term problem: the most significant generational shift of the 20th century. Birth rates had fallen during World War II, but with post-war prosperity and suburban lifestyles in the 1950s came an unprecedented surge in the number of new babies. During the 1930s, around 2.5 million babies were born a year in the US.

Between 1946 and 1964, this number was between 3 and 4 million a year. By 1964, 40 per cent of the US population was 18 or younger, and yet Hollywood was still being run by aging studio bosses making films for the baby-boomer generation's parents.

In 1967, the baby boomers made their presence felt in cinemas. Over the next 10 years or so, the big hits of American cinema were of an altogether different flavour to *The Sound of Music:*

- *Bonnie and Clyde* **(1967):** A crime caper featuring sexy young stars Warren Beatty and Faye Dunaway and a harrowing violent ending.

- *The Graduate* **(1967):** A sex comedy with a young Jewish lead (Dustin Hoffman), a disaffected counter-culture tone and a folk-rock soundtrack.

- *Easy Rider* **(1969):** A low-budget rock-and-roll biker movie with several sequences of drug-fuelled psychedelic hallucinations.

- *The Godfather* **(1972):** A decidedly non-biblical epic, telling the bloody tale of an Italian-American crime syndicate through the generations.

- *The Exorcist* **(1973):** A nightmarish vision of demonic possession featuring a swearing, blaspheming and vomiting 12-year-old girl.

These films and their contemporaries became known as *the New Hollywood.* They smashed taboos around sex, drugs and violence and told largely contemporary stories about multicultural America. They showed clear stylistic influences from European art cinema, including experimental editing practices, narrative ambiguity and downbeat endings. They were made by a new generation of young, cine-literate directors who considered themselves *auteurs* in the European sense: radical, creative risk-takers (see Chapter 14).

From the Hays Code to the ratings system

During the 1950s and 60s a series of racy foreign films imported from Europe, including *La Dolce Vita* (1960), were popular with American audiences, demonstrating a demand for adult material. In 1966, Warner Bros. tested the creaking Hays Code with its film of the stage play *Who's Afraid of Virginia Woolf?*, which was full of profanity and obscenity. It was released uncertified but carried a warning pointing out its unsuitability for under-18s. The film was a hit.

The floodgates were opened for all kinds of content and the Motion Picture Association of America (MPAA, formerly the MPPDA) was forced to introduce a national ratings system to avoid legal challenges. Many of the hits of the New Hollywood era were rated 'R' for restricted or even 'X' – such as *Midnight Cowboy* (1969), the only X-rated film ever to win the Oscar for Best Picture.

For about a decade, many of these creative risks, surprisingly, paid off, not only with the new generation of film critics, but also with the American public. But uncontrolled creativity can also spell danger, as famously demonstrated by Michael Cimino's financially disastrous *Heaven's Gate* (1980), which nearly bankrupted its studio, United Artists. Clearly relying on maverick directors to produce surprise hits was too risky for studios. Seeking financial stability, the studios turned to the biggest hit of the 1970s, *Jaws* (1975) – check out the later section 'Eating Hollywood: Jaws'.

Heading Back to the Future: Blockbusters, Franchises and Indiewood

Hollywood has always thought big. DW Griffith's controversial Civil War epic *The Birth of a Nation* (1915) was the longest and most expensive film of its era, but it also happened to become an enormous hit; the same applies to *Gone with the Wind* (1939) and *Titanic* (1997).

However, the foundation of Hollywood's power during the studio era was in producing a whole range of films, including cheap B-movies and shorts, and packaging them into mixed programmes of entertainment (see 'Running the Dream Factory' earlier in this chapter). When audiences fell and viewing patterns changed, family roadshows and then adult New Hollywood films came and went, but what Hollywood needed most was a new business model.

Eating Hollywood: Jaws

Arriving in summer 1975, *Jaws* certainly was a monster hit. According to film historians Sheldon Hall and Steve Neale, in its first two weeks of release in the US, the movie brought in $21 million in box-office receipts, topped $100 million after two months and after 5 months had taken $150 million. Not only were these record receipts, but also most importantly they were made in record time. For a little bit of context, the biggest hit of the 1960s, *The Sound of Music* (1965) took four years to make as much as *Jaws* took in four months.

But *Jaws* was no surprise hit: it was the result of a careful marketing and release strategy that was in the process of reinventing Hollywood. The key elements of the *Jaws* model are:

- ✔ **Use of a well-known pre-sold property:** The novel *Jaws* by Peter Benchley had been the publishing phenomenon of 1974, spending most of the year on the bestseller lists.

- ✔ **Well-publicised production history:** The making of *Jaws* became news-worthy in itself, building audience awareness and anticipation. Bad publicity? Pah.

- ✔ **Heavy promotion on TV networks:** Universal paid for 30-second spots in 23 primetime shows during the three days up until the film's release, which was the biggest advertising campaign yet seen in Hollywood.

- ✔ **Quick and wide release:** *Jaws* opened on more than 400 screens across America in June 1975 and was showing on almost 1,000 a few months later. By contrast, the big hit of 1973, *The Exorcist*, opened on only 24 screens.

The producers of *Jaws* at Universal didn't invent this strategy. Pre-sold properties had always been popular, and generating publicity during shooting was an old trick. Using TV for publicity had become commonplace as well, although *Jaws* took it to the next level. The release of *Jaws* was wide compared to earlier hits, but by the 1970s other studios were also experimenting with blanket releases, such as United Artists who put out the previous three Bond films on 600 screens.

Jaws is the first modern blockbuster not because it *invented* these strategies, but because it *perfected* them.

Of course *Jaws* benefitted greatly from its talented director, Steven Spielberg. But Spielberg wouldn't have been in charge of *Jaws* had Lew Wasserman not been the head of Universal. Wasserman started out as an agent, and his company MCA profited from the end of the studios' contracts. (He made James Stewart super-rich by negotiating profit share deals rather than upfront salary.) MCA moved into TV production first and then purchased Universal's back catalogue and eventually its entire business.

Under Lew Wasserman, Universal became a *horizontally integrated* major studio. Horizontal integration differs from the vertical integration of the old studio system in important ways as Table 9-2 details.

Table 9-2	From Vertical to Horizontal Integration
Vertical Integration	*Horizontal Integration*
Studios did their own production and owned distribution wings and cinema chains to maximise revenues.	Studios outsource production to independents and are primarily distributors and agents.
Different companies were merged together, but all with the aim of getting movies into cinemas.	Movie studios are part of large entertainment conglomerates with interests across many media sectors.
Stars, directors and production crew were under long-term contracts for efficient in-house production.	Stars and creative talent are essentially freelancers, and movies are packaged by the studios (read the following section for more details).
All profits came from selling cinema tickets, and popular films were re-released over and over again.	Profits come from a range of revenue streams including publishing (book and music), TV and theme parks.
Movies were the product.	Intellectual property is the product; a popular character or story can produce all kinds of media and merchandise.

Deciphering agent-speak: Packaging, high concept and synergy

Lew Wasserman, the man who taught Hollywood how to make money again, began his career as an agent (which is no coincidence). As the studio system broke down, turning everyone into freelancers, the agents found themselves holding the balance of power. As audiences declined and production costs rose, stars assumed new importance as a means of insuring against box-office failure. Agents were the ones who nurtured the talent and had the contacts needed to bring the best people together.

Under the studio system, production was financed internally, and the production heads assembled the basic elements of the feature-film project: the script, the director and the cast. By the 1970s and 80s, powerful agents were increasingly playing this role, and they gave it a new name: *packaging*. The goal of the package was to attract finance for the project, through a major distribution deal or via smaller independent companies. After the package was financed (either by the studio or by a combination of other sources, such as private financiers) and approved, the agents received their commission and went to work on the next big project.

For instant major just add cash

Packaging of films enabled smaller players with access to big finance to compete with the majors for the first time. Several companies achieved so-called instant major status during the 1980s, but most failed within a decade:

✔ Carolco Pictures was formed by entrepreneurs in the 1970s and made its name through big-budget action films such as *Rambo: First Blood, Part II* (1985), *Total Recall* (1990) and especially *Terminator 2: Judgement Day* (1991). Extravagant overspending in the early 1990s brought down the company.

✔ Cannon made a killing selling dubious exploitation movies such as *Death Wish II* (1982) and *Lady Chatterley's Lover* (1981) to overseas markets. The company held considerable assets in the British film industry, which were unceremoniously sold off due to financial mismanagement.

✔ Vestron began by buying home video rights for films just as the format took off and then moved into film production. Not even the huge hit *Dirty Dancing* (1987) prevented it from being sold off just a year later due to cash-flow problems.

The easiest types of films to finance in this way are ones that can be described quickly and grasped easily. Such films are sometimes called *high concept,* because they're all about a strong and simple idea. Steven Spielberg famously aimed to describe his movies in 25 words or less, and so here are a few attempts to do it in 10:

✔ *Beverly Hills Cop* (1984): Street-smart Detroit cop transferred to wealthy white neighbourhood; stays sassy.

✔ *Home Alone* (1990): Noisy child accidentally left home for Christmas repels burglars. Violently.

✔ *Speed* (1994): Bomb on bus will explode if slows. Sandra drives quickly.

✔ *Face/Off* (1997): Cop and crook switch faces. Both annoyed. Lots of shooting.

✔ *Snakes on a Plane* (2006): Surely no explanation required.

Along with being useful for pitching your package, a high-concept idea is also perfect for marketing purposes. The horizontally integrated majors of the 1980s worked to sell a strong idea across several media formats, ideally each cross-promoting the other – bringing about another agent-speak word: *synergy.* For example, *Purple Rain* (1984) was carefully marketed to ensure that its star Prince's singles were in heavy rotation on MTV, selling the soundtrack album and the film. The producers of both? Clever Warner Bros.

If you want to understand how Hollywood worked in the 1980s, you can do a lot worse than watch Robert Altman's satire *The Player* (1992). Here the industry is run by slick but interchangeable entrepreneurs in suits, who pitch ridiculous high-concept ideas to each other, like 'It's *Out of Africa* meets *Pretty Woman*'. The film does have a murder plot, but the real fun is spotting the amazing array of cameo appearances and seeing the film-within-a-film *Habeas Corpus* change from a gritty, worthy legal drama to an action flick where Bruce Willis rescues Julia Roberts from the gas chamber with a shotgun.

Acting like kids: Family franchise fun

For most of its history, Hollywood was in the business of producing wholesome family entertainment. The restrictions placed on adult content under the Hays Code (see the 'Appealing to everyone, offending no one' section earlier in this chapter) ensured that the vast majority of films from the studio era were suitable for children to watch, even if the grown-ups understood that more was going on just off screen.

But then the old moguls of the studio system gave way to a new generation of film-makers, the baby boomers grew up and for a brief time adult films were Hollywood's big hitters. Many of these films were certainly not kids' stuff, most notably *The Exorcist* (1973).

Fast-forward just ten years from *The Exorcist* and you find that the biggest movie of 1983 was *The Return of the Jedi*. The year before that it was *E.T. the Extra-Terrestrial* (1982) and the year after *Ghostbusters* (1984). Clearly, the economics of the industry had shifted once more, away from an unusual run of adult-themed films and back towards family entertainment. But this was family entertainment of a different order to *Gone with the Wind* (1939) or *The Sound of Music* (1965). Instead of parents taking their children along to the movies, now the kids were dragging their parents in and demanding merchandise as well as popcorn.

Hollywood's return to family entertainment in the 1980s has several explanations:

- ✔ As with New Hollywood, demographics played a part. In 1967 almost half of the US adult population was aged 16–24. Fifteen years later, the baby boomers were having kids of their own, the so-called echo boom phenomenon, and these youngsters loved the movies.

- ✔ The rapid growth of multiplex cinemas in the US during the late 1970s and 1980s meant that the viewing experience was now more comfortable and safer for families with young children.

✔ Although the US domestic market was relatively stable, the explosive growth of international markets during this period meant that, by 1994, Hollywood was bringing in more money from overseas than it made at home. And marketing *E.T.* internationally is much easier than *The Exorcist.*

But probably the most significant change during this period was the uptake of home entertainment technologies, particularly home video. After overcoming the format war between VHS and Betamax (see Chapter 16) and concerns over home taping of movies from television, the studios all entered the home video market in the early 1980s. Table 9-3 illustrates the rapid growth of Hollywood video revenues over the following decade.

Table 9-3	Growth of Home Video in Hollywood		
Video Release	*Title*	*Domestic Rentals* *	*Video Revenues*
1983	*Raiders of the Lost Ark*	$116 million	$30 million
1986	*Top Gun*	$79 million	$40 million
1987	*E.T.*	$187 million	$175 million
1989	*Batman*	$250 million	$400 million
1995	*The Lion King*	$173 million	>$500 million

* Domestic rentals is the amount returned to the distributor after cinema release in the US and Canada. The figure is typically around a half to two-thirds of total box-office receipts.

The revenues that home video brought in were essentially pure profit for the studios, because they'd already recovered the cost of producing the film from the theatrical run. Family blockbusters also bring in additional revenue streams, such as merchandising. George Lucas made his billions not just from cinema box office, but from shrewdly retaining the rights to his *Star Wars* characters as toys. Further synergistic opportunities also open up through tie-in promotions with fast-food restaurants or product placement within the films themselves. Spielberg's shot of the *Jurassic Park* (1993) toy stall in his 1993 film is partly a joke, but it certainly helped to sell sweatshirts and lunch boxes.

Film sequels and series have always played a part in Hollywood's production slates, most notably with the James Bond films dating back to *Dr No* in 1962. But the economic importance of the franchise rose markedly throughout the 1980s and beyond. During that decade, three sequels were the top grossing films of their year (both *Star Wars* sequels plus *Beverley Hills Cop II* (1987)) and the top tens of the year are filled with more examples. By 2014, franchise films took up 15 of the top 20 highest grossing films of all time. Critics may complain about the lack of original scripts, but Hollywood is a business and you can't argue with that kind of profit.

Disney does it first

Walt Disney began as a small independent studio making animated shorts in the 1920s. It created hugely popular characters (including that mouse), but everything changed with the first animated feature, *Snow White and the Seven Dwarfs* (1937), which was (for a few years) the biggest grossing film of all time. At this stage Disney needed the major RKO to release its films, limiting its profit share.

After a string of successful animated features for RKO, Disney created its own distribution arm, Buena Vista, in 1953. Instead of taking on the majors directly, the company diversified into television and theme parks. The first Walt Disney World in Florida was an enormous success, making Disney a horizontally integrated company long before Paramount attained this status in the 1970s.

The return to family entertainment and the rise of home video in the 1980s shifted the odds further in Disney's favour. The biggest-selling home videos are family entertainment, because anything that keeps children quiet for a couple of hours is like gold dust for parents. Disney's 2006 merger with Pixar and acquisition of Marvel in 2009 and Lucasfilm in 2012 have probably assured the company's future.

Behaving like grown-ups: Indiewood

Even though family franchise films dominate the blockbuster end of the market, Hollywood continues to produce a variety of films each year. For one thing, blockbusters are incredibly expensive to produce, and so studios have to offset profits against high production costs. And when blockbusters fail, they can be crippling for a studio's balance sheet. So Hollywood studios also produce or distribute a range of lower budget genre films, such as comedies or horror movies, which entail less risk but still have the potential of becoming *crossover hits* (movies which make the leap from niche to mainstream audiences).

The low-budget end of the spectrum has always been the most accessible for independent production companies. Even during the peak of the Hollywood studio system, tiny 'poverty row' producers were churning out cheap B-movies. After World War II, independent producers such as Roger Corman made cheap but popular genre movies and provided a vital early training ground for major directors such as Francis Ford Coppola and Martin Scorsese (see Chapter 14). In the 1980s a few independent companies briefly achieved instant major status before over-spending themselves into oblivion (see the sidebar 'For instant major just add cash').

Independent cinema today isn't just a reference to the size and status of production companies relative to the major conglomerates; it also means a style of film that's unusual or risk-taking. Independent films are supposed to bring new aesthetic forms and styles into the mainstream and to provide opportunities for young up-and-coming film-makers. They seek and often receive positive critical attention and win awards, which makes them particularly attractive to film stars. They may not be hugely profitable, but they generate kudos and raise profiles.

This type of film-making has its origins in the American avant-garde film of the 1950s and 60s and is also often influenced by European art cinema. Some key examples to check out include:

- ✔ *Shadows* **(1959):** John Cassavetes used his acting salary to self-finance and produce his low-budget features, such as this one, which are loose-limbed and largely improvised.

- ✔ *Badlands* **(1973):** Terence Malick's slow-paced and beautifully shot tale focuses on young killers on the run in South Dakota.

- ✔ *Blood Simple* **(1984):** Joel and Ethan Coen's debut is a brutal, noir-ish thriller, which was a winner at one of the first Sundance Film Festivals.

- ✔ *sex, lies, and videotape* **(1989):** Steven Soderbergh's film won the Palme d'Or at the Cannes Film Festival and put Miramax into the big league.

- ✔ *Rushmore* **(1998):** Wes Anderson's debut set the stage for a series of comedic indie hits and re-launched the career of Bill Murray.

Even this short list indicates the importance of film festivals for American independent cinema. Especially vital is the Sundance Film Festival due to its patron Robert Redford's passionate support for indie film-makers. The growth of this festival in the late 1980s and early 1990s provided a space for individual films to coalesce into movements, most notably *New Queer Cinema,* which kick-started the careers of Gus Van Sant, Todd Haynes and producer Christine Vachon. Sundance's subsequent mainstream impact significantly blurs the boundaries between Hollywood and independent cinema.

The 'independent' status of these films in financial terms is also increasingly blurry. Miramax under Harvey Weinstein provides the perfect example. His strategy of combining US indie releases with international imports was extremely successful in the early 1990s. Along with *sex, lies and videotape,* Miramax also had hits with *The Crying Game* (1992), *Clerks* (1994) and *Pulp Fiction* (1994). A notoriously forceful personality, Weinstein also has a fantastic record of securing Oscar wins for his releases such as *Shakespeare in Love* (1998). The fact that the Disney company bought Miramax in 1993 makes the 'independent' status of these films problematic.

The Oscars go indie

Hollywood's Academy Awards have always been a balancing act between art and commerce. During the studio era and into the 1960s, the Best Picture winner was often the biggest hit of the year, such as *Mutiny on the Bounty* (1935), *Gone with the Wind* (1939) or *Ben-Hur* (1959). Even during the New Hollywood phase (roughly 1967 to 1976), the Academy rewarded hits such as *The Godfather* (1972), *The Godfather Part II* (1974) and *Rocky* (1976).

Since 1976, however, the only three films to be both the biggest grossers and Best Picture of their year are *Forrest Gump* (1994), *Titanic* (1997) and *The Lord of the Rings: The Return of the King* (2003). Instead Best Picture has tended to go to Indiewood titles such as *The English Patient* (1996), *No Country for Old Men* (2007) and *Argo* (2012). Contemporary franchises such as the *Dark Knight* trilogy or the *Harry Potter* films win only in technical categories. The Academy seems to have fallen out of love with blockbusters.

As Hollywood and the independent sector became increasingly intertwined, the term *Indiewood* was coined to describe this growth area of the modern movie industry. Its most obvious home is the studio-created subsidiaries of the majors, such as Sony Pictures Classics or Fox Searchlight, or in companies acquired by the majors such as Miramax. Being involved in Indiewood production brings the majors several advantages including building relationships with tomorrow's major directors, providing unusual vehicles for stars and, of course, winning awards.

Chapter 10

Enjoying the British Invasion: From Brit-Grit to Frock Flicks

*W*hen screenwriter Colin Welland accepted his Oscar for *Chariots of Fire* (1981), he declared optimistically that 'The British are coming!' A full-scale invasion of Los Angeles by Brits in shorts has yet to take place, but the story of competition, complicity and collusion between the British and American film industries is as dramatic and satisfying as any Richard Curtis rom-com.

Instead of attempting to compete with Hollywood glitz and glamour, British film-makers have often taken the opposite approach by turning the camera onto the grittier side of life. Although these social realist film-makers originally saw television as the enemy of cinema, they soon came to enjoy its increased production funding.

The British film industry has survived ups and downs and continues to enjoy success in film adaptations of classic literature and vital participation in two of the most successful film franchises of all time – James Bond and Harry Potter. And yet, these successes raise the question: just how 'British' is British cinema these days anyway?

Getting Real: Brit-Grit

If you happen to be in the UK, try finding a friendly person of a mature vintage (perhaps at a bus stop) and ask them what they think of British films. Chances are they say something along the lines of 'Well, they're all a little bit miserable, aren't they dear? Horrible housing estates, criminals, all that shouting. I do like that nice Judi Dench though.'

What is it about British cinema that leads people to think first of dour *kitchen-sink dramas* (about the domestic lives of working class characters)? Do British film-makers set out deliberately to create something distinctively different from Hollywood glitz and glamour or is it simply because these films tend to be cheaper to produce for a perennially cash-strapped industry? Is it even down to the British weather, because drizzle and grey skies make the perfect backdrop for misery – or at least melancholy?

This section ponders these mysteries while examining the history of Free Cinema, the New Wave and more recent award-winning examples of Brit-grit.

Paying for Free Cinema

Britain's distinguished tradition of documentary film-making was forged during the 1920s when the British Empire was at its widest extent. Film-makers such as John Grierson and Herbert Ponting were fired up by the drive to study the world and its peoples and bring a little slice of them back to cinemas at home (for more on these documentary films, turn to chapter 8). For a while in the 1930s these film-makers even worked together for a government body known as the Empire Marketing Board.

But by the 1950s the British Empire was in decline, and the formerly noble desire to study the peoples of the world on film became tainted by the difficult history of the colonised nations. If, as some native peoples believed, a still camera can steal your soul from your body then what can a movie camera wielded by an imperial superpower take away?

In 1951, Clement Atlee's post-war Labour government tried to wipe the slate clean and look to the future with a national celebration: the Festival of Britain. The Festival turned out to be a key turning point for the British Film Institute (BFI), which had been around since the 1930s but made little impact outside of education and film archiving. The BFI commissioned and built a futuristic concrete 'Telecinema' on London's South Bank centre to showcase new cinema technologies such as (gasp) 3D.

After the Festival was over, the BFI repurposed the Telecinema into a National Film Theatre (NFT), bringing about a new era of film culture. Of course a British cinema culture had always existed, but this time it was all grown up and intellectual.

Eager wannabe *cinéastes* (that is, passionate and well-informed film fans) queued up outside the NFT in their turtle-neck sweaters to see the latest Italian neo-realist effort (see Chapter 11 for examples) or hear talks from the Grand Old Men of British cinema, such as Grierson himself. Several of these articulate and educated young people began to think that British film needed a jolly good shake-up and that they were just the fellows to do it.

Lindsay Anderson, Karel Reisz and Tony Richardson were already involved in film criticism and programming films for cinema exhibition, and had started to make short documentary films using newly portable cameras on the streets of London and farther afield. A new public scheme known as The Experimental Film Fund (also under BFI administration) paid for several of these films. Still struggling to get their films seen by the public, Anderson, Reisz and Co. came up with the brilliant idea of screening them together at the NFT under the intriguing banner of 'Free Cinema' (as in free from the commercial bounds of the wider film industry). And thus they engineered an important cinematic movement.

The Free Cinema films were mostly short documentaries shot with black-and-white handheld cameras. They avoided old-fashioned voiceover commentary and were experimental with both image and sound. Here are three good examples (in chronological order):

- *O Dreamland* (1956): Lindsay Anderson tours a fairground in Margate. Although the film features no commentary, impressionistic sound was added in post-production. Watch out for the creepy laughing clown.

- *Momma Don't Allow* (1956): Karel Reisz and Tony Richardson film an evening at a jazz club in London's working class district of Wood Green.

- *Nice Time* (1957): Two young Swiss film-makers Claude Goretta and Alain Tanner create this bright and lively impression of a night out in Piccadilly Circus.

Breaking the New (British) Wave

Free Cinema may have made a big splash among the cosmopolitan film culture vultures of Soho and the South Bank, but reaching the general public of cinema-goers across Britain required a different approach. Just across the

English Channel, radical young French filmmakers organised themselves into a movement known as the *Nouvelle Vague* (New Wave) in the late 1950s (see Chapter 11 for more), and their British peers were only too keen to follow suit.

The subsequent New Wave films built on the spare, documentary aesthetic of Free Cinema to create bigger stories about working-class characters who challenge the social status quo. As narrative films, they took one step away from Free Cinema's engagement with reality, but are still 'realist' in the sense of attempting to recreate everyday life, warts and all. Their working class protagonists were generally men who expressed clear dissatisfaction with their lot.

Yorkshire-born but Oxford-educated Tony Richardson was already an experienced theatre director, and his English Stage Company staged the first production of John Osborne's controversial play *Look Back in Anger* in 1956, creating a storm of publicity and the so-called angry young man movement. Richardson then set up Woodfall Films to produce a film version starring brooding Welshman Richard Burton.

Here are two films featuring wound-up young men:

- *Look Back in Anger* (1959): Jimmy Porter (Burton) has a wife who's from a social class higher than his own, and boy does he make her suffer for it. When he's not letting off steam playing jazz trumpet in the local clubs, his favourite pastime is having a go at the missus. He's abusive and unfaithful, and he never stops talking about how angry he is.

- *Saturday Night and Sunday Morning* (1960): Karel Reisz's film offers a more sympathetic example of the angry young man protagonist. Arthur Seaton, played with real swagger by Albert Finney, is a disaffected factory worker with a boring family life, but his response is to get out and grab what he wants (which is mainly pints of beer and women). Hedonism being infinitely more attractive to audiences than petty marital abuse, the film was a surprise hit and created a vital new star in Finney.

These and other stories of boys taking out their feelings on girls understandably attracted charges of misogyny, both from contemporary critics such as Penelope Gilliat and from film historians looking back at the movement (notably John Hill). But some films of the British New Wave were ground-breaking in their depictions of sexuality and gender. *Room at the Top* (1959), a steamy story of sex and social climbing, was given an X rating by the British Board of Film Classification. This rating placed it in the same category as pornographic films, but the Associated British Cinemas chain nonetheless agreed to show the film, and it turned out to be a huge success. Seen from today's perspective, *Room at the Top* is hardly pornographic, but its script and Simone Signoret's performance acknowledge female sexual pleasure in a manner that was genuinely taboo-breaking.

Tony Richardson's *A Taste of Honey* (1961) is unusual among the New Wave films in having a central character who's neither male nor particularly angry. Salford teenager Jo (Rita Tushingham) finds herself pregnant and homeless and then almost succeeds in setting up an extremely radical family unit featuring a gay male father figure. Jo's friend Geoff's sexuality, although unnamed, is clearly articulated through Murray Melvin's mannerisms and costume, and even though the family unit fails at the film's conclusion, the film doesn't punish him for being gay.

Another memorable female character was found in John Schlesinger's *Billy Liar* (1963). Julie Christie's Liz is so luminously beautiful that she seems straight out of a Hollywood movie, and the film's balancing of Northern grit with wild escapist fantasy also signalled a way forward for the New Wave directors who each eventually moved away from the realist style that they memorably championed.

Finding poetry in common places

As the British New Wave film-makers grew in stature or moved off in different directions, an increased level of visual and narrative experimentation crept back into serious British cinema.

Tony Richardson's Woodfall Films had their biggest international success with *Tom Jones* (1963), a free-wheeling adaptation of the Henry Fielding novel that used tricks borrowed from avant-garde theatre, such as allowing Albert Finney's Tom to address directly the cinema audience. For Lindsay Anderson, European art cinema (see Chapter 11) was the model that inspired his later films, including *If . . .* (1968) and *O Lucky Man!* (1973).

Whereas the political baton of the New Wave films passed from film to television during the 1970s and 1980s (see the nearby sidebar 'Brit-grit on the box'), the 1990s and 2000s saw a revival of interest in specifically cinematic visions of working-class life. This revival was part of a wider upturn in the fortunes of the British film industry enabled by increased production funding from public sources, including tax breaks and the National Lottery.

A good example here is the work of Shane Meadows, whose early short films and features found support from BBC Films, EM Media (a regional funding body) and the Arts Council's Lottery fund, though Meadow didn't really find his audience until *Dead Man's Shoes* (2004) and especially *This is England* (2006). Using recognisable realist techniques including actor improvisation, handheld camera work and location shooting, Meadows adds a particular blend of warm characterisation undercut with savage moments of violence.

Brit-grit on the box

In the 1960s, British television was growing in stature commercially and artistically. The BBC's series of one-off long-format television plays began to look more and more like serious alternatives to cinema, especially as they nurtured new talent such as Tony Garnett and Ken Loach. The Wednesday Play format ran from 1964 to 1970 and championed new writers with overt political agendas. Loach's most provocative work as part of this series was *Cathy Come Home* (1966), which placed the issue of homelessness onto the national agenda.

Such plays were able to draw on distinctively television-specific qualities, such as those connected with news broadcasts. These programmes had a sense of urgency and 'liveness' that was missing from cinema. The 'drama-documentary' format continued to produce controversial TV films such as *Threads* (1984), which visualised a nuclear attack on the Northern city of Sheffield, and Jimmy McGovern's *Hillsborough* (1996), a controversial attempt to revise the officially sanctioned history of the 1980s football stadium disaster.

Of course another British television genre owes a great deal to the working-class focus and kitchen-sink style of the New Wave films – the soaps. When *Coronation Street* was first broadcast in 1960, viewers considered it gritty and realistic; the same can be said for *EastEnders* and *Brookside* that followed in the 1980s. However Lindsay Anderson would no doubt have been horrified to hear that his aesthetic legacy includes *Hollyoaks*.

For more on the relationship between British television and British films, check out the later section 'Meeting of the Screens: Big and Small'.

Grim and unsettling violence, particularly of the domestic kind, plays a key role in other Brit-grit films including Gary Oldman's *Nil by Mouth* (1997) and Paddy Considine's *Tyrannosaur* (2011). Here the characters are very angry men indeed, but they're much older than their New Wave equivalents – and they often turn their rage upon their own families. Nonetheless, these films seem to play well with critics and awards juries, maybe because such gatekeepers see so many films and only remember the truly shocking. Both these films, as well as Tim Roth's equally challenging *The War Zone* (1999), were first directorial efforts from well-established actors. Perhaps actors love creating roles that their peers can really get their teeth (and their fists) into.

In contemporary Brit-grit, the angry young men of the New Wave have given way to displaced or disaffected people of all ages, genders and races, but the issues of poverty and social injustice remain. The recent revival of social realist cinema also differs from the New Wave in that it has enabled several female directors to emerge as major figures, including the following:

✔ **Andrea Arnold:** This director's *Fish Tank* (2009) treads familiar ground in its housing-estate setting, but she's subsequently applied her realist style to period costume drama with an adaptation of *Wuthering Heights* (2011).

✔ **Lynne Ramsay:** This Scottish director's films are infused with a visual sensibility that she developed as a photographer. Her *Ratcatcher* (1999) and *Morvern Callar* (2002) are as surreal and dreamlike as they are gritty. Ramsay's career then stalled due to an aborted attempt to adapt one bestselling novel, *The Lovely Bones,* before being spectacularly reborn with another adaptation, *We Need to Talk About Kevin* (2011).

The next time you watch a Brit-grit film, either from the classic New Wave era or any of the more modern examples, try and think about the ways that the screenwriter, director and actors work together to produce an impression of real life. Pay attention to the dialogue, which is often in British regional dialects and may be improvised by the actors themselves. Try to notice the elements of film style that make up the effect of realism, such as the use of natural lighting or handheld shaky camerawork. A comparison across historical periods will clearly illustrate that what is considered realistic in one era becomes obvious or mannered in another.

Meeting of the Screens: Big and Small

This book is called *Film Studies For Dummies*, right? So you could be forgiven for wondering why I'm suddenly talking about television. Well, Britain is a good example of a small-ish country that was only really able to support a viable film industry of its own for a short period when cinema audiences were at their peak (between around 1930 and 1950). Since then, film financing has relied upon international co-productions, government initiatives and, particularly, money from television. This means that separating the film industry from the television industry in the UK is an extremely difficult and not especially useful exercise.

Along with the financial and creative connections between TV and film in the UK, British television is also an important force because of the particular make up of its national broadcasting service. The British Broadcasting Corporation (the BBC, known colloquially as Auntie, or the Beeb) is the world's oldest and largest broadcaster, and the fact that it's funded by a licence fee rather than by advertising makes it an international model for public service broadcasting. Of course the BBC is no longer the only force in British television, but its influence casts a long shadow.

In this section I explore how television transformed itself from dangerous young upstart to sympathetic funding partner of the film industry, as well as casting a (confused) eye at the often bizarre offspring of the two media: TV spin-off movies.

Assessing British television's influence on film

If you want to know how the British film industry felt about the upstart medium of television in the 1950s, you can look at how the gogglebox features in films of the era.

In Ealing Studios' *Meet Mr Lucifer* (1953), popular comic Stanley Holloway plays a stage actor in a show with no audience. He falls, bumps his head and has a hallucination where the devil tells him that he invented television to make people miserable! The rest of the film vividly illustrates this theory through a series of episodes in which regular folk have their lives ruined after receiving televisions. A housewife becomes so enthralled by the telly that she neglects her chores and family duties! An impressionable young man falls in love with a singing TV presenter and is driven mad with jealousy! *Meet Mr Lucifer* is a strange little film, but its message is unambiguous: TV is the spawn of the devil.

Or consider this small moment from a more famous film: Arthur Seaton (Albert Finney), the hard-drinking, womanising (anti-) hero of *Saturday Night and Sunday Morning* (1960), returns home from a hard day at work to his parents' house, where his dad is avidly watching the telly. Conversation proves impossible, infuriating Arthur to the extent that he has to go out on the lash.

You can read such depictions of TV on film as representing the views of the educated middle classes towards the newer media, a belief that it was a new 'opiate of the masses' and a debased form of mind-numbing entertainment with the potential to seriously damage family life. But you also need to consider them as signs that film-makers and producers were seriously worried that the new medium would destroy their regular audience of habitual cinema-goers.

Cinema-going habits in Britain did indeed change dramatically between 1950 and 1980. Admissions to cinemas rapidly declined from the incredible peaks reached during World War II, when more than 1.6 billion tickets were sold annually, to a desperate low of less than 100 million admissions a year by the mid-1980s. That's a fall in sales of around 95 per cent, enough to bring any industry to the brink of collapse.

But television wasn't entirely to blame for this remarkable change in consumer behaviour. Demographics played a large role, for example, because the 'baby boom' of the late 1940s and 1950s meant that more adults were caring for children and probably unable to get babysitters. Rapid population growth also changed cities, with new suburbs being built to accommodate growing families. This left city centre cinemas farther away from their target audience, resulting in many closures and shabby upkeep of those that survived.

In essence, people had a choice: take a bus trip into town to a run-down, flea-pit cinema, or stay at home in the warm with the telly. Unsurprisingly, many voted with their cosy, slippered feet. (For more on the baby boom's influence upon American cinema, head to Chapter 9.)

Coming to the British film industry's rescue: Channel 4

The early 1980s were desperate times for the British film industry. Cinemas were run-down and mostly empty, the major film production companies such as Rank and ABPC were dropping like flies, and the new Conservative government was merrily dismantling the bodies and policies that had previously offered limited public support.

British film-makers with commercial potential were generally forced to relocate to Hollywood, and so the UK waved cheerio to the talents of Alan Parker and brothers Ridley and Tony Scott. The outspoken Parker also wrote scabrous newspaper articles about the terminal lack of artistic ambition in British film, and particularly the limited scale and viewpoint of kitchen-sink-style dramas that were better suited to television.

Whether you agreed with Parker or not, British cinema had a clear and desperate need for an injection of new ideas and exciting young talent. When it eventually arrived, that boost came from the very source that Parker blamed for the industry's state of decline. More specifically, it came from a new TV channel with a chartered responsibility to innovate and cater to previously under-served minority audiences: Channel 4.

In 1982, Channel 4's first CEO Jeremy Isaacs followed the lead of European broadcasters by offering small amounts of finance for films to appear on TV in the UK and in cinemas abroad, in order to create content for the new channel. A few years later changes in media legislation meant that it became possible to offer theatrical release deals to these 'TV films', and Film Four really took off as a new force in the British film industry.

My Beautiful Laundrette (1985) seemed on paper to be the kind of uncommercial 'politically correct' project that was only suited to minority television, being a love story between a white male skinhead and a Pakistani businessman. However upon its release it became not only a critical success, earning BAFTA and Oscar nominations, but also a surprise box-office hit in the UK and internationally. It launched the theatrical film career of Stephen Frears and gave the (now multiple Oscar-winning) actor Daniel Day Lewis his big break. Most importantly, it represented new hope for the beleaguered British film industry, and it established a finance model that proved remarkably successful over the coming decades.

Practically every successful British film since 1985 has something to do with Channel 4 in one way or another, whether fully financed by the channel, bought for TV rights or made through co-production deals with bodies such as the BFI and British Screen. A few more key examples amply illustrate how Channel 4 saved the British film industry:

- ✔ *The Crying Game* (1992): Irish director Neil Jordan's noir-ish thriller about the IRA became an Oscar-winning crossover hit. Its now infamous gender-bending twist generated enormous publicity.

- ✔ *Four Weddings and a Funeral* (1994): Richard Curtis, Working Title and Hugh Grant all owe their later successes to this classic English rom-com with an American female lead.

- ✔ *Trainspotting* (1996): Danny Boyle's hyper-kinetic visuals and dance music soundtrack made British (well, Scottish) cinema genuinely cool again.

Leaping from TV to cinema screen

Beginning in the 1970s, things began to get really weird in the relationship between television and film:

- ✔ Hammer Film Productions, world-renowned producers of gothic horror films, had their biggest domestic success not with a *Dracula* or *Frankenstein* adaptation but with a big-screen version of the mundane British sitcom *On the Buses* (1971).

- ✔ The most recognisable character to emerge out of 1990s British cinema is probably Rowan Atkinson's grotesque Mr Bean.

- ✔ The most profitable 2011 film by far was Channel 4's comedy spin-off *The Inbetweeners*, which grossed more than £41 million from a budget of just £3.5 million.

Critics may hate them, but audiences just can't seem to get enough of British TV spin-off movies. The 1970s was the golden era of the sitcom spin-off, with *On the Buses* being followed by *Steptoe and Son* (1973), *Are You Being Served?* (1977) and *Porridge* (1979) to name but a few.

So what accounts for often unglamorous TV stars such as Reg Varney and Wilfred Bramble invading the big screen? Principally, these films were commercial safe bets in an era when the film industry was going through serious financial difficulties. Spin-offs are cheap to make, have a built-in audience appeal and offer the (rather dubious) pleasure of watching your favourite small-screen stars in glorious cinematic colour.

Most big-screen versions took advantage of slightly higher production values by shooting on location (still rare in 1970s TV), and the most common narrative conceit was to place a familiar cast of characters in an unfamiliar setting (preferably in Spain).

These films may not stand up to much critical scrutiny, but you can at least defend them as the last gasp of genuinely popular British films made primarily for British audiences, because most other types of British films have to be made with international audiences in mind. The sense of humour of TV spin-offs is also often in the direct lineage of the great British music hall and variety tradition. And they now exist as a kind of memory vault for sitcoms that would otherwise have been long forgotten. *For the Love of Ada,* anyone?

The strategy of production company Working Title in the 1990s was entirely different. British films now had to succeed *internationally* in order to make a profit – witness *Four Weddings and a Funeral* and all the Richard Curtis rom-coms with American lead actresses. By extension, when Working Title realised that Rowan Atkinson's weird little TV character Mr Bean was something of a cult star across the world, they polished him into an international hit by setting *Bean* (1997) in America. And the strategy paid off, with global box-office takings to put Hollywood to shame.

The 'coming to America' trope was also exploited by Sasha Baron Cohen's surprise hit *Borat* (2006), albeit to much less sanitised effect. Cohen's previous attempt to cross over into cinemas with his Ali G character had been a failure, but *Borat*'s confrontational guerrilla-style shooting and exploitation of gullible American bystanders resonated with the then dominant sitcom mode: the documentary-style comedy of embarrassment typified by *The Office* (2001).

But Borat's success was nothing compared to Channel 4's *The Inbetweeners,* which is currently the highest grossing comedy of all time in UK cinemas. With its sympathetically drawn oddball characters and especially the sunny holiday setting, this film brings the British sitcom spin-off back to its 1970s roots.

Adapting Great Works: 'Oh, Mr Darcy!'

Pop quiz: name the two characters who've been portrayed most frequently in film and television around the globe? Need a clue? Think silly hat and weird teeth. No, it's not Zorro and Austin Powers. In 2012, the clever people at Guinness World Records announced that the two characters you're most likely to see on screen are Sherlock Holmes and Dracula. The king of fictional sleuths has appeared 254 times and been played by more than 70 actors including Basil Rathbone, Robert Downey Jr and Christopher Lee. Holmes is just pipped at the post, however, by the blood-sucking Count who's appeared in a staggering 272 films or TV shows.

Meanwhile the most adapted writers are William Shakespeare and Charles Dickens. In my unscientific poll of the Internet Movie Database writers' credits, Shakespeare has a whopping 975 credits and Dickens has an impressive 339. (Check this out yourself at www.imdb.com.) These stats can of course be endlessly debated and quibbled over, but the overall trend is beyond question: when creating literary characters that continue to resonate with readers and audiences across many different types of media, the tiny British Isles punches way above its weight. So why, forsooth, is this the case? I dig deeper in this section.

Reviving the classics, over and over

The British Empire's cultural and educational reach, the development of the novel and other literary forms, and the status of English as a world language all play a significant role in the success of British literary adaptations. But as regards the simpler question of why make yet another screen version of *Romeo and Juliet* or *Oliver Twist,* the answer is . . . because audiences continue to enjoy them.

The pleasures of the familiar costume drama have a great deal in common with those associated with all film or TV genres (see Chapter 5). You return to these stories again and again because they're simple to recognise, they balance repetition with originality and they provide an opportunity to reach beyond the plotline to explore character, performance or other production values such as costume and setting.

But another important factor is at work here that separates these adaptations from popular genres such as action films or romantic comedies. The difference is what French sociologist Pierre Bourdieu describes as *cultural capital.* Put simply, watching these films makes you feel cleverer and more powerful due to the high status of the original literary works. If you studied the texts yourself in school or college, you probably feel even more smug and self-satisfied! From the film-makers' point of view, the cultural capital embodied in these reworkings can often translate into financial capital (box-office pounds and dollars), as well as increased respect and status within their notoriously fickle industry.

So everyone's a winner, right? Well, not quite, because all systems of capital have winners and losers. Think how you felt in school the first time you were presented with a page of Shakespeare's blank verse. Stupid, right? That's because cultural capital has to be earned via education, and that isn't equally distributed across society. Simply put: Shakespeare and Dickens are real turn-offs for some audiences.

But some adaptations effectively translate the original text into another form altogether. Amy Heckerling's 1995 rom-com *Clueless* is a great example of this type of 'invisible' adaptation. The film is loosely based on Jane Austen's *Emma,* but the central characters of spoiled, manipulative rich girl, stupid best friend and initially annoying and superior male love interest are plucked from their context in Regency England and placed in 1990s Beverly Hills. The fact that *Clueless* works so well is partly down to an implied similarity between the two historical eras and locales, with Beverly Hills being just as socially stratified and divided by wealth as Austen's 19th-century Surrey. Of course you have to know that the film is based on Austen's novel to enjoy this kind of reading, which brings me back to Bourdieu.

The majority of those who bought a cinema ticket to see *Clueless* were entirely unaware or uninterested in the fact of its inspiration. But the movie still resonated with audiences. Why? I suggest because of notions of essential character types reaching across human narrative history. But that's way too big a story for this chapter. (See the section on Levi-Strauss and character archetypes in Chapter 13.)

The past today: Heritage films

Academics love to argue about what to call things. They fill entire articles and even books with attempts to define and refine conceptual frameworks, often creating careers in the process of coining a new and persuasive key term. *Heritage films* is a case in point. The film industry and audiences already have plenty of names for this type of cinema – costume dramas, period films, prestige pictures, even the slightly derogatory 'frock flicks' – so why invent another one?

The main reason why the term has become commonplace in scholarly circles is that it connects the films with other related areas of study and debate. For instance, when Merchant Ivory films such as *A Room with a View* (1985) were wowing audiences around the world, historians and sociologists were also discussing a trend among politicians, charities and museum curators towards an increased *commodification* (being turned into profit-making concerns) of British historical artefacts and buildings. Margaret Thatcher's Conservative government even had a Department of National Heritage whose remit included the whole of the arts, not just museums and stately homes.

So the use of the term 'heritage' connects such films to broader debates about the value of British history, how it's preserved and crucially how it should be exploited economically. Of course, you can view commodification in more or less positive terms. Marxist-informed scholars (see Chapter 13) tend to see it as a Very Bad Thing, given that history should be freely available to all, not just those who can stump up the cash for a membership to charities such as English Heritage. Other interpretations are more forgiving. You can argue that monetising history at least makes it available to some people, as opposed to it being completely lost.

When you think through the value of heritage in relation to films, these debates tend to focus upon whether the fictional worlds are authentic in historical terms. For example:

- You can argue that the pretty, ornate aesthetic of a heritage film such as *A Room with a View* stultifies its audiences and trivialises the serious undercurrents of class, gender and race that run beneath the frocks.

- Or you can say that the pleasure audiences take from these films – whether from costume, setting or props – is just as significant as the intellectual debate they stimulate. And what's more, these appreciations are often undervalued by critics because they associate them with female audiences.

Whether you criticise heritage films for superficiality or celebrate their democratic, accessible approach to history and narrative, you can't deny that they're a vital cornerstone of the British film industry. Here are just a few more examples (in chronological order) that demonstrate these films' economic importance:

- *The Private Life of Henry VIII* (1933): Charles Laughton's jolly monarch produced a massive international hit for Alexander Korda. Sadly, Korda failed to reproduce this success.

- *Chariots of Fire* (1981): Hugh Hudson's Oscar-winning sporting drama turned its producers Goldcrest into major Hollywood players. Sadly, Goldcrest failed to maintain this success.

- *Atonement* (2007): This sweeping epic of love set against World War II featured a narrative twist. Sadly, Keira Knightley continues to enjoy considerable success.

So the next time you sit down to watch a heritage film (perhaps on TV with your mum) by all means enjoy the extravagant costumes and detailed period settings. But also be aware that there is always more going on behind the (beautiful) scenes, and that representations of gender roles and class divisions always say far more about the moment the film is made than the time it's set.

Beating Hollywood at Its Own Game

A beggar woman steals a baby! But wait, the family dog is on the case. Rover tracks down the thief and then brings father along to reclaim his child. The day is saved, hurrah! Such is the simple but exciting plot of *Rescued by Rover* (1905), which was a hit for British producer Cecil Hepworth. Today film historians consider the film to be a crucial aesthetic innovator because it uses editing (see Chapter 4) to build a sense of space and a thrilling race against time.

Despite pioneers such as Hepworth, Britain's position as a world leader in cinematic art was severely inconvenienced by World War I. By the time the 1920s were roaring and cinema was becoming a fully fledged industry, the expanding British cinema circuits were already chock-a-block with American movies.

In this section, I celebrate popular British genres and analyse the Britishness of the internationally beloved creations James Bond and Harry Potter. I dedicate this section to Rover!

Producing local films for local people

From today's perspective, in this multimedia, multichannel Internet age, you can easily forget that cinema-going was once the principal source of entertainment and information about the world for the majority of people in Britain.

During cinema's heyday, between 1930 and 1960, going to 'the pictures' was such a popular pastime in Britain that most people attended several times a week, watching a mixed programme of shorts, cartoons, newsreels and feature films. As a result, the relatively small-scale British film industry easily survived and even prospered while making films primarily for its domestic audience. Much of this modest, home-grown cinema has specific elements designed to appeal to British audiences, which don't necessarily translate to international cinema-goers. For this reason, these films are often great for revealing British national tastes and character.

Make 'em laugh, make 'em laugh

The most popular British films of the 1930s and 40s were musical comedies starring British singers, dancers and comedians. This status isn't altogether surprising when you consider the early history of film as an entertainment form.

Cinemas didn't just spring up out of nowhere and start showing feature films. At first short novelty films were shown in other entertainment venues such as fairgrounds and music halls beginning in the late 1890s. So, many of Britain's first film stars began their careers belting out sing-a-longs from the music-hall stage. Just think of George Formby, the ukulele-strumming, toothy Lancashire lad whose goofy looks and high, nasal singing voice were no barrier to him becoming a major film star. Or consider Gracie Fields, whose cheery, down-to-earth manner and natural rapport with her stage audiences translated into films such as *Sing as We Go* (1934) and *Keep Smiling* (1938), which were just the tonic for Depression-era Britain.

George and Gracie excelled at making British audiences laugh, using jokes and local references that undoubtedly baffled international audiences. (No wonder that people often cite comedy as the least exportable of film genres.) Yet more respectable British comedy of the type Ealing Studios produced can often tickle the funny bones of foreigners too. The comedies produced by Michael Balcon at Ealing have clever, literary scripts and a more realistic aesthetic, and are often built around stories of plucky little chaps overcoming corrupt institutions, which chimed particularly well with immediately post-war audiences.

By the late 1950s and 1960s, however, the cheeky, seaside postcard humour of the *Carry On . . .* films was getting Britain chuckling. Filled with staple comedy characters such as naughty nurses and randy patients, the *Carry On . . .* team managed to build a series of 31 films from double-entendre gags and reassuringly familiar performances from its regular stars.

Scare 'em stupid

As genres, musicals and comedies are particularly adaptable to local cultural traditions, but often more difficult to appreciate out of cultural context. By contrast, successful horror films (see Chapter 5) seem to seep easily across national borders and into the international arena.

The films made by tiny British production house Hammer in the 1950s and 60s are excellent examples of horror's transnational appeal; they were hugely profitable at home and overseas. Hammer's versions of the gothic literary classics *Dracula* (1958) and *The Curse of Frankenstein* (1957) are rich in period detail, shot in lurid full colour and played seriously by reputable actors such as Peter Cushing and Christopher Lee.

Next stop: The 'Lost Continent' of British cinema

Not so long ago (as recently as the 1990s), the main focus for scholars of British cinema were documentaries and the realist films of Free Cinema and the New Wave (see the 'Getting Real: Brit-Grit' section earlier in this chapter). This preference was partly because the most vocal and persuasive critics of the New Wave period were often the film-makers themselves (step forward, Lindsay Anderson).

But critics and scholars valued realism over fantasy for other reasons, many of which had to do with building an argument for cinema as a potent social force, not just as frivolous entertainment. Although this argument is important, it resulted in the vast majority of British films being ignored and consigned to what academic Julian Petley called 'the lost continent' of British cinema.

During the last 20 years, film scholars have shifted towards reclaiming the genuinely popular, however silly and apparently superficial, as the most important focus for study and debate. After all, the movies that audiences actually choose to see have a greater impact on society than highfalutin films that don't attract an audience. There must be something important and potent about popular cinema that allows it to connect with so many ticket buyers.

Alongside this broad shift, scholars have taken a second look at several previously disreputable genres, such as horror and the *Carry On . . .* films. Many people once considered the latter risqué comedies at best an embarrassment for British cinema and at worst horrendously reactionary and sexist. But recent alternative readings suggest that these films may also represent liberating spaces where audiences are able to explore or disrupt restrictive gender stereotypes. Ooh err matron, indeed!

The company continually modified its house style to match consumer taste and demand, famously ramping up the sexual content of later films such as *The Vampire Lovers* (1970). And when cinema audiences went into steep decline in the 1970s Hammer moved out of film production and into TV with *Hammer House of Horror* (1980). Hammer's business sense was just as scary as its movies.

Bonding with Bond, James Bond

As is perhaps fitting for a globe-trotting playboy spy, the production of the James Bond films has always been a truly international affair. The rights to Ian Fleming's bestselling novels were bought by a Canadian producer, Harry Saltzman, who teamed up with an American, Albert (Cubby) Broccoli, to make the films for Hollywood studio United Artists. The first one, *Dr No* (1960), cast a Scottish lead, Sean Connery; a Swiss love interest, Ursula

Andress; and another Canadian, Joseph Wiseman, as the titular villain. Exotic locations in Jamaica and the West Indies feature prominently. Nonetheless, many fans describe the long-running series as 'quintessentially English', pointing to Bond as one of the true icons of British cinema.

But if this Britishness is absent from its production, where does it reside exactly?

One suggestion is that Bond's attitude towards the rest of world marks him out as truly British, especially given his birth during the era following World War II, a time properly described as the end of the British Empire. Bond appeals to British audiences, so this logic goes, because he represents a bygone age when the British thought of themselves as the moral backbone of the entire world. But this nostalgia for a colonial past doesn't explain Bond's popularity with international audiences, nor can the colonial considerations truly be considered a potent force today.

Nonetheless Bond's longevity as a cinematic action hero is remarkable and is largely thanks to the producers' brave decision at the end of Connery's career as the sexy spy to cast another actor in the role. Thus the character became bigger than any individual star who plays him. This replaceability means that Bond can be periodically reborn with a different physical presence and a different set of moral imperatives suitable to the age at hand.

So Connery's cocky and violent Bond gave way to the suave charmer Roger Moore whose Bond outings borrowed from sci-fi and horror films. By the time of Pierce Brosnan's Bond in the mid-1990s, the films were ramping up the explosions to compete with other stars of the era, such as Bruce Willis and Arnold Schwarzenegger. Brosnan's descent into campiness was reversed by casting Daniel Craig as a world-weary spy somewhat adrift in the information age. Craig's Bond films are also visually muted with a realist aesthetic found in contemporary films such as the *Bourne* trilogy. The huge success of *Skyfall* (2012) has appropriately reinvigorated the franchise at a time when British cinema is also full of renewed confidence.

Try to watch Bond films from different periods and compare the lead performances as well as the supporting roles and villains. You can learn a great deal from the ways that sex and violence are portrayed over the many decades of the franchise's existence.

Casting a spell: Harry Potter and the magical franchise

The cultural phenomenon of JK Rowling's boy wizard translated with unbelievable ease from page to screen, and the eight films in the resulting franchise have grossed almost $8 billion. A neat trick indeed.

But those box-office billions largely go to Hollywood, because the films were produced entirely with American finance, and the rights to exploit the franchise in other ways are held by the canny Rowling herself or by Warner Brothers. Fans in the UK can tour the production studios at Leavesden, but if you want to experience the Wizarding World of Harry Potter theme park, you need to fly to Florida, and not by broomstick.

The film rights to Rowling's books were sold in a flurry of publicity in 1999, when the press reported that the author had insisted on British actors in the coveted roles. The public is unlikely ever to know whether Rowling's preference was a genuine deal-breaker or simply a useful public relations exercise, but Warner Bros. paid unusual respect to the designated nationality of the films' characters. They also made the decision to base production entirely within the UK, which was actually a far more significant coup for the British film industry as a whole. Producers chose Leavesden Studios, an enormous former aircraft hanger near Watford, as the films' production base, and so began a decade of intensive and overlapping pre-production, shooting, post-production and publicity that employed huge numbers of technical and support staff.

The huge amounts spent on production don't only benefit those directly employed by the film industry. Contractors and suppliers across the country were able to bid for a piece of the Potter pie. Now that this activity has ended, a positive legacy of increased levels of skills and experience within the industry is likely for many years to come.

So how do the Harry Potter films sit in relation to the history of British cinema? Many people see them as a pinnacle of quality ensemble acting, for which British films are often praised. They certainly contain occasional flashes of the rich tradition of popular film-making in Britain, from Ealing Comedy (Harry as the little chap standing brave against the corrupt establishment) to Hammer Horror (the sinister Death Eaters are as wreathed in fog as many a Bray set, where Hammer were based). (I discuss Ealing and Hammer in the earlier 'Producing local films for local people' section.)

The films also have a great deal in common with heritage films (check out the earlier section 'The past today: Heritage films'), including the period feel of the settings and costumes, and the films' version of boarding school often feels straight out of the 1950s. Above all, the Harry Potter films stand for a period of hugely successful collaboration between British creativity and international finance and marketing that seems likely to set the pattern for what becomes of the British film industry as the 21st century progresses. For example, the Oscar and BAFTA-winning *Gravity* (2013) was also shot in the UK with overseas finance.

So next time you plan a Harry Potter movie marathon, try to watch them as examples of British cinema made on an international scale. As above, consider comparing the films to classic British comedies, horror films or period dramas. The films' ten-year production period provides a very human and real example of its young stars aging on screen, but you should also think about the development of the franchise's visual style, from the glossy and brightly-lit *Philosophers Stone* (2001) to the darker, grittier feel of the final episodes.

Chapter 11

Admiring European Films: Culture and Commerce

* *

In This Chapter

▶ Defining European cinema nationally and transnationally

▶ Making major advances in European film language

▶ Contrasting popular and art cinema

* *

Many people in the US and the UK see European cinema as being intellectual, arty and difficult, and it can be all these things (the kinds of films that Europe exports often are). But if you take a closer look at the sort of films that people in Paris, Berlin or Madrid watch (and sometimes make), you see that European cinema also contains silly comedies, exhilarating thrillers and glossy star vehicles. Just like Hollywood in fact – though sometimes with exotic settings and sexier dialogue.

In this chapter I spend time on the best-known intellectual and art-cinema movements, including Italian Neorealism and German Expressionism, but I also look at popular genre films and exploitation cinema. You get to meet some familiar and less familiar film stars, and examine the workings of the industry including national film policy and international film festivals.

Answering a Not-So-Simple Question: What Is European Cinema, Anyway?

The most obvious definition of *European cinema* is films produced by the countries within Europe. Simple, right? Well, not really. To begin with, you have to address the issue of which countries belong within the constantly changing and shifting borders of the European continent. Is Turkey in Europe or Asia? How about Russia? Then you also have to consider the fact that Europe as a political entity comprises other groupings such as the financially integrated Eurozone and the larger European Union. Not to mention the fact that co-production arrangements mean that several nations (often within and outside of Europe) produce many European films.

If simply counting the number of films made within the region doesn't do the situation justice, how can anyone conceive of national or regional cinema instead? As Andrew Higson discusses in an often-cited film studies article from 1989, people use the term *national cinema* to mean three different things:

- ✔ **The film industry of a particular country that produces movies for audiences to consume at home or abroad:** National governments most often use this model to design policies that protect or promote domestic production.

- ✔ **The kind of films that a country produces, the themes these films explore and how they conceive of national identity:** This text-based approach is common within film studies (see Chapters 10 and 12 of this book), but it can also be unfairly selective about which films qualify as being nationally significant.

- ✔ **The ideas of art over commerce and of personal, auteur projects over mass-produced movies:** The problem with this critical focus on art cinema is that it results in too little attention being paid to popular films that European audiences actually watch.

Cool cinema: Nordic film

The recent international success of so-called Nordic noirs such as *The Killing* (*Forbrydelsen*) (2007–12) and *The Girl with the Dragon Tattoo* (*Män som hatar kvinnor*) (2009) has brought fresh attention to film and TV made in the northernmost parts of the European continent. But cinema from the Nordic nations has always been cool.

Denmark produced one of the first genuine auteurs of European cinema in the shape of Carl Theodor Dreyer. With its stylised cinematography and stunning close-ups, Dreyer's *The Passion of Joan of Arc* (*La Passion de Jeanne d'Arc*) (1928) is considered one of the great artistic achievements of early cinema.

Not to be outdone, the Swedish director/writer/producer Ingmar Bergman was a giant of postwar European art cinema. If you've ever wondered where the image of death as a tall, gaunt man in a long black cloak with a penchant for playing chess comes from, blame Bergman's *The Seventh Seal* (*Det sjunde inseglet*) (1957).

In the 1990s, Danish directors blazed a trail for brutal realism with the *Dogme 95* movement. Lars von Trier and Thomas Vinterberg published a 'Vow of Chastity', which outlawed any artificiality in shooting and declared that the director wasn't to be credited. Ironically this approach turned out to be great publicity for von Trier, who continues to enjoy his place as the (aging) enfant terrible of European cinema.

Higson recommends that film studies shift its focus away from film production to include film consumption. In this sense, all films distributed and enjoyed by audiences within a particular country are part of its national cinema culture. For example, one important question facing the national cinemas of the former Eastern-Bloc countries (for instance Poland or what used to be East Germany) is the effect of the sudden rise of Hollywood imports in the 1990s. If you look only at local film production, you don't get the bigger picture on this issue. See the nearby sidebar 'Raising the Iron (Cinema) Curtain' for more.

One of the advantages of a consumption-led approach is that is avoids the need to give films a clear-cut national identity – because in reality, many films are products of several nations working together. Film financing and co-production arrangements are particularly complex across Europe, where pan-European structures bring together nations of different sizes and with different agendas.

For all these reasons many film scholars now discuss European film-making as a *transnational* cinema, where borders between countries have become increasingly insignificant. However, this approach makes structuring an analysis involving many countries rather tricky. So, in the interests of clarity I have used a traditional national categorisation in this chapter, but have tried to emphasise areas of crossover and exchange wherever possible. The countries I focus upon – France, Germany, Italy and Spain – are the largest film producers and the most historically significant cinemas from the European region.

Raising the Iron (Cinema) Curtain

Admittedly, Eastern European cinema has a bit of reputation for serious and dour realism. Critics and film festivals adore Hungary's Béla Tarr, probably the best-known contemporary director from the region, but a 150-minute black-and-white film about a horse featuring only 30 shots (*The Turin Horse* (*A torinói ló*) (2011) is never going to be an easy sell in the multiplexes.

But if you want to be an open-minded film studies student, you need to be suspicious of such sweeping generalisations. Not only do they neglect huge swathes of film history, but they also reflect little more than prejudices and stereotypes of other regions. Delve into the films of this complex and fascinating part of the world, and you also find plenty of black humour, subversive surrealism and even whimsical children's animation.

To forever banish the stereotype of Eastern European film drabness, get hold of a copy of Vera Chytilová's joyous and anarchic *Daisies* (*Sedmikrásky*) (1966). This Czech film is anything but dour, from its madcap, slapstick performances to its lovely colour-filtered visuals. Two teenage girls (both called Marie) decide to 'go bad' by making merry with men, food and booze. The Czech government of the time banned the film, which by the way is awesome (the film, not the government!).

Making a Rendezvous with French Cinema

Although the French probably didn't invent film – Mr Edison has the strongest claim on that front – they almost certainly invented *cinema,* in the sense of projected moving images. They were definitely the first to industrialise film-making fully, because Pathé Frères was the global leader in world film distribution long before the Hollywood majors got into their stride. The French have had a natural affinity with cinema ever since.

In this section I guide you through the key moments of French cinema history, check out how the French have defended their film industry from Hollywood and don my tux for a trip to the Cannes Film Festival.

Travelling from poetic realism to new extremism

Trying to get to know the output of a prolific national cinema like that of France can feel daunting. If you're a film enthusiast, you may have seen a good number of recent French films and maybe even a few of the classics. But putting it all into context can be challenging.

Luckily, the history of European cinema tends to be constructed out of *movements:* moments when everything comes together to produce a distinctive body of films.

The preponderance of movements is partly because production levels in Europe can be sporadic, but also because critics love finding the current hot directors or uncovering hidden gems from the past. Either way, you can't claim to know much about French cinema unless you recognise the most important movements or periods. The following are good places to start:

✔ **Belle époque:** From the beginnings of cinema to World War I, France led the way. The Lumière brothers ran public screenings as early as 1895, and by 1910 Pathé Frères was a global film distributor. Georges Méliès produced spectacular fantasies (see Chapter 5), Alice Guy-Blaché was a pioneering female director (check out Chapter 19) and thrilling crime serials such as *Fantômas* (1913–4) entertained the world.

✔ **Poetic realism:** Critics applied this term to a group of popular and well-received French films of the 1930s, linked by a stylistic darkness and pessimistic narrative tone. Key examples include Jean Vigo's dreamlike *Zero de Conduite* (*Zero for Conduct*) (1933); Jean Renoir's dark comedy of manners *La Règle du Jeu* (*The Rules of the Game*) (1939); and Marcel Carné's *Les Enfants du Paradis* (*Children of Paradise*) (1945), often voted the greatest French film of all time.

✔ *Nouvelle vague:* The original 'New Wave' broke in France in 1959. A group of critics and directors with a passion of cinema rallied against so-called quality films to produce fresh and experimental movies full of youthful vigour. Check out the freewheeling spontaneity of François Truffaut's *Jules et Jim* (*Jules and Jim*) (1962), the choppy jump-cuts of Jean-Luc Godard's *À Bout de Souffle* (*Breathless*) (1960) and the Hitchcockian chills of Claude Chabrol's *Le Beau Serge* (literally, *Handsome Serge*) (1958).

✔ *Cinéma du look:* A glossy, stylised and genre-driven set of films from the 1980s to the 2000s. They foreground visual spectacle and advertising influences the colour, lighting and composition as much as film. Jean-Jacques Beineix's *Betty Blue* (*37°2 le matin*) (1986) was responsible for millions of posters on students' walls, Leos Carax's *Les Amants du Pont Neuf* (1991) launched the career of Juliette Binoche and Luc Besson's *Nikita* (1990) gave audiences a stylish and deadly hit-woman.

✔ **New extremism:** A brutally violent and sexually explicit set of films made around the start of the 21st century by a group of male and female directors in France (and elsewhere). Beware, these films aren't for the faint-hearted. If you think you can take it, try Gasper Noé's *Irréversible* (2002), a non-linear rape revenge narrative, or Catherine Breillat's *Romance* (*Romance X*) (1999), which shows porn actor Rocco Siffredi doing what he's normally paid to do.

Making an exception for French cinema

The French have always had a love/hate relationship with Hollywood. The critics of the influential French film journal *Cahiers du Cinéma* were basically responsible for the idea that critics and scholars should take Hollywood cinema seriously. They made auteurs out of Charlie Chaplin, Howard Hawks and John Ford (see Chapter 14) while dismissing their own directors. Bizarrely, serious French cinéastes also love daft American comedians such as Jerry Lewis and Jim Carrey. But does this mean that Hollywood is welcome to dominate French cinema screens? *Mais non!*

The French are adamant in defending their precious cinema culture from too many outside influences. Since the 1990s, they've expressed this protection in terms of *l'exception culturelle* (the cultural exception), which French film-makers use to justify film policies during trade negotiations. Whenever the Americans cry foul against restrictive quotas or unfair advantages for subsidised film, the French call upon their exception, often backing it up with the imperative to protect the French language itself.

Why does the French government feel the need to protect its cinema – and what measures does it use?

- ✔ In 1928, the French film industry had all but disappeared, decimated by World War I and American and German imports. As a result the government introduced an import/export ratio to benefit French producers. It tightened up this measure over the coming decades, specifying a maximum number of foreign imports per year.

- ✔ After the complete isolation from American movies imposed by World War II, an exhibition quota was put in place, forcing cinemas to show French films for 4 weeks out of every 13.

- ✔ The *Centre National de la Cinématographie* (CNC) was also established following World War II. This film body is responsible for stimulating film production and promoting film heritage and education. The CNC financially supports all French films produced via a levy on box-office receipts, as well as offering larger loans to selected high-quality or otherwise valuable projects.

In theory, these film policies and others assure the health of the domestic film industry by reducing competition from imported titles, providing a guaranteed place on local cinema screens and assisting with the difficult early stages of film finance. In practice, however, they rarely seem to work exactly as planned. For example, the French quota system struggled from its inception in the late 1920s due to the rapid expansion of cinema screens during the following decade. Good quality French films simply didn't exist in sufficient quantities to fill the required proportion of an expanding number of screens.

Even if its film policies don't always have the planned effect, the French film industry today is in relatively good health. The French produce more films per year than any other European country and have higher cinema attendances than at any point since 1946. A recent run of highly successful French films including *The Intouchables* (*Intouchables*) (2011) has put the French share of box-office receipts up to almost 50 per cent. This figure is way above the share of the domestic market captured by other European nations, including Italy (around 30 per cent) and Spain (only around 12 per cent). So the French are doing something right.

Untranslatable French Cinema?

Bienvenue chez les Ch'tis (2008) is a raucous fish-out-of-water farce from established French comedy star Dany Boon. It broke all box-office records in France and is the most successful French film of all time. It played well in some European countries but was barely released in the UK and didn't reach cinema screens in the United States.

Its title translates as *Welcome to the Sticks*, but this misses its regional point of reference. Similarly, the film as a whole is a fascinating example of the untranslatable nature of popular comedy films. It derives much of its humour

from the regional stereotype of people from the Pas de Calais region of Northern France (colloquially, *les Ch'tis*), which is basically impossible to understand outside of the country – unless you live in Belgium.

Most interestingly of all, *Bienvenue*...received an Italian remake *Benvenuti al Sud* (*Welcome to the South*) (2010) and an American version starring Will Smith is rumoured. Although specific regional stereotypes aren't funny abroad, clearly many countries have their own to chuckle at.

Appreciating a glamorous business: The Cannes Film Festival

Each May, a strange cinematic pilgrimage occurs. Practically the entire film industry dusts off its tuxedos and gowns and jets off to the south of France for two weeks of back-to-back film screenings and glamorous photo opportunities. Cannes media coverage is pure glamour, as the biggest stars and directors dazzle fans on the famous Croisette runway, and films compete for the main prize: the Palme d'Or. But behind the scenes, the Cannes Film Festival is about cold hard cash: deals are done, contacts are made and rooms are 'worked' to within an inch of their lives.

Behind all this frivolity, you can forget that the major European film festivals grew out of the international tensions of World War II. The Venice Film Festival came before Cannes, launching in 1932 as fascism was rising across Europe. Not surprisingly, German and Italian films tended to win the awards, but when Jean Renoir's *La Grande Illusion* (*Grand Illusion*) (1937) lost out to films made by Nazi Minister Goebbels and Mussolini's son, the French were understandably outraged.

Their response, the inaugural Cannes Festival of 1939, was unfortunately timed, running for only one day before the outbreak of war shut it down. After the war, the Cannes Festival played an important role in rebuilding the infrastructure of the French film industry. It was also vital in building the reputations and launching the films of the French New Wave and the other movements of European art cinema (see the earlier 'Travelling from poetic realism to new extremism' section).

Here are just a few of Cannes's defining moments over the years:

- **1953:** Nubile French star Brigitte Bardot poses for photographs on the beach at Cannes, cementing the Festival's star-making status.

- **1959:** François Truffaut's film debut *Les Quatre Cents Coups* (*The 400 Blows*) (1959) wins Best Director, launching the French New Wave.

- **1968:** Directors Louis Malle and Jean-Luc Godard bring the Festival to a halt when they protest in support of the student uprisings in Paris.

- **1993:** Jane Campion is the first female director to win the Palme d'Or for *The Piano*. In 2014 she returned to head the festival jury.

- **2004:** Michael Moore wins the top prize for *Farenheit 9/11,* the first documentary to win for almost 50 years. The French never miss an opportunity to antagonise US politicians.

In today's film industry, festivals play several important roles. They're fantastic publicity for films and film-makers: many reputations and careers have been built out of the exposure and prestige the festivals can generate. The major festivals (Cannes, Berlin, Sundance) are like huge conferences for industry folk and have marketplaces where people finance and sell films into distribution. Smaller festivals can help regenerate local arts activity or tourism, or even act as a forum, drawing attention to political issues (for example, look up the lively gay, lesbian and queer cinema festival circuit). Finally, as the number of festivals continues to grow, you can consider the festival circuit as an alternative means of distributing films and reaching audiences.

Stepping Out of the Darkness: German Cinema

For a brief period between the two world wars, German cinema came close to rivalling Hollywood as an industrial-scale dream machine – and far surpassing it in terms of artistic ambition. The films of *German Expressionism* employed stylised set design, shadowy lighting and broken narratives, and were widely admired and imitated across the world.

Germany lost most of its film-making talent during the tragic years of Nazi rule, but by the 1970s it found a new voice. Since reunification of East and West Germany in 1990, many German film-makers have faced and explored the darkness of their recent history on the cinema screen.

Lurking in the shadows: German Expressionism

Many of the most vivid and unforgettable images of early cinema come from German Expressionist films. The horrible shadow of Count Orlok the vampire creeping up the stairs to feed (*Nosferatu: A Symphony of Horror* (*Nosferatu: eine Symphonie des Grauens*) (1922)), the angular, disjointed world of Dr Caligari (*The Cabinet of Dr. Caligari* (*Das Cabinet des Dr. Caligari*) (1920)) and the beautiful but deadly female cyborg from *Metropolis* (1927) were all brought to life during this amazingly fertile period. The influence of this moment upon the development of cinema as an art form is immense, especially because many of its film-makers and technicians were forced to leave Germany soon afterwards to work across Europe and in Hollywood.

Expressionist is one of those terms that more pretentious film critics and bloggers love to throw around without always understanding its meanings. Don't fall into this trap. Here's a solid film studies definition:

- Expressionism was a broader artistic movement that flourished in Germany in the early 20th century, including painters, writers and even architects. One way to think of it is as the opposite of *Impressionism,* which is concerned with surface reality, whereas *Expressionism* sees the world through the filter of human perception and emotion.

- Expressionism in film creates stylised worlds using clearly artificial, often geometric set design, elaborate costuming and unnatural makeup. The cinematography emphasises bold contrasts of dark shadows and bright highlights. The acting style is heightened and (to modern tastes) rather theatrical.

- Expressionist film protagonists experience extreme psychological states, which are reflected in their strange environments. Key themes are madness, criminality and the fracturing of identity.

Film scholars have argued that a conflict between traditional notions of German identity and modernity characterise Expressionist cinema, embodied by machines and technology. Nowhere is this conflict more evident than in Fritz Lang's proto-sci-fi *Metropolis* (1927). Its convoluted story boils down to two elements. The first is a traditional love story: boy meets girl, girl gives her face to an evil cyborg, boy watches evil cyborg getting burnt at the stake. The second has something to do with man versus machine in a huge futuristic factory. It's seriously confusing.

Do watch *Metropolis:* it has so much going on that you're unlikely to notice that the story doesn't make sense. The enormous sets of beautiful art deco machines are crammed with thousands of marching extras (see Figure 11-1). The gleaming cityscapes are clear influences on the visual design of later sci-fi films, particularly *Blade Runner* (1982), and the transformation sequence that creates the woman/robot was endlessly copied in Hollywood horror movies such as *Frankenstein* (1931). *Metropolis* throws so many ideas at the screen at such a bewildering rate that you can forgive a bit of incoherence.

Figure 11-1:
Fritz Lang's
Metropolis
(1927)
explores the
beauty and
the horror of
machines.

Courtesy Everett Collection/REX

Recreating (New) German Cinema

World War II caused the majority of German film-makers to emigrate, split the country into two halves and destroyed international demand for German films. East German film-makers inherited the country's formerly glorious UFA studios (which produced Lang's *Metropolis* in 1927), but the Soviet-aligned Stasi secret police assumed control of all production. In West Germany, genre cinema recovered to some extent, with the nostalgic and rural *Heimatfilm* (literally 'homeland-film') remaining popular, but underlying economic problems and rapidly falling cinema attendances brought the industry to the brink of collapse by the 1960s.

If ever a national cinema needed a radical break with the past, it was postwar Germany's – not least because the question of German national identity remained a toxic and largely taboo issue. So, in 1962, with New Waves breaking all over Europe, German film-makers got together to produce a bold statement of intent for a new national cinema. The Oberhausen Manifesto called for a new method of film production, one free from the conventional film industry and the outside interests of commerce.

As with many political manifestos, the detail of how film-makers would achieve their goals was somewhat lacking. But its signatories succeeded in lobbying the West German government to set up a funding stream driven by artistic impulse rather than commercial demand. Thus *New German Cinema* was born. Here are its main leaders:

- **Wim Wenders:** His accessible fiction films rework American genres such as the road movie or the crime thriller. His 1987 fantasy *Wings of Desire* (*Der Himmel über Berlin*) was a crossover hit internationally, and he's also made successful documentaries.

- **Rainer Werner Fassbinder:** The most abrasive and individual of the New German Cinema directors. Fassbinder was openly gay and worked prolifically to produce avant-garde reinterpretations of the Hollywood melodrama. For example *Fear Eats the Soul* (*Angst essen Seele auf*) (1974) is effectively a remake of Douglas Sirk's *All That Heaven Allows* (1955). He died in 1982 from a drug overdose.

- **Werner Herzog:** His films of the New German Cinema period are grandiose epics starring his volatile best friend and occasional enemy Klaus Kinski, including a remake of Expressionist classic *Nosferatu: The Vampyre* (1979). He remains an important voice in world cinema, working between fiction and documentary films (see the section 'Weighing Documentary Ethics' in chapter 8), and has probably the best accent in cinema.

Cinema after the wall

In the 1990s, as the former East Germany grew used to Western consumerism post-reunification, a new generation of German film-makers were more commercial in their outlook than the directors of the 1970s and 1980s. A so-called cinema of affluence emerged with directors making successful middle-class comedies and thrillers for the domestic market, such as *Stadtgespräch* (*Talk of the Town*) (1995).

Good Bye Lenin! (2003) was an international hit comedy about the impact of reunification on a family living in former East Berlin. Its main plot device requires its hero Alex (Daniel Brühl) to recreate carefully the outmoded fashions, food and even TV shows of East Germany for his mother who was in a coma as the wall fell. Thus the film indulges in what has become known as *Ostalgie*, nostalgia for the East German way of life.

By contrast, another crossover hit, *The Lives of Others* (*Das Leben der Anderen*) (2006), is a thriller about life under Stasi surveillance. *Ostalgie* is absent in this taut and terrifying tale of political allegiance and betrayal.

Melding Style and Substance: Italian Cinema

If Italian cinema was to be remembered only for the handful of revolutionary Neorealist films made after the devastation of World War II, it would still be one of the most influential in the history of world cinema. But Italy has much more to offer, including a rich tradition of popular genre film-making, *autori* (Italian for auteurs) such as Federico Fellini, eccentric exploitation movies and comedy stars such as Toto, who's a comedy saint in his home nation but virtually unknown overseas.

Finding heroes on the street: Neorealism

Neorealism means 'new realism', and the term was first applied to film-makers working in the devastation of post-World War II Italy. All realist movements claim to be more realistic than what came before, and so what were the Neorealists reacting against?

Before Neorealism, Italian cinema was known for historical spectacles such as *Cabiria* (1914), and, after 1922, Benito Mussolini's Fascist government engineered a safe and uncontroversial genre cinema. The period of post-war reconstruction saw Italian film-makers and audiences keen to overthrow the past and re-embrace the world.

As its name suggests, Neorealism was a new form of realism, but it shares some of the stylistic characteristics and concerns of earlier films, particularly the poetic realism of French cinema during the 1930s (see 'Travelling from poetic realism to new extremism' earlier in this chapter). Unlike the bleak pessimism of earlier realist forms, however, the Italian writers and theorists who contributed to Neorealism were driven by a more optimistic humanism, which emphasises emotional connections between people as a force of narrative and historical change. Marxist ideals, such as giving voice to the repressed proletariat (see Chapter 13), and Catholic notions of guilt and redemption also have a place.

The key films of Italian Neorealism include the following:

- ✔ ***Ossessione (Obsession) (1943):*** An uncredited adaptation of the hard-boiled novel *The Postman Always Rings Twice*. Director Luchino Visconti shot this steamy tale of adultery and murder entirely on location in Italy's Po Valley, giving it a similar gritty look to later Neorealist films. The Fascist regime hated it so much that they destroyed the original negative, but Visconti saved one print and his film for later generations.

- *Roma, città aperta (Rome Open City)* **(1945):** Roberto Rossellini's tale of heroism among the Italian resistance movement was an enormous popular hit at home and won international prizes including the Palme d'Or at Cannes. The film's an exciting thriller with established stars, including comedian Aldo Fabrizi, and features the debut of fiery Anna Magnani who became one of Italy's best-loved actresses. Its championing of the common man (and woman) makes it a Neorealist classic.

- *Ladri di biciclette (Bicycle Thieves)* **(1948):** A moving fable of poverty on the streets of Rome and probably the most famous Neorealist film. Director Vittorio de Sica used non-professional actors for a naturalistic feel, although Neorealist theorist Cesare Zavattini's screenplay is tight and controlled (the nearby sidebar 'Neorealism according to Zavattini' contains more on Zavattini's theories).

- *La Strada (The Road)* **(1954):** Federico Fellini developed his film-making craft with Rossellini, and his first international success displays elements of Neorealist style, including location shooting and a narrative interest in the margins of society. But *La Strada* also has a fantastical quality that foreshadows Fellini's later magical-realist films. A wonderful, childlike performance from Fellini's wife Giulietta Masina, whose face is as expressive as any great silent comedian, drives the film.

The importance of Neorealism for international cinema was profound. Many of the films associated with the movement benefitted from critical attention gained through the European film festival circuit, which developed around the wartime period. Popular films such as de Sica's *Ladri di biciclette* received very wide international exposure and influenced later New Waves across the world, including Britain, Brazil and India (check out Chapter 12).

Neorealism according to Zavattini

Cesare Zavattini was an important screenwriter of the Neorealist movement and also its foremost theorist. His article 'Some Ideas on the Cinema' was published in 1953 and is essential reading if you want to understand the movement fully. It's available for free online, and so you have no excuse. Here's one of Zavattini's notable claims:

- *No doubt one's first and most superficial reaction to everyday reality is that it is tedious. . . . One shouldn't be astonished that the cinema has always felt the* natural, unavoidable necessity to insert a 'story' in the reality to make it exciting and 'spectacular'. . . .

- *Now it has been perceived that reality is hugely rich, that to be able to look at it directly is enough; and that the artist's task is not to make people moved and indulgent at metaphorical situations, but to make them reflect (and, if you like, to be moved and indignant too) on what they and others are doing, on the real things, exactly as they are.*

A good recent point of comparison is with Iranian cinema since 1997, with directors including Abbas Kiarostami (see Chapter 19) producing films that bear comparison with the best of Neorealism in terms of style and ethos.

Featuring swords, sandals and naughty nuns: Italian genre and exploitation films

The Neorealist directors won international renown, but they didn't always set the box office on fire at home in Italy. The movement did, however, provide a confidence and global profile for Italian cinema, which grew during the decades after World War II.

Although the deposed Fascist regime had restricted the freedom of cinema, it had at least provided a strong infrastructure for film-makers, particularly the studio set up at Cinecittà just outside Rome. Although damaged during the war and used for a time as a camp for displaced persons, by the 1950s it had been rebuilt and become a favourite shooting location for Hollywood epics such as *Ben-Hur* (1959).

But not only international productions filled Cinecittà's sound stages. Italian cinema also had a strong tradition of genre film-making that was enormously popular at home and (in some cases) abroad. Here are the most significant genres:

- **Peplum films:** Named after the distinctive toga costumes their stars wore, these 'sword and sandals' movies were lively and light-hearted adaptations of classical mythology boasting scantily clad muscle men and buxom beauties fighting mythical creatures of all shapes and sizes. They were relatively cheap to make and sold well overseas: for example: *Le Fatiche di Ercole (Hercules)* (1958) starring American body-builder (and former Mr Universe) Steve Reeves.

- *Commedia all'italiana*: Literally 'comedy Italian style' – with a dark satirical bite. International hits include *Divorzio all'Italiana (Divorce, Italian Style)* (1961) starring Marcello Mastroianni as a Sicilian nobleman who forces his wife into adultery so that he can murder her; *Una Giornata Particolare (A Special Day)* (1977) again featuring Mastroianni playing against type as a gay man; and *Travolti da un insolito destino nell'azzurro mare d'agosto* (which becomes a much more concise *Swept Away* in English) (1974), remade in 2002 by Madonna to absolutely no acclaim whatsoever.

- **Spaghetti westerns:** Between 1963 and 1973 more than 400 westerns were made in Italy, driven by the international success of Sergio Leone's trilogy of films starring Clint Eastwood. Leone took elements of the classic Hollywood western and added gratuitous violence, stylised close-ups and Ennio Morricone's atmospheric music.

> ✓ *Giallo* **films:** Named after the yellow cover of pulp-fiction books published in Italy, these schlocky thrillers or gory, visually ornate horror films pre-date the American slasher movie. See the films of Mario Bava or Dario Argento.

Within commercial film industries worldwide, the boundary can blur between fairly respectable genre film-making and the rather less reputable *exploitation cinema:* low-budget films with an emphasis on spectacle, sex or violence. For example, 1970s Italian cinema featured a distinctive cycle of films referred to as 'convent-sexy' in their home market and 'nunsploitation' movies by cult-film fans. You can guess what happens in these films from their (English) titles: *Sinful Nuns of St Valentine* (1974), *Behind Convent Walls* (1977) or – best of all – *Killer Nun* (1978). It may be tough to take such trashy films seriously, but they can be read as a kind of safety valve for a deeply Catholic culture that routinely represses female sexuality.

Meeting the prince of laughter: Totò

Think 'Italian movie stars' and you probably see a mental image of sultry Sophia Loren or suave Marcello Mastroianni. You probably don't picture a skinny, aging comedian with sad eyes and an unnerving puppet-like quality. Well, you may after reading this section.

Totò was an unlikely looking movie star, but for a period between the 1940s and 1960s he was the biggest draw in the Italian film industry. Italians continue to remember Totò fondly, and his films play regularly on Italian TV. Yet practically nobody outside of Italy has heard of him.

Totò is the stage name of Antonio De Curtis, who was born into poverty in Naples. His tough start in life and his strong connection to the Neapolitan region are important elements of his star image or persona (see Chapter 3). On screen, the Totò character is usually poor, hungry and scheming, but fundamentally honest. The trademarks of his performance style are physical dexterity, a talent for mimicry and impersonation, and an odd, disjointed walk that brings to mind a puppet or marionette.

Totò made more than 100 movies during his long career. Among the best known are the following:

> ✓ *Totò a colori* (*Totò in Colour*) (1952): The first Italian film made in colour was such a big hit that it still features among the top-grossing films of all time in the Italian market when adjusted for inflation.

> ✓ *L'Oro di Napoli* (*The Gold of Naples*) (1954): Made up of six stories set in Naples, the hometown of Totò and the film's director Vittorio de Sica. As a sign of de Sica's international profile, the film was entered into competition at the Cannes Film Festival.

Italian cinema reborn

As in most other European countries, the Italian film industry went through a depression and crisis in the 1970s when production levels and audiences dropped off. But since the 1980s and 1990s Italian film-makers have reclaimed their position as producers of some of the most respected and popular European films in the international market.

The world-wide success of so-called nostalgia film *Nuovo Cinema Paradiso* (*Cinema Pardiso*) (1988) led the rebirth of Italian popular cinema, which was consolidated by black comedy *La vita è bella* (*Life is Beautiful*) (1997), whose writer-director-actor star Roberto Benigni won legions of fans after his over-excited Oscar acceptance speech.

Italian cinema still produces recognisable art cinema autori (auteurs) such as Nanni Moretti (*La stanza del figlio* (*The Son's Room*) (2001)) and Paolo Sorrentino (*La grande bellezza* (*The Great Beauty*) (2013)). But the new generation of film-making talent is more diverse than in previous decades, as illustrated by Turkish-Italian director Ferzan Ozpetek's comedies of (gay) manners including *Mine vaganti* (*Loose Cannons*) (2010) and several emerging female directors, such as Asia Argento, daughter of horror-movie maestro Dario Argento.

✔ *Uccellacci e uccellini* (*Hawks and Sparrows*) (1966): Directed by radical poet and film-maker Pier Paolo Pasolini, this film illustrates Totò's ability to unite low and high culture. It's also a showcase for his physical skills, as Totò hops around like the titular sparrow with remarkable agility for a comedian of his advanced years.

Given Totò's special status in Italian popular culture and his apparent lack of appeal outside his home nation, he arguably fulfilled a valuable social function for Italian audiences. In a country where Catholicism still exerted control over cinema through censorship, he was favoured by the Vatican as the embodiment of a traditional type of Italian-ness for most of his career. For audiences living through post-war reconstruction, Totò must have been a reassuring figure, an emblem of tradition in the face of rapid social change.

Watching Freedom Explode: Spanish Cinema

Spanish cinema-goers represent one of the largest national groupings within Europe, and Spanish-speaking people worldwide add further potential audiences for Spanish films. But the country's film industry remains somewhat of a poor relation to those of France, Germany and Italy, and the box-office takings captured by local films in Spain are only around 12 per cent, which is among the lowest in Europe.

Losing Luis Buñuel

If you want to understand how difficult the situation was for Spanish film-makers, you only need to look at the career of their most talented and radical director, Luis Buñuel. Buñuel was born in Northern Spain and raised as a devout Catholic before studying in Madrid, where he met the artist Salvador Dalí. Both men moved to Paris to find the inspiration and the finance to make their incendiary surrealist films, including *Un Chien Andalou* in 1929 (see Chapter 7).

After the Civil War cut short a brief return to Spain in the 1930s, Buñuel relocated to the US and then to Mexico where he worked prolifically in the commercial film industry until the 1960s. An enormous scandal greeted his 1960 film *Viridiana,* which the Catholic Church considered blasphemous and the Franco government banned, bringing down its production company. Buñuel then produced his best-known art films including *Belle de Jour* (1967) for the French film industry.

For much of its history, Spanish film was doubly marginalised, left out of the Hollywood mainstream and the exclusive European art-cinema club. This section considers why this is the case.

Considering Fascism and Catholicism

The Spanish film industry struggled while its French and Italian counterparts thrived for several key reasons:

- ✔ During cinema's early years, Spain was economically unable to sustain large-scale film production and instead relied on imports from its neighbouring countries. Historians estimate that only six fiction films were made in Spain from 1896 and 1905, compared to hundreds from its European neighbours.

- ✔ By the 1930s Spain had developed a genre cinema, focused upon the distinctively Spanish folk tales or *españoladas,* full of bull-fighting and flamenco dancing. But the brutally violent Civil War of 1936–9 and then the immediate onset of World War II destroyed the Spanish economy, and the country took much longer to recover than other regions of Europe.

- ✔ General Franco's fascist government maintained power for more than a third of the 20th century (1939–75) and also kept strict control over Spanish culture including cinema. The Catholic Church joined Franco's censors to exercise one of the most repressive regimes of recent history.

Evading the censors, metaphorically speaking

Placing strict controls over what you can and can't say and show is a red rag to a bull for many artists, and the few notable serious film-makers of the Franco period are no exception. One way to avoid falling foul of the censors' scissors is to construct your story out of metaphors, which allow audiences to draw radical interpretations while retaining plausible deniability.

Historians of Spanish film have identified a metaphorical style of film-making that includes Carlos Saura's *La Caza* (*The Hunt*) (1966) and José Luis Borau's *Furtivos* (*Poachers*) (1975).

But perhaps the best-known metaphorical film is *El espíritu de la colmena* (*The Spirit of the Beehive*) (1973). This gently moving and beautifully shot film is full of metaphorical images that viewers can interpret politically or otherwise, including a young girl's fascination with Frankenstein's monster.

You can consider Guillermo del Toro's Mexican-Spanish co-production *El laberinto del fauno* (*Pan's Labyrinth*) (2006) as an heir to this tradition, because it mixes its tale of bloody Civil War violence with metaphorical fantasy elements.

The fascist government and the Church imposed their control over cinema in three important ways:

- ✔ **Censorship:** The government and the Church had to approve screenplays, which along with the finished films were often cut or altered. Decision-making was arbitrary but without appeal. When official guidelines were put in place in 1962, film-makers were at least able to work out ways around them.

- ✔ **Compulsory dubbing:** Foreign films had to be dubbed into Spanish, which became a subtle form of censorship. For example, the Spanish dub of John Ford's *Mogambo* (1953) turned a married couple into brother and sister to legitimise the wife's adultery. Although forced dubbing was intended to protect the Spanish language, the move only strengthened the audience appeal of Hollywood cinema.

- ✔ **State newsreels:** Cinemas were legally obliged to begin every film programme with an official newsreel from the Franco government, which were a mix of explicit propaganda and other subjects including sport and entertainment. Cinemas were unable to screen supplementary material such as shorts or animation, and so film-making training suffered as a result.

Returning of the repressed: Pedro Almódovar

Historians often discuss what happened in Spain and with Spanish cinema after Franco's death in 1975 in psychoanalytical terms. Sigmund Freud claimed that humans can never fully repress their darkest and most secret desires, because in the end they emerge more powerful than ever (see Chapter 13). In the same way, the conventional history goes that after years of repressive fascist rule, Spain entered a period of non-stop sex, drugs and rock and roll.

Of course this behaviour was literally true for only a small section of the Spanish population living in wealthy urban areas. But one of the reasons why this image of a hedonistic Spain became so widespread is that it provides the compelling setting for many of the early films of Spain's first internationally recognised auteur (who didn't have to work abroad): Pedro Almodóvar. For many audiences outside Spain, Almodóvar *is* Spanish cinema.

In fact Almodóvar's earliest experiments with film-making happened well before the liberalisation of Spanish society in the early 1980s. Moving from rural La Mancha to Madrid in 1969, he became part of an underground scene of artists, musicians and other radical types who inspired many of his eccentric characters, as well as providing his early film's recognisable punky aesthetic. He's a self-taught film-maker who gradually replaced the rough edges of his early work with an accomplished style.

Almodóvar's films are characterised by the following concerns:

- ✔ **A female perspective:** Many of Almodóvar's stories are based around the experiences of strong female characters, often played by his favourite actresses Carmen Maura and Penelope Cruz. For example, *Mujeres al borde de un ataque de nervios* (*Women on the Verge of a Nervous Breakdown*) (1988) was his breakthrough international hit. His films about men, such as *Carne trémula* (*Live Flesh*) (1997), tend to be less well received.

- ✔ **Queer as folk:** Almodóvar is openly gay and many of his films feature assertive, well-rounded gay characters. Film critics and academics, however, often discuss his films from a broader queer perspective (see Chapter 15) due to their fluidity around gender. For example, *La ley del Deseo* (*Law of Desire*) (1987) is about a gay film director whose brother is a transgender lesbian.

- ✔ **Expressionistic visuals:** Although Almodóvar has worked across a variety of visual styles, he's best known for his brightly coloured compositions achieved with bold décor and costuming. Credit here also goes to his regular art director Antxon Gomez and cinematographer José Luis Alcaine.

Although Almodóvar is certainly one of the most respected directors in international cinema, as his many prizes and accolades demonstrate, several film scholars have noted an ambivalence in his reputation in his native Spain. He has suffered a backlash, with some critics tiring of his frivolity and calling for a more serious engagement with Spain's difficult recent history. His dominant status can also tend to eclipse other ambitious Spanish film-makers such as Alejandro Amenábar or Julio Medem. Perhaps one director can't bear the weight of an entire national cinema alone, but Almodóvar wears his responsibilities lightly and with charismatic flair.

Chapter 12

Mixing Monsters, Musicals and Melodrama: World Cinema

*W*hen you browse the category lists of online distributors such as Amazon and Netflix, you find an odd mixture of groupings. Recognisable genres such as 'comedy' appear alongside media types, such as 'television shows' or 'documentaries', as well as broader, audience-driven categories such as 'cult films'. But ever since the appearance of the humble video store, all distribution outlets have separated out international films into their own category of 'world cinema'. Why is this?

In terms of the now sadly defunct video shop, the world-cinema section was kept separate for practical reasons. First, doing so allowed most video renters to avoid having to read subtitles, which is a genuine dislike of many viewers. Second, in the opposite sense, a distinct section allowed cine-literate types to go straight for those titles, which made them feel clever and cosmopolitan. Finally, the world-cinema category borrowed the slightly sexy, dangerous connotations of art cinema, so that these titles were often kept away from the kid's cartoons, safely up on the top shelves.

So much for the grubby practicalities. As I discuss in this chapter, clearly more is going on when you lump together and dedicate a decidedly small space to films produced by every part of the world except Hollywood. Additionally, much bigger issues are at stake regarding the structure of the international film industry, the unequal access to funding streams and distribution networks across the globe, as well as the complexities of taste and film form in different national and transnational contexts.

Expanding Vision: World Cinema and Third Cinema

First off: the idea of getting audiences in the US and Europe to watch more films produced from different bits of the world is 'a good thing'. People around the globe have so many different ways of telling stories, fascinating local cultural traditions and interesting landscapes to experience, why not explore the world from the safety of your cinema seat or sofa? Also, giving film-makers around the world more equal access to equipment, funding and distribution networks helps to level out the playing field.

Given this noble agenda, why is world cinema such a tricky term in film studies circles? Several reasons create this discomfort:

✔ The term *world cinema* means the world as viewed from the perspective of the developed Western world. So world cinema is in essence everything except films made in the West. Why shouldn't action films from Hong Kong compete directly with action films from Hollywood without being placed in their own tiny ghetto of film culture?

✔ Who decides on the tiny number of world titles that do receive support in Western markets? Mainly Hollywood controlled distributors. Film festivals offer an alternative route to international recognition, but this process privileges a certain style of film-making: serious art cinema.

✔ Ambitious film-makers from non-Western countries are always going to be tempted to adopt Hollywood practices of style and form, or to produce films that cater for Western prejudices or look like adverts for the local tourist industry. Neither strategy is likely to produce the best quality films.

Film-making wizards of Oz

I can't pretend that the language barrier isn't an issue with world cinema. Many people just don't like reading subtitles and can't accept the artificial weirdness of dubbing. As a result, English-speaking cinemas from far-flung parts of the world are often allowed into the Western club more quickly than their 'foreign language' counterparts.

Australia is a good example. Much like the UK, its openness to Hollywood imports has often stunted home production, although with government support it had a healthy documentary sector and occasional bursts of art cinema activity (for instance, *Picnic at Hanging Rock* (1975)). Since the 1980s, Australian film-makers have sometimes broken international markets with comedies, such as *'Crocodile' Dundee* (1986) or *Muriel's Wedding* (1994), or horror movies such as *Wolf Creek* (2005). Successful Australian actors (such as Russell Crowe and Nicole Kidman) and directors (including Peter Weir) often leave home for Hollywood, becoming part of the transnational flow of film-making talent.

Why does Western culture exclude so much of world culture? Theorists Ella Shohat and Robert Stam suggest that Western culture is deeply Eurocentric. *Eurocentrism* is a way of thinking and speaking (also known as a discourse, see Chapter 15) that helps to create identity. For example, most Westerners have a Eurocentric view of history, which begins with the Greeks rather than any early Islamic or Chinese civilisation. Eurocentrism doesn't rule out the urge to be cosmopolitan, which may appear to be a positive step in the right direction. But in reality, world cinema and its close relatives world music and world literature provide ways for Western audiences to ease their conscience while continuing to ignore the rest of the world.

The most concerted attempt to overcome the West's Eurocentric film culture came in the form of the *Third Cinema* movement. Beginning in Latin America in the late 1960s, international film-makers set out to destroy the dominance of Hollywood (First Cinema) and European art cinemas (Second Cinema). These film-makers reject the commercial approach of Hollywood and the auteur approach of Europe, instead preferring a workers' collective model. Argentinean directors Fernando Solanas and Octavio Getino published a Third Cinema manifesto in 1969, which proposed the construction of a radical new film language to attain goals such as the 'decolonisation of minds' in the Third World.

Clearly these ambitious aims have yet to be fully achieved, but nonetheless the Third Cinema movement did serve as a platform for a generation of film-makers including:

- **Nelson Pereira dos Santos:** A leader of the Cinema Novo movement in Brazil during the 1960s and 1970s (check out the later sidebar 'Opposing Hollywood: Cinema Novo' for more details). His most famous film is a black comedy about cannibalism with the fantastic name *How Tasty Was My Little Frenchman* (*Como Era Gostoso o Meu Francês*) (1971).

- **Ousmane Sembène:** A writer and film-maker from Senegal, which Europeans repeatedly colonised. Sembène made realist films in French and in his native Wolof language, which gained recognition via the French film festival circuit. His *La Noire de . . .* (*Black Girl*) won the Prix Jean Vigo for features in 1966 (see Chapter 19).

- **Ritwik Ghatak:** A Bengali film-maker whose left-leaning political films such as *Meghe Dhaka Tara* (*The Cloud-Capped Star*) (1960) later inspired a brief Third Cinema movement known as New Indian Cinema in the 1970s (for more, travel to the later section 'Pondering Bengali film: World or parallel cinema?').

Be honest, have you heard of any of these film-makers before? How about Jean-Luc Godard, Roberto Rossellini or Wim Wenders? I hope that you can see what I'm getting at here. Film studies has traditionally been as guilty of Eurocentrism as any other aspect of Western culture, which is why everyone knows about the French New Wave but hardly anyone has heard of Cinema

Novo. This critical favouritism becomes a self-fulfilling prophesy owing to the availability of film titles and research materials. For example, if (like me) you're licking your lips at the prospect of seeing whether *How Tasty Was My Little Frenchman* lives up to its title, you're going to be disappointed: it's not currently available on DVD in the UK.

All things considered, *Third Cinema* carries too much political baggage for it to work within this chapter, which considers mainstream commercial films alongside more radical work. In the absence of a clearer, more recognisable term, I stick with *world cinema* instead, but please try to bear my initial reservations in mind when reading this chapter, whether you're from the Eurocentric West or elsewhere.

So, with these considerations in mind, join me as I take a tour of a few of the more fascinating corners of world cinema, taking in exotic monster movies from Japan, rousing Bollywood musicals and dynamic contemporary thrillers from Mexico along the way.

Journeying into Japanese Cinema: Godzilla, Anime and More

Of all the cinema traditions from around the world, Japanese cinema seems to have a particular appeal for audiences in the West, and especially for young audiences. Contemporary Japanese films often gain cult status, attracting devoted followers who become part of fan sub-cultures obsessed with Japanese *anime* (animation) and *manga* (comic books).

A major attraction of Japanese films for Western audiences has always been their distinctive difference to Hollywood cinema. They represent a culture that feels alien and exotic in many ways – but also shares (and in some senses generates) the West's rampant consumerism and love of new technology.

Reaching back to classical cinema, Japanese style

Although Japan's film industry was busy producing films as early as many of their European counterparts, Western audience didn't 'discover' Japanese cinema until 1951. When Akira Kurosawa's *Rashomon* (1950) won the Golden Lion at the 1951 Venice Film Festival, European and American critics raved about its experimental structure and vivid imagery. Kurosawa quickly became the most celebrated Japanese director outside of his home country, although only his period films found favour, especially those depicting warring Samurai culture. He became an exemplar of Japanese culture in the West, while in Japan, although commercially successful, he was criticised for being too Westernised.

The contradictory status of Kurosawa at home and abroad raises fundamental issues with the West's response to Japanese cinema, or in fact any cinema from a culture that's separate to and different from your own. As a Western viewer, you clearly lack contextual information, may misread culturally specific content and run the risk of applying film theory based largely on European philosophy to these films. At its worst, according to British film theorist Paul Willemen, reading Japanese films from a Western film studies perspective represents an attempt to impose cultural practices and place the 'foreign' culture in a subordinate position.

Many film studies texts claim that Japanese cinema represents a kind of mirror image of Hollywood, which also enjoyed a classical period. Consider these details:

- Japan industrialised cinema on a scale comparable only to Hollywood's classical period of the studio era between 1930 and 1960 (check out Chapter 9). In the late 1930s, Japan was probably the most prolific producer of films in the world, with between 500 and 2,000 films being made per year. It also had an extremely healthy exhibition sector with annual audiences of more than 400 million in 1940.

- Japanese film-makers did adopt and adapt elements of the Hollywood classical style (based on strong narrative cause and effect and continuity editing (see Chapter 2)), but to what extent is difficult to assess. Japanese audiences certainly loved the comedies of Charlie Chaplin, and the notion of slapstick entered the local film vocabulary. Kurosawa was a student of Western art and loved Hollywood movies.

- Several formal traditions in Japanese films, however, are specific to Japanese culture. *Kabuki* theatre was a strong influence on early Japanese film, and a narrator or *benshi* often accompanied silent films, thereby avoiding intertitles and leading to more static framing and longer takes than commonly found in Western cinema.

The best-known examples of classical Japanese cinema are the contemporary set domestic dramas (or *shomin-geki*) of Yasujiro Ozu. For example, *Tokyo Story* (1953) demonstrates Ozu's distinctive visual and narrative style. The story's main characters have a loose goal (as grandparents travelling round visiting their ungrateful children) but things end up in a similar place to where they started. People talk and are busy eating or doing other domestic chores, but rarely does anything dramatic happen.

Ozu's typical camera placement is lower down than in comparable Hollywood films, roughly at the head height of the traditional Japanese sitting position. The camera is usually static, which allows careful composition of characters within the geometric features of Japanese domestic space. Above all, Ozu's films have a stillness and elegance, which combined with their engaging human qualities, raises them into the canon of established world-cinema classics.

Facing an incredible, unstoppable titan of terror!

The title for this section borrows (okay, steals) from one of the marketing taglines used to promote the original 1954 *Godzilla* movie. It represents the sensationalist, campy tone that became associated with 1950's monster movies in general, and certainly the equally unstoppable Godzilla franchise in particular.

The originators of the series, Toho Studios in Tokyo, produced a further 27 Godzilla films over the next half century, with the character evolving from a terrifying destroyer of Japanese cities to a benevolent guardian angel figure. Hollywood has twice attempted to capture the lumbering magic of the Japanese original, most recently with Gareth Edwards's 2014 film.

Although some critics found Edwards's version of the mythological creature too dour and serious when compared to the somewhat cheesy reputation of the Japanese series, in fact his tone is strikingly similar to the original 1954 release. *Godzilla* was conceived in a period when Japanese society was still traumatised by the atomic bombs that the US dropped on Hiroshima and Nagasaki in 1945. Even more directly, the film was inspired by further nuclear accidents caused by US testing of nuclear weapons in the sea around Japan during the early 1950s.

This reading isn't a case of film studies scholars layering social context onto popular genre films; *Godzilla* is absolutely explicit in referring to nuclear paranoia:

- ✔ The opening sequence depicts a fishing boat destroyed by an underwater explosion, echoing the results of a recent nuclear accident widely reported by the Japanese media.

- ✔ Godzilla is awoken by the nuclear testing and emerges from the sea, breathing 'atomic breath' (grab the mouthwash) and wreaking havoc across Tokyo.

- ✔ The ethical dilemma at the film's climax, where a scientist wrestles with whether to use a new 'weapon of mass destruction' against Godzilla demands to be read in the context of Hiroshima.

J-Horror (not J-Lo movies)

In recent decades Japanese horror (or *J-Horror* among fans) has become increasingly popular internationally, spurred by VHS and DVD releases as well as legal or pirated Internet distribution. In the UK, this popularity was evidenced by the growth of niche labels such as Tartan's Asia Extreme. Hollywood has of course produced remakes of *kaidan* films, including *The Ring* (2002) and *The Grudge* (2004).

The West's repeated adoption of Japanese horror opens up some interesting issues. Is horror, being primarily visual and visceral, simply among the most translatable of genres? Or is this trend part of an ongoing *orientalist discourse* (something I discuss in Chapter 15), which suggests that Japanese society remains a terrifying, monstrous 'other' for audiences in the West?

Japanese critics at the time spotted this allegorical treatment of the nuclear issue and the film faced criticism for cynically exploiting the recent tragedies. Nonetheless it was a commercial success, prompting a US re-edited version, which – remarkably – inserted a new lead character played by the American Raymond Burr and removed many of the explicit references to Hiroshima and Nagasaki. This version, *Godzilla: King of the Monsters!* (1956), introduced the prehistoric monster to Western audiences and was also a hit. But its radical re-engineering of the original film's ideology represents one of the clearest examples of Hollywood exercising its *hegemony* (powerful influence, see Chapter 13) over world cinema and politics.

The monster movie genre (or *daikaiju eiga*) that *Godzilla* sparked off is a major strand of the Japansese horror film. Other common forms include:

- **The *kaidan* (avenging spirit) film:** Features the return of (usually) a female spirit force to avenge wrongs done to her. The *kaidan* often has long black hair and wide staring eyes, parodying female beauty, and may be associated with a haunted house – a notably domestic, feminine realm. Examples include *Onibaba* (1964) and *Ringu* (1998).

- **The techno/body horror film:** Japanese society underwent a rapid industrialisation, largely during the 20th century, and combined with its military culture these changes created tensions around the human body. In these films, technology repeatedly violates and invades bodies in monstrous ways. Examples are *Matango* (*Attack of the Mushroom People*, 1963) and *Tetsuo: The Iron Man* (1989).

Agreeing that anime rules, okay

The term *anime* generally means Japanese animated films. But it's also part of a much larger culture within and outside of Japan, as well as the hub of a multimedia entertainment industry estimated to be worth around $6.5 billion a year and encompassing TV shows, video games, toys and merchandise. For example, the hugely profitable *Pokémon* franchise began in 1996 with games for handheld video devices and spread like wildfire through international markets. Although anime feature films remain a niche product in the West compared to Hollywood animation, anime has long-dominated the world TV markets.

From the Western perspective, Japanese animated films burst into international consciousness in the late 1980s, largely due to the international theatrical distribution of Katsuhiro Otomo's *Akira* (1988). Thanks to the influence of this film, the best-known examples of anime internationally are cyberpunk-inspired apocalyptic sci-fi films. But this genre is only the tip of the anime iceberg. You can find children's classics such as *Heidi, Girl of the Alps* (1974), romantic comedies such as *Aa! Megami-sama* (*Oh My Goddess!*) (2000) and mainstream family blockbusters such as *Princess Mononoke* (1997). Within Japanese visual culture, the breadth and variety of anime is equivalent to that of live-action narrative film in the West.

Scholar of Japanese studies Susan J Napier identifies three major *modes,* or expressive frameworks, within the enormous variety of anime:

- **Apocalyptic:** Drawing upon Japan's traumatic war experiences during the 20th century, visions of the end of the world feature across Japan's cultural output, including novels and films. Miyazaki's *Nausicaä of the Valley of the Wind* (1984) is one example of a post-apocalyptic fantasy with a vision of hope and rebirth.

- **Festival:** Festivals are essential elements in Japanese social life, when the normal rules of repressive society are temporarily suspended and play with identity and behaviour can occur. You can see the festival mode in the wild fantasy, sex and violence common within anime. The mode is similar to what Marxist theorist Mikhail Bakhtin called the *carnivalesque* in Western culture.

- **Elegiac:** This mode is a wistful nostalgia for passing traditions, as well as lost love, beauty and youth. It's often associated with nature, such as cherry blossoms or water imagery. For example, the romantic *Whisper of the Heart* (1995) has this recognisable sweet but sad tone.

Napier is clear that not all anime fit neatly within one of these modes. In fact many crossover between them. For example, the cyberpunk classic *Ghost in the Shell* (1995) has an apocalyptic tone, because its complex narrative ends on a point where cybernetic life no longer requires humanity to survive and replicate. With its more transgressive ideas about identity and its strong violent content, it also operates within the festival mode. Finally, the film contains powerful elegiac moments, such as the famous sequence when its female cyborg protagonist travels down a canal through the city in the rain, wistfully contemplating what being human means.

Too cute! *Kawaii* culture

Kawaii is one aspect of Japanese culture that feels particularly strange for Westerners. The love of all things cute extends from pop culture into fashion and even behaviour, particularly for young women. Within anime narratives, super-cute *shojo* character types are widespread. *Shojo* originally referred specifically to girls aged around 11 or 12, but it has come to stand for the wider phenomenon of feminine identity caught between childhood and adulthood. Anime master Hayao Miyazaki's films are often based around *shojo* girls, such as *Kiki's Delivery Service* (1989).

Investigating Indian Cinema: Bollywood and Beyond

One coherent 'Indian cinema' doesn't exist. Instead, speaking of multiple cinemas and industries within the Indian subcontinent makes much more sense. The enormous diversity of religions, cultures and languages have created multiple sites of production and cinematic traditions.

In 2009, the Indian film industry produced 1,288 films in 24 different languages. Even the third most significant 'regional' cinema in India – Tamil language film – has an audience of 60 million people across India and a further 10 million ex-patriot, or *diasporic,* speakers across the world (check out the later sidebar 'The importance of diaspora'). These audience numbers are comparable to a large European country such as France or Germany – yet no one ever refers to Germany as merely a 'regional' producer of European cinema.

Making a song and dance of Bollywood

The term *Bollywood* has created much confusion around Indian cinema. With its obvious echoing of Hollywood, the term is a patronising Westernised view *and* a back-handed compliment, in the sense that Bollywood films are considered the commercial equal of Hollywood in some ways.

Bollywood is a Hindi language cinema, which is the largest language grouping of Indian films, but not all Hindi films are Bollywood. The term refers precisely to the big-budget, star-driven films made in Mumbai (formerly Bombay), though Western journalists and critics often misuse the term as a catch-all for the entire range of Indian film production.

This confusion is partly because Bollywood films have achieved the highest visibility outside of India, thanks to aggressive international distribution and marketing. But also because Bollywood films are so distinctive and so unlike the classical Hollywood mode (see Table 12-1).

Table 12-1	Comparing Hollywood and Bollywood Cinema
Hollywood	*Bollywood*
Tight narrative structures that are goal-oriented and driven by cause and effect.	Stories are just pretexts for creating spectacle and emotion.
Plots triggered by disruption to equilibrium, which the heroic protagonist has to restore.	Plots structured around social problems, which are resolved with emotion rather than logic.
May use musical numbers within generic constraints of the musical.	Song and dance sequences are vital within all genres.
Genres are defined by content (such as crime film) or emotional effect (such as comedy).	Genres relate only to content (historical), because all emotions should be blended – the *masala* principle.
The dramatic unities of space and time create consistent pace and style.	Visual style can change depending on the *rasa* (emotion) of that moment.
Cinema audiences are usually silent and watch each film only once.	Films are longer, audiences often interact with songs and dances, and multiple viewings are common.

The mother of all Hindi movies

Mother India (1957) is perhaps the best-known example of the classical Bollywood style and is famous for its blend of heightened emotions, particularly love and sorrow. The film is an epic story spanning several generations of a family, united by a powerful maternal figure Radha, played by the great Indian film star Nargis. The film's social problem is the coming of modernity represented by an industrial canal destroying farmland.

Mother India's sorrowful *rasa* centres on Radha's suffering through poverty and her relationship with her beloved son, whom she must sacrifice at the end of the film. This conclusion ignores a plausible narrative for emotional effect, highlighting the importance of blending emotional flavours into a tasty *masala*.

Imposing Westernised theory upon films from different cultural contexts can be difficult, and so theorists of Indian cinema have looked to ancient Indian aesthetics for ways to understand Bollywood films. One important idea concerns audience emotional response, known as *rasa*. Some *rasa* seem universal (such as mirth or fear), whereas others have specific meanings within Indian culture (heroic energy). The text needs to signal each *rasa,* for example by using music to create a romantic effect.

Another particularly Indian ingredient is *masala,* a term from Indian cooking meaning a blend of spices. The *masala* principle means blending several *rasa* into each text, and creating the correct balance of emotional flavours.

Pondering Bengali film: World or parallel cinema?

Pop quiz: where does *The Simpsons*'s endearing shopkeeper Apu get his name from? If you know that Apu is also the central character from Satyajit Ray's *Apu Trilogy,* you clearly know your world cinema classics (or you're a complete *Simpsons* geek, but congratulations either way!). The fact that Matt Groening and his team pay homage to the Bengali director Ray is revealing for at least two good reasons:

- ✔ Ray was the first (and for several decades, the only) Indian director to achieve international renown.
- ✔ Ray's films feel accessible to Western audiences due to their realist style and universal philosophy of humanism.

The first film in Ray's Apu trilogy, *Pather Panchali* (1955), demonstrates a very different sensibility to the spectacle, high emotion, and song and dance of Hindi classics such as *Mother India* (1957) (turn maternally to the earlier sidebar 'The mother of all Hindi movies'). *Pather Panchali* is shot in simple black and white, using only natural locations and a mixture of theatre and non-professional actors. No spectacular dance numbers interrupt the narrative flow; like all Ray's films, however, *Pather Panchali* is intensely musical. It has a melancholy, haunting score by the (later famous) sitar musician Ravi Shankar and several characters sing folk songs at key moments in the drama. Most importantly, the film rewards humanist readings due to its wide-eyed and engaging child lead Apu (Subir Banerjee) and its universal themes of family and poverty.

Ray's films aren't representative of the whole of Bengali cinema, just as not all Hindi cinema is as populist as the biggest Bollywood titles. Both industries produce a range of products. Ray's status as a prototypical world cinema auteur, however, did help to establish a route to international recognition for subsequent Indian film-makers, as well as creating a space for alternative film within India itself.

The Bengali city of Calcutta is home to an Indian intellectual culture dating back many centuries, and two of Ray's contemporaries, Ritwik Ghatak and Mrinal Sen, form part of this tradition.

Ghatak and Sen's films are more explicit in their political engagement than Ray's – for example, their critical stance towards the partition of Bengal in 1947. For this reason, they're seen as being vital in instigating a Third or *parallel* cinema movement known as *New Indian Cinema:*

- ✔ Indian film has its own First Cinema in the shape of Bollywood and a Second Cinema in the auteur tradition influenced by Europe and characterised by Ray. Check out the tripartite categories of Solanas and Getino in the earlier 'Expanding Vision: World Cinema and Third Cinema' section).

- ✔ The widespread political turmoil in India during the 1970s led the government to set up a Film Finance Corporation aimed at supporting the development of more international auteurs like Ray. The result, though, was to allow more politically oriented directors to flourish, enabling the parallel cinema of Ghatak, Sen and others.

- ✔ This radical, modernist film-making movement failed to attract audiences domestically or abroad, however, and the movement stalled. Government funds were diverted to less confrontational middle-brow films suitable for a growing domestic middle-class audience.

The career of the successful female director Aparna Sen offers a good demonstration of the legacy of Bengali parallel cinema. Born in Calcutta, her father was the renowned critic and film-maker Chidananda Dasgupta. She acted in many of Satyajit Ray's films as a teenager and young woman before making her directorial debut in 1981 with *36 Chowringhee Lane.* Although not a commercial success, this film attracted critical attention through its open portrayal of female sexuality and the role of women in modern Indian society. Sen's later films treat themes such as sectarian violence and mental illness – without a dance routine in sight.

Taking Bollywood global

Bollywood is *not* the whole of the Indian film industry, and Bollywood films are certainly *not* the kind that international critics tend to take seriously, but these facts result in a rather limp definition – commercially minded Hindi cinema produced in Mumbai – which doesn't do Bollywood justice.

For some observers and (more recently) film scholars, Bollywood is much more. Just as Hollywood can't be contained within a suburb of Los Angeles, *Bollywood* is increasingly coming to stand for a glittering array of globalised popular entertainment forms, not just film but also TV, music and advertising.

The importance of diaspora

The concept of *diaspora* refers to a worldwide community of people who have moved away from their homeland but who nonetheless continue to share a common culture and/or language. People from across the Indian subcontinent have been displaced by colonialism or chosen to migrate for economic reasons, often to the UK or other English-speaking countries.

For the globally ambitious Bollywood film industry, diasporic populations across the world are important markets for its films. In the UK, British Film Institute figures illustrate the vitality of this market, with 94 films from the South Asian continent released in 2012 alone, capturing a larger market share than that of European cinema.

The international distribution of Indian films, and especially Hindi cinema, isn't a new phenomenon. In the 1970s for instance, the Middle East became a significant export market for Indian films to satisfy the demand of a large transplanted community of Indian workers. But this export was piecemeal and largely controlled by state institutions.

In recent decades, this situation has changed beyond all recognition. The Indian government removed the previously restrictive tax and funding regimes in 1998, allowing national and international finance to create full-scale corporatisation within the industry. India has always had a very healthy production and exhibition sector, but the increased involvement of international partners opened up serious potential for overseas revenue.

As a case study, take a look at a typical Bollywood hit, *Dhoom 2* (2006):

- *Dhoom 2* was produced and distributed by Yash Raj Films, one of the major forces in the Indian entertainment industry, with subsidiaries in television, music, home video and even a fashion chain. The film was relatively big budget for the Bollywood industry at around $6 million, including the cost of extensive location shooting in Brazil and major stars such as Aishwarya Rai (see Figure 12-1).

- As a sequel to a surprise hit of 2004, the film uses the Hollywood model of franchise building and borrows marketing strategies familiar from the international action film, such as posters displaying the abbreviated logo *D:2*. The film was cross-promoted with tie-ins including Coca-Cola and Pepe Jeans.

- The film broke box-office records in India and went on to gross $26.9 million in its home territory. It received theatrical releases in the US, the UK, the Netherlands, Australia and New Zealand, bringing in a further $5.5 million. Its soundtrack was also the biggest of the year in India, selling 2 million copies. It has been released more widely on DVD and is available to stream on Netflix in the UK.

Figure 12-1: Aishwarya Rai helps to sell *Dhoom 2* (2006) in India and overseas.

But even the strong performance of *Dhoom 2* was dwarfed by the next instalment of the franchise, *Dhoom 3* (2013), which was the most expensive Indian film ever produced and at $88 million is currently the highest grossing Indian film of all time at the box office worldwide. For Bollywood's global prospects, apparently the only way is up.

Looking to Latin America Cinema

In the 21st century, the film-makers of Latin America (comprising Central and South America as well as the Caribbean) have made big splashes on the international independent circuit. Stylish thrillers such as *Amores Perros* (2000) and *Cidade de Deus* (*City of God*) (2002) have broken out of the world cinema ghetto and into mainstream multiplexes in many territories. Stars such as Salma Hayek and Gael García Bernal bring glamour and sex appeal, while directors such as Alfonso Cuarón win awards aplenty, including Oscars. Although Latin America has traditionally been a key market for Hollywood films, these film-makers and stars have turned the tables by appealing to a growing Hispanic population in the US.

Latin America is a large and varied area with many linguistic and cultural traditions, as well as a difficult history of colonial rule. Covering all countries and trends within this section is impossible, and so instead I focus on three key moments in three different areas:

✔ **Brazil:** As the largest country in the region, Brazil has produced the closest thing to a vibrant popular cinema independent of Hollywood.

✔ **Cuba:** This Caribbean island is a fascinating case study of a small national cinema supported consistently by a politicised state.

✔ **Mexico:** The three amigos of contemporary Mexican cinema – Cuarón, Alejandro González Iñárritu and Guillermo del Toro – demonstrate the continued value of auteurism within a contemporary world cinema context.

Brazil: Hollywood in the tropics?

As the largest and most economically significant of the Latin American countries, Brazil's film industry benefits from a huge domestic audience. Of course its demographics also make it a key target of Hollywood films and a favourite location for American movies. Hit comedies such as Bob Hope's *The Road to Rio* (1947) and musicals such as *That Night in Rio* (1941) exploit the exotic allure and carnival atmosphere of Brazil's biggest city. The country has also produced Hollywood stars such as Carmen Miranda, known as 'The Brazilian bombshell' thanks to her show-stopping performances and extravagant fruit-filled hats (she starred in *That Night in Rio*).

Carmen Miranda's career began in Brazilian popular films of the 1930s, which, as elsewhere in the world, grew out of vibrant local traditions. This popular cinema was genre-based, with the most popular types of film including the following:

✔ The *chanchada* took elements from Brazilian carnival culture, blended them with bits of the Hollywood musical and added local comedy stars. *Alô, Alô Brasil!* (1935) helped to launch Carmen Miranda, and the genre remained popular into the 1960s when it morphed into sex comedies, known charmingly as *pornochanchada*.

✔ The *cangaceiro* was a Brazilian variant of the Western cowboy film, often with a strong musical element. The genre produced an international hit *O Cangaceiro* (*The Bandit*) (1953), which won prizes at the Cannes Film Festival.

✔ Brazilian melodramas such as *O Ebrio* (*The Drunkard*) (1946), a morality tale dealing with alcoholism and adultery, was hugely popular in Brazil and remains a touchstone for popular cinema culture to this day. Melodrama is also a vital element of the *telenovela* soap-opera format that dominates Latin American television worldwide.

Opposing Hollywood: Cinema Novo

Cinema Novo was a new-wave cinema comparable to those that spread across Europe in the 1950s and 1960s, but with a tougher political agenda. It became associated with the pan-Latin American Third Cinema movement after Brazilian director Glauber Rocha wrote a manifesto called 'The Aesthetics of Hunger', which argued that films had to reveal the hunger, poverty and violence inherent to Latin American society in order to free its peoples from waves of colonial rule.

This radical movement found some favour with mainstream audiences in Brazil, for example with Rocha's own *Deus e o Diabo na Terra do Sol* (*Black God, White Devil*) (1964), a bleak and violent version of the *cangaceiro* genre, and with the allegorical comedy *Macunaíma* (1969). You can also detect elements of the Cinema Novo aesthetic in the hard-hitting violence of the breakthrough hit *Cidade de Deus* (*City of God*) (2002).

The large size of Brazil's domestic market prompted several attempts to stabilise film production within a studio system. An Italian producer Franco Zampari set up one notable example, the *Companhia Cinematográfica Vera Cruz,* in 1949. The company had the ambition of matching MGM's production values as a self-styled 'Hollywood in the Tropics'. Despite occasional successes, including *O Cangaceiro,* the studio fell foul of Brazil's economic turbulence and closed just five years later.

Meanwhile a new generation of Brazilian film-makers were digesting the lessons of Italian Neorealism (see Chapter 11) and experimenting with a more authentic film-making style known as Cinema Novo (see the nearby sidebar 'Opposing Hollywood: Cinema Novo' for more).

The impact of Cinema Novo on popular cinema was short-lived, largely because government censorship forced the film-makers into ever more allegorical and experimental forms. Film scholars Stephanie Dennison and Lisa Shaw have described the continuing mutation of the *chanchada* genre throughout the 1970s and 1980s, including sex comedy and melodrama variants. The Brazillian horror film was much enlivened by the eccentric character of Coffin Joe (José Mojica Marins) who made inventive low-budget chillers in the 1960s and then became a popular television personality. In recent decades, the director Walter Salles has made quality films such as *Central do Brasil* (*Central Station*) (1998), which found a wide international audience.

Cuba: Small cinema, big ideas

Imagine a country where the government makes all the films, controls their distribution and even runs the cinemas in which they're shown. Sounds like a dystopian sci-fi nightmare along the lines of Terry Gilliam's *Brazil* (1985) right?

Well, this situation was basically in place in Cuba for the latter part of the 20th century. You're probably imagining poor Cubans being forcefully subjected to awful propaganda films and tedious documentaries about Marxism. But the fascinating thing about Cuban cinema is that it survived and even creatively flourished under these extremely unusual conditions. And it did so right under the nose of the world leader in free-market economics, the US of A.

Even before the Cuban Revolution of 1959, Cuba had a relatively well-developed cinema-going culture. Film historian Michael Chanan describes how the country's sugar industry created a working-class audience hungry for cinema and a transport infrastructure capable of sustaining distribution. In the 1920s, Cuban audiences apparently thrilled to fast-paced action films and Hollywood stars such as Mary Pickford and Douglas Fairbanks. After the coming of sound, Mexican and Argentinian melodramas made some headway against Hollywood thanks to the shared language, but American films remained popular. Of course this situation changed after the Revolution, when the Cuban state became communist and allied itself with the Soviet Union.

After the Revolution, Cuba had only one producer, distributor and exhibitor in the market: the official body *Instituto Cubano del Arte y la Industria Cinematográficos* (ICAIC). The ICAIC produced five to ten features and many more documentaries per year until the early 1990s, when its state funding was slashed. Contrary to expectations, these films weren't all sterile propaganda, because film-makers sympathetic to the state ran the ICAIC and they were allowed relative artistic freedom. Here are three of the more unusual examples:

- *Cuba Baila* (*Cuba Dances*) (1961) uses the conventions of popular melodrama but offers a gentle satire of middle-class pretentions when Cuban street musicians take over a family party.

- *¡Vampiros en La Habana!* (*Vampires in Havana*) (1982) is a popular adult animated film. The symbolism around vampires and capitalists is fairly obvious, but it's great fun nonetheless.

- *Cecilia* (1982) is an expensive and glossy adaptation of a classic Cuban novel set in 1930s Havana. The film caused great controversy due to its reinterpretation of the original text to emphasise Afro-Cuban identity and religious practices.

Although the ICAIC lost most of its state funding in the 1990s, it continues to operate as a producer/distributor of a smaller number of films, largely thanks to international co-production treaties with the Latin American countries. Cuba has experienced a gradual opening up to Western ideas since that point, as evidenced by the popular comedy *Fresa y Chocolate* (*Strawberry and Chocolate*) (1993). Its gentle treatment of gay identity and sub-culture was bound to be controversial in Cuba given General Castro's well-known homophobic policies, but the film has also been criticised from the other perspective, for downplaying gay rights issues. But some critics point out that its ending, which sees its central gay character leave Cuba, has a tone of sadness for Cuba's unwillingness to change.

Mexico's modern auteurs

When the Mexican director Alfonso Cuarón won an Academy Award for directing *Gravity* (2013), the Mexican press was somewhat conflicted.

Having a Latino director at the top of the Hollywood tree was seen as beneficial, perhaps bringing fresh public attention and finance to the struggling Mexican film industry. And yet *Gravity* is clearly a transnational film production, featuring US finance and stars but shot and post-produced by an international crew in the UK. Fellow Mexican director Arturo Ripstein was widely quoted as saying that *Gravity* was a Mexican achievement as much as *Rosemary's Baby* (1968) was a Polish one, referring to the nationality of its director Roman Polanski (in other words, not at all).

Together with Alejandro González Iñárritu and Guillermo del Toro, Cuarón is part of a trio of directors linked by their nationality, talent and ambition. They're also friends and professional collaborators, earning them the nickname 'the three amigos'. Film historian Deborah Shaw sees them as representing the value of auteurism in contemporary world cinema: del Toro and Cuarón have created distinctive visual styles across a range of popular genres (check out Chapter 14 for more on del Toro's auteur status), Iñárritu is the very model of transnational independent film-making.

But all three amigos rely on an impressive grasp of the conventions of international cinema in its different incarnations.

In particular, a closer look at Iñárritu's films shows his career-building savvy:

- *Amores Perros* (2000) combines three separate stories into one narrative structure linked by a central event, a car crash in Mexico City. Film theorist Eleftheria Thanouli identifies this type of narrative structure as a key element of an international postclassical style of film-making, also found in the films of Danny Boyle, David Fincher and Wong Kar-wai.

- *21 Grams* (2003) uses a similar narrative structure but this time across multiple locations including Mexico City and Memphis. A multinational cast of character actors speak English, and despite its Mexican creative crew, the film is effectively an American indie rather than a Mexican film.

✔ *Babel* (2006) goes even farther afield with multiple stories taking place in Mexico, Morocco and Japan. Its title refers to the Biblical myth of universal humanity, suggesting that people all around the world are essentially the same. The film therefore incorporates the humanism essential to notions of world cinema. Its cast includes major stars Brad Pitt and Cate Blanchett.

The key element uniting these three films is director Iñárritu's background in communications and marketing: he's a consummate publicist. The marketing strategy of launching *Amores Perros* at the Cannes Film Festival paid off handsomely, with his Critics Week Grand Prize leading to a string of further awards and nominations, including Best Foreign Language Film at the Academy Awards. Iñárritu was then able to use this prestige to secure financing and distribution deals with Focus Features and Paramount. He became the kind of director whom stars such as Brad Pitt love to work with in order to keep them artistically fresh and commercially credible.

So where does this leave the 'Mexican-ness' of Iñárritu and his fellow amigos? During Cuarón's big moment, his Oscar acceptance speech, he chose to poke humour at his own thick accent by telling an amusing anecdote about Sandra Bullock mishearing the word 'earpiece' as 'herpes'. Thus he turned his accent, which for some ex-patriot people is a source of shame or discomfort, into an endearing character trait. Clearly this playful engagement with regional stereotypes is a long way from the confrontational stance of Cinema Novo (see the sidebar, 'Opposing Hollywood'), but Cuarón's self-effacing persona is vastly more marketable in the competitive marketplace of transnational cinema.

Part IV
Bringing In the Big Ideas: Theories and Beyond

Courtesy Everett Collection/REX

Ocean's Eleven (2001) is cool fun – but what does it say about modern men and masculinity? Find out at http://www.dummies.com/extras/filmstudies.

In this part . . .

- Talk the language of film theory.
- Explore the relationship between the film text, its context and the spectator.
- Audit the auteur theory as well as some directors who may well qualify for this lofty title.
- Consider the role of theory in the new digital age.

Chapter 13

Theorising about Film: How Movies Work

I'm going to be upfront with you: film theory isn't easy. Most theory involves outdated, jargon-laden language, and even after you decode the written style, the central concepts can be tricky to get your head around. Add to that the fact that many of the important film-theory books and articles take part in a philosophical conversation with other complex, jargon-heavy ideas that you've probably never heard of, and you have a recipe for giving up, throwing your film-theory book across the room and going to watch *The Hunger Games* movies on Netflix to work through your frustration. So, why bother?

As the saying goes, nothing good ever comes easy. Film theory can be difficult, but if you really want to understand how movies *work*, the effort is well worthwhile. Film theory aims to help answer the seriously big questions of film studies, such as: why do you enjoy watching films? Does a film reflect the culture that creates it – or does it help to shape that culture?

If you don't think these questions are worth thinking about, you can skip this chapter. But then again you're reading this book, and so I hope that you do care about this stuff. Plus, millions of film students around the world have grasped these ideas successfully and you can too. So stick at it, soldier. One day you'll be glad that you read this chapter and therefore know how film connects to some of the great ideas of the last hundred years or so: formalism, Marxism, structuralism and psychoanalysis.

Building a Foundation of Film Theory: Text, Context and Spectator

All film theory is about the relationship between three elements: a *film text* (the object of your study), its *context* (or place within wider culture and society) and the *spectator* (yes, that's you).

Not all types of film theory engage with all three elements to the same extent: some focus on just one (such as formalism) and others concern themselves with the relationship between two elements. For example, as well as formalism, in this section I describe notions of realism, which are largely about the relationship between the text and its context, and reception theory, which examines the relationship between the spectator and the text.

Formalism: What is a film?

In order to understand something, you have first to know what it is. This statement may sound blindingly obvious – it's a film, you fool. But how do you *know* it's a film? What are its basic formal properties and how are these similar or different from other cultural forms?

Formalism attempts to answer these questions by studying structure and technique as the basis of an art form. Unlike many other methods of theorising a text, this type of film theory isn't particularly concerned with content or meaning. Instead of subjective interpretation, formalism attempts to impose scientific objectivity by establishing methods for rigorous analysis.

Questioning your textuality

Hold on a minute. Why use the word *text* instead of *film* or *movie*?

Film theory tends to refer to *the text* for a couple of reasons. First, much of film theory is borrowed and adapted from literary theory, where the object of study is literally text on a page. Applying literary theory terminology to film isn't laziness; it reinforces the idea that people need to take films as seriously as literature.

Second, *text* is a more open and flexible word than the other possibilities, particularly *work*, which implies that an individual artist labouring alone in a studio produces a film. The auteur theory may try to assert this position (as I describe in Chapter 14), but it's by no means the only way of thinking about authorship in cinema.

Formalism takes its name from a group of Russian academics and critics who, inspired by the 1917 Revolution, decided to overthrow traditional methods of discussing art and literature. The Russian formalists were interested mainly in literature, but their method of analysing structure, and especially narrative patterns, can be applied to film. Several well-known film-makers were also involved in this vigorous outpouring of ideas, particularly Sergei Eisenstein who used the formalist framework to come up with his theory of montage as a radical editing style (you can meet Sergei in Chapter 4).

Formalism tries to address several specific issues, notably:

- ✔ **What makes art different from communication?** The formalists identified that poetry and metaphor are vital elements of literature. Viktor Shklovsky argued that artists _defamiliarise_ the everyday world by making it seem strange and unfamiliar. This idea often relates to avant-garde film or art cinema (check out Chapter 7).

- ✔ **Do groups of texts work in similar ways?** Several formalists laid the foundations for genre theory and structuralism (see Chapter 5 and the later section 'Taking Films to Bits: Structuralism', respectively) by linking groups of texts together. They analysed folk tales, for example, and yielded common characters and narrative elements. Literary theorist Tzvetan Todorov applied psychoanalysis (flip to the later section 'Getting into Your Head: Psychoanalysis and Film' for details) to discover new genres, such as _the fantastic,_ which blurs the lines between reality and fantasy.

- ✔ **How is a text affected by its context (how it is made, for example)?** More recent neoformalist critics such as Kristin Thompson rethink formalist ideas with renewed focus on production context. Thompson points out that the notion of defamiliarisation requires you to first understand the everyday world of a film's contemporary audience.

Few examples of defamiliarisation beat the opening sequence of _Blue Velvet_ (1986), which features a clear blue sky before gently panning down to reveal crimson red roses and a white picket fence. Bobby Vinton croons 'Blue Velvet' on the soundtrack as happy firemen wave, children cross wide streets and a middle-aged man waters his garden with a hose: the perfect picture of sunny suburbia. But then . . . the man clutches his neck in agony before collapsing on the grass. His dog plays with the spraying hose regardless. The camera gets closer to the grass until you see an extreme close-up of beetles and insects living off garden decay. From familiar to defamiliarised in just a few shots – that's David Lynch.

Realism: Does film reflect reality?

Whereas formalism is mainly about the film text itself, the many theories that come under the banner of _realism_ investigate the complex relationship between a text and its context.

A *realist* approach to making or analysing films assumes that a real world exists, separate from human understanding of it. If that sounds like stating the obvious, don't forget that some philosophies do question the existence of reality outside of perception. Just think about the well-known philosophical riddle: if a tree falls in the forest and nobody's around to hear it, does it make a sound? But don't ruminate for too long, because I need to keep this section moving along.

In early writing about film, the ability of the camera to capture reality mechanically was a vital element of what made film special as an art form. Realism became the focus of debates about film after World War II, in the wake of the films of Italian Neorealism and French Poetic Realism (see Chapter 11). As a result, critics came to think of techniques that minimised intervention from the film-maker as more realistic than the more stylised film-making of Soviet montage or German Expressionism. Subsequent theorists, however, disputed the cinema's ability to reflect reality by emphasising its nature as a cultural construction, as well as noting that conventions of realism change over time and across different cultural contexts.

Some key debates around realism include:

- ✔ **Which of film's particular qualities are more realistic than others?** André Bazin was a key critic of the French film journal *Cahiers du Cinéma* and a firm advocate of realism as the destiny and the goal of cinema. Bazin praised not only the documentary-style aesthetics of Neorealism, but also commercial film-makers such as Orson Welles for his use of deep focus and long takes, which both avoid the artificial intervention of editing.

- ✔ **What's the relationship between realism and fantasy in cinema?** Early film historians noted two primary drives of film represented by the *actualities* (everyday scenes) of the Lumière brothers on the one hand and the fantasy of George Méliès on the other. In particular, Jewish German sociologist Siegfried Kracauer argued that the Expressionist flight from reality in 1920s films indicated a fear of chaos and disorder within German society that made it vulnerable to fascist control (for more on Nazi aesthetics in documentary film, see Chapter 8).

- ✔ **How does digital film-making relate to the real world?** Film theorist Stephen Prince suggests that computer-generated imagery (CGI) compromises the direct relationship between photographic cinema images and reality, and that a different kind of *perceptual realism* will replace photographic realism, asking: do the images look real or move realistically?

At first glance, *Russian Ark* (2002) appears to be an exercise in taking Bazin's notions of realism to extremes. Alexander Sokurov's film is a 99-minute-long single take with no editing to disrupt its reality effect. Although other film-makers have attempted single-shot films in the past (including Hitchcock with

Rope (1948)), the use of light digital cameras that can shoot for long periods made it achievable. But this film is no exercise in documentary style realism. The film explores different periods of history within the same location, requiring complex mise-en-scène (something I discuss in Chapter 4) to produce its overlapping effects. In the end, *Russian Ark* demonstrates that long takes aren't inherently realistic after all.

Reception: What is a spectator?

The obvious danger of the formalist approach to cinema (check out the earlier section 'Formalism: What is a film?') is that if you spend too much time thinking about what a film is, you can forget that a film doesn't provide the same experience for each individual spectator.

Reception theory puts the spectator at the heart of the film experience with the aim of avoiding simplifications and generalisations. No single theory of reception exists: you can discuss the vital relationship between text and audience in many different ways. Crucially though, all models of reception place a greater emphasis on what a spectator does with a text than what a text does to her.

Literary theory was the inspiration for film studies to pay greater attention to the spectator rather than just the film text. Roland Barthes was particularly influential with his provocative claim that the author was dead: he meant that readers produce meaning by working within the codes of the text. Reception studies are also influenced by ideas drawn from sociology, such as Pierre Bourdieu's notion of *cultural capital*. For Bourdieu, a spectator's ability to interact with and make sense of a text is related to her level of power within society, with some types of spectatorship (such as understanding avant-garde film) requiring greater levels of cultural capital than others.

Other important questions that reception theory poses include:

- ✔ **How do individual spectators respond to real texts?** Early film theory presented a model of a passive spectator who believed everything she saw. In contrast, cultural theorist Stuart Hall argues that spectators can read a film in many possible ways, including in an *oppositional mode* where the viewer rejects prescribed meaning and creates her own.

- ✔ **What's the role of viewing context in understanding a film?** Major currents of film theory, such as structuralism (see 'Taking Films to Bits: Structuralism' later in this chapter), remove spectators from their historical context. Film theorist Janet Staiger argues instead for a focus on context as the fertile middle ground between the text and spectator, and for historical rigour when collecting evidence.

> ✔ **How do people remember their viewing experiences?** Research on memories of cinema-going suggests that people remember snippets rather than entire films, and that where you see films and with whom can dominate your recall. Annette Kuhn's work on *cinema memory* combines autobiographical and historical approaches.

Janet Staiger's study of *The Silence of the Lambs* (1991) and its effects on audiences is a great example of how reception theory can explain what spectators do with a film. This multiple Oscar-winning horror film provoked intense debate upon its release, mostly around issues of gender and sexuality. For example, gay rights groups actively picketed the film's screenings, claiming that it depicted gay men as monstrous. Staiger analyses the written and spoken responses to the film as evidence that spectators produce many responses to a film depending on their social positioning, gender identity and historical context.

Janet Staiger and Annette Kuhn make use of their own personal responses to particular films or images in their work on reception. So using yourself as a guinea pig for a reception study is quite appropriate. However, you need to think of your memories only as raw data that isn't necessarily meaningful in itself. You have to analyse this data in order for it to be useful.

So you can think through your responses in relation to Stuart Hall's reading strategies – or follow Bourdieu and consider your levels of cultural capital at different points in your life.

Shaping Society with Film: Marxism

American president John F Kennedy was apparently fond of an anecdote about the revolutionary philosopher Karl Marx. Marx struggled financially for most of his life, working mainly as a journalist, and while employed by the *New York Herald Tribune* as a foreign correspondent he repeatedly complained about his meagre salary. When his complaints fell on deaf ears, Marx quit journalism to write books including *Das Kapital* (1867–1894), which, directly or indirectly, led to the Russian Revolution, Stalinism and the Cold War. If only the editor of the newspaper had been a little more generous, the 20th century may have turned out a little differently.

This section comes over all radical, as I describe how film theorists have employed Marx's ideas, fortunately to less violent ends.

Dialectics, or agreeing to disagree

How does society change? How do ideas develop over time? The *theory of dialectics* tackles these questions – and influenced Marx's work. For the ancient Greeks and Hindus, disagreements between two parties were resolved through open discussion and debate, with each party arguing its case until a middle-ground solution was reached. Even today, the mark of 'balance' on news shows is about getting two people with opposite ideas to argue.

The 18th and 19th century German philosopher Georg Hegel took up this idea and extended it into an entire model of history and thought. This model is often expressed as a three-stage process: *thesis* (the current state of affairs), which is challenged by an *antithesis* and eventually results in a new *synthesis.* This synthesis then becomes the next dominant thesis, which in turn invites a challenge.

Meeting Marx (Karl, not Groucho)

You don't have to be a revolutionary communist in order to make use of Marx's theories of civilisation, which are based on a model of human society that considers what you produce and how (see Figure 13-1). Marxism holds that under capitalism, a minority of wealthy capitalists control the means of production (the *base*) and they exploit the workers' labour. The workers put up with this situation because of systems of thought (the *superstructure*) such as religion, education and culture – including the movies. Marx argues that the base shapes the superstructure, rather than the other way round. As a result, structural reform is necessary to reshape society, and not just new ideas.

The most important implication of Marx's model of society when studying culture is that you have to consider any practice or text in terms of the historical conditions that produce it. This idea is particularly relevant for film studies, because film is a large-scale industry, which requires raw materials, technology and workers in order to function (see Chapter 2). Film is clearly not only about economics, however, and so you need to try to maintain a balance between the creative freedom of artists and producers and the structure that enables or frustrates them.

For Marx, Hegel's model of history was used to explain the development from medieval feudalism (where lords and kings controlled serfs) to capitalism, and to predict that capitalism would eventually give way to communism.

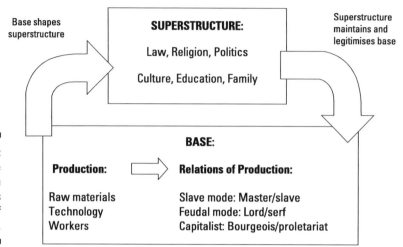

Base shapes superstructure

SUPERSTRUCTURE:

Law, Religion, Politics

Culture, Education, Family

Superstructure maintains and legitimises base

Figure 13-1:
The place of culture in Karl Marx's model of society.

BASE:

Production: → **Relations of Production:**

Raw materials   Slave mode: Master/slave
Technology   Feudal mode: Lord/serf
Workers   Capitalist: Bourgeois/proletariat

For example, a classic Marxist analysis of Warner's successful talking picture *The Jazz Singer* (1927) needs to take into account:

- ✔ The structure of the Hollywood studio system during the 1920s, including the dominance of Paramount, against which new competitors such as Warner Bros. were forced to take risks with new technology.

- ✔ The amount of leisure time and disposable income of the film's large urban audiences.

- ✔ The celebrity of Al Jolson, a Broadway star who drew on long traditions of Jewish theatrical performance that pre-date US society.

- ✔ The tension between family and fame that drives the narrative, including the importance of family within Jewish immigrant populations.

Spending time with the Frankfurt School: Fun is bad

As part of doing film studies, you may be required to watch lots of so-called bad films. Say, Adam Sandler rom-coms or action movies starring Dwayne 'The Rock' Johnson. While you're engaged in this serious research, your friends or parents may say, 'What are you doing watching that rubbish? Don't you know that bad movies rot your brain!' Here's a possible response: 'That was indeed the assumption of the Frankfurt School of Marxists who were influential in the establishment of cultural theory, but their pessimistic view of popular culture has since been debunked by cultural relativism.' You may get a slap, but at least you can demonstrate your intellectual superiority in the process.

Take a look at Marx's model of society for a moment (in the preceding section and Figure 13-1). Concentrate on the idea that the superstructure 'maintains and legitimises' the base. One possible extension of this notion is to suggest that culture, as an important element of the superstructure, basically exists to keep the workers in their place. In a nutshell, this was the main argument of the Frankfurt School of Marxist thinkers, established in (duh) Frankfurt in 1923 and moved to New York's Columbia University during the rise of Hitler in the 1930s and the war-ravaged 1940s. The writers and academics of the Frankfurt school developed a system of *critical theory*, which combined Marxism with psychoanalysis, but in this section I just focus on the Marxism aspect.

Theodor Adorno and Max Horkheimer described popular entertainment forms as a product of the *culture industry*. These products were basically all the same and entirely predictable. So you can choose to read a superhero serial in a comic book or watch it at the cinema, but either way you have the same experience and you know exactly what you're getting. Most importantly, the products of the culture industry reflect and impose social conformity. For example, the backstage musical *Gold Diggers of 1933* (1933) presents a team of sparky, likeable chorus girls. But they're all in essence subservient to a millionaire's ambitions to become a writer. The songs are just an entertaining distraction from the girls' powerless economic position.

Here's another important element of the Frankfurt School's critique: high art is okay. These critics see opera, serious literature and classical music as full of genuine imagination and encouraging of audiences to be active participants rather than passive consumers. You can see how avant-garde or art cinema is defendable along similar lines. This position is clearly elitist and reveals a major flaw within the Frankfurt crowd's thesis. Intellectuals – who are arguably complicit with the superstructure's elite – are basically telling the *proletariat* (in Marxist terms, the poorest of the classes) that what they enjoy is rubbish.

Answer in the affirmative

Even slightly less depressing approaches of the Frankfurt School, such as that of Herbert Marcuse, end up confirming the dominance of the culture industry. Marcuse suggested that pop songs, novels and films can be seen as *affirmative culture*. They function as escapism and lift people's spirits, especially during hard times. To give just one of many possible examples, the bright, glitzy musicals of the 1930s offer a perfect example of escapism as the Great Depression raged outside the cinemas.

However, ultimately this affirmation is also repressive because it only allows for certain types of fantasy and playfulness. Anything too radical is dismissed as running counter to the drives of entertainment. Nobody really wants to watch a radical political movie, do they? Well, maybe art-house audiences.

The Frankfurt Marxists' account of culture also suffers from a disregard for the individual spectator and what she may do with a text. The Frankfort critique of mass media assumes that people simply accept what they're told at face value and then go about their proletariat business. This approach is sometimes called a *hypodermic needle model* of the audience, because they remain passive while being injected with culture, to which, as with an illegal drug, they may become addicted.

Subsequent Marxists maintained their belief in Marx's model of society, but sought to correct this imbalance by paying greater attention to how the spectator engages with the text.

Negotiating between culture and behaviour: Ideology

If James Brown is the Godfather of Soul, Louis Althusser is the Godfather of film studies (though with less sweating!). Althusser recast the Marxist critique of culture with an absolutely essential additional concept: *ideology*.

You need to get a grip on the notion of ideology, otherwise 90 per cent of film theory makes no sense whatsoever. So if you digest and remember only one part of this chapter, please make it this section.

Althusser rejected Marx's idea that the base of society (its forms and means of production) shapes its superstructure (its laws, culture, politics and so on). (Check out the earlier section 'Shaping Society with Film: Marxism' for more detail.) Instead Althusser saw the relationship between the two as a practice, a system through which people understand their lives. This practice is *ideology*. In a broader sense, ideology is behaviour – rituals, customs and so on – prescribed by the *ideological state apparatus* of education, religion and the media.

Show me the hegemony!

Italian Marxist Antonio Gramsci looked at Althusser's notion of ideology and wondered: if the capitalist system is so oppressive, why don't people carry out more revolutions? He concluded that the oppressed masses must be actively agreeing to be led by the oppressors, and he called this process of negotiation *hegemony*. Of course, conflicts exist in society, but they're expressed in safe, non-revolutionary ways.

When applied to culture, the concept of hegemony avoids the rigid, prescriptive feel of much ideological criticism in favour of a negotiated middle ground between high and low culture, authenticity and commercialisation, resistance and incorporation. For example, you can think of Hollywood's dominant position within cinema as being hegemonic, because audiences around the world participate in its pleasures.

Living under capitalism, people constantly encounter logical contradictions or tensions between opposing ideas. Ideology works by dispelling these tensions with false but convincing solutions. For example, managers often find that the needs of their business conflict with their workers' personal lives, but they can rely on the ideology of 'competitiveness', which is encouraged by government policy, to help them sleep at night.

Cultural texts are complicit in this process of offering false solutions to irresolvable contradictions. The most obvious examples in narrative cinema tend to arrive at the end of a film, when closure demands that film-makers 'paper over the cracks' of the dangerous ideas that they may have been exploring. Hitchcock's *Rebecca* (1940) is a steamy tale of adultery, sexual intrigue and murder, all extremely damaging to the social superstructure of the family. But all this nasty mess is stuffed back into its box at the end as the protagonists' house burns down and the couple are reunited. How exactly does this solve all the real issues? It doesn't.

One important effect of the climactic fire in *Rebecca* is that the housekeeper Mrs Danvers (Judith Anderson) is destroyed in the blaze. Why was this necessary? What big problem is the film attempting to resolve? Althusser suggests that when a film offers a solution to a problem that it doesn't name, the problem is a *symptom* of ideological practice at work. Thus a *symptomatic* reading of a text looks for the gaps, the looming subtext that's never mentioned. In *Rebecca*, the missing problem, or *structuring absence,* is lesbianism. Mrs Danvers is coded as masculine and domineering, and is clearly in love with her former mistress, the murdered Rebecca. Under the Production Code (see Chapter 9), homosexuality could only ever function as an unnamed problem; the result was often unconvincing solutions.

Taking Films to Bits: Structuralism

The formalists (see 'Formalism: what is a film?' earlier in this chapter) tried to understand how films work by thinking about the techniques and choices film-makers make when constructing texts. In doing so, they often concluded that texts tend to work in similar ways within a given context. For example, the formalist Vladimir Propp analysed Russian folk tales and found that the same characters cropped up again and again and had similar functions within the narratives. You can think of this common narrative form as a *structure,* which is embedded within a particular culture – or is even universal throughout human society.

Structuralism grew out of formalism, but instead of studying individual texts it takes groups of films to bits to discover their underlying commonalities. The following sections break apart the pieces.

Linking linguistics and film: Saussure

Here's a word: 'cinema'. When you read this word, you probably conjure up an image in your mind of a large, dark room where people go to watch films together in public. But why? Nothing about the word 'cinema' directly links it to that darkened room. In itself, 'cinema' is just a sequence of six letters, a collection of individual sounds that join together to form the word. If you're an English speaker, at an early age you connect the large dark room with the sequence of sounds that is cinema, and then later you discover how to read and write the word. This process becomes instinctive.

The science of *linguistics* breaks down the instinctive behaviours of language to expose its structure. The influential Swiss linguist Ferdinand de Saussure developed a theory of linguistics that is known as *semiotics* (after the Greek for sign: *semos*), which argues that words are *signs* that are made up of two elements:

- ✔ The *signifier* is the set of letters on a page or the sounds made when the word is spoken.
- ✔ The *signified* is their meaning.

The relationship between the signifier and signified is arbitrary. The word 'cinema' contains nothing inherently cinema-like about it. Other languages use different signifiers for the same sign (for example, *kino* in German). Language also creates meaning through difference, and so 'cinema' isn't 'the-atre' or 'museum'.

So what does all this talk about language have to do with film? Well, a sign doesn't have to be a written or spoken word – it can also be an image. If a film opens with a shot of the Empire State Building, you probably assume that the story is set in New York City. Here the image of the famous building functions as a signifier for the larger sign of New York. If the following shots are streets filled with yellow cabs, you know that you were correct in your assumption. But if, on the other hand, the Empire State is followed by shots of Big Ben in London and the Eiffel Tower in Paris, you guess that the story is international in setting, such as a James Bond film.

This example illustrates that meaning isn't only produced by individual signs, but also by signs linked together, as with a sentence on a page or a sequence within a film. Saussure pointed out that these meanings can be changed in two ways (see Figure 13-2). Meaning and, in this case, narrative accumulates through the combinations on the *syntagmatic* axis (derived from the more familiar term 'syntax', meaning sentence structure), whereas different choices made on the *paradigmatic* (from 'paradigm', or pattern of thought) axis can create very different narrative outcomes.

Whereas in theory Harry could choose to kiss either Hermione or Voldemort, we know that these choices have already been set by JK Rowling and the film's screenwriters. Nonetheless, less conventional possibilities exist, thanks to the variety and flexibility of language and storytelling. Consider the phenomenon of internet *fan* or *slash fiction,* which takes well-known characters in unpredictable directions.

Figure 13-2:
Saussure's
semiotic
possibilities
applied to
the Harry
Potter
universe

Harry Potter	fights with	Voldemort	P A R A D I G M A T I C
Albus Dumbledore	saves	Severus Snape	
Ron Weasley	kisses	Hermione Granger	

SYNTAGMATIC

Signs as icons, symbols and indexes

If a film opens with the Empire State Building and you conclude that it's set in New York City, the relationship between signifier and signified isn't purely arbitrary, as Saussure claimed it was for individual words. The Empire State Building obviously exists as a part of the New York skyline. Here the work of Charles Sanders Pierce comes into play.

Pierce differentiated between different types of signs:

✔ An *icon* is a sign that visually resembles what it stands for. Therefore photographs and cinema images are iconic because

they look like an object in reality. The shot of the Empire State looks like the actual building.

✔ A *symbol* has no obvious connection with what's signified. For example: the words 'Empire State Building'.

✔ A sign can be considered *indexical* if some meaningful connection exists between the signifier and the signified. In this sense, the establishing shot of the Empire State Building is an *index* of the larger meaning that *this film will be set in New York City.*

Sampling film semiotics: Metz

Saussure's theories of semiotics were designed to be applied to written and spoken language. Applying the theories to other types of communication presents exciting possibilities for new critical interpretations – but also highlights the differences between language and other cultural forms.

French theorist Christian Metz was the first to think through the complex implications of applying semiotics to film. His work is driven by two central questions:

- ✔ Is film really a language?

- ✔ If so, how do you map the constituent elements of the two systems (language and film) onto each other?

Metz's first attempts to apply semiotics to film produced mixed results:

- ✔ With Saussure's sign, the relationship between the signifier and the signified is arbitrary. Metz argued that the mechanical reproduction of reality found in the photograph and hence cinema image meant that this relationship wasn't down to chance. Cinema directly reflects reality instead of recreating it in symbolic fashion as language does.

- ✔ Saussure's rules of language (which he called *la langue*) depend on difference between a limited number of options (for instance, cinema isn't theatre). But cinema images are potentially infinite in variety, meaning that the paradigmatic axis is open, not closed as with *la langue*. In other words, we can't define an image of a dog by saying that it isn't a cat, or a pig, or a hamster, because this process could potentially go on forever.

- ✔ Metz argued that an image of a revolver in cinema means not just 'revolver' but 'here is a revolver!', which raises the question: does this make an image more like a sentence than a single sign or word? The problem here is that an individual image can't be broken down into smaller units of meaning.

Despite the complicating issues, Metz concluded that the syntagmatic axis of language, where meaning accumulates sequentially, *is* applicable to narrative cinema, because it constructs time and space using shots that produce meaning in relation to one another (again, consider the New York City establishing sequence).

By focusing on the syntagmatic axis of cinema, Metz came up with a detailed classification of filmic structure called *la grande syntagmatique*. This hierarchy of eight different levels has 'autonomous shots' at the top and 'ordinary sequences' at the bottom. In between come parallel intercutting, scenes and episodes. It's an impressive model, but even film theorists have struggled to apply it to actual texts. For example, John Ellis's attempt to apply the system to *Passport to Pimlico* (1949) concludes that the categories are too broad or too similar to each other to be easily separated. Even though the results are complex and challenging, Metz did found an entirely new way to think about film – which is pretty amazing.

Meeting mythic structures: Lévi-Strauss

As well as producing hard-wearing jeans (no, not really), the anthropologist Claude Lévi-Strauss was so impressed with Saussure's linguistic structuralism that he decided to apply it to entire cultures. He claimed that you can discuss anything from cooking to clothing as a language in terms of its use of signs and structure.

But here I'm most concerned with Lévi-Strauss's structural analysis of mythology, because it examines the status of stories within culture. His argument is pretty straightforward:

- ✔ Myths and legends told across the globe are hugely diverse but can all be boiled down to similar structures in their essence.

- ✔ Myths work like language in that they're comprised of individual units of meaning, or *mythemes,* combined into particular patterns.

- ✔ The underlying structures of myths are organised as *binary oppositions,* such as culture/nature, man/woman, good/bad and so on.

- ✔ The purpose of myths is to solve magically all the tensions and oppositions that you observe in the world and make you feel better.

Although culture has moved on a little since the days of myths and legends, clearly people still tell stories to make themselves feel better. Therefore, suggesting that film-making has taken on this function within society isn't much of a leap, particularly when you consider that film genres exhibit remarkably similar basic structures over time and across different cultures.

As Table 13-1 illustrates, *fundamental* (that is, defining) binary oppositions exist in any genre, but each one also develops its own variations on these themes. With the three examples in the table, each genre has a clear focus on one particular set of oppositions: for example, westerns are often about the tension between nature and civilisation with issues of gender being much less important, whereas rom-coms focus on the battle of the sexes and have weak or absent antagonists to represent evil.

Table 13-1   Lévi-Strauss's Binary Oppositions in Three FilmGenres

Genre and Example	Nature/ Civilisation	Man/Woman	Good/Bad
Western: *True Grit* (2010)	Mattie, Cogburn and LeBoeuf ride across the river into lawless Native-American territory.	Mattie emulates her father, not her mother. Narration reveals that she never marries.	The climactic showdown between Mattie and her father's killer.
Romantic comedy: *When Harry Met Sally* (1989)	Autumn leaves in Central Park illustrate time passing. Free love versus marriage.	Men want sex, and women want marriage. Marriage based on friendship wins out.	Social mores, such as pro-miscuity is bad, monogamy is good. Healthy and unhealthy relationships.
Horror: *Friday the 13th* (1980)	The abandoned campground where the killer stalks.	Sexual activity causes teens to get killed. The killer is a deranged mother.	Alice, the good 'final girl' over-comes the evil killer.

Lévi-Strauss's mythic structures operate at an unconscious level, and so bear in mind that storytellers aren't necessarily aware of why they use them or why audiences enjoy them.

Getting into Your Head: Psychoanalysis and Film

Psychoanalytic film theory is a way to uncover the hidden meaning from a text and a means of understanding the complex processes of film spectatorship. It *doesn't* aim to psychoanalyse film characters in order to work out why they behave the way they do – that would be crazy: characters aren't real people.

As a method of criticism, psychoanalysis works for all films, not just those that use the therapeutic process as a storytelling device or seek to explain the behaviours of heroes or villains through reference to traumatic childhoods.

Also, a film doesn't need to be explicitly surreal in visual style or dreamlike in structure. If psychoanalytic film theory works, it works universally. In this section I discuss the connections between dreaming and cinema, and how films may help to create our sense of ourselves. I also trace the importance of psychoanalysis within feminist film theory.

Delving into dreams: Freud and film

Sigmund Freud is credited with creating the practice of psychoanalysis, and his ideas on how the mind works are so influential that many of them have seeped into common usage. If someone unwittingly says something revealing, you attribute the slip to Freud. If a middle-aged man pulls up next to you in a bright red sports car, you roll your eyes and conclude that he's overcompensating for a lack of sexual prowess.

Pop psychology is fun. So why ruin it by trying to apply Freud's ideas to films? What's the logical connection between the study of human behaviour and understanding a movie? Consider these basic ideas of psychoanalysis:

- ✔ The human condition is an eternal conflict between your own drives and desires and the requirements that civilisation and culture impose.

- ✔ This conflict helps to create the three-part structure of your psyche: the id, the ego and the superego. You're born with your *id,* which is a seething mass of unregulated desire. Becoming an adult means developing a conscious and rational *ego* to moderate the id, as well as a strict *superego,* which is the internalised voice of authority.

- ✔ The poor, overworked ego spends its days negotiating between the chaotic, unruly id and the dry, authoritarian superego in order to keep just about sane. In the process, much of what your id desires is repressed into your psyche. But repression doesn't destroy desire, it merely delays it or converts it into other drives.

- ✔ While your rational ego is asleep, your dark, repressed desires escape into your dreams, typically in disguised, symbolic forms. Therefore, interpreting dreams can provide the key to understanding your psyche.

- ✔ Cinema can be viewed as a kind of collective dream, and so applying Freud's methods of interpretation to films can reveal the hidden desires of the author, or, more interestingly, those of the audience, who use the film as a fantasy space to play out their own desires.

Freud started this work by analysing myths, most famously the story of Oedipus from Greek legend. Oedipus is a tragic figure who, due to a long sequence of events, ends up killing his father and marrying his own mother.

Freud claimed that this narrative was an analogy for psychological development in children, with all people going through phases of desiring their mothers and wanting to kill their fathers. As disturbing and bizarre as this sounds, you can easily find similar structures in mainstream cinema when you choose to look for them: *Luke, I am your father. . . .*

Leaping through the looking glass: Lacan

Okay, take a deep breath, because in this section things start to get complicated. Jacques Lacan was a French psychoanalyst who picked up Freud's ideas about how human consciousness develops (such as the Oedipus analogy) and reformed them into a much more complex system. Why bother with it? Well, because a great deal of film theory already does.

Lacan, rather than Freud, was in vogue in the 1960s and 1970s, during the formative stage of much modern film theory. If you read classic film theory from that period, you almost certainly come across Lacan or his ideas. These discussions become incredibly annoying unless you can grasp the basics beforehand.

The most important element of Lacan for the purposes of film studies is his discussion of the *mirror stage* of psychological development. At this moment, an infant aged around 12 months first recognises her own image in a mirror. Just think for a second how profound this change is. Before you recognise your image, you just exist with no concept of self or the exterior world. Lacan calls this earlier state of pure existence *the real.* After the mirror stage, you understand that you have a body and are separate from the world. He calls this new phase of development *the imaginary.* You have yet to acquire language by entering *the symbolic,* and so you relate to the world primarily through images.

You can probably see some tempting connections to draw between Lacan's notion of the imaginary and the experience of cinema. Christian Metz (see 'Sampling film semiotics: Metz' earlier in this chapter) is responsible for opening this particular can of worms:

✔ Metz drew on Lacan's notion of the mirror phase with one important qualification: what you see in the mirror isn't yourself but an idealised notion of what you may be. As a baby, you can't yet control your own body. So the image is a fiction, and babies soon realise and accept that images are different to themselves.

✔ Metz proposed that the cinema screen operates as a kind of mirror, reflecting idealised versions of yourself. This idea is one possible explanation for the process of identification with fictional characters that you experience when involved with a film.

✔ Alternatively, Metz suggested that you identify not only with people on screen, but also with the *cinematic apparatus* itself. Sitting in the cinema watching a film, you feel as if you somehow create the images on screen, functioning as camera and projector. Yet you also know that this is an illusion, just like babies misrecognising themselves in mirrors.

All these ideas may sound sweet and innocent – babies and mirrors, how adorable! But don't worry, Lacan also gives plenty of messy ideas about sex and death to come to terms with. He follows Freud by discussing the Oedipus complex as the encounter with sexual difference that turns you into an adult. Lacan states that after you make it through this stage, you're forever in a state of *lack,* wanting subconsciously to go back to being baby, united with your mother's body. This impossible desire defines your entire life, leading you into relationships that can never fully satisfy. Cheery, huh? But just think about Hollywood's version of romance – such as Jerry Maguire proclaiming 'You complete me!' in the 1996 film named after him – and tell me that Lacan doesn't have a point. Even if it's buried beneath layers of interminable psychobabble.

Rejecting the male gaze: Mulvey

Film theorist Laura Mulvey investigates what she calls *the male gaze* at work in mainstream narrative cinema. Mulvey's work is vital to feminist film theory, partly because it formalises and explores a self-evident problem with film: male characters tend to act and female characters are passive, just there to look pretty. The concept of the male gaze draws on elements from Freud and Lacan's models of sexual pleasure (see the preceding two sections) to help explain women's 'to-be-looked-at-ness', the cinematic treatment of their bodies as display. Mulvey argues that this system of visual pleasure needs to be destroyed if women are ever to be considered equal in society.

The first of the *Transformers* movies (2007) contains a great example of the male gaze at work. Hapless hero Sam (Shia LaBeouf) picks up the gorgeous Mikaela (Megan Fox) in his car, only to find that it breaks down on the dusty highway. Sam is reduced to a gabbling wreck by the presence of Mikaela, who takes the initiative by tying her hair back, stepping out of the car and taking a look at the engine. Leaning her arms on the open bonnet she describes how the carburettor 'squirts the fuel in so you can go faster'. This pose displays her well-toned figure so perfectly that Sam is rendered almost speechless. The camera lingers on her midriff as he gazes uncontrollably at her.

The pleasure of the male gaze comprises two elements:

✔ **Scopophilia:** The pleasure of looking at a sexual object, which according to Freud is associated with power, because doing so subjects the object to a *controlling* gaze.

✔ **Narcissism:** The pleasure of looking at an image of oneself, drawing on Lacan's mirror stage (see the preceding section) to imply identification between male audience members and male characters on screen.

These two looks are magnified as men in the audience look at men on screen looking at women.

But here's a twist in the tale for the male bearer of the look. The image of the woman being looked at means sexual difference, which creates a primal fear in the male viewer – that of castration. No, seriously. Fear of castration is a big deal in psychoanalytic theory. It's important because the castration fear helps to explain the common and unsettling link between sex and violence on cinema screens, such as in slasher movies. Even if this fear doesn't manifest in real violence, it can justify the narrative 'punishment' of sexuality that crops up in most films noir, where the femme fatale has to die. Alternatively, women are *fetishised* and turned into abstract objects, for example in those famous Busby Berkeley dance routines of the 1930s.

Sisters, doing it for themselves

Much film theory is dominated by a succession of men: Marx, Freud, Lacan and so on. You need to see Laura Mulvey's radical attack on mainstream cinema and its male gaze in the context of a period when female academics and theorists shunted the great men aside and found their own voices. The cultural feminism of the 1970s and 1980s incorporated not only psychoanalysis, but also Marxism, literary theory and reception studies. The concept of *patriarchy* (the rule of the father) was added to capitalism as a force of ideological control over society. Feminist readings of film texts developed Louis Althusser's symptomatic approach to rich and productive ends.

In short, you can think of feminist film theory as a bridge between the grand theories of modernism (such as Marxism and psychoanalysis), and the hybrid approach to culture that typifies the various post-theories that I explore in Chapter 15.

Chapter 14

Praising Great Directors: Auteur Theory

*B*efore auteur theory emerged in the 1950s, so-called serious art critics considered movies as rubbish. Now they're often thought of as great works of art. How did this happen?

Well, many people argue that before you can talk about art, you need to have an artist, someone whose personal stamp you can detect on everything that they produce. Poets, authors, composers and painters all create the more 'respectable' art forms. In cinema, *auteur theory* places creative responsibility with the director.

After I define, dissect and debate auteur theory, in this chapter I also explore some good examples of individual auteurs of film history and of today. For ease of reference I have roughly grouped these film-makers chronologically: firstly, those who worked in the classical period of 1930 to 1960; secondly, those who emerged throughout the 1960s to the 1990s (most of whom are still active today); and, finally, some contemporary 21st century examples. In serving up these profiles, I had room to include only a select few, so how did I choose which made the grade and which were left aside?

  ✔ Firstly, there are several examples who have received so much attention within film studies that to leave them out would have been crazy. Stand up, Alfred Hitchcock, John Ford and Orson Welles, for example.

  ✔ Secondly, I have included directors who've had less written about them but who have all produced a substantial legacy of films which are recognisably *theirs* in some interesting way or another.

  ✔ Finally, I have broadened my focus to include both commercially successful Hollywood film-makers (notably Steven Spielberg) and more idiosyncratic directors with well-known art house appeal (such as David Lynch).

Seeing the Director as God

Some directors may well see themselves as gods (still think you're 'king of the world', Mr Cameron?), but plenty of humbler metaphors exist. You can think of the director as the conductor of an orchestra, making sure that all the creative elements synchronise perfectly and work in harmony. Or directors may function like creative blueprints, with all the people involved in the production trying to bring to life their own idea of 'a Spielberg film' or 'a Scorsese film'.

Whichever metaphor you prefer, clearly the director is an important figure in today's film culture. In order to understand why this is the case, you need to take a look back to the *cinéphiles* (film-lovers) of 1950s Paris, who analysed the themes, genre and mise-en-scène of popular movies to create the figure of the auteur.

Digging to the roots of auteur theory

As cinema flourished in the first half of the 20th century, critics writing about literature were free to examine poems, novels and plays in the light of an author's biography and personality. These analysts of high art never thought to look for personal expression in the picture houses. For old-school elitists, movies were cheap and vulgar; for radical Marxists (see Chapter 13), they were mindless fodder that industrial overlords churned out to keep the workers' minds off their dreary lives. Either way, nobody took film seriously.

The Romantics: This time it's personal

The idea that art is personal expression may seem obvious now, but this notion only became widespread over the last couple of centuries. Prior to the 18th century, painters and composers worked for the church or wealthy families, and poets were bearers of folk-art traditions. Assigning full creative control of great art to the artists themselves was illogical, even blasphemous.

Then the Romantic movement arrived (between around 1780 and 1850), with luminaries including poet William Wordsworth, composer Ludwig van Beethoven and painter William Blake. All their works demanded to be discussed as creations of very human geniuses. Ever since, artists (including film-makers) have been suffering to express their inner demons for the advancement of humanity.

Early avant-garde film-makers, such as Sergei Eisenstein (see Chapter 4), and artists from other mediums who experimented with film, such as Jean Cocteau, considered their work to be the polar opposite of corporate studio film-making (see Chapter 7). But the reach of their films was limited and had little impact on the general perception of Hollywood films as an industrial product (which I discuss in Chapter 9).

One country's intellectual culture, however, was sympathetic to cinema – France. So *that's* why they get to name all the key film studies terms in their own language.

François Truffaut started the whole auteur discussion. As a troubled, rebellious teen growing up in Paris in the 1940s, Truffaut took inspiration from the glut of American movies filling European cinemas after World War II. He gorged on films directed by John Ford, Alfred Hitchcock and Howard Hawks. Having been expelled from countless schools, he often watched three movies a day. This intensive viewing experience was vital for his later views on the stylistic and thematic connections between particular films.

Truffaut became a self-styled film critic and published an influential manifesto for cinema in 1954. His essay 'A Certain Tendency of the French Cinema' argues that:

- ✔ 'Quality' French cinema (mostly literary adaptation) was stultified, artistically bankrupt and dull, dull, dull. He didn't mince words, old Truffaut.

- ✔ Most French directors were merely *metteurs-en-scène* (literally 'someone who puts stuff into a shot'), meaning that they simply implemented the ideas of completed scripts passed to them by producers.

- ✔ Directors who had greater control over dialogue and story can be considered *auteurs* ('authors') of their work. This privileged list included serious film-makers such as Jean Renoir and Max Ophuls, but also the popular comedian Jacques Tati.

Truffaut's case was hardly free from self-interest; he wanted a new film industry filled with young bucks such as himself. And that's basically what happened: the French New Wave (for more see Chapter 11). But turning himself into an auteur only helped to strengthen Truffaut's case.

Linking auteur, theme and genre

For Truffaut and his French New Wave chums such as Andre Bazin and Jean-Luc Godard, the true artists of the cinema weren't the old-timers making respectable, quality films, but the Hollywood directors. The critical journal to which they all contributed during the 1950s, *Cahiers du Cinéma*, made a point of taking Hitchcock and Hawks as seriously as any European avant-garde film-maker, something that was genuinely revolutionary for film culture.

Working as a director in Hollywood during the studio era was a very different experience from shooting cheap films with your buddies on the streets of Paris. Most directors were employees of the studios, working under contract (see Chapter 9). They rarely wrote their own scripts, and so weren't literal auteurs like Truffaut's select few, and they almost never had the final say as to the content or style of their films. Nonetheless, the *Cahiers* critics argued that their bodies of work contained notable consistencies.

Auteur critics read recurring themes in a director's work as *an authorial signature,* placed upon the films in question as if they were paintings. So for example:

- ✔ John Ford's films are about the American landscape – and particularly the tension between domesticity and the wilderness.

- ✔ Hitchcock's films often feature 'ice maiden' female leads: cool, blond women who are as much of a mystery as the twisting plotlines.

- ✔ Charlie Chaplin's films often depict technology taking on a life of its own to comic effect.

Yet, perhaps perversely, the fact that many Hollywood auteurs worked within the confines of genre film-making (check out Chapter 5) only enhanced their claims to authorship. The auteur critics compared Ford's westerns and Chaplin's comedies to their contemporaries and found them to be superior due to their complex thematic content. In addition, if a film-maker was able to overcome restrictions, such as generic constraints or studio interference (as happened throughout Orson Welles's career) then the auteur critics concluded that they must qualify as an artistic genius.

American critic Andrew Sarris gave 'the auteur theory' its catchy title in an article for New York's *Village Voice* in 1962. Sarris made an explicit connection between recurring themes across a director's body of work and the director's own personality, or – to use Sarris's own term – the artist's '*élan of the soul*'. Sarris used this extremely Romantic criterion (see this chapter's sidebar 'The Romantics: This time it's personal') to create his own selected band of auteurs, including Hollywood and European avant-garde film-makers.

Seeing the auteur in mise-en-scène

As I discuss in Chapter 4, mise-en-scène is the stuff of film-making – sets, props, actors and so on – as well as how everything looks up on the screen. These elements are certainly the parts of the film-making process over which the director has most control, and so unsurprisingly auteurist film critics most closely scrutinise these aspects. Detailed, careful analysis of style within mainstream popular film-making was just as ground-breaking in the 1950s and early 1960s as the notion of directorial authorship – and was vital in the development of film studies as a discipline.

Although you can criticise the use of themes as authorial signatures or stamps (on the grounds that they're narrative elements often present in the script, over which the director may have very little control), in contrast, mise-en-scène analysis with an auteurist bent examines visual motifs and other stylistic elements to establish authorial presence.

Take a closer look at the mise-en-scène in a still (Figure 14-1) from Charlie Chaplin's *Modern Times* (1936). The setting is clearly industrial, a modernist factory with art deco fixtures that bring to mind Fritz Lang's *Metropolis* (1927). The grid lines of the large windows create a sense of imposing space, which diminishes the human figures in the frame. The workers are dressed in dirty uniforms that expose their arms, providing visual contrast between machinery and the human body.

Figure 14-1: Charlie Chaplin's *Modern Times* (1936).

Courtesy Everett Collection/REX

But the most important element of the mise-en-scène here is the director/star himself. Chaplin is smaller than the other actors, setting him apart. His physical performance in this sequence is one of increasing mania, as his rapidly repeated movements take over his body and bring chaos to the factory floor. The character Chaplin plays is literally crushed by the wheels of industry, but Chaplin the comedy star and director remains firmly in charge of the mechanical mise-en-scène, imposing his physical presence to wildly comic effect.

As this example demonstrates, nothing of what you see on screen is accidental, and you can read all elements as signalling authorial presence. Chaplin the actor, director, screenwriter and producer is probably as close to being the author of his films as possible within the Hollywood system. In this scene, he may be referencing German Expressionist films to construct a satire of the dehumanising effects of technology, but he's also, fundamentally, being very, very silly indeed. And that's the true nature of Chaplin's genius.

Debunking auteur theory

Auteur theory was an important step in order for film studies to become a standalone discipline. It provided a critical framework that allowed critics to take popular cinema as seriously as avant-garde or art films and generated some fantastic close readings of film style and form. It also enabled the French New Wave by handing creative control to ambitious young directors, as well as inspiring plenty of other film-makers around the world. But does it stand up as a rigorous methodology?

One of the most interesting effects of auteur theory is that it sparked many arguments in the public sphere of film criticism. Andrew Sarris, the critic who brought Truffaut's ideas to the American public (and incidentally was the first to call it an actual 'theory') was soon locked in a productive debate with the lead critic of *The New Yorker,* Pauline Kael. Table 14-1 summarises their entertaining face off.

To be fair to auteur criticism as a whole, Sarris's essay, although influential, is a bit of an easy target. The writings of auteurist critics in the British journal *Movie* (1960–1990) are much more clearly argued and based upon detailed analysis of evidence from the film texts. The *Movie* method was also established as the foundation of film studies as an academic discipline in the UK after its main critics VF Perkins, Robin Wood and Charles Barr became the first film professors (for more on these pioneers, see Chapter 17). Meanwhile Peter Wollen and others substantially developed the basic ideas of auteur theory (see the sidebar, 'Reshaping Auteur Theory').

Table 14-1   Andrew Sarris Versus Pauline Kael on Auteur Theory

Andrew Sarris	*Pauline Kael*
The joy of auteur theory is in noticing vital similarities across a director's body of work.	All directors borrow and steal from each other and their own work. Some repeat themselves incessantly.
Auteurs are directors of sublime technical competence and ability.	Why prefer technically competent films to exciting experimental ones?
The mark of an auteur is the distinguishable personality of the director.	The smell of a skunk is more distinguishable than a rose; does that make it better?
Auteurs have an '*élan* of the soul' that other directors lack.	This statement isn't criticism, it's a vague, subjective feeling at best.
The auteur's 'inner meaning' comes from the tension between his material and his personality.	Why waste time watching mediocre films to find a bit of personality? See all the great work instead.

Critical debate is never a bad thing, and despite the backlash auteur theory helped to legitimise the serious study of popular culture, for which everyone – not least the writer of this particular book – is very grateful.

Reshaping auteur theory

The auteur theory always was a controversial idea. Film critics in the 1950s and 60s and, eventually, film scholars in the 1970s and onwards continued to argue about its usefulness, resulting in several important revisions to the original theory. For example, in the late 1960s film theorist Peter Wollen pointed out that there was an important difference between real-life film-makers – say, Alfred Hitchcock – and their artistic identities, which he put into inverted commas to separate the two. So, rather than being a real person, 'Alfred Hitchcock' is a term that refers to his directorial persona accumulated across many films.

Wollen also borrowed bits from the structuralist approach to culture made famous by Levi-Strauss (see Chapter 13). The earlier auteur critics focused on *similarities* between a director's films as signals of artistic genius, but Wollen's new 'auteur-structuralism' searched for *tensions* between binary oppositions, such as nature versus civilisation. Importantly, this allowed films of completely different styles or genres by the same film-maker to be considered alongside each other, resulting in fruitful readings of directors such as Howard Hawks whose creative legacy is very diverse.

Encountering Old-School Auteurs (1930s to 1950s)

The first directors that auteur critics took seriously were those who worked during the studio era of Hollywood (and elsewhere). They didn't necessarily set out to be great artists, but they all produced inspiring bodies of work within industrial and generic constraints. Whatever you feel about auteur theory, the following directors' careers helped to shape the discipline of film studies, and they each made films that easily stand the test of time.

John Ford: The American landscape

When a young, over-enthusiastic Jean-Luc Godard interviewed John Ford for *Cahiers du Cinéma* in the late 1950s, he asked 'What brought you to Hollywood?' and Ford responded 'a train'. This bit of industry legend survives because it sums up Ford's bluff, no-nonsense response to the many accolades he received throughout his long career. Ford directed more than 140 movies, won four Oscars for directing (still an industry record) and was the first recipient of the American Film Institute's (AFI) Lifetime Achievement Award in 1971.

Themes and style

Key aspects of Ford's work include:

- **Absent family:** In Ford's films the home is a vital touchstone, and so when family members go missing someone must find or avenge them. See: *My Darling Clementine* (1946), *The Searchers* (1956), *Donovan's Reef* (1963).

- **Cowboys and Indians:** Although Native Americans are bad guys in most of his westerns, during his later career Ford spoke of his sympathies for the Native American cause. The jury is still out. See: *Stagecoach* (1939), *Cheyenne Autumn* (1964).

- **The Wild West:** Ford's favoured wide compositions place human figures against nature and history. He often shot on the spectacular location of Monument Valley in Utah and Arizona. See: *Fort Apache* (1948), *She Wore a Yellow Ribbon* (1949).

- **Playing the fool:** Many of Ford's staunch heroes are set against foolish sidekicks, often played by his brother Frank. See: *Steamboat Round the Bend* (1935), *Young Mr Lincoln* (1939).

Critical reputation

John Ford's importance for Hollywood history can hardly be overstated. His status within film studies was secured as soon as the auteurist critics turned their attention to Hollywood and found unifying themes and style across so many popular and influential films. His powerful personality is certainly stamped upon his best work. Ford is often cited as an influence on other directors; Orson Welles claimed to have watched *Stagecoach* 40 times while making *Citizen Kane* (1941) – check out 'Orson Welles: The self-styled genius' later in this chapter.

Where to start

The Searchers has it all: spectacular, burnt orange landscapes; a moving child kidnap plot; a classic Max Steiner score; and John Wayne being John Wayne. Oh, and one of the best endings ever shot.

Howard Hawks: Screwball and highballs

Howard Hawks was born in 1896 to wealthy industrialists. He was an Ivy League graduate in engineering, but from an early age was more interested in fast cars and racing. He also flew planes in his military service. Upon moving to Hollywood he consolidated his network of 'men's men', produced his own silent shorts and was soon taken on by Fox as a director. He later moved from studio to studio with unusual freedom. He went on to write, produce or direct around 50 films, but only won an Honorary Oscar in 1975.

Themes and style

Key aspects of Hawks's work include:

- **Variety is the spice of life:** Unlike most auteur directors, Hawks was renowned for work in many different genres, including war films such as *Only Angels Have Wings* (1939), musicals like *Gentlemen Prefer Blondes* (1953) and even sci-fi – he certainly produced *The Thing from Another World* (1951) and probably directed it, although he gave the official credit to Christian Nyby so he could get Directors Guild membership.

- **One of the guys:** His films often contain scenes of male bonding within macho groups – see *Hatari!* (1962) – but he also gives screen time to strong (some may say) masculine women, including Lauren Bacall in *To Have and Have Not* (1944).

- **Role reversals:** Many of Hawks's screwball comedies play with switching roles: male/female (*I Was a Male War Bride* (1949)), adult/child (*Monkey Business* (1952)), controlled/chaotic (*Bringing Up Baby* (1938)).

- **Snappy dialogue:** Hawks worked closely with his favourite screenwriters to produce rapid-fire, often overlapping dialogue that creates pace and zip. In *His Girl Friday* (1940), Cary Grant and Rosalind Russell trade lines such as: 'You're wonderful, in a loathsome sort of a way'.

Critical reputation

If Hollywood's true genius is found in its professionalism, fun and sheer unbridled energy then Howard Hawks *is* Hollywood. He hated 'message movies' which preached to their audience, was unconcerned with visual style and repeated the same plot devices over and over again – but he knew how to entertain an audience. Actually, Hawks's tendency to repeat plots across different genres makes him a darling of the auteur-structuralist approach (see Chapter 15). His powerful female characters have also received attention from feminist film scholars.

Where to start

If you don't get a kick out of watching kooky Katharine Hepburn torturing uptight Cary Grant in *Bringing Up Baby,* you're probably clinically dead. The movie even has a leopard wandering down the street in Connecticut for heaven's sake.

Alfred Hitchcock: The master of suspense

With his portly frame and haughty demeanour, Alfred Hitchcock is surely the most recognisable of all film directors. This fame is no accident, because Hitchcock was a master showman and self-publicist, appearing in trailers, TV shows and often within his own films as an uncredited extra. His status as a celebrity director leant him great power over his own career. Hitchcock was English and worked in the British film industry for nearly 20 years before moving to Hollywood in 1940. His legacy of popular and artistically ambitious thrillers produced on both sides of the Atlantic make him a heavyweight auteur.

Themes and style

Key aspects of Hitchcock's work include:

- ✔ **Guilt and innocence:** Hitchcock's heroes are often falsely accused men as in *The 39 Steps* (1935) and *North by Northwest* (1959), whereas his heroines are mysterious or guilty women as in *Blackmail* (1929) and *Vertigo* (1958).

- ✔ **The killer inside:** Psychopaths and sociopaths lurk within domestic environments, not just in *Psycho* (1960), but also in *The Lodger* (1927) and *Rope* (1948).

- ✔ **Dissecting stardom:** Hitchcock explores the darker sides of several much-loved and wholesome stars including Jimmy Stewart in *Rear Window* (1954) and Ingrid Bergman in *Notorious* (1946).

- ✔ **Look *and* listen:** Hitchcock's visuals are influenced by German Expressionism as in *The Wrong Man* (1956) and Soviet montage in *that* shower scene, but his experimental use of sound was just as striking, especially in early British sound film *Blackmail.*

Critical reputation

In interviews, Hitchcock deliberately played with ideas derived from psychology, including sadism (torturing the audience) and voyeurism (looking at things you shouldn't). So unsurprisingly a fair proportion of the many critical readings of his films are psychoanalytical in nature, some of the best being those by Robin Wood. Hitchcock's American films received far more attention from early auteurists than his British ones, an imbalance that Tom Ryall and Charles Barr have since corrected.

Where to start

If you've already watched *Psycho,* check out *Vertigo.* It has a gorgeous expressionistic use of colour, an icy (dyed) blonde heroine and an incredible score by Bernard Herrmann. But most of all, it's utterly deranged and disturbed.

Michael Powell and Emeric Pressburger: Two for the price of one

Wait a minute, who exactly is the auteur here? The answer is both. English director Michael Powell and Hungarian screenwriter Emeric Pressburger were very different personalities, but they worked so closely together on a series of great British films that they took joint credit for writing, directing and producing. Alexander Korda brought them together at the start of World War II and they set up The Archers production company in 1943. They produced a string of popular and acclaimed films before Powell's career (without Pressburger) was destroyed by the failure *Peeping Tom* (1960).

Themes and style

Key aspects of Powell and Pressburger's work include:

- ✔ **Poetry and propaganda:** During World War II they produced films with propaganda agendas; *49th Parallel* (1941) aimed to bring the US into the conflict. They also caused controversy by making a sympathetic German soldier the true hero of *The Life and Death of Colonel Blimp* (1943).

- ✔ **Flights of fantasy:** Their films stand out from the realist tradition of British cinema (see Chapter 10), because they're wildly imaginative and fantastical, notably *A Matter of Life and Death* (1946) and *Black Narcissus* (1947).

- ✔ **Highbrow ambitions:** They were unafraid to tackle opera in *The Tales of Hoffmann* (1951), ballet in *The Red Shoes* (1948) or even Geoffrey Chaucer in *A Canterbury Tale* (1944).

- ✔ **Technicolor dreams:** Powell gave legendary cinematographer Jack Cardiff his first major feature in *A Matter of Life and Death*, and his Technicolor photography gives many of their films a dreamlike beauty.

Critical reputation

Powell's joint authorship with Pressburger is still so unusual in the film industry that it creates an interesting and important challenge to the auteurist cult of the individual (you could also think about the Coen Brothers and the Wachowskis in this light). Powell and Pressburger's love of myth and escapist fantasy also undermines the commonly held view that the Brits only make grim realist films. Surviving relatives have tended their legacy: Powell's widow is Martin Scorsese's editor Thelma Schoonmaker and Pressburger's grandsons are the film-makers Andrew and Kevin Macdonald.

Where to start

If you think you don't like classic British films, just try *A Matter of Life and Death*. It's funny and deeply moving, looks incredible (thanks to Jack Cardiff) and its brilliant use of colour serves as a twisted mirror image of *The Wizard of Oz* (1939), in that here reality is in gaudy Technicolor and heaven in pearly black and white.

Orson Welles: The self-styled genius

Orson Welles didn't need auteur theory to turn himself into a genius, but it helped. Born to an influential Chicago family, he was a prodigious child musician but later rejected a Harvard scholarship in order to travel to Europe. In Ireland he bluffed his way onto the stage where he became an instant success, and he was directing major stage shows in New York by his early 20s. His radio broadcast of *The War of the Worlds* in 1938 reportedly prompted national panic. RKO then granted him an unprecedented level of freedom for an unproven director, and the result was *Citizen Kane* (1941). His career was troubled, but the films he left behind are among the most ambitious in Hollywood's history.

Themes and style

Key aspects of Welles's work include:

- **Tragic heroes:** Welles knew what to steal from Shakespeare – heroes with grand ambitions but also tragic flaws that bring them down in the end. See: *Citizen Kane, The Magnificent Ambersons* (1942).

- **Actor-director:** Welles acted in many of his own films but also took work for other film-makers, playing memorable villains in *The Third Man* (1949) and *A Man for All Seasons* (1966).

- **Deep focus:** Andre Bazin loved Welles for his deep framing, which often has several planes of action going on simultaneously. Look at an early scene in *Citizen Kane,* which frames its hero as a child playing outside in the snow while his fate is decided by his poor parents inside the house.

✔ **The illusionist:** Welles was a well-known amateur magician, and his love of theatrical illusion crops up in his films. Check out the transformation of the house in *Magnificent Ambersons* from a winter's day to a summer's evening through clever lighting effects.

Critical reputation

Two words: 'Citizen' and 'Kane'. Welles's first film was audacious, and it came along at precisely the right time, when auteurist critics were looking for the classics of cinema to rank alongside other art forms. It has since reigned almost unchallenged as 'the greatest film ever made'.

Welles is the perfect Romantic auteur (see the sidebar 'The Romantics: This time it's personal'), because his genius burned brightly but not for long, and he was practically martyred by his biggest fans. As ever, Pauline Kael (see the earlier section 'Debunking auteur theory') provided some measure of reason to the debate; although she was a fan, she argued convincingly not to overlook the contributions of his collaborators.

Where to start

Welles was great as a stage impresario in *The Muppet Movie* (1979). I'm kidding. Just watch *Citizen Kane* and see what the fuss is all about.

Meeting the Essential Modern Auteurs (1960s to 1990s)

Auteurism opened up a conversation about the cultural status of cinema and the role of the director that continued from the 1960s onwards. As this section demonstrates, modern auteurs had the artistic freedom to combine influences from Hollywood, Europe, world cinema and avant-garde films. Most of these directors are still working today, and longevity certainly helps cement their auteur status. If you're familiar with their recent films, looking back to their earlier work will give you a much richer understanding of their creative personalities.

Stanley Kubrick: An epic perfectionist

Stanley Kubrick grew up in a middle-class Jewish family in New York City. His great love from an early age was photography, and in the 1940s and early 50s he became involved in the city's modern art movement. He shot documentaries and low-budget war and crime films before a brief foray into Hollywood with *Spartacus* (1960). He moved to England to shoot *Lolita* (1962) and enjoyed the experience so much that he never permanently returned to the US. A notorious perfectionist, who shot hundreds of takes, and a virtual recluse, Kubrick produced challenging and controversial films until his death in 1999.

Themes and style

Key aspects of Kubrick's work include:

- ✔ **Behind the mask:** Disturbing images of the human body obscured by masks or prosthetics recur in Kubrick's films, including *The Killing* (1956), *A Clockwork Orange* (1971) and *Eyes Wide Shut* (1999).

- ✔ **Pushing boundaries:** Kubrick's adaptation of *Lolita* challenged the censors and had to exclude explicit eroticism, while *A Clockwork Orange* wasn't banned but was rather withdrawn from circulation in cinemas by the director himself after it was linked with a copycat killing.

- ✔ **Careful composition:** Kubrick lends his images a sense of heightened, composed reality, which makes them iconic, notably riding the bomb in *Dr Strangelove* (1963) and the star child of *2001: A Space Odyssey* (1968).

- ✔ **A chilly distance:** Don't worry if you feel yourself held at a distance from his characters. Kubrick didn't particularly care whether you care or not.

Critical reputation

As a self-styled 'serious' film-maker, Kubrick wasn't loved by the original auteurists, but his reputation has grown in recent decades. Film critics and scholars commonly discuss Kubrick's intellectual and arty films as part of grand ideas such as 20th-century modernism. However he also attracted charges of misogyny from feminist critics over his challenging representations of female sexuality.

Where to start

2001 is the original new-age sci-fi epic. Watch it and be impressed. And puzzled.

Martin Scorsese: Storyteller of the streets

Martin Scorsese was born in New York in 1942 to second-generation Sicilian-American parents and grew up in Manhattan's colourful Little Italy district. He spent much of his childhood indoors suffering from severe asthma, and so trips to the cinema were a powerful escape. He planned to be a priest and enrolled in Catholic College aged 14 before being kicked out for teenage behaviour. In 1966 he was one of the first graduates from New York University's new Film School. B-movie producer Roger Corman was his early mentor, and he became friends with the influential 'movie brats' (a group of young, film-literate directors) including Francis Ford Coppola. He has been married five times and conquered cocaine addition, but now into his 70s he's as popular and acclaimed as ever.

Themes and style

Key aspects of Scorsese's work include:

- ✔ **New York, New York:** Scorsese's most personal films are firmly rooted in the city and Italian-American community where he grew up. Before the 1990s clean-up, those streets were pretty mean. See: *Mean Streets* (1973), *Taxi Driver* (1976), *Gangs of New York* (2002).

- ✔ **Guilt and redemption:** Scorsese's characters are morally ambiguous, and many are involved in crime or violence. Guilt requires redemption, involving penance or suffering. In *Raging Bull* (1980), Jake la Motta hits rock bottom in prison before he shows any remorse for his violence.

- ✔ **Moments in time:** Freeze-frames mark moments of character development or disrupt the flow of time for dramatic or comedic reasons, such as the dwarf tossing in *The Wolf of Wall Street* (2013).

- ✔ **Pop music:** *Mean Streets* was one of the first movies to use well-known pop songs as a score, and his later films feature tracks from The Rolling Stones, Cream and Ray Charles.

Critical reputation

Scorsese is extremely movie-literate and modelled himself as an auteur after the European model of personal, independent film-making. His early films can therefore be compared to those of Italian Neorealism and the French New Wave (see Chapter 11). In his later career, his gangster films are ripe for discussions of masculinity and contemporary ethics. He's a noted champion of film preservation, overseeing the restoration of many classics including films by Powell and Pressburger and Akira Kurosawa. Despite almost unanimous acclaim and popularity, he didn't win an Oscar until 2006.

Where to start

Goodfellas (1990) is the perfect first Scorsese film with its tale of the rise and fall (or fall and rise) of a blue-collar gangster in New York. It's funny, violent and stylish all at the same time.

Steven Spielberg: The kid who never grew up

Steven Spielberg was born in 1946, making him part of the post-World War II baby-boom generation. As the child of divorced orthodox Jewish parents he faced prejudice at school and started making (and exhibiting) his own 8 mm films at an early age. He was unsuccessful in applying to film school in California, but while working as an intern for Universal Studios, he made a short that won him a job directing for TV. His first feature film flopped, but his second, *Jaws* (1975), became such a huge hit that it forever changed the way studios release their films (check out Chapter 9 for details). His subsequent career has seen unparalleled popularity and profits.

Themes and style

Key aspects of Spielberg's work include:

- ✔ **The inner child:** Spielberg's films aim to capture the wonder and excitement of childhood and often have child (or childish) protagonists, as in *E.T. the Extra-Terrestrial* (1982), *Hook* (1991) and *A.I. Artificial Intelligence* (2001).

- ✔ **High concept:** Hollywood likes ideas that can be grasped immediately. What if someone brought back the dinosaurs? What if Peter Pan grew up? What if the authorities were able to catch murderers *before* they killed? That'll be *Jurassic Park* (1993), *Hook* and *Minority Report* (2002) in a nutshell.

- ✔ **Emotional storytelling:** Spielberg isn't afraid of big emotional moments and often uses close-ups to capture actors' awestruck reactions to off-screen events. See: *Close Encounters of the Third Kind* (1977), *Jurassic Park*.

- ✔ **Keep on moving:** Spielberg's films are packed with movement, most obviously from his action-hero characters, but also generated by his fluid camera, which often moves rather than cuts, as in the Omaha beach sequence in *Saving Private Ryan* (1998).

Critical reputation

Spielberg's enormous popularity came before his critical rehabilitation. For a long time he was blamed for the 'dumbed down' blockbuster mentality of contemporary Hollywood. But being this successful for so long doesn't happen by insulting your audience's intelligence. Spielberg is a master craftsman and a highly effective storyteller. If you want to understand Hollywood cinema, with all its associated pleasures and political compromises, his films are a perfect place to start.

Where to start

Spielberg's films are so familiar that engaging with them critically can be challenging. So try watching his early made-for-TV movie *Duel* (1971) to spot those Spielberg moments of tension, surprise and kinetic excitement.

Quentin Tarantino: Uber-movie-geek

Quentin Tarantino came from humble beginnings in Tennessee and grew up in Los Angeles. He hated school and left as soon as possible, but he was obsessive about movies from an early age. He was taken to R-rated movies by his mother and her boyfriends. Later, as an employee of a porn theatre and then famously a video store, he was exposed to all varieties of extreme and cult films. He had some training as an actor but is a self-taught director. His debut, the heist movie *Reservoir Dogs* (1992) was an immediate hit, and although he's not the most prolific of directors, his films have generally matched critical approval with bankable success.

Themes and style

Key aspects of Tarantino's work include:

- ✔ **Stuck in the middle:** Tarantino's scripts are often nonlinear in structure, and so they start somewhere in the middle and may end with the beginning. In *Reservoir Dogs,* the audience sees events before and after the bungled heist but never the heist itself.

- ✔ **Talk the talk:** Characters chat about all kinds of banal stuff, with banter and pop-culture references filling entire sections of *Pulp Fiction* (1994) and the tense 'guess who' scene of *Inglourious Basterds* (2009).

- ✔ **Pleasure and pain:** Extreme violence is never far away in Tarantino's universe and is often visualised in excruciating detail, including decapitations in *Kill Bill: Volume 1* (2003) and the car as weapon in *Death Proof* (2007).

- ✔ **Hollywood and beyond:** Tarantino's role models are wide-ranging, from the French New Wave to Hong Kong action cinema to legendary B-movie producer Roger Corman.

Critical reputation

If you want to try and explain postmodernism to someone, probably the easiest way is to say: 'You know *Pulp Fiction*? Like that.' Tarantino's films tick all the postmodern boxes: generic deconstruction, check; pop culture meets high culture, check; nostalgia, check. His films are also vital examples in debates around cinema violence and its impact on audiences. Although Tarantino is a vocal critic of film school, he's a clear advocate for engaging with the whole of film history, from cult films to great classics. He's also probably the most-cited director in current film-student essays and dissertations.

Where to start

Reservoir Dogs has all the Tarantino trademarks but none of the self-indulgence: horrific violence, hilarious dialogue, clever structure, perfect use of cheesy music. It's all right there.

David Lynch: The American nightmare

Lynch grew up moving from small town to small town in Middle America, which provided him with the settings of many of his later films. He didn't get on with formal education but thrived as a student of painting in Philadelphia.

He moved to Los Angeles with his wife and young daughter and received a small grant from the AFI to make *Eraserhead* (1977), a disturbing surrealist vision of parenthood. Despite his idiosyncratic style he has produced notable commercial successes, including *The Elephant Man* (1980) and his TV murder mystery *Twin Peaks* (1990–1). His odd personality and strange behaviour make him the subject of much intrigue.

Themes and style

Key aspects of Lynch's work include:

- **Small-town America:** Lynch's films and TV shows reveal dark desires lurking behind brightly painted facades. *Blue Velvet* (1985) and *Twin Peaks* are notably creepy, but Lynch also made the affectionate and quietly moving *The Straight Story* (1999) about a dying man's travels through Americana.

- **Dream logic:** Nothing is what it seems, different actors may play the same character and stories shift inexplicably in space and time. See: *Mulholland Dr.* (2001), *Inland Empire* (2006).

- **Symbolic motifs:** Lynch uses visual motifs that are repeated across his films, such as lighting matches, moving road markings lit by headlights and female torch singers. These invite endless speculation as to their meaning, partly because Lynch steadfastly refuses to explain them.

- **Music lover:** Lynch has released his own weird music and the sound in his films is equally distinctive. He blends 1950s pop tunes with jazz and melodramatic classical scoring, while industrial white noise throbs in the background.

Critical reputation

Lynch has never been short of critical attention, though he generally refuses to offer explanations for his mysterious work. His films and TV shows fit well within an understanding of postmodernism, in that they smash the barriers between high and low culture and constantly question stable identity and meaning. Lynch's surrealism also invites psychoanalytical readings around sexuality and violence. In his more recent films, the narrative logic has become more and more complex, inviting comparisons with other *puzzle films* such as Christopher Nolan's *Memento* (2000) – check out the later section 'Christopher Nolan: Worlds within worlds'.

Where to start

Blue Velvet is a remarkable, candy-coloured film noir with a square-jawed hero, a sadomasochistic femme fatale and a terrifying villain played by Dennis Hopper. Just don't watch it at home alone.

Turning Attention to 21st Century Auteurs (1999 to today)

Only time will tell whether the film-makers in this section join the ranks of the greatest auteurs, but the early champions of Hitchcock and Welles didn't let that bother them, so why should you.

Plenty of contemporary film-makers aside from those I include in this section have serious auteur potential: David Fincher, Sofia Coppola and Peter Jackson to name but a few. Try to keep track of your favourite director's work, the awards they win, how critics and audiences talk about them, and whether their films seem to become more important as time moves on, and you could watch them blossom into fully fledged auteurs.

Ang Lee: The hidden dragon

Ang Lee's life and films are the very definition of transnational. He grew up in Taiwan, to Chinese parents, but was a theatre student in the US. Experiments with film-making gained him entrance to Tisch School of the Arts of New York University, where he trained alongside another famous Lee (Spike), but he didn't release his first feature until he was 37. His surprise hit *The Wedding Banquet* (1993) opened doors in Hollywood, where he worked in diverse genres and styles. In 2006 he became the first Asian director to win an Oscar for directing *Brokeback Mountain* (2005), and he won a second for *Life of Pi* in 2012.

Themes and style

Key aspects of Lee's work include:

- ✔ **Unspoken desires:** Lee's films are fuelled by repression, be it sexual in *Brokeback Mountain* and *Lust, Caution* (2007), emotional in *The Ice Storm* (1997) and *Sense and Sensibility* (1995), or, erm, something to do with gamma rays in *Hulk* (2003).

- ✔ **East meets West:** Lee's early films are about characters caught between Chinese and American culture, and in his third, *Eat Drink Man Woman* (1994), a traditional Taiwanese family faces pressures from globalisation.

- ✔ **Global Chinese Cinema:** *Crouching Tiger, Hidden Dragon* (2000) is by far the highest grossing foreign language film in the US, establishing a market for Zhang Yimou's *Hero* (2002) and stars such as Zhang Ziyi.

- ✔ **The third dimension:** Lee was the first director to win an Oscar for a 3D film with *Life of Pi,* which considered alongside *Hugo* (2011) and *Gravity* (2013) represents a new critical acceptance of the technology.

Critical reputation

Although Hong Kong action films and international epics such as *The Last Emperor* (1987) established Western awareness of Asian cinema, Ang Lee's career represents a new phase in this relationship. His image as a softly spoken intellectual proves that you don't have to be a bullish egomaniac to qualify as a contemporary auteur.

Where to start

The Wedding Banquet is a charming and effective culture-clash comedy. It's sadly lacking in flying sword fights though.

Christopher Nolan: Worlds within worlds

Christopher Nolan was born in England but grew up on both sides of the Atlantic and has dual British-American citizenship. He taught himself to make films using basic 8 mm equipment, and although he studied English Literature at university he used his student years to develop 16mm short films. He self-financed his first feature *Following* (1998), which attracted enough attention on the festival circuit to get him a deal for *Memento* (2000), a mind-bending indie thriller that was a critical and commercial hit. His dark and gritty reboot of the Batman character has been so successful that he now has the power to produce challenging films with blockbuster budgets.

Themes and style

Key aspects of Nolan's work include:

- **Memories are made of this:** Nolan's films play with the relationship between stories and memory, and his characters are often psychologically damaged. In *Memento,* his hero has no long-term memory and *Inception* (2010) is about implanting fake memories.

- **Russian dolls:** In Nolan's short *Doodlebug* (1997), a man squishes a bug only to find that it's a miniature version of himself and that he's next for the boot. A similar, infinitely expandable logic structures *Inception's* multiple parallel worlds.

- **Realistic fantasies:** *Batman Begins* (2005) cuts out the baroque archness of superhero movies to produce something raw and believable, whereas *The Dark Knight* (2008) blends hand-held camerawork and improvisation with enormous spectacular set pieces shot on large-format and high-definition IMAX film stock.

- **Moral uncertainty:** Nolan's films have few clear-cut heroes and villains, and threats are sudden and mysterious in origin – inviting comparisons with American society's climate of fear and uncertainty post-9/11.

Critical reputation

Nolan is a key postmodern auteur because he appears to make personal, distinctive films within the Hollywood mainstream. He has legions of passionate supporters, demonstrating that directors are clearly considered the primary authors of their films within popular film culture. Fans and students discuss Nolan's nonlinear stories alongside those of Tarantino, David Lynch and others as puzzle films, which deconstruct themselves for the pleasures of a postmodern audience.

Where to start

You need to watch *Memento* at least twice to understand its intricate plotting. Luckily the steamy, noir-ish story is well worth the required effort.

Kathryn Bigelow: Boys and their guns

Kathryn Bigelow is certainly not the only acclaimed female director. That list would also include Jane Campion, Mira Nair and many others. However, Bigelow is an unusual case of a female auteur, in the sense that she has produced a body of distinctive and (some would say) personal films – within the Hollywood mainstream. Bigelow came to film-making through painting and avant-garde film culture and was tutored by auteur-structuralist scholar Peter Wollen (see sidebar 'Reshaping Auteur Theory' above). A string of successes put her on the directing A-list, until the commercial disaster of *Strange Days* (1995). For her comeback film, *The Hurt Locker* (2008) she was not only the first woman to win Best Director at the Academy Awards, but also beat fellow nominee and ex-husband James Cameron.

Themes and style

Key aspects of Bigelow's work include:

- ✔ **Boys' films:** Bigelow made her name working in genres traditionally seen as masculine – horror, cop thrillers and war movies. Some critics claim that her films deconstruct these genres through excess: too much of everything that audiences love about them (guns, explosions and so on).

- ✔ **Packing a pistol:** Guns are cinema's primary phallic symbols (honestly). So in *Blue Steel* (1989), when a female cop and a male thief battle for possession of a pistol, more is clearly at stake than just weaponry.

- ✔ **Points of view:** Bigelow frequently employs shots that reflect characters' points of view, playing with perception and notions of first-person narration. This theme is the entire plot of *Strange Days,* but also features in the chase sequences of *Point Break* (1991).

- ✔ **Casualties of war:** Although Iraq war drama *The Hurt Locker* was a legendary comeback, Bigelow's follow-up, *Zero Dark Thirty* (2012), split critics over its apparent support of torture in the war on terror.

Critical reputation

Bigelow's awareness of film theory (and ability to cite it in interviews) means that her apparently glossy and superficial movies are ripe for alternative readings. Her concern with looking and vision, particularly around issues of gender and violence, are easily connected to Laura Mulvey's theories about the 'male gaze' of cinema (see Chapter 13). The big question posed by Bigelow's career is: why is she the only recognised female auteur of popular cinema? Well, others might qualify, such as Penny Marshall – actor, prolific producer and director of *Big* (1988) and *A League of Their Own* (1992) – but unfortunately Marshall's aren't the kind of films that get (mostly male) film critics excited. Bigelow plays the big boys at their own game.

Where to start

Point Break is perfect for film students in that it's supremely entertaining and deceptively smart. Also, don't Keanu Reeves and Patrick Swayze make a lovely couple?

Guillermo del Toro: Monster moviemaker

Guillermo del Toro was born in Guadalajara, Mexico, and raised a strict Catholic. While working as a special-effects make-up artist, he was also busy writing and directing short films and setting up film festivals in his home town. His first feature *Cronos* (1993) was an international film-festival favourite that led Miramax to fund his second film. After an initial unhappy encounter with Hollywood, he made his next two films as Mexican-Spanish co-productions to great acclaim. For *Hellboy* (2004), del Toro was given greater control by the film's producers, and since then has worked successfully on big-budget international projects, as a writer-director and as a producer.

Themes and style

Key aspects of del Toro's work include:

- ✔ **Metaphorical monsters:** His remarkable monsters, including the Pale Man from *Pan's Labyrinth* (2006), whose eyeballs are in his hands, and the gigantic Kaiju of *Pacific Rim* (2013), are modern fairy tale creations, rich in symbolic meaning.

- ✔ **Comic-book guy:** He considers comic books as great popular literature and has adapted and directed *Blade II* (2002) and the *Hellboy* franchise.

- ✔ **Mexican movies:** Together with his friends Alfonso Cuarón and Alejandro González Iñárritu, del Toro brought Mexican cinema to new international audiences and created strong links with Hollywood (see Chapter 12 for more on these 'three amigos').

- ✔ **Director-producer:** del Toro is just as happy producing films as directing them, and his recent production credits include *The Orphanage* (2007), *Biutiful* (2010) and the upcoming *Kung Fu Panda 3*.

Critical reputation

Guillermo del Toro's status as an auteur straddles both senses of the term. He has made critically adored art films (*Pan's Labyrinth* featured high on many lists of the best films of the 2000s lists) and Hollywood genre movies that nonetheless reflect a coherent artistic vision. His complex and visually intricate horror films reward socio-political readings. Del Toro's success highlights the transnational reach of Hollywood, which has a long tradition of adopting the best film-makers from around the world, but he has maintained strong links with his native Mexico as well. Above all, del Toro confirms cinema's connection to fairy tales, which need fantastic and horrific monsters.

Where to start

Yes, everyone loves *Pan's Labyrinth*. But if you're avoiding *Hellboy* because you're tired of lame comic-book movies, you're just wrong. Ron Perlman's wisecracking cigar-smoking demon is an absolute hoot.

Chapter 15

Exploring New Approaches to Film Theory – and Beyond

*W*hat's going on with film studies' fascination with all things theory? No sooner have you grasped classical film theory and then managed to get your head around structuralism (I discuss both in Chapter 13) than you have to deal with *post*-structuralism and post-colonialism, not to mention post-feminism and postmodernism, which for some reason doesn't normally require a hyphen.

Film theorists love sticking *post* in front of everything. In regular usage, the prefix *post-* simply means 'after', which makes it a useful add-on when discussing historical periods or other processes. So in this sense, post-structuralism is a label for a period of theorising that came after the time when everyone was into structuralism. Simple, right?

Well, unfortunately not: this *post-* also implies a kind of opposition to the ideas of the earlier period. It's not quite as strong as *anti-* (against) but it comes pretty close in some cases. Just to confuse matters further, in strictly chronological terms, film theorists started to use structuralist and post-structuralist ideas around the same time, during the 1960s and 1970s. So instead of a clear development from one idea to the next, you have to see this time as more like a messy period of overlap, conflict and exchange. But then history is always like that when you think about it.

Multiplying Meaning: Post-Structuralism

Linguistics teaches that the word 'pig' is a sign, made up of a *signifier* (the letters 'p', 'i' and 'g' arranged in that order) and a *signified* (a pink, hairy four-legged creature that lives on a farm). Linguistics is the basis of structuralism (see Chapter 13), which is a way of interpreting texts that assumes a fixed relationship between signifier and signified. A pig is a pig, right? Yes, unless you're speaking informally about 'a greedy person' or, in British slang, 'a police officer'. These meanings are all related to each other, but many, many of them exist. *Post-structuralism,* which extends *and* challenges structuralism, accepts and explores the multiplicity of meaning in language and in culture.

Discerning the difference between structuralism and post-structuralism

The idea that meaning is multiple, flexible and unstable has profound implications for the way you understand and study texts (see Table 15-1).

Table 15-1	Structuralism versus Post-Structuralism
Structuralism	**Post-Structuralism**
Meaning is a noun; it's fixed and stable.	*Meaning* is a process; it flows continually onwards.
Like languages, you can boil down a text to an essential underlying structure.	Underlying structures aren't natural – they're imposed, and they change over time.
Binary oppositions (for instance, male/female) are equally weighted. They structure myths and narrative.	Binary oppositions are unequal and related to power (such as male dominates female).
Even though their connection is arbitrary, a signifier always produces a signified.	Signifiers don't produce signifieds; they just produce more signifiers.
A text is an individual example of larger systems of meaning.	A text is produced only through the active process called reading.

To clarify the difficult concept that signifiers produce only more signifiers, consider how a dictionary works. If you look up the signifier 'pig', you find that it has several possible signifieds including the farm animal, the greedy person and the police officer. But how do you know what a 'farm animal' is? You need to look up the signifiers 'farm' and 'animal', which themselves have several further possible signifiers. And so it goes on.

Post-structuralism states that meaning is constantly put off, or *deferred.* Only when you read or hear a word used in context can you determine its meaning. But even then, each word carries traces of its other meanings and uses.

These insights connect to studying films, because in some ways the film image feels closer to the post-structuralist model of a sign than the structuralist one. Think of a familiar motif such as the cowboy riding off into the sunset. This image has no single fixed meaning in itself. It only acquires meaning in a narrative sense due to its *context,* its place within a chain of other images. Even then the traces of its previous uses inevitably colour its meaning, because audiences familiar with westerns have seen this device used over and over again. Not to mention the specific associations of the sunset, or the horse. Watch those meanings multiply. . . .

Deconstructing texts and discourses

The 2002 documentary *Derrida* includes a riveting moment when the white-haired French philosopher and post-structuralist Jacques Derrida is asked to provide the origin of his critical method called deconstruction. Sat in a conventional academic pose, surrounded by bookshelves, Derrida reacts immediately against the question itself, pointing out the artificiality of the interview situation and the impossibility of knowing who the audience for the documentary will be. He chooses to underline the fact that he's speaking within the frame of a documentary rather than ignore it. Here Derrida isn't just being a grumpy academic; he's answering the question by deconstructing it and exposing some of the assumptions behind it.

Given this startling demonstration from Derrida himself, you can understand why defining deconstruction as a critical approach is rather difficult. In fact some people claim that doing so is impossible, because to define it is to shackle it to convention, which is the opposite of deconstruction.

However, this section is likely to disappear entirely up its own *derrière* if I don't at least try defining it:

- ✔ **Deconstruction aims to open up a text to multiple readings by overturning commonly accepted interpretations.** For example, when analysing a text, you can easily fall back on a Freudian explanation for a male character's behaviour (see Chapter 13). But deconstruction forces you to take apart your assumptions, for example by acknowledging that Freud's ideas were – in themselves – a teeny bit misogynist.

✔ **When analysing a text, deconstruction looks out for *axioms,* or self-evident truths.** Popular movies are full of these neat moments or lines that you're not supposed to question, such as 'life is like a box of chocolates' or 'love means never having to say you're sorry'. Take these to pieces, and you find new ways to read the film (see the sidebar, 'Deconstructing *Forrest Gump* (1994)').

✔ **By exposing the power relations in commonly accepted readings, deconstruction creates space for marginalised social groups.** Therefore it's a useful strategy for feminist readings, queer theory and post-colonial theory (see the later 'Going for girl power! Post-feminism', 'Moving beyond gender: Queer theory' and the following section, respectively).

Okay, so deconstruction is a tough one. Luckily, other post-structuralist thinkers take elements from Derrida's strategy but make them easier to apply.

Philosopher Michel Foucault shares Derrida's deconstructive attitude to culture, although the two famously argued about their critical methods. Foucault's central idea is known as *discourse,* which begins with what people say or express about a particular topic. But a discourse is more than just idle chatter: it also manages knowledge and power within society, and therefore governs behaviour. Ultimately, even your own identity comprises discourses around gender, nationality and so on.

Deconstructing *Forrest Gump* (1994)

One fruitful method of deconstructing films is to look for *axioms* (self-evident truths) that encapsulate the film's worldview – and then smash them to pieces. Doing so should help to unmask the systems of thought that prop up the film's narrative and themes.

The most notable axiom of the 1992 Oscar-winner *Forrest Gump* was also one of its marketing taglines: 'Life is like a box of choco-lates . . . you never know what you're gonna get'. This piece of folk wisdom passed down from mother to son is used to explain the worldview of mentally challenged Forrest (Tom Hanks), and particularly his stoicism and belief that life appears random but is actually predetermined in some way. Both these characteristics are important within the broadly Christian outlook that the film favours (indeed, Forrest has been seen as a Christ-like figure by some critics).

Everything works out fine for Forrest, so what's the problem with seeing the world in this way? Well, maybe we need to consider other charac-ters too, such as Forrest's true love (and briefly his wife) Jenny (Robin Wright). What Jenny 'gets' from life's 'box of chocolates' is bitter and unpalatable. She moves to the big city, is seduced by political activism, sexual liberation and drugs and then dies of an unnamed condi-tion, which is likely to be understood by audi-ences as AIDS.

In other words, the film tries to cover up the high price that some disadvantaged mem-bers of society have to pay for railing against the system. And this makes it ripe to be deconstructed.

Of killer cyborgs and office politics

When analysing a text through its discourses, context is particularly important because the discourse exists within *and* outside the text. For example, *The Terminator* (1984) clearly presents the belief that humankind is heading for a future where the machines get smart and kill all the people. But this story about technology is also intertwined with gender discourses in interesting ways. Arnie's hyper-masculine body becomes contaminated by technology, whereas the mother Sarah Connor (Linda Hamilton) is the character who survives and thrives.

You can therefore read the film in relation to discourses about the 1980s workplace, where traditionally masculine jobs in heavy industry were being lost to automation and replaced by 'feminised' service sector roles. After all, where does the climactic showdown take place? In a factory. I rest my case.

Discourse differs from Althusser's notion of *ideology* (see Chapter 13) in that discourse is not simply an instrument of control imposed upon the masses. Instead, discourse is a site of conflict, negotiation and debate. The nearby sidebar 'Of killer cyborgs and office politics' takes a stab at the discourses of technology and gender in *The Terminator* (1984).

Dismantling empires: Post-colonialism

If, as I describe in the preceding section, post-structuralism is about instability and multiplicity of meaning, as well as giving voice to the voiceless, you can see why it became a suitable framework for studying the current and former colonies of the Western powers.

In film studies, *post-colonialism* allows detailed consideration of films produced by countries that are (or were) colonised. It also examines the representation of colonised nations and people within Western cinema. A key process within post-colonialism is that of *othering*: the ways that one group defines itself against what it isn't – often people who are different in particular ways.

The literary theorist Edward Said lived the experience of colonialism from childhood, being born in Jerusalem to Palestinian and American parents. Later, as an academic working in the US university system, he wrote the book *Orientalism* (1978), which helped to set the agenda for post-colonial studies. Said draws on Derrida and especially Foucault to create his notion of an *orientalist discourse* that characterises the representation of the East within the culture of the West. Here the East functions as the mysterious, sexualised other to the West's rationality. His primary examples are from visual art and literature, including the novels of Joseph Conrad, but his ideas are flexible enough that you can apply them to popular cinema.

A classic example of Hollywood's orientalist tendency is *Indiana Jones and the Temple of Doom* (1984) – the one set in India, with the cute/annoying Chinese kid sidekick and Spielberg's wife as the love interest. Indy (Harrison Ford) needs to save a village's children, whom a cult has kidnapped and enslaved. The film implies that the locals are incapable of providing strong father figures to protect their own children, and so an American with a whip has to save the day. It also depicts Indians as being only superstitious primitives or brutal cannibals. I'm sorry, you probably loved this film as a child (I know I did), but it's really racist.

The other side of the post-colonial coin is to give a voice to people deprived of one by the processes of colonisation. Here the Indian critic Gayatri Chakravorty Spivak provides useful terms to open up the debate:

- **Subaltern:** Spivak adopts the lowly military ranking to refer to colonised peoples who have no access to the tools of Western culture. More than simply being a repressed minority, the *subaltern* literally has no cultural voice, identity or history.

- **Epistemic violence:** Spivak borrows Foucault's term 'episteme' to refer to the power structures that make knowledge possible. Therefore *epistemic violence* is knowledge and truth that colonising powers use as social control (for instance, imposing religion or education upon indigenous populations). In order to escape epistemic violence, the subaltern have no option other than to abandon their cultural heritage and adopt Western modes of culture and behaviour.

Here's an example of this process at work within the international film industry: Western critics adopted many of the best-known world cinema directors, such as Satyajit Ray and Akira Kurosawa (whom you can meet in Chapter 12), only *after* they won prizes at European film festivals. You can argue that they found such favour only because they adopted the narrative and visual style of Western art cinema, such as Italian Neorealist films. Indeed Kurosawa, adored by the festival circuit, was widely criticised on his own turf for pandering to European sensibilities, suggesting that Hollywood cinema isn't the only one guilty of epistemic violence against indigenous cinemas.

Realising Nothing Matters Anymore: Postmodernism

Postmodernism is the critical theory that everyone pretends to know about. People apply the adjective *postmodern* willy-nilly to everything from pop videos to home décor. In its most vague and general usage, the word seems to be synonymous with the notions of irony and self-consciousness.

Modernism's moment

To understand postmodernism, you need to know a bit about *modernism*. Confusingly, the 'modern' of modernism is now very old. The modernist moment happened around the end of the 19th century and the beginning of the 20th, and was marked by dramatic developments in all types of culture from the visual arts to the written word.

The modernist radicals wanted to shake up traditional art forms and rewrite the aesthetic rulebook. They favoured formal experimentation and abstraction over realism. Think of the stream of consciousness prose of James Joyce, the atonal music of Arnold Schoenberg or the cubist paintings of Pablo Picasso.

But over time the radical paintings and books that were so shocking in the 1920s became the intellectual mainstream of the 1950s. The avant-garde stance of modernism was hostile towards popular culture as a corrupting influence, as the Marxists of the Frankfurt School (see Chapter 13) also argued – but pop culture nonetheless advanced unconcerned.

The beginnings of postmodernism as a reaction to the elitism of modernism can, perhaps, date to 1962 when Andy Warhol put prints of Marilyn Monroe and Campbell's soup cans into art galleries, thereby collapsing the boundary between high art and popular culture.

These ideas of postmodernism aren't necessary problematic – in fact they're strangely appropriate given the term's connotations of rampant populism. But if you want to be taken seriously as a film student, you need to understand some of the depths hiding within this wilfully superficial term. Fortunately, you can do so while reading this section and watching some fascinating films.

Narrating the end of history

You can view the loss of faith in the world-changing philosophy of modernism in the 1950s and 1960s (read the nearby sidebar 'Modernism's moment') as symptomatic of a larger crisis facing all the heroes and big ideas of Western culture. According to literary theorist Jean-François Lyotard, this crisis is the essence of the *postmodern condition*. Lyotard had a fancy name for these big ideas: *metanarratives,* literally stories about stories.

You can think of all the theories I cover in Chapter 13 – Marxism, structuralism, psychoanalysis – as metanarratives, because they offer overarching ways to understand the grand sweep of human history and experience. You may therefore expect postmodern cinema to abandon large ambitious ideas and focus on banal spectacle. *Transformers* (2007) anyone? Yet, as the following sections attest, this isn't the case: big ideas are still plentiful.

Another key postmodern thinker Frederic Jameson disagrees with Lyotard on metanarratives, because he considers Marxist theory still applicable to today's stage of late capitalism. He does, however, share Lyotard's pessimism about popular culture with regard to its ambition and sense of history. Jameson argues that the main features of postmodern cinema are:

✔ **Pastiche:** Unlike parody, which copies to mock convention, *pastiche* is the pointless quotation of other films, genres and periods. No one has anything new to say, and so culture endlessly recycles and quotes other culture.

✔ **Nostalgia:** In the 1980s, Hollywood looked back to the 1950s in films such as *Back to the Future* (1985), as it attempted to relive the vitality of pop culture of that period. Even *Star Wars* (1977) evokes nostalgia, not for a historical period but for a lost style of storytelling and viewing.

✔ **Waning of affect:** *Affect* is the raw experience of emotion before it is given a label such as 'happiness'. Jameson argues that postmodern culture has lost touch with emotional expression. This idea is close to the philosophical term *nihilism:* the sense that nothing has meaning.

Quentin Tarantino's *Kill Bill* films (2003 and 2004) blend many different styles of action film together: Hong Kong martial arts movies, Japanese anime, low-budget 'grindhouse' revenge thrillers. Tarantino isn't parodying these styles – indeed, he clearly has great affection for them – and he's aware that mainstream audiences aren't as familiar with their conventions as he is. And yet, affect (emotion) is weak. Revenge is a conventional motivation rather than a personal one, and violence is slick and spectacular rather than painful and tragic. Most of all, the *Kill Bill* films are nostalgic for a particular kind of video-store cinephilia, where exploitation movies from across the world used to rub their VHS-shaped shoulders together.

Getting super-excited about hyper-realism

Jean Baudrillard, who died in 2007, always gave good headline. The title for his 1991 book *The Gulf War Did Not Take Place* was thoroughly provocative for the political elites of America and its allies, and his views on 9/11 were equally inflammatory, inviting accusations that he was defending terrorists' actions. As a theorist of the media itself, not just its products, he was always on hand for a spiky, counter-intuitive quote or a controversial statement. He was also a master at turning news items or anecdotes inside out to expose their theoretical meaning. But mostly, he really enjoyed an argument.

Baudrillard's central idea emerges from the ruins of semiotics and post-structuralism (check out the earlier section 'Multiplying Meaning: Post-Structuralism'). Under structuralism, the sign has meaning because it refers to a signified, an essence of meaning drawn from reality (see Chapter 13). But if post-structuralism is correct, and a signifier creates only more signifiers rather than a signified, where does reality fit into this equation? Everything becomes a copy of a copy for which no original exists. Baudrillard calls this copy of a lost original the *simulacrum*. In place of reality, postmodernism creates a *hyper-reality* where you can't identify a meaningful difference between a simulation and a real object.

I know, this argument sounds completely nuts, right? But bear with me for a moment and consider a few of Baudrillard's persuasive examples:

- ✔ **The Gulf War:** As the first conflict of the modern media age, TV images of the 1990 Gulf War serve as the war itself for Western audiences. One moment of news coverage became a Baudrillard anecdote to illustrate the hyper-real: a CNN news anchor cut live to reporters in the Gulf only to find them watching CNN to find out what was happening.

- ✔ **Disneyland:** As a perfect simulation of the idea of 'America', the theme park is actually more real than the confusing experience of being in a modern US city, such as Los Angeles.

- ✔ **9/11:** Come on, didn't you feel like you were watching some kind of low-budget version of *Independence Day* (1996) the first time you saw the planes hit the Twin Towers on TV?

Luckily, Baudrillard loved the movies and spoke and wrote a great deal about them. His favourite thing about cinema is its joyful avoidance of the real, its ability to act as pure, beautiful simulation. He was also interested in films that blur real and virtual identities, such as *Mulholland Dr.* (2001) and *The Truman Show* (1998).

Perhaps understandably, he considered realism to be a complete waste of energy and despaired that cinema was drifting towards an obsession with the illusion of reality, particularly with regard to digital special effects. But definitely the most interesting case of overlap between Baudrillard and cinema is *The Matrix* (1999).

The Wachowskis claimed to be heavily influenced by the concept of the simulacrum when writing *The Matrix* and even feature a close-up of Baudrillard's book in one scene. When Morpheus (Laurence Fishburne) shows Neo (Keanu Reeves) the post-apocalyptic Earth, he cites Baudrillard's phrase 'the desert of the real'. But Baudrillard later denounced the film as a misreading of his work. The clear separation between the matrix and the 'real' world is actually the opposite of hyper-reality where the two collapse together. Plus, Baudrillard found the film's negative view of virtual reality inconsistent with its heavy investment in digital special effects.

True to form, Baudrillard came up with a perfect sound bite to leave you with: '*The Matrix* is the kind of the film about the Matrix that the Matrix itself could have produced.' Ouch. My brain hurts.

Going for girl power! Post-feminism

To be clear, don't take this (or any) discussion of *post*-feminism as implying that the feminist project is over or that it's a job well done. In Western culture, women continue to face inequality in the workplace, sexual discrimination and domestic violence. In other parts of the world, women have barely any human rights whatsoever.

Why then do many people think that feminism is something that their mothers and grandmothers had to worry about? Even worse, why are people – including many young women – so uncomfortable with the term *feminism* itself? Critiques of *post-feminist* culture are concerned with these kinds of questions.

Waving at feminists across history

If you do any reading around feminist theory, you may find reference to various periods of feminist thought, which are often called *waves*. Take a moment to identify these waves:

- **First Wave feminism** has its roots in the 18th century, but took on a new momentum around 1900 with discussion of the 'New Woman' in art and literature. Women's groups campaigned against legal inequalities, including access to education, property rights and particularly the right to vote.

- **Second Wave feminism** was active from the 1960s until the 1980s. Informed by counter-culture and debates around political oppression, Second Wave feminists argued against sexual discrimination and negative representations of women. The negative stereotype of the bra-burning, man-hating feminist originates from this era.

- **Third Wave feminism** argues for greater diversity and incorporates queer theory and post-colonial studies. This wave began around 1990 and is informed by academic debates around post-structuralism and breakdown of stable gender identities. Some scholars still consider the Third Wave active.

- **Fourth Wave feminism** is still a matter of debate. Some feminist critics claim that the internet and social media have sparked a new grass-roots movement supporting women's rights. Webzines, blogs and Twitter campaigns also have a part to play here. Meanwhile, less techno-savvy feminists decry the internet for its fracturing and personalising of the debates.

And where does post-feminism fit into this story? Well, first we need to separate the waves of feminism, which were movements or projects brought about by theorists with explicit political agendas, and post-feminism, which is an aspect of contemporary culture. Historically speaking, post-feminism became widespread in Western society after Second Wave feminism, in the 1980s and 1990s.

Cultural theorist Angela McRobbie advises against considering post-feminism as a simple victory for the conservative backlash against feminism itself: things are more complicated than that. She discusses the box-office hit *Bridget Jones's Diary* (2001) as an example of the post-feminist conflicts facing modern young women:

- Bridget (Renée Zellweger) has benefitted from the apparent freedoms of choice for women, in that she's able to relocate to London and forge her own career – albeit one at which she's not particularly good.

- These freedoms serve only to create new anxieties however: being a 'singleton' in a world of happy couples, not finding the right man and handling the ticking biological clock. She also deals with comedic neuroses, including an obsessive monitoring of weight and alcohol consumption.

- Bridget fantasises about marrying her sexy boss (Hugh Grant), but the white wedding dress and traditional trappings seem ridiculous, because feminism dictates that women aren't supposed to want that anymore. The film ends, however, on a very conventional romantic clinch with the sensible, marry-able Mark (Colin Firth).

Figure 15-1:
Brave and capable but revealingly dressed Cameron Diaz in *Charlie's Angels: Full Throttle* (2003).

Courtesy Moviestore Collection/REX

The contradictory ending of *Bridget Jones's Diary* is typical of post-feminist culture. Women may be well aware of feminist ideals but choose to flout them, sometimes ironically. Just think about the debates around female pop stars such as Madonna, the Spice Girls and more recently Rihanna, who all claim or claimed female empowerment while presenting themselves as sexual objects for a male gaze. Film scholar Sarah Projansky has named this brand of post-feminism as 'sex-positive' in that it decries Second Wave feminism as being 'anti-sex'.

A similar process is clearly at work in *Charlie's Angels: Full Throttle* (2003). The film's beautiful female stars play the roles of tough women, but they're frequently displayed in demeaning activities such as pole dancing. Of course, they're also required to wear skimpy, figure-hugging outfits while saving the day (see Figure 15-1). You go, girls.

Moving beyond gender: Queer theory

First, the 'Q' word. Inappropriate much? *Queer* may cause a bit of discomfort and squeamishness, but that's entirely the point of using it. The term has been used as a derogatory affront against gay men for decades. Turning the word around from an insult into a celebration is suitably camp and politically radical. What's more, queer is now an extremely inclusive term, describing not only gay men and women, but also the whole rainbow spectrum of non-normative sexualities and gender identities. Most importantly, it rhymes as part of the famous battle cry: 'We're here, we're queer, get used to it!'

Post-structuralist Michel Foucault's ground-breaking *History of Sexuality* (1976) sparked theoretical work on sexuality as a set of conventions within society. Here Foucault takes a common assumption – that Victorian society repressed sexuality – and turns it on its head. By naming, pathologising and criminalising homosexuality, repressive institutions in fact created the discourse that became gay identity.

The idea that sexuality is a discourse (see 'Deconstructing texts and discourses' earlier in this chapter), instead of natural and predetermined, is also explored at length by gender theorist Judith Butler. Butler goes further than Foucault by arguing that gender itself is a performance:

✔ Early feminists argued that you're born male or female, but have to learn to become a man or a woman. Butler disputes that even your physical sex is a predetermined binary, citing examples of transgender identities.

✔ After your sex is ascribed one way or another, you're taught gender as a way to behave: from your parents, schools, the media and culture. This process is like a ritual, which creates an illusion of being natural and essential. But nothing is inherently natural about femininity or masculinity.

✔ Butler discusses the practice of *drag*, or playing a different gender role to your given gender, as a way of demonstrating that *all* gender identities are performed, straight or otherwise. The explicit performances of drag artists help to bring this to light.

Well, his real name *was* Marion

Film theorist Richard Dyer describes camp as a way of approaching culture, instead of a particular quality inherent in texts such as films or TV shows. Therefore, you can perceive even a butch 'man's man' figure such as John Wayne as camp, even though he seems to represent the very opposite.

Dyer argues that the Wayne persona is a 'production number' with overemphasised masculine traits, including the famous walk and drawling accent.

But even the nostalgia and affection for Wayne within mainstream culture is a sort of camp. Along these lines, you can see camp as a feature of postmodernism more generally, a way of interpreting culture that allows ironic reclaiming of bad films, terrible actors and washed-up star personas. Have you *seen* David Hasselhoff lately?

So queer theory suggests that all gender identity is performed, something that you *do* rather than something that you *are*. In the same way, you can apply queer readings to any cultural text, not just those created by gay people or featuring gay characters.

A vital strategy here is *camp,* which is derived from the knowing, theatrical style of behaviour common to gay sub-cultures. Author and critic Susan Sontag called camp a 'sensibility' with many elements, including artificiality, extravagance and debunking the pretentious. Film critic and author Jack Babuscio refined Sontag's definition, emphasising irony, wilful superficiality and humour. Within the gay community, humour is a coping mechanism for social alienation and tragedies such as the 1980s AIDS epidemic. For another take on camp, check out the nearby sidebar 'Well, his real name *was* Marion'.

Reaching the End of Everything: Post-Theory?

Post-theory can mean one of two things. Firstly, it can be used as a catch-all term for the group of theories which begin with the prefix *post-,* such as most of the frameworks I examine in this chapter. Secondly, and more controversially, post-theory can refer to the period after high film theory has run its course. Clearly, not all film scholars believe that this has happened yet, or that it ever will. Nonetheless, this chapter dares to ask: is film theory dead? And if so, what next?

The glory days of film theory were the 1960s to the 1980s. During this extremely productive period (which Chapter 13 explores), film theory cross-fertilised with linguistics, Marxism and psychoanalysis to produce many of the classic texts students still read today. Film studies was still an upstart discipline with plenty to prove to older, more familiar fields of study, and so dense, challenging ideas were a suitably highbrow response to those who doubted that film was worth studying at all.

From the 1990s to the present day, the field of film studies has grown in size and confidence, and so naturally a greater diversity of approaches is now on offer. This section discusses the place of film theory in this new order and whether you even need it anymore.

Smashing the SLAB: Bordwell takes aim

In 1996, possibly the most famous film scholar on the planet David Bordwell published an edited collection with the attention-grabbing title *Post-Theory: Reconstructing Film Studies.* In the introductory essay, Bordwell conceded that his title was a bit of a tease. He wasn't intending to argue that *all* film theory was useless, but instead that High Theory had had its day.

The kind of Theory (with a capital T) that Bordwell aimed to dismantle carries the suitably weighty acronym SLAB:

- ✔ **S is for Saussure:** His study of linguistics gave rise to film semiotics.

- ✔ **L is for Lacan:** Psychoanalyst of choice for film theorists.

- ✔ **A is for Althusser:** His concept of ideology is vital for film studies.

- ✔ **B is for Barthes:** Particularly his productive post-structuralist reading strategy.

So what exactly is Bordwell's beef with High Theory?

- ✔ Bordwell objects to *top-down inquiry,* the tendency of film scholars to start with the theory and then move down to a text as illustration. The task of research should be to pose a problem and gather data, instead of simply attempting to prove a theoretical model works. Bordwell also claims that film theory suffers from an over-reliance on French philosophy, to the detriment of schools of thought from different countries, which often aren't even translated into English.

- ✔ Bordwell claims that theorising is too eclectic in its sources, drawing from a wide range of positions that may be logically opposed to one another. He cites the fact that High Theorists discuss some ideas of the favoured theorists while overlooking others. Theories that refute the commonly held position are simply ignored: for example Noam Chomsky's work on linguistics that overturns Saussure.

✔ Bordwell mocks the loose, associative style of argument characteristic of the least intelligible film theory. Instead of classical rhetorical strategies such as *inductive reasoning,* which posits evidence to substantiate a claim, film theory often performs bizarre leaps of logic and offers eloquent but unsupported conclusions.

✔ Bordwell critiques theorists who over-rely upon evidence drawn from film texts themselves. He suggests that instead of evidence, the film theorist has only interpretation. By this logic, a theory is given weight simply by generating a fresh reading of a film.

Bordwell's preferred way forward for film theory is what he calls *middle-level research.* This approach asks questions that have factual *and* theoretical implications. Studies of particular film-makers, genres and national cinemas are good examples, as are the variations of film history that investigate production, exhibition or stylistic developments over time. Most importantly, Bordwell suggests that middle-level research projects don't require a 'Big Theory of Everything' in order to be worthwhile and valid. Phew, thank goodness for that.

Striking back at Bordwell

Not everyone agrees with David Bordwell on the passing away of High Theory. Many theorists refute Bordwell's argument that research doesn't need a 'Big Theory of Everything', by insisting that any claim around knowledge, truth and power is inherently about culture, identity and politics. If you choose not to make these assumptions explicit, you're basically kidding yourself. More importantly, plenty of interesting ideas are still waiting to be explored at the level of Bordwell's High Theory. Should theorists abandon attempts to rethink the discipline of film studies just because they're busy studying films? Doesn't the field of film studies have room for pragmatism *and* ambition?

In recent decades, few cinematic thinkers have been more ambitious than Gilles Deleuze. Yes, he was another French philosopher – but don't hold that against him. The most fascinating thing about Deleuze is that he doesn't just philosophise *about* cinema and how it works, instead he uses cinema *as* philosophy. In other words, Deleuze claims that films actively produce new ideas and new ways of seeing the world. They're not simply representation; they're events in themselves.

You can see why Deleuze's ideas are an attractive starting point for film scholars, who've taken them in a variety of directions:

✔ Deleuze's dissection of the complex relations between time and movement are useful frameworks for film scholars to analyse a wide range of film styles and genres, including classical Hollywood and European art cinema.

✔ Deleuze influences studies of national identity through the idea of *minor cinema*. For example, films from post-colonial nations may use the dominant cinematic form but play it 'in a minor key', subverting its meanings. This approach is more optimistic than that of subaltern studies (see 'Deconstructing empire: Post-colonialism' earlier in this chapter).

✔ Deleuze's free-floating ideas on affect (emotion) provide a focus for studies of visceral effects upon the body in cinema, in an avant-garde context (for instance, Andy Warhol) and in mainstream horror films (George A Romero).

Deleuze was a reclusive figure, believing that his books spoke for him. By contrast, Slavoj Žižek is somewhat of a rock star – at least by film-theorist standards. His frequent media appearances, journalistic contributions to political debates and, most recently, the documentaries he stars in, all capitalise on his entertaining and engaging persona. Žižek takes two of High Theory's biggest ideas – Marxism and psychoanalysis – and fuses them into a radical critique on contemporary consumer society. He's particularly influenced by Jacques Lacan's notion of fantasy as the way people experience the world and the social construct of ideology.

If you want to get a quick grasp of Žižek's ideas and experience his unusual rhetorical style, take a look at one of his documentary films, such as *The Pervert's Guide to Ideology* (2012). He takes clips from many films and intersperses them with shots of himself explaining his theories. But instead of capturing the interviews in the studio, director Sophie Fiennes shoots him on location and with lighting and cinematography to match the film itself. So when discussing frustrated fantasy and violence in *Taxi Driver* (1976), Žižek is sprawled out on Travis Bickle's military cot bed. This amusing and thought-provoking device literally places the theorist within the text.

Thinking about thinking: Cognitive theory

If you ever (bravely) try to read Deleuze or simply watch Žižek doing his quirky thing in his documentaries, you may well end up thinking: wait a minute here. That's a brilliant theory, delivered convincingly. I even understand some of it. But where's the evidence? Can you prove that the theory works in practice? If you have this kind of rational brain, cognitive film theory may well be for you.

Cognitive film theory is extremely diverse, drawing on aspects of psychology, biology and neuroscience. But it's united in its use of scientific methods and its implicit opposition to the High Theory of psychoanalysis.

Unsurprisingly, as the lead opponent to High Theory, David Bordwell is a committed cognitivist. His fascination with storytelling and narration has neo-formalist qualities (see Chapter 13), but in recent years it led him further and further down the cognitive route. Bordwell describes how he came to reject top-down inquiry (taking big ideas from other fields and attempting to apply them to film), in favour of asking specific, detailed questions and then looking for broader theoretical frameworks if necessary.

For example, Bordwell examines film characterisations, noting that audiences tend to make snap judgements about characters based on their actions, as soon as they're introduced. These reactions are useful for screenwriters because they allow economy of storytelling. But why does this process work?

- ✔ Bordwell argues that clinical psychology offers several convincing answers. The *primacy effect* suggests that you're trained to rely heavily upon the first pieces of information you receive, which shape your future responses.

- ✔ Bordwell also notes the *fundamental attribution error,* which leads you to interpret other's behaviour as attributable to their personalities, even while you excuse your own through environmental factors. So if someone shouts in a meeting, they're bossy; if you do it, you're stressed out.

Taken together, these two factors help to explain superficiality when grasping character. Of course film-makers can use this straight, or choose to subvert it to provide narrative twists.

Philosopher Noël Carroll argues that the increased interest in cognitivism within film theory circles creates challenges for film theory's long-standing love of psychoanalytic theory (see Chapter 13). He uses the analogy of psychoanalysis as a clinical practice, which is only considered necessary in medicine *after* rational explanation for behaviour is at an end. Carroll's implication is that when two theories about film clash, one of which is cognitive and one psychoanalytical, the burden of proof is with the psychoanalytical response. Carroll also notes that, although the practice of psychoanalysis has data generated by patients, psychoanalytic film theory seems to exist with no evidential basis.

So does cognitivism spell the end of High Theory? Or does it simply replace the problems of one method with those of another? One thing's for sure, you can bet film theorists across the globe are thinking about issues like this right now. Thinking really, really hard. . . .

Chapter 16

Outliving Celluloid: Cinema in the 21st Century

. . . .

In This Chapter

▶ Charting changes in cinema-going, technology, distribution and more

▶ Tracing the effects of new technology on viewing patterns

▶ Considering what happens to distribution and copyright when media converge

. . . .

*T*he first decade of the second century of cinema was one of dramatic and rapid technological change. During this period, film-making transitioned from a physical, chemical process to an almost entirely digital one, the Internet revolutionised distribution and viewing practices, and the blockbuster business model came under increasing strain. But those who predicted that cinema wouldn't survive these changes were left eating their words.

In this chapter, I explain these technological changes and explore their effects upon the cinema experience in all its developing forms.

Revising Rumours of Cinema's Death: Still Watching, Just Differently

Way back in the 1990s, you barely opened a magazine or newspaper without encountering an article proclaiming that cinema was dying or already dead. Even clever literary theorists such as Susan Sontag joined in, arguing that each new wave of audiovisual technology had so eroded the magic of cinema that *cinephilia,* or the love of cinema, was gone forever.

I'm sorry, Susan, but you were wrong. Twenty years later, cinema is still alive and kicking. Technological change has continued apace, and going to the cinema is now only one of a range of options for film fans. But audiences continue to choose that option. In the UK for example, 2012 was a record-breaking year for cinemas, with attendance at its highest level for more than 30 years. Purists may lament the end of *celluloid* (the plastic used to create film prints for projection; see the later section 'Shifting from celluloid strips to hard disk drives' for more details), but clearly people still love going to the pictures.

Cinema-going over the decades

Although in many ways cinemas are in good health today, pretending that film is still the dominant force of popular culture that it used to be is foolish. Just take a look at Figure 16-1, which illustrates the spectacular change in the scale of cinema-going in the UK.

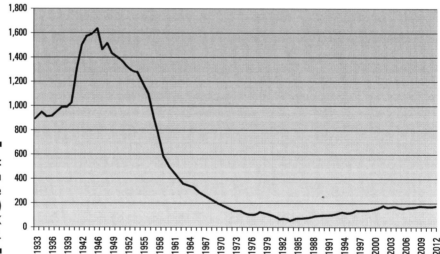

Figure 16-1: Cinema attendance (in millions) in the UK since 1930.

Cinema-going in the UK reached an incredible peak during World War II, with 1.6 *billion* tickets being sold a year. After all, other opportunities for entertainment were thin on the ground during blackouts and cinemas offered a great way to get your fix of patriotic newsreel footage or pure, invaluable escapism. Although British film-making activity was severely hampered by rationing, its cinema managers had never had it so good.

These audience levels were clearly unsustainable after life returned to something like normal. Historians often attribute the gradual and then extremely steep drop off in cinema-going in the 1950s and 1960s to competition from television, but a range of other factors were also at play:

✔ Post-war 'baby boom' meant fewer cinema trips for young parents.

✔ Redesigned cities moved urban populations into suburban ones, shifting them away from city-centre cinemas.

✔ Poorly attended cinemas rapidly turned into disreputable fleapits, or were repurposed as bingo halls or nightclubs.

By the early 1980s, things were pretty desperate for film industries across the world, and even Hollywood was looking shaky thanks to a string of multinational corporate takeovers. But then (as Figure 16-1 illustrates) things began, slowly but surely, to improve.

A key turning point for the UK was the opening of the first *multiplex* cinemas in 1985. These enormous new screening venues were built in suburbs with ample parking, many screens for a range of films and surrounding leisure or retail complexes. Critics called multiplexes soulless and corporate, but audiences soon realised that convenience, comfort and choice were more important than the decaying romance of the old-fashioned picture palaces.

Meanwhile many smaller, single-screen cinemas were saved from extinction by shifting upmarket to provide a more personal alternative to the multiplexes. More mature audiences often prize these venues and willingly pay a premium to avoid the popcorn-munching teenage crowd.

Global cinema-going trends

The Western world has experienced a similar pattern of cinema attendance to that of the UK since the Second World War. US annual attendance peaked at 4.7 billion in 1947 and then plunged down to around 1 billion by the 1970s, but recovered gradually and currently sits at around 1.5 billion tickets sold per year. This trend is repeated across Europe and in other countries with large, well-developed film industries, such as Japan.

In other parts of the world, cinema is still booming. According to data gathered by the United Nations, admissions to Chinese cinemas more than doubled between 2005 and 2011, with the Russian Federation and Brazil nearly matching these spectacular growth rates. Clearly the world still wants the cinema experience.

Shifting from celluloid strips to hard disk drives

For almost a century, cinema remained an *analogue system,* which means that it created physical objects *analogous* (or corresponding to) to reality (notably image negatives, sound waves), which were then used to recreate 'reality' on screen.

The knowable, tactile nature of celluloid is most obvious when you get hold of a film strip and hold it up to the light; you can see a tiny image frozen from the stream of movement, clear and sharp. Although the pattern of sound waves that make up the synchronised sound aren't intelligible to the naked eye, you can at least perceive them as loud and dense or sparse and quiet when looking along the film itself.

Digital recording is different to its analogue predecessors in that it represents sound and images in the form of information (numbers), which bear no direct physical resemblance to the original source: light and vibrations. Table 16-1 explores several other differences that have implications for film-making.

Table 16-1	Differences between Analogue and Digital Film-making
Analogue Cinema	**Digital Cinema**
Film reels are expensive, requiring careful planning during the filming process to minimise costs and obtain desired effects.	Digital storage is very cheap, and so film-makers can produce much more footage with practically no extra cost.
Film must be developed before you can view it, and so film-makers don't know for sure whether they've captured the desired shot for several hours or days.	Digital footage is available to view instantly, and so any reshoots can take place immediately.
Film is *sequential* (you must view it from beginning to end), making editing laborious and slow.	Digital video is *random access,* and so you can complete editing much more quickly.
Colour, brightness and contrast are difficult to modify, placing greater importance on good cinematography.	Images can be easily modified and retouched, making post-production crucial.
Film negatives and prints degrade over time, and copies of copies lose definition.	In theory data doesn't degrade, and can be copied perfectly with no loss of quality.

Digital systems first made an impact on film editing, where its advantages are most obvious. Shooting on *digital video* (DV) rather than film began to be possible in the mid-1990s, but the relatively low quality of the images meant that it wasn't suitable for mainstream commercial film-making. At least not until George Lucas upped the high-definition ante with *Star Wars Episode II: Attack of the Clones* (2002). The *Star Wars* prequels are also overwhelmingly digital in the sense that many action sequences aren't recorded at all, but created digitally by computers.

Transitioning to digital, holding onto analogue

Throughout film history, technological change tends to lead to changes in the ways films look and feel. Thus, a profound shift such as the recent change-over to digital production and exhibition has had a significant impact on film aesthetics. Many early DV feature films were experimental in nature, and explored the possibilities offered by the new medium:

- ✔ *Timecode* (2000): Director Mike Figgis was an early convert, using the increased flexibility and storage capacities of DV to produce a split-screen vision of events happening simultaneously from four different viewpoints.

- ✔ *Dancer in the Dark* (2000): Lars von Trier used up to 100 digital cameras to shoot his star Björk's musical numbers, creating a kaleidoscopic effect in editing.

- ✔ *28 Days Later* (2002): Danny Boyle's zombie film employs the surveillance camera feel of DV to create dramatic irony – the cameras are still watching, but all the people are dead. The blocky, jerky quality of movement on DV represents the terror of being chased by the undead.

Of course big-budget blockbuster cinema already had digital elements by this point thanks to *computer-generated imagery* (CGI). From the tipping point of *Jurassic Park* (1993), which first convinced audiences that digital was able to recreate organic living creatures, to the digital excess of the *Star Wars* prequels beginning in 1999, CGI went from a spectacular draw to commonplace technology.

One noticeable effect of this digitisation is that the virtual camera (which provides the point of view upon digital worlds) is free to move around space in unnatural ways. This ability enables the spectacular extreme zooms of films such as *Moulin Rouge!* (2001) and *Hugo* (2011), as well as more surreal moments when the camera appears to pass through solid objects, including human bodies (*Fight Club* (1999), for instance). In theory, digitised sequences never need to cut, and long, fluid takes are possible. But in practice many digital films continue to build and explore space through traditional *continuity editing* (flip to Chapter 4 for details).

As the survival of continuity editing suggests, not everything about digital film-making is new and radical. Nicholas Rombes argues that the changeover to digital has been accompanied by a backlash of 'analogue nostalgia', as some film-makers mourn the loss of celluloid. For example, the Dogme 95 films of Lars von Trier and Thomas Vinterberg were shot on low-definition DV cameras, but according to a strict aesthetic code that bans all cinematic artifice. As a result, these films feature shaky camerawork, mistakes and chaotic improvisation – the opposite of the eerie perfection of digitised imagery.

For the clearest demonstration of analogue nostalgia, watch the Grindhouse films produced by Quentin Tarantino and Robert Rodriguez. In *Death Proof* and *Planet Terror* (both 2007), the film-makers deliberately insert imperfections and mistakes, including *unmotivated cuts* (edits that seem unintended by the film-makers), *burnouts* (where the celluloid appears to catch in the projector and disintegrate) and inset cards notifying the audience that reels are missing. You can understand this attempt to recreate the experience of watching exploitation movies in the 1970s as a longing for an earlier cinematic experience, one bearing the sticky, human fingerprints that are absent from digital film-making.

Changing Where, How and When You Watch

In these days of digital archives and 'instant everywhere' moving images, you have to remind yourself that access to film was, not so long ago, much more restricted. During the early years of film studies (in the 1970s and 1980s), students had to know how to perform all sorts of physical tasks, including how to handle celluloid, how to project using multiple reels and how to operate a Steenbeck viewing machine. Film studies meant dealing with the materiality of film itself. These days, you can get a degree in film studies without ever encountering a strip of celluloid.

Experiencing cinema nowadays

The experience of cinema in the 1920s or 1930s was so intense and unusual that it invoked regular comparisons with dreaming. Both activities involve darkness, a degree of physical comfort and being transported into different imaginary realms. Try to imagine the experience of seeing a film for the first time during cinema's early days. It must have felt so separate from everyday existence as to be almost magical.

Classical Hollywood films worked hard to maintain a glossy, luxurious facade and to avoid revealing their artificiality. Huge, epic films such as *Gone with the Wind* (1939) and *Ben-Hur* (1959) demanded nothing less than awestruck reverence from their audiences, who were generally happy to oblige. Of course avant-garde experimental films have always existed (see Chapter 7), but these remained firmly on the fringes of film culture and were just as far removed from everyday experience as the grandest epics.

Watching films today is clearly hugely different:

- ✔ You can watch films anywhere, from huge IMAX screens down to tiny mobile devices.

- ✔ Home film-making equipment becomes cheaper and better quality by the day, meaning that everyone can have a go at making films.

- ✔ The Internet offers huge databases of moving images to stream and download, collapsing film's past into its present.

- ✔ DVDs and Blu-Ray discs typically contain a bewildering array of supplementary material ('making of' documentaries, commentary, deleted scenes), which lay bare the construction of cinema.

- ✔ Even relatively mainstream films such as *Memento* (2000) or *Eternal Sunshine of the Spotless Mind* (2004) deconstruct themselves (see Chapter 15) in a manner that used to be reserved for radical avant-garde cinema.

Digital disruption

In her work, film theorist Dina Iordanova suggests that *digital disruption* has already restructured many industries (publishing, music, photography) and may be about to do the same for Hollywood. Iordanova identifies a period prior to 'radical disruption' (the crisis point when dramatic changes occur) in other industries that bares similarities to today's film industries: many new technologies are available, numerous possibilities bubble away under the surface and pressure is building on the established business models. Perhaps only when Hollywood studios start to go bust will the radical potential of digital cinema be fully realised.

Audiences now are so soaked in moving images and so well versed in how they're put together that the awe-inspiring mystique of early and classical cinema is difficult, if not impossible, to maintain. Today's sophisticated audiences don't necessarily have to be seen as A Bad Thing, though. The democratisation of film-making can, in theory, lead to a revolution in the possibilities of cinema. This change hasn't happened yet, but you never know. Yep, still waiting. . . .

Watching films amid the comforts of home

Technically speaking, you've always been able to watch films at home, and indeed lower-quality prints on film formats such as Super 8 or 16mm were produced for domestic use as recently as the 1970s (check out the later section 'Elevating everyone to film-maker status (sort of)' for more). But in practice, the cost of projection equipment and the skill required to present it reliably meant that very few people had home cinemas based around celluloid. Most non-theatrical film-screening venues were instead film clubs or schools.

The big game changer for home cinema was videotape. Video systems record onto magnetic tape that's cheap to produce and convenient to use, packaged on neat cassettes. The first major 'format war' of home cinema was between Sony's Betamax system and rival JVC's VHS system in the late-1970s. Although Betamax offered a higher-quality video image, the larger VHS format recorded for longer and eventually became the industry standard.

VHS created two new subsidiary markets for the film industry: video rental and video sell-through. Rental became widespread first, with stores stocked with VHS tapes popping up across the US and UK in the 1980s. Video rental stores offered a new space for film culture that had little to do with the cinema experience. Film geeks were able to access dozens of films in their favourite genres, leading to thriving markets for international horror movies or kung fu action films.

VHS sell-through was initially prohibitively expensive, because the studios were afraid of destroying the rental market. The Disney Corporation led the charge towards sell-through, wisely realising that families could re-watch their classic children's movies over and over again at home, easily justifying a premium cost. Partly for this reason, *The Lion King* (1994) remains the best-selling VHS of all time, with more than 30 million copies sold in the US alone. Other 'must-own' titles were *Star Wars* (1977), or perfect Christmas gifts for your mum, such as *Titanic* (1997).

Home video was a wildly successful venture for the major studios, to the extent that the cinema release soon became a minor contributor to a film's eventual profitability. But the relatively poor image and sound quality of magnetic videotape meant that a clear distinction remained between home and 'real' cinema viewing experiences. An early attempt to introduce digital quality on LP-sized laserdiscs never took off. DVD, on the other hand, was a different story.

The DVD format uses compression algorithms to squeeze a high-quality movie onto a single, CD-size disc. Apart from the obvious increases in image and sound quality, DVD offers *read-only access,* which eliminates one of the most irritating aspects of VHS tapes: you never need to rewind the discs. This flexibility also enables distributors to include additional material, often as an incentive for fans to re-purchase titles they may already own on VHS. Plus DVDs are a lot cheaper to produce than videocassettes, and so the format was an apparent win-win for the industry. At least until DVD piracy arrived (see 'Stealing pleasures' later in this chapter).

Play the movie, watch the game

Arguably the most radical new possibilities for the traditional film-viewing experience have come not from television or any of the successive home-cinema formats, but from video games. Gaming offers increasingly movie-like aesthetics with franchises such as *Grand Theft Auto* and *Final Fantasy,* but with the crucial added element of interactivity. Even if you're not a gamer yourself, game culture has altered the ways you think about *identification* with characters on screen (flip to Chapter 3 for more on identifying with actors and characters). For example: the plugging in of human consciousness into artificial bodies forms the basis of digital cinema's biggest hit, *Avatar* (2009).

Hollywood used to think of games as just another merchandising opportunity. Each blockbuster needed an accompanying (often less-than-great) spin-off game. Similarly, early attempts to adapt popular games into films, such as *Super Mario Bros.* (1993) and *Street Fighter* (1994), were poorly conceived cinematic failures. But in recent years, the sci-fi and horror genres have produced narratives that seem to work equally well in either format. The foremost example is the *Resident Evil* franchise, which by 2014 has produced six video games and five movies.

From humble beginnings, the game industry now generates revenues that are comparable with Hollywood blockbusters. In 2013, *Grand Theft Auto 5* sold 32.5 million copies, at a cost per unit typically 3 or 4 times higher than an average cinema ticket or DVD. No wonder Hollywood is increasingly making films that look like games rather than the other way around.

Collapsing the release window

The number of ways in which the film industry makes money from films has steadily increased since the 1950s (when older films began appearing on network television). By the late 1990s, a complex system of staggered *release windows* developed. Under this system, films worked their way through the following stages in two to three years:

- Theatrical release (in cinemas)
- Non-theatrical (such as airlines, hotels)
- Pay-per-view TV, and then cable TV
- Video rental, and then video sell-through (see the preceding section)
- Network TV

This complex system was built up over many years of careful negotiation between producers, distributors and exhibitors. In post-1970s Hollywood, the producer of the biggest films also tends to be the distributor, and so the main resistance to change has typically been from the exhibition industry. Cinemas, so the argument goes, have the most to lose from the 'cannibalising' effect of allowing products down through the revenue streams too quickly. Why bother going to watch something in the cinema when you can see it just as easily at home?

But the economic logic of this system has come under increasing strain. When sell-through DVDs typically made several times more money than cinema tickets, the question arose: what was the theatrical release for? Was it just a highly expensive advertising campaign for the real money generators: shiny plastic discs? Meanwhile, technology stepped in and provided impatient consumers with what they wanted: instant access to films and television shows. The problem was that consumers could also easily avoid paying for their viewing experiences – and many did.

Alice, through the release window

In the UK, Tim Burton's *Alice in Wonderland* (2010) became something of a test case when the major cinema chains threatened to boycott the film due to Disney's plan to release it on DVD just 12 weeks after it debuted in cinemas. The Cineworld chain eventually caved in and agreed to present the film in their cinemas, citing strong audience demand for 3D as the deciding factor.

In the end, the film performed strongly across all formats, suggesting that the reduced delay didn't damage the initial theatrical release. Perhaps the inherent advantages of a cinema release, the spectacle and the social experience are enough to protect this privileged window after all.

Internet piracy has turned the logic of release windows on its head (see the later 'Stealing pleasures' section). If studios wait for ages after releasing a film in cinemas to provide a home entertainment option, they give audiences more incentive to download it illegally and immediately. This factor led studio distributors to push more and more aggressively for a shorter window between cinema and DVD release.

The most recent challenge to the release window system has come from the development of Internet *video on demand* (VoD), enabled by increasingly widespread broadband services. Producers of smaller films are now experimenting with radical release strategies. In 2006, Steven Soderbergh's microbudget feature *Bubble* went into movie theatres and subscription TV on the same date. On 5 July 2013, the arty horror film *A Field in England* was the first film released across all platforms simultaneously in the UK: in cinemas, on sell-through DVD and Blu-ray, on free-to-air digital TV and via the Internet on demand. The strategy seems to work well for low-budget niche releases, allowing producers to maximise limited marketing budgets.

Converging on the Next Phase: Film and Everything Else

Early cinema was such a radical shock for audiences because it was an entirely new experience. Nobody had seen images move in such a lifelike way before and the effect was mesmerising. Nowadays, moving images are everywhere, on screens of all shapes and sizes, on websites which inform us about the news, entertain us, or sell us products, even on billboards on major public transport systems.

Older media, such as books, newspapers, phonographs and even the cinema were resolutely separate from each other. New media *converge*. In this section, I look at the implications of media convergence for blockbuster cinema, TV, DIY film-making and copyright protection.

Reassessing event movies

Ever since *Jaws* (1975) and *Star Wars* (1977) rewrote the rulebook on how to release and market blockbuster films, the Hollywood film industry has become more and more reliant upon *event movies* – films that create such an unstoppable buzz and momentum that everyone feels as if they sort of *need* to see them. These films are also known as *tentpole releases,* because they reach higher than all around them and also provide financial shelter for other films of more modest stature.

The most successful event movies tend to work to the following formula:

- ✔ They're based on a pre-sold property, such as a bestselling novel, a popular comic book or often just a previously successful film.

- ✔ Their marketing begins as soon as they're in pre-production, with teaser material being made available long before the film's release date. They use tie-in merchandising and cross-promotional strategies with all kinds of products from soft toys to fast-food restaurants.

- ✔ They aim for very wide releases, often simultaneously across many international territories.

As financially successful as this business strategy has been over the last 30 years, it isn't without its flaws. The drive to release the biggest and best films leads to inflated production costs, with key personnel such as directors and stars commanding larger and larger salaries. The budgets of the first modern blockbusters were relatively modest compared to today's behemoths. *Jaws* cost around $8 million to produce in 1975, which is equivalent to about $34 million today, adjusted for inflation. To produce a Batman movie in 2012, you don't get much change from a quarter of a billion dollars (*The Dark Knight Rises* cost around $250 million to produce and an estimated $100 million to market).

Ever growing production costs means that the risks associated with releasing such films has also become bigger and bigger. In 2012 Disney suffered a rare humiliation with *John Carter,* a pre-sold, heavily marketed special-effects spectacular that cost as much as *The Dark Knight Rises* but took only around $180 million worldwide in cinemas. When event movies bomb, they really bomb.

Although the event-movie system has always produced the occasional high-profile flop, the more worrying trend for producers is that the fundamentals of how the film industry works are going through rapid change. In 2004, the journalist and author Chris Anderson popularised the concept of *the long tail* in the new media landscape. Anderson starts by arguing that the old Hollywood business model – the event-movie strategy – was based upon limitations in the industry that no longer exists. Cinemas as a means of distributing films have a very limited 'shelf space' or number of screens. Not so long ago, blockbusters were able to force other releases out of business by severely restricting their capacity to reach audiences.

But when you take a look at DVD sales, downloads and streaming (which don't have to contend with shelf-space limitations in a world with Amazon, iTunes and others), you get a sense of what the long tail means. Figure 16-2 shows that major titles such as Disney/Pixar's *Monsters University* (2013) always sell bucketloads, but down the other end of the scale, obscure art house movies and classic titles are still finding space. In this new era of theoretically infinite shelf space, businesses are making money by selling small amounts of many items instead of relying on blockbusters.

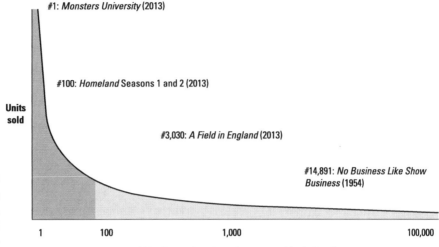

#1: *Monsters University* (2013)

#100: *Homeland* Seasons 1 and 2 (2013)

Units sold

#3,030: *A Field in England* (2013)

#14,891: *No Business Like Show Business* (1954)

Figure 16-2:
The long
tail of digital
distribution.

1   100   1,000   100,000

DVD chart ranking from *Amazon.co.uk* (12/11/2013)

Elevating everyone to film-maker status (sort of)

Regular folk have been able to make their own films using low-quality equipment for many decades, at least since the consumer electronics boom of the 1950s and 1960s. Film formats such as Super 8 (8 millimetre-wide images recorded onto the film) brought costs within the reach of many amateur film-makers, although it wasn't a mass-market phenomenon.

Nonetheless, amateur film-makers' films are of huge interest to social historians, and collections are regularly found in national film archives. Amateur films, and later home videos shot on magnetic tape, clearly have a different place in people's lives from professional features or documentary films:

- ✔ Anthropologists study them as a form of *social practice,* in that their use connects to domestic rituals and communication.

- ✔ They often commemorate significant family events and milestones such as holidays, weddings and children's birthdays, which gives the films a special relationship with emotional memory.

- ✔ Super 8 and other domestic formats employed in feature films often draw upon these formats' nostalgic feel, such as scenes of childhood in *My Own Private Idaho* (1991), which are shot in Super 8.

Of course domestic film or video recording equipment can be used for more than just making family memories. Cheaper film formats have always played an important role in avant-garde film-making, with few experimental films requiring the expensive gloss of 35 mm stock. Cheap VHS camcorders also allowed a generation of children and teenagers to pretend to be Steven Spielberg and direct their own epic productions at home. Check out the small British film *Son of Rambow* (2007) for a warm, funny recreation of this moment.

The biggest challenge for fledgling directors working with VHS was editing. The only way to reorder scenes shot on magnetic tape is by recording from one VHS player to another, which degrades quality significantly. These limitations led to the rise of digital video. Home film-makers first converted VHS into digital formats to play around with on a computer and later started shooting directly onto digital. Ambitious home film-makers can now do almost anything that the professionals can, including distributing their work to audiences via YouTube.

Although home film-makers can now produce material that looks and feels relatively professional, watching a few amateur films on YouTube instantly illustrates the essential ingredients remaining largely beyond their reach. Good sound design and editing remains a challenge. More importantly, you can't fix weak storytelling with digital editing software. No doubt a few talented, instinctive directors exist, artists who can pick up cameras and make wonderful films. But many more need to study and work at their craft. Which is why in order to make films, you also need to study films.

Amateur films that changed the world

The most famous piece of 8 mm film in existence was recorded by amateur film-maker Abraham Zapruder in Dallas, Texas, on 22 November 1963. Zapruder set out to record the passing of President Kennedy's motorcade, but instead accidently documented the President's assassination. The resulting 26 seconds of silent colour footage have been endlessly analysed and become the subject of countless conspiracy theories.

Fifty years later, standard issue smartphones can capture much higher resolution video than Super 8 and practically everyone has them. Passers-by and eyewitnesses with the ability to capture and distribute video via the devices in their pockets were largely responsible for documenting the revolutionary and violent Arab Spring in 2011. These events were a watershed moment of 'citizen journalism' in which people tell their own stories to the news networks.

Raising the bar: TV catches up with cinema

In the 21st century, TV has finally thrown off its image as being somehow second rate compared to cinema and taken its place as a screen offering entertainment of equally high quality as the silver variety. In the US, cable channel HBO led the shift towards cinematic drama with an amazing run of critically acclaimed and internationally popular series starting with *Sex and the City* in 1998 (until 2004) followed swiftly by *The Sopranos* (1999–2007). Networks such as AMC followed HBO's lead with glossy, expensive shows, for instance *Mad Men* (2007–) and *The Walking Dead* (2010–).

Television executives scheduled these hit shows on TV in the time-honoured way, carefully managing timeslots to catch and hold onto audiences. But the shows also found large new audiences through DVD box set releases. The popularity of reasonably priced box sets created a new way of consuming TV series, known informally as *binge-watching*. Good consumers used to wait patiently for the next dose of favourite shows; now you can watch the whole series back to back in a weekend, if you have the stamina.

The binge-watching phenomenon is part of a broader trend away from scheduled programming and towards an audience-driven, on-demand model. This shift is significant within media studies, which used to theorise that the never-ending *flow* of programming (where shows become part of larger schedules) was the key difference between TV and the discrete viewing experience of film. In Britain, the BBC's iPlayer service was launched in 2007, offering 'catch up' viewing of the previous week's programmes. It proved so successful with audiences that within a year it was responsible for 5 per cent of total Internet traffic in the UK. By 2012, 40 per cent of British adults were regular iPlayer users.

DVD box sets and the on-demand streaming model of catch-up services (such as iPlayer) and subscription services (such as Netflix) levelled the playing field between films and TV shows. Films and TV are now easily interchange-able options for an evening's entertainment, with drama series offering lon-gevity and films a comparatively quick, two-hour hit of viewing pleasure. The boundaries between the two media in terms of cultural prestige and personnel have now almost completely evaporated.

At the time in the late 1980s, many people saw David Lynch's decision to make *Twin Peaks* for US network TV as a radical and surprising move from an avant-garde film director. Conventional logic said that directors started with TV and then graduated to film-making. Nowadays many directors and produc-ers work in both media:

✔ Joss Whedon directed the megahit big-screen version of *The Avengers* (2012) and its TV spin-off *Agents of S.H.I.E.L.D.* (2013).

✔ Todd Haynes was at the forefront of the 'New Queer Cinema' movement of the late 1980s and early 1990s, but he also directed the TV miniseries *Mildred Pierce* (2011), starring Kate Winslet.

✔ Veteran film-makers such as Martin Scorsese now feel comfortable working in TV drama. Marty executive-produced and directed the first episode of *Boardwalk Empire* (2010). For HBO, natch.

✔ Indie film-maker Steven Soderbergh has claimed that he will quit cinema for TV permanently after the experience of making the award-winning Liberace biopic *Behind the Candelabra* (2013) for (who else?) HBO.

Stealing pleasure

Every new step forward in home cinema or film-making technology is a double-edged sword for the film industry. On the one hand, new opportunities for revenue streams are created and happily exploited, such as the vital cash injection from DVD sales in the late 1990s. On the other, with each new product the industry's previously watertight grip on its own intellectual property inevitably loosens. Before home video, practically nobody was able to own a copy of *Gone with the Wind* (1939). Now you can buy one on DVD for just £3.99.

Using VHS to capture film content (by sneaking a camcorder into a cinema screening or duplicating existing original tapes) was hampered by poor quality and the necessity to sell the taped copies illegally. DVDs really let the cat out of the bag due to one crucial property of digital video: you can copy it perfectly with no loss of quality. The industry's attempts to restrict this huge potential for loss of revenue, such as copy protection algorithms, were largely unsuccessful. Within a couple of years, DVD piracy was rampant across the globe and Hollywood in particular was very, very cross.

But things were about to get a whole lot worse. Start with a physical format you can copy perfectly onto a computer, add an easy means to share that data with anyone around the world, and you have a serious copyright problem. File sharing through BitTorrent is fast, efficient and relatively anonymous, although authorities can track and prosecute very heavy users, notably large servers holding huge amounts of illegal material.

With Internet file sharing, image quality is no longer a disincentive, and you don't even have to sneak up to a dodgy dealer at a street market to get your hands on a copy anymore. But probably the most significant factor convincing consumers to share illegally is early availability. Viewers can watch films at home while they're still in the cinemas, and see TV shows across international networks immediately after their US screening – something that often takes years otherwise.

The story remains the same?

With the seismic changes going on in technology and industry practices, you may be wondering whether films are really that different from what they were in the 1980s and 1990s:

✔ Despite talk of 'the long tail' creating opportunities for smaller films and niche marketing (see the earlier section 'Reassessing event movies'), blockbusters still dominate the market.

✔ Audiences remain attracted to familiar but different-enough products: genre films, literary adaptations and star vehicles, for example.

✔ Story structures, character development and screen performance styles remain largely unchanged.

✔ Digital aesthetics and style employs a virtual camera that allows unlimited camera movement, but even purely digital films such as *Toy Story* (1995) construct space with traditional continuity editing (which I describe in Chapter 4). Indeed, David Bordwell (see Chapter 17) argues that rather than a radical break in aesthetic styles, contemporary films *intensify* existing conventions, with more and faster cuts.

Meanwhile those elements highlighted as being new or different in digital film culture, such as the importance of moments rather than entire stories, and spectacle rather than narrative, have arguably always been present in one form or another. For example, film theorist Tom Gunning's description of very early film as a 'cinema of attractions' feels completely relevant to the current moment (check out Chapter 17). And the huge archives of digital video history such as YouTube are dominated by home videos of singing cats.

Of course the international film industry wasn't going to take this situation lying down. The Motion Picture Association of America (MPAA) launched a global propaganda offensive to reinforce the criminal nature of this activity:

✔ The MPAA claims $6.1 billion of revenue was lost in 2008 alone.

✔ The FBI now produces anti-piracy warnings and seals for official products.

✔ Cinema and TV adverts aim to dispute the widely-held notion that piracy is a 'victimless crime', even linking it with international terrorist organisations.

Yet the MPAA figures have been widely disputed, because they're based on estimates and predictions of behaviour that can't be accurately tracked. In particular they assume that one pirated copy equals one lost sale of a copyrighted version, whereas evidence suggests that many consumers use pirated versions to 'try before they buy'. Lecturing consumers about illegal behaviour is unlikely to be effective, with the endless copyright notices on DVDs actually making the 'clean' pirated downloads more attractive.

While Hollywood was busy spending money telling file sharers how naughty they were, other sectors of the entertainment industry accepted that they were probably fighting a losing battle and instead focused on experimenting with business models to adjust to the new reality. One key strategy is to challenge the release window model (see the earlier section 'Collapsing the Release Window') to minimise or eliminate delays. Most consumers are willing to pay a reasonable amount to access something legally, provided the other incentives (such as earlier access) are removed. All that's needed is a bit of innovation and experimentation with modes of delivery and pricing to make sure that consumers behave ethically with regard to copyright.

Part V
The Part of Tens

For a list of the ten topics film students love to debate, head to http://www.dummies.com/extras/filmstudies.

In this part . . .

- Read up on ten film writers guaranteed to expand your views on film studies.

- Add ten essential films to your watch-list.

- Meet ten fantastic film-makers who haven't received the attention they deserve – yet.

- Survive and prosper as a film student.

Chapter 17

Ten Film Writers You Need to Read

*T*hroughout this book, I make constant use of other people's ideas. So this chapter is an opportunity to give a little back and pay respects to some inspirational film scholars. Obviously, the work of the ten writers I include barely scratches the surface of the huge variety of methods, approaches and styles that make up film studies. But hey, you have to start somewhere, and each of those featured here are great introductions to a range of approaches when writing about film. So get ready to meet ten fascinating film writers and thinkers, explore their contributions and chew on great quotes from their most notable works.

The books that I mention below are generally widely available through public libraries or booksellers. The majority remain in print, and those that are older can be picked up through used or second-hand shops or websites. Film journals can be trickier to access, but your local library should be able to help you track them down.

VF Perkins: Analysing Film Style

To discover how to write precise, elegant and weighty film analysis, you can do a whole lot worse than study the writings of Victor Perkins. Perkins began his career as a film critic for the film journal *MOVIE*. He later co-founded one of the first academic film departments in the UK at Warwick University in 1978, where he taught until he retired in 2004. He's still an occasional lecturer and active researcher.

Key concepts and where to find more:

> ✔ **Auteurism:** As a critic for *MOVIE*, which followed the French *Cahiers du Cinéma* in celebrating the work of popular film and film-makers, Perkins was an auteurist (see Chapter 14) with a particular interest in

mise-en-scène (which I discuss in Chapter 4). His favourite directors include Max Ophüls, Nicholas Ray and Jean Renoir. Check out his article 'The Cinema of Nicholas Ray', *MOVIE* 9 (May 1963).

✔ **Film as Film:** This influential book argues for film to be judged on its own merits instead of worrying about whether or not it's an art form. See: *Film as Film: Understanding and Judging Movies* (Penguin, 1972).

In the movies we have to accept the point of view given to us. Our activity in the cinema, discounting the extra-curricular enjoyments of courtship, arson and malicious damage, is very limited. We can watch. We can listen. All the rest is in the mind.

—VF Perkins (Film as Film)

Richard Dyer: Watching Stars and Developing Queer Theory

If you love films, you can't help but be fascinated by the glamour of film stars (find much more on stars in Chapter 3), which means you have to read Richard Dyer at some point. Luckily his writing is witty and intellectually rigorous. Dyer has held professorships in film studies at universities including Warwick, King's College London and St Andrews. He has been actively involved in gay and lesbian politics in the UK, and he organised one of the world's first film festivals about homosexuality at London's National Film Theatre in 1977.

Key concepts and where to find more:

✔ **Starry-eyed:** Dyer argues that stars are constructed not only from an actor's performances, but also from publicity material and gossip columns. You can then examine the resulting *star image* in relation to the politics of identity. Check out *Stars* (British Film Institute, 1979).

✔ **Here and Queer:** Dyer's work in queer theory examines the repression of gay identity in popular culture and celebrates strategies of resistance, such as the camp sensibility: for example, *The Culture of Queers* (Routledge, 2002).

Looking at, listening to [Judy] Garland may get us inside how gay men have lived their experience and situation, have made sense of them. We feel that sense in the intangible and the ineffable – the warmth of the voice, the wryness of the humour, the edgy vigour of the stance – but they mean a lot because they are made expressive of what it has been to be gay in the past half century.

—Richard Dyer (Heavenly Bodies: Film Stars and Society, 2nd edition, Routledge, 2004)

Tom Gunning: Reassessing Early Cinema

If the idea of watching early cinema fills you with the fear of being bored out of your mind, take a look at the work of Tom Gunning. He brings the more outrageous and sensational aspects of early film practice to wider attention. Gunning is currently a professor in cinema studies at the University of Chicago. He has published widely on early cinema, film cultures and the history of film exhibition.

Key concepts and where to find more:

- ✔ **Cinema of attractions:** Gunning highlights the status of cinema as a fair-ground novelty instead of as an early version of today's narrative film. The *cinema of attractions* is about visual spectacle and sensory experience rather than storytelling. Some critics (such as Leon Gurevitch) have extended this model into contemporary blockbuster cinema. Check out 'The Cinema of Attractions: Early Film, Its Spectator and the Avant-Garde', *Wide Angle* 8 (Fall 1986).

- ✔ **The newness of the old:** Gunning emphasises that early cinema was radical, shocking and outlandish, as well as a vital part of modernism in European culture. See *The Films of Fritz Lang: Allegories of Vision and Modernity* (British Film Institute, 2000).

  From comedians smirking at the camera, to the constant bowing and gesturing of the conjurors in magic films, this is a cinema that displays its visibility, willing to rupture a self-enclosed fictional world for a chance to solicit the attention of the spectator.

  —*Tom Gunning ('The Cinema of Attractions')*

Molly Haskell: Engaging with Feminism and Film

Molly Haskel is a journalist, film critic and film scholar, making her among the most accessible of writers on feminism and film. Like her late husband, Andrew Sarris, Haskell wrote for *The Village Voice* in the 1960s. She has taught at Barnard College and Columbia University. She continues to have a voice on the cultural politics of women and you can follow her on Twitter.

Key concepts and where to find more:

- ✔ *Her-*story of cinema: Haskell identifies a trend towards more derogatory representation of female characters in film, which the title of her note-worthy book spells out. But she also identifies examples of women who resist or break out of negative stereotyping, such as Katharine Hepburn. Check out *From Reverence to Rape: The Treatment of Women in the Movies* (University of Chicago Press, 1974).

✔ **(Not) Gone With The Wind:** Haskell takes a detailed look at Hollywood's greatest movie of all time to revise common perceptions of its sexism and racism. She also challenges the auteurist focus on directors by examining the contributions of author Margaret Mitchell and star Vivien Leigh. See: *Frankly, My Dear: 'Gone With The Wind' Revisited* (Yale University Press, 2009).

It's a fitting irony that the example par excellence of this studio-confected world was Gone With The Wind, a celebration of caste and class from the New World's most democratic medium, the portrait of a never-never land whose harmony and grace depended on the smoothing out of much that was ugly and uncomfortable.

—*Molly Haskell (Frankly, My Dear: 'Gone with the Wind' Revisited)*

Yvonne Tasker: Analysing Action Cinema

Yvonne Tasker writes clever things about (occasionally) stupid movies. Her work on the muscle-bound action stars of the 1980s has been widely influential, and she's also written about images of women in the workplace and the military. She's a professor of film studies at the University of East Anglia.

Key concepts and where to find more:

✔ **Musculinity:** Tasker's work analyses the images of absurdly beefy bodies of both genders that are common in action films. Their importance is related to *discourses* (what you say and think) of race, class and sexuality. Check out *Spectacular Bodies: Gender, Genre and the Action Cinema* (Routledge, 1993).

✔ **Feminism/post-feminism:** Tasker's work tackles the debate around these two controversial terms. She investigates the differences and similarities between them and outlines their relative usefulness for discussions of popular culture, notably films and television. See Yvonne Tasker and Diane Negra, editors, *Interrogating Postfeminism: Gender and the Politics of Popular Culture* (Duke University Press, 2007).

The visual spectacle of the male body that is central to muscular movies puts into play the two contradictory terms of restraint and excess. Whilst the hero and the various villains of the genre tend to share an excessive physical strength, the hero is also defined by his restraint in putting his strength to the test. And it is the body of the male hero which provides the space in which a tension between restraint and excess is articulated.

—*Yvonne Tasker (Spectacular Bodies)*

Michel Chion: Speaking Up for Film Sound

Film began as a visual medium, and film criticism has tended to relegate sound and music to a secondary position ever since. This neglect is clearly a great injustice, because sound is crucial for film storytelling and good film music is one of the major pleasures of watching films. As a musician and composer, Michel Chion is well qualified to theorise about film sound. He works and teaches at the Sorbonne in Paris.

Key concepts and where to find more:

- ✔ **Voice training:** Chion's work explores the strange power of the voice in cinema, drawing on a range of examples from *Psycho* (1960) to *2001: A Space Odyssey* (1968). He distinguishes between *visualised* voices (where the source is on-screen) and *acousmatic* ones that are disembodied from their source. Check out *The Voice in Cinema* (Columbia University Press, 1999).

- ✔ **Sound argument:** Chion urges film audiences to think of sound as not simply a slave to the image and to narrative, but as an aesthetic force in its own right. Sound and image can and do work together, but this interaction requires a complex 'contract' negotiated between film and audience. See *Audio-Vision: Sound on Screen* (Columbia University Press, 1994).

This work [understanding sound] is at once theoretical and practical. First, it describes and formulates the audiovisual relationship as a contract – that is, as the opposite of a natural relationship arising from some sort of pre-existing harmony among the perceptions. Then it outlines a method for observation and analysis that has developed from my teaching experience and may be applied to films, television programs, videos and so forth.

—*Michel Chion (Audio-Vision)*

Richard Maltby: Investigating Cinema History

Film history has traditionally been about the films themselves. The method has tended to involve looking for key classic film texts as 'milestones' and tracing aesthetic developments between them. Richard Maltby encourages viewers to return films to their social and economic contexts. His own history of Hollywood cinema is an important text for film students. He has taught film studies in the UK and Australia.

Key concepts and where to find more:

- ✔ **Consider the Code:** Maltby's history of Hollywood emphasises the importance of the Hays Code's self-regulation (see Chapter 9), which shaped classical storytelling into ambiguous narratives where film-makers signalled adult content without showing it. Check out *Hollywood Cinema,* 2nd edition (Blackwell, 2003).

- ✔ **Cinema history:** Maltby argues that *film* history misses what's most vibrant and interesting about cinema-going. Instead, you should focus on *cinema* history, examining real buildings and their audiences. See: 'New Cinema Histories' in Richard Maltby, Daniel Biltereyst and Philippe Meers, editors, *Explorations in New Cinema History* (Wiley-Blackwell, 2011).

The [Hays] Code's regulation of movie content can, therefore, best be understood as a generic pressure, comparable to the pressure of convention in a romantic comedy or a Western. 'Sophisticated' viewers, familiar with the conventions of representation operating under the Code, learned to imagine the acts of misconduct that the Code had made unmentionable.

—*Richard Maltby (Hollywood Cinema)*

Nicholas Rombes: Discovering Digital Cinema

The digitisation of cinema is one of the most important and urgent issues of contemporary film studies (as I discuss in Chapter 16). But given that digitalisation is a current and ongoing phenomenon, you can't easily pick out which theorists are going to be the most influential. So I go with the scholar who's had the biggest impression on my understanding of the topic.

Nicholas Rombes is something of a renaissance man, being a novelist, music critic and film theorist. He's also professor of English at University of Detroit Mercy. As you'd expect from a digital guru, he has an excellent blog at www. thehappinessengine.net.

Key concepts and where to find more:

- ✔ **New punk:** Rombes finds parallels between the raw, stripped back aesthetic of punk music from the 1970s and the film-makers of today. Important film-makers in this regard include those of the Dogme 95 movement such as Lars von Trier (see Chapter 11) and the army of YouTubers doing it for themselves.

✔ **Digital dreaming:** Rombes is fascinated by the deliberate imperfection of early film shot on digital video, such as David Lynch's *Inland Empire* (2006), or films displaying a nostalgia for old technology, notably Quentin Tarantino's *Grindhouse* project (2007). He also makes provocative claims that film theorists no longer need to deconstruct cinema because contemporary cinema deconstructs itself.

> *[I]n the ruptures and gaps that have opened up as cinema transitions from the traditional analogue apparatus to the digital, there has been an unexpected resurgence of humanism – with its mistakes, imperfections and flaws – that acts as a sort of countermeasure to the numerical clarity and disembodiment of the digital code.*
>
> —*Nicholas Rombes (Cinema in the Digital Age, Wallflower Press, 2009)*

Hamid Naficy: Exploring Accented Cinema

As I note in Chapter 11, the study of world cinema in film studies has moved away from questions of national identity and towards issues of transnationalism. This shift provides space to discuss the many films made across national borders, or the films made by migrant or displaced populations. Hamid Naficy suggests that the latter's films can be considered 'accented' in a similar way to your voice when speaking a language with which you didn't grow up. Naficy is Iranian and has worked at home and in the West.

Key concepts and where to find more:

✔ **Accented cinema:** The 'accented' films of displaced film-makers working in other countries share common thematic concerns and stylistic elements, such as stories about journeys and fragmented narrative structures. His examples include Arabic or *beur* cinema in France and Asian cinema in Britain. Check out *An Accented Cinema: Exilic and Diasporic Filmmaking* (Princeton University Press, 2001).

✔ **Film-making in Iran:** Naficy's enormous four-volume history details the particular ways that Iranian society shapes its films. The book covers all periods from the silent era up to 2010, including the upheavals of both Iranian revolutions. See *A Social History of Iranian Cinema, Volume 1: The Artisanal Era* (Duke University Press, 2011).

In the best of the accented films, identity is not a fixed essence but a process of becoming, even a performance of identity. Indeed, each accented film may be thought of as a performance of its author's identity. Because they are highly fluid, exilic and diasporic identities raise important questions about political agency and about the ethics of identity politics.

—Hamid Naficy (An Accented Cinema)

Charles Barr: Battling for British Cinema

British cinema used to have a sorry reputation among film scholars, even British ones. This impression is partly François Truffaut's fault, because he claimed that the words 'British' and 'cinema' were incompatible. One of the first scholars to challenge this reputation was Charles Barr. He also helped to set up the pioneering school of film studies at the University of East Anglia where he taught for many years. He is now a visiting professor and remains an active researcher.

Key concepts and where to find more:

- **Ealing Studios:** Barr was one of the first film scholars to study an institution rather than individual films and film-makers. He suggests that Ealing Studios' post-war films can be seen as a 'cinema of consensus', securing national identity during a period of trauma and recovery. Check out *Ealing Studios* (University of California Press, 1977).

- **English Hitchcock:** Although Hitchcock is perhaps the most discussed film-maker in film studies, his early films made in England receive little attention. Barr corrects this imbalance through a detailed study of the 23 English films, grouped according to their scriptwriting collaboration. See: *English Hitchcock* (Cameron & Hollis, 1999).

I see Hitchcock's absorption in the London stage as a mark of his rootedness within the culture, and the cinema, of that time and place. To the end of his life, he would remain very English in his public image – dress, speech, deportment, humour – and this Englishness was more than just a facade. My concern is not to deny the cosmopolitanism of his cinema in a spirit of cultural nationalism, but simply to redress a balance.

—Charles Barr (English Hitchcock)

Chapter 18

Ten Must-Watch Movies

*B*oy, this was tough. Having to choose just ten essential films from the entire history of world cinema is incredibly difficult. I try to maintain a balance across genres, historical periods and national cinemas, but inevitably I leave many areas uncovered here.

In the end, I put self-torture aside and simply go with the films that mean the most to me, as a film student and now as a (very lucky) film academic. I'm not saying the following ten are the greatest films of all time, just that they're great places to start studying film.

Don't feel like you have to start at the beginning of this list and work through it to the end. Jump around to what interests you most and start from there. Hopefully this list will make you want to watch (or re-watch) many of these films, and, luckily, all of them are easily available to rent, download or stream.

Sherlock, Jr. (1924)

If you're new to film studies, you may well struggle a bit with early, pre-synchronised sound cinema. The obscure jokes, the mannered acting style and the static compositions can be alienating. So whenever I want to show a film to students that can help them overcome their reservations, *Sherlock, Jr.* usually does the trick. Charlie Chaplin may be better known, but Buster Keaton's understated dry wit as a performer and his visual inventiveness as a director make him the silent comedian most accessible to contemporary audiences.

Often the biggest revelation for students watching *Sherlock, Jr.* is that clever *meta cinema* (films about films) doesn't begin with *Pulp Fiction* in 1994. In fact playing around with what film is and does was a defining characteristic of early cinema, and here Keaton takes this play to spectacular extremes. The moment when his projectionist character falls asleep on the job, leaves his earthly body behind and then tumbles into the action on the cinema screen is simply jaw-dropping.

The sequence that follows is a tour de force of physical precision and clever editing, as Keaton's hapless projectionist finds the scenery constantly changing around him. The film was clearly a ridiculous, insanely dangerous project to take on. Keaton's entire persona (and 'Buster' nickname) was based around his apparent immunity to injury while performing stunts, and you see some doozies here. The common knowledge that Keaton broke his neck while performing one of them (look out for the water tower!) only adds to their thrilling allure.

But is it still funny 90 years on? Of course humour is a matter of personal taste, but I've seen it many times and it still makes me smile. In the final scene, the earnest look on Keaton's face as he studies the leading man on screen in order to find out how to woo his girlfriend is touching and sweetly comical, like the rest of this surprising little film.

Casablanca (1942)

Smart literary theorist Umberto Eco was spot on when he said that *Casablanca* isn't just *a* movie, it's *the* movies. He means that this film seems to be the perfect embodiment of classical Hollywood cinema, that golden era of confidence, glamour and escapism (see Chapter 9). If you need an example to illustrate any of the key elements of the classical Hollywood style, such as continuity editing, narrative economy or the visual treatment of stars, it's all right here. It may not be as grandiose or ambitious as *Gone with the Wind* (1939) or *Citizen Kane* (1941), but *Casablanca* is practically flawless.

Of course the apparent perfection of classical Hollywood is in itself a carefully crafted illusion. Film historians have uncovered *Casablanca*'s troubled production history, consisting of compromises and last-minute changes. The original choice to play Rick was none other than (later President of the United States) Ronald Reagan. Imagining the clean-cut Reagan in the role is nearly impossible, because Humphrey Bogart is so good at world-weary cynicism. But if Reagan *had* played Rick, well, American history may have worked out rather differently.

Casablanca is also a great example of how big-budget, prestige Hollywood pictures typically try to offer something for everyone to maximise their audience. It's both a genuinely thrilling and suspenseful wartime drama, pitting noble freedom fighters against sinister Nazis, and a swooningly romantic love story. *Casablanca* is meaty, adult drama, while staying true to the letter of the Hays Code and so ensuring that it's technically suitable for children. Yet the film leaves enough space for grown-ups to infer violence, infidelity and possibly homosexuality in their imaginations.

This sense of openness and ambiguity is most obviously felt in *Casablanca*'s famous final scenes, which bring all the film's thorny issues to a head without resolving them. The biggest dilemma of all is whether Ilsa (Ingrid Bergman) should have left with her husband or stayed with her true love Rick. Even other movies can't decide. In *When Harry Met Sally* (1989), Ilsa's choice is a bone of contention between the mismatched central couple. Sally (Meg Ryan) supports her choice 'because women are very practical, even Ingrid Bergman', whereas Harry (Billy Crystal) can't believe Ilsa would want a passionless marriage over her chemistry with Rick. See it and pick a side.

Singin' in the Rain (1952)

Singin' in the Rain is the crowning achievement of that most showbiz of genres: the Hollywood musical. MGM's dream team under producer Arthur Freed created the film from scratch, combining catchy numbers from the back catalogue of classic 1930s and 1940s musicals and showcasing Gene Kelly at his most athletic and least pretentious (compared, say, to *An American in Paris* (1951)). The film's historical setting, during Hollywood's transition to sound in the late 1920s, allows the film to poke gentle fun at the silliest aspects of the musical genre (see Chapter 5 for my take).

Of course any musical stands or falls on the quality of its numbers. Luckily, *Singin' in the Rain* has the perky and energetic 'Good Morning', as well as comedian Donald O'Connor back-flipping through 'Make 'Em Laugh' and an incredibly slinky dance solo from leggy former ballerina Cyd Charisse. Not to mention *that* soggy title number from Gene Kelly, which is simply one of the most joyful five minutes of celluloid ever created. See it, and be forever tempted to start dancing with your umbrella and splash passing policemen.

The film's view of 1920s Hollywood is mostly warm and affectionate, with plenty of fun in the forms of vampish Dietrich-alike actresses and chorus girls jumping out of cakes. Take its account of the coming of sound to the industry with a fairly large pinch of salt, however. For a start, converting studios into sound stages took much longer than the 'couple of weeks' cited here. Plus the visual style of many of the numbers (particularly the 'Broadway Melody' ballet) weren't possible in late 1920s Hollywood.

Also, the conclusion to the film's storyline sees the beautiful but vocally unappealing Lina Lamont (Jean Hagen) exposed as a fraud because homely but talented Kathy Selden (Debbie Reynolds) has been dubbing her voice. In reality many Hollywood stars (including Cyd Charisse) had singing doubles throughout their careers without being treated as phonies. Of course, as ever with Hollywood, the film's ending is the emotionally satisfying conclusion rather than the logical one. In the end, historical inaccuracies mean little in the face of *Singin' in the Rain*'s barrage of pure unadulterated entertainment.

Rear Window (1954)

Although I resist the temptation to include many of the most obvious 'Greatest Films Ever Made' on this list – notably *Citizen Kane* (1941) – I just can't leave out Alfred Hitchcock. In fact, Hitchcock's achievements are so many and varied that I could easily devote the entire list of ten just to his films. Chapter 14 digs deeper into Hitchcock's legacy.

So why choose *Rear Window* from an unparalleled body of work? Well, primarily because it's a great film to introduce film theory – particularly the notion of voyeurism. In psychoanalysis, *voyeurism* is the pleasure of looking at people without their knowledge, which clearly comes into play in cinema spectatorship.

Hitchcock was well aware of this psychoanalytical idea and its relation to cinema, and *Rear Window* is the ultimate expression of this visual perversity. Its hero, Jeff (Jimmy Stewart), is a photographer who's currently wheelchair-bound and spends his days gazing at people in apartments across the courtyard. But when he apparently uncovers foul play, the act of looking puts him and his loved one into mortal danger.

Hitchcock is also known as the 'master of suspense', and *Rear Window* certainly doesn't disappoint on this score. In one key scene, Jeff's girlfriend Lisa (Grace Kelly) bravely breaks in to the suspected murderer's apartment to search for evidence. Jeff looks on from his rear window and is horrified to see the murderer return home. Hitch generates tension by keeping the perspective with Jeff, withholding important information, and so reinforcing his and the spectators' impotence. More than 60 years on, the sequence is still edge-of-your-seat viewing.

Jeff's stalled relationship with Lisa provides the emotional context for this tense murder mystery. Although the beautiful socialite clearly adores the wounded photographer, he fears marriage and the loss of excitement this brings. In typically kinky Hitchcockian fashion, Jeff only displays real desire for Lisa after she steps into the drama happening across the courtyard – and into his gaze. After overcoming the resulting dangers, the film ends with the suggestion of marriage (or at least domestic bliss). But the film's final look isn't from Jeff but from Lisa at Jeff as he sleeps. For those who just like to watch, *Rear Window* dares to stare right back.

À Bout de Souffle (Breathless) (1960)

If you want to understand why French cinema (which I cover in Chapter 11) is so effortlessly cool, look no further than *À Bout de Souffle* (literally 'out of breath'). Jean-Luc Godard's explosive debut takes the essential elements of the American gangster movie – the girl, the gun, the car and the disaffected hero – shifts them to the lovely streets of Paris, and adds jazz music, loads of cigarettes and sexy philosophising. The film is instantly recognisable as the work of an ambitious film-maker bursting with new ideas and a passion for cinema, which is why it continues to inspire film-studies students to this day.

Godard and his fellow cinéastes and critics at the influential *Cahiers du Cinéma* journal were notable early champions of Hollywood genre film-making. True to form, *À Bout de Souffle* pays homage to the hard-boiled anti-heroes of American film noir (see Chapter 5). Michel (Jean-Paul Belmondo) openly models himself upon his idea of Humphrey Bogart – and his French pronunciation of 'Bogey' is utterly charming. But Michel is an amateur crook, self-deluded and high on Hollywood nonsense. Face it, modelling yourself on a film-noir hero isn't the most sensible of lifestyle choices.

Only a film-maker who understood classical Hollywood style as well as Godard could deconstruct it so effectively. The film opens in a provincial French town, where Michel promptly steals a car and heads off to Paris. Belmondo improvises wildly while driving, even addressing the camera directly. He takes out a gun and pretends to shoot the sun, accompanied by gunfire on the soundtrack. The effect is disorienting and exhilarating.

À Bout de Souffle shatters the illusion of coherent time, which is the intended by-product of classical continuity editing (check out Chapter 4 for details). Jagged jump-cuts chop up the dialogue scenes set in the bedroom of love interest Patricia (Jean Seberg). These moments may have taken place over minutes, hours or days. This disorientation has the effect of giving weight to the couple's sexy sparring. But nearly every scene has small shifts and stylistic surprises in store. It's like a movie, only different.

Don't Look Now (1973)

Confession time: I admit that the first time I saw *Don't Look Now* on late-night TV in the dark, it scared the bejesus out of me. Watching it now, at a more, ahem, mature stage in my life, the film's moving portrayal of grief is what gets me. The film is still devastating, but in a completely different way. It may be a bit of a left-field choice, but for me *Don't Look Now* proves that the films that really get to you are the ones most worth revisiting.

Director Nicolas Roeg is one of the unsung heroes of British cinema. He spent his long career making idiosyncratic and formally experimental films that don't fit easily into any of the familiar genres of British film (which I discuss in Chapter 10).

Don't Look Now is the story of a married couple, John and Laura Baxter (Donald Sutherland and Julie Christie), who are struggling to come to terms with the death of their daughter. John begins to see things that are impossible to explain; they may be ghostly apparitions of his daughter or hallucinations brought on by grief.

Only at the end of the film – spoiler alert! – do you realise that John has second sight and was foreseeing his own grizzly murder. Until this point, *Don't Look Now* exists on the borderline between fantasy and reality, and as a result everyday objects take on a disorienting strangeness. Everything feels like an omen. The film is set in Venice, but grand vistas are avoided in favour of claustrophobic walkways and dank tunnels.

On reflection, *Don't Look Now* repays my repeated viewing because it's a strange mix of chilly art cinema, emotional melodrama and gothic horror film. The film's frank and grown-up portrayal of marriage is surprisingly rare in cinema – see the famous scene where John and Laura's lovemaking is intercut with them getting dressed to go out. Its imagery and atmosphere are distinctive and difficult to shake off. Ignore the title's warning, but don't watch it alone.

Blade Runner (1982)

Suggesting that *Blade Runner* is a film ahead of its time has become a cliché. The original release was greeted with critical hostility and audience indifference. But since then the film's reputation has grown and grown. Today many people credit its dark and grungy view of the future for dominating the look of sci-fi films for the coming decades. This reading is somewhat ironic, given that *Blade Runner* is a film so clearly influenced by the history of cinema, from the vast skyscapes of *Metropolis* (1927) to the dark smoky rooms of film noir. (Chapter 5 has more on sci-fi and film noir.)

Who'd have thought that sci-fi and film noir would prove such productive partners? Jean-Luc Godard for one, whose *Alphaville* (1965) displays elements of both. But *Blade Runner*'s narrative, adapted from sci-fi scribe Philip K Dick's short story, is a natural fit for this generic blending. In particular it offers a fascinating reworking of the femme-fatale figure in Rachael (Sean Young) who's cold, aloof and damaged because (unknown to herself) she's an android. This revelation opens up the disturbing possibility that the world-weary hero Deckard (Harrison Ford) is also non-human.

One significant stylistic borrowing from film noir, however, was largely responsible for the critical hostility that greeted the film's original release: Harrison Ford's incredibly wooden noir-style voice-over. Along with an equally unconvincing happy ending, this aspect frustrated many viewers. The voice-over and the ending were removed in the 1992 'director's cut' attributed to Ridley Scott, sparking off a short-lived trend towards multiple versions of films that privileged the director's vision over that of the studio. In effect this revised version was the industry's delayed recognition of the cult of the auteur, which began in film criticism in the 1950s (and which I write about in Chapter 14).

Pulp Fiction (1994)

When I saw *Pulp Fiction* in the first year of my film studies degree, it was like a vindication of my (somewhat unorthodox) choice of subject. This film was so exciting and provocative, so enthralled with the cinema of the past and so confident about the cinema of the future, that I began to wonder why anyone would choose to study anything else. Watching it again recently with students, during its 20th anniversary year, the film feels absolutely of its time, and admittedly it isn't without flaws. But it remains a milestone of a film, and for that reason, it has to be on this list.

In the 1950s and 1960s, *cinephilia* (the obsessive love of film) was somewhat of an elitist hobby. You could see films only in cinemas, or occasionally on television. For example, pioneering film scholar Victor Perkins admits that the detailed textual analysis in his book *Film as Film,* which came out in 1972, was based on film screenings from the 1950s. By the 1990s, things were very different. Quentin Tarantino's humble job as video store manager enabled him to see films from all corners of the world and all moments of film history (see Chapter 14 for more on Tarantino). The result is *Pulp Fiction*.

Whereas the previous generation of cine-literate directors (such as Martin Scorsese) was inspired largely by European art-house cinema (see Chapter 11), Tarantino's influences are a heady mix of genres from martial arts films to blaxploitation movies to B-movie thrillers (to name but a few). In fact his entire fictional world is made from other movies. For this reason, some accuse him of empty, meaningless pastiche or namechecks for namechecks' sake. But when his style works best, for example in the Jack Rabbit Slims sequence featuring John Travolta and Uma Thurman's dance routine, the result is electrifying.

Today, thanks to the Internet, practically anyone can achieve a level of film geekery equivalent to Tarantino's with much less effort. I'm constantly surprised by the breadth and diversity of my students' influences. But as many of them go on to discover, knowing this stuff is one thing – making it into something as awesome as *Pulp Fiction* is quite another.

Spirited Away (2001)

As an introduction to the sweet and strange world of Japanese anime, *Spirited Away*, by the master of the form, Hayao Miyazaki, is pretty hard to beat (check out Chapter 12 for more on Miyazaki and Japanese cinema). It begins in the real world, where Chihiro is having a tantrum about changing schools. For reasons that seem logical only when watching, her childlike selfishness manages to get her parents turned into giant, meat-gobbling pigs.

Chihiro is then plunged into a wildly imaginative fantasy realm based around a traditional Japanese bathhouse – one staffed by animals and witches and visited by spirits. She must survive in this world alone, discovering that she does need the support of adults after all, and growing up a great deal in the process. The section of the film where she gets a job in the bathhouse actually offers some pretty decent advice on becoming an adult. Be grateful, work hard and don't step on the super-cute soot sprites.

Spirited Away is so compelling because you have no idea what to expect next. Unless you always anticipate meeting an enormous spirit shaped like a radish in a lift. Admittedly, the film's narrative structure and outlandish characters are most surprising (and occasionally disturbing) from a Western point of view. Viewers in the West are accustomed to a certain style of fairy-tale storytelling, and *Spirited Away* certainly isn't it. *Alice in Wonderland* is the only thing that comes remotely close.

Miyazaki's character animation is comparable to that of Walt Disney (see Chapter 6), but instead of cute little puppies, Miyazaki can make you fall in love with tall, silent ghost figures or bouncing disembodied heads without the use of dialogue. You find dazzling sequences packed with dozens of beautifully drawn and distinctive creatures, all doing their own weird little thing. But the truly memorable moments in *Spirited Away* are the sections of quiet contemplation where nothing much happens, such as the train journey through a flooded land. The whole film is a gorgeous visual treat.

Cidade de Deus (City of God) (2002)

Cidade de Deus appears on this shortlist because it proves that world cinema (the subject of Chapter 12) doesn't have to be obscure and arty. Instead it can be breathlessly exciting and as adrenaline-filled as the best Hollywood action movies. This Brazilian co-production won rave reviews at international film festivals and went on to gross more than $30 million worldwide.

As a marker of its reputation with regular movie fans, the film is currently at number 21 on IMDb's Top 250 chart, level-pegging with Kurosawa's *Seven Samurai* (1954) as the highest rated foreign-language title.

Cidade de Deus is about growing up on the mean streets of the *favela* slums in Rio de Janeiro, which are infamous for gang violence and organised crime. It centres on young Rocket (Alexandre Rodrigues) who dreams of a life as a photographer but keeps getting dragged back into violence. Co-directors Fernando Meirelles and Kátia Lund trained up a large cast of young unknowns from the local area to ensure authentic performances. If all this is starting to sound like dour gritty realism, don't worry. The hyper-kinetic visual style and carefully crafted fight sequences are more *Kill Bill* (2003) than *The Killing* (2007–2012).

The style of *Cidade de Deus* is clearly indebted to American cinema. It uses the freeze-frames of Martin Scorsese, the chapter titles of Quentin Tarantino and the retro-chic visuals of Wes Anderson. These elements have led some critics to identify it as another victory for globalisation and a further loss of distinctive national cinema cultures. But this reading does an injustice to a film with such an original and important voice. You can equally read the film as a signal that American cinema's long period of domination over popular screens is finally coming to an end. Come in, Hollywood, your time is up?

Chapter 19

Ten Film-Makers You Need to Know Better

In This Chapter

▶ Rating the most underrated film-makers
▶ Encountering new voices and visions
▶ Stepping outside the mainstream

*O*ne of the great joys of practising film studies is coming across a film-maker you've never heard of, but who just blows your socks off. As you dig deeper into film studies, I hope that you find some yourself, but in the meantime, here are a few film-makers I think are well worth getting to know.

I stay away from the best-known directors (who are nearly all men from Hollywood, as I discuss in Chapter 14), and try to share the spotlight with women film-makers and those from less well-charted areas of world.

I present these film-makers in no particular order, so dip in and out of the list as you please. However, please don't be put off if the names here are ones that you've never heard of – that's the point of this chapter. As you may expect with less well-known directors, some of these films are widely available, and some less so, but all can be tracked down if they take your fancy.

Feng Xiaogang

Feng Xiaogang is China's most commercially successful film director of the last 20 years, earning him the accolade of 'the Chinese Spielberg'. He trained in television before making popular films of a specifically Chinese genre: the New Year celebration film. Since then Feng has made Chinese/Hong Kong co-productions and 'Main Melody' films, sanctioned by the Chinese government and reaffirming traditional values. Despite these patriotic successes, he continued to struggle with issues of censorship in the state-controlled film industry of mainland China.

Several of Feng's slick and popular films are now available on DVD outside China:

- **Be There or Be Square (Bu jian bu san) (1998):** A romantic comedy about two migrants living in the US. It features Feng's favourite male star, You Ge, and the actress who became Feng's wife, Fan Xu.

- **A World Without Thieves (Tian xia wu zei) (2004):** A hit action comedy featuring Hong Kong action star Andy Lau. Set on a train travelling across China, it offers fight sequences, romantic subplots and visual spectacle made with high production values.

- **Aftershock (Tang shan da di zhen) (2010):** About the Tangshan earthquake of 1976, combining blockbuster computer-generated imagery (CGI) effects with an intimate story of twins separated by the disaster. A huge box-office success in China, it was entered for the foreign-language Oscar category in 2011.

Alice Guy-Blaché

To paraphrase Jane Austen, it is a truth universally acknowledged that film history suffers greatly by ignoring the contributions of female film-makers. So what if I told you that one particular woman was instrumental in the early film industry, went on to direct and produce more than a thousand films throughout a long career, and even set up and ran her own successful movie studio?

That woman is Alice Guy-Blaché. She started out as a secretary for Gaumont Film Company, became a director in 1896 and worked prolifically in Paris and later New York for the following 25 years. So why isn't she celebrated alongside the Lumière Brothers or Georges Méliès? Well, it isn't called film *his*-story for nothing.

As is common with early cinema, the majority of Guy-Blaché's films are lost forever. But the following are a few that survive (and which you can view online):

- **La Fée aux choux (The Cabbage Fairy) (1896):** A simple scene of a fairy birthing babies from a cabbage patch that may well be the first fiction film ever made. It depends which historical source you consult and how you define a 'fiction film'. In any case, it certainly predates the much more celebrated films of Georges Méliès.

- **La Vie du Christ (The Birth, the Life and the Death of Christ) (1906):** An ambitious production with a large budget that was obviously spent on spectacular sets and hundreds of costumed extras. It was released specifically to compete with a similar film from rivals Pathé, demonstrating Guy-Blaché's keen business sense.

- *A House Divided* **(1913):** A lively comedy telling the story of a married couple living in separate areas of the same house, which sounds very much like Tim Burton and Helena Bonham-Carter's 'modern' arrangement. It was made in New York by Guy-Blaché's extremely successful Solax studio.

Ousmane Sembène

Can you name a single film made by an African film-maker? Or name an African film-maker for that matter? At least after reading this section you know one: Ousmane Sembène.

Sembène was born in Senegal in 1923 but moved to France to find work. He began to write novels, but seeking a better way to communicate with people in Africa, where literacy rates remain low, he turned to film-making. His films were sometimes supported by French subsidies and found favour at European film festivals (see Chapter 11), but they were often critical of French colonialism. He remained a prolific writer and occasional film-maker until his death in 2007.

Sembène's notable films include:

- *La Noire de . . . (Black Girl)* **(1966):** Tells the story of a girl from Senegal who moves to France seeking a better life. Instead her French employers abuse her and treat her like a slave. The film was the first feature film by an African director to gain international recognition.
- *Xala* **(1975):** *Xala* is a Wolof (that is, a Senegalese language) word meaning temporary sexual impotence, which is important in this satire about failed masculinity among the wealthy business class in Dakar.
- *Moolaadé* **(2004):** Film-makers from several French-speaking African nations co-produced this powerful and disturbing film protesting against female genital mutilation. It won the *Un Certain Regard* prize at the Cannes Film Festival in 2004.

Roger Corman

In cult cinema circles, Roger Corman is a colossus. In his autobiography he claims to have directed or produced well over a hundred films without ever losing money, which (if true) is a remarkable feat. Most of his movies were low-budget genre films made in the 1950s and 1960s, shot very quickly and distributed as exploitation films to low-rent movie houses. He's a notable champion of young film-making talent and gave early opportunities to Martin Scorsese, Francis Ford Coppola and James Cameron. Now into his late 80s, he shows no sign of retiring and is still working in Hollywood as an executive producer.

Corman's back catalogue is enormous, but the following are a few representative titles:

- *Attack of the Crab Monsters* **(1957):** One of Corman's earliest hits. This black-and-white sci-fi-comedy-horror film was made for just $70,000 but reportedly grossed more than $1 million in the US.

- *The Tomb of Ligeia* **(1964):** Part of Corman's series of Edgar Allen Poe adaptations, which are among his most critically respectable films. Robert Towne, later an Oscar winner for *Chinatown* (1974), wrote the script. Corman shot the film in England, in a spooky ruined castle in rural Norfolk.

- *Piranha* **(1978):** A loving tribute to/rip off of *Jaws* (1975), this schlocky B-movie itself sparked several increasingly postmodern remakes, most recently in 2010. Corman produced it, John Sayles wrote the screenplay and Joe Dante directed before becoming one the most successful directors of the 1980s.

Lynne Ramsay

Okay, so Lynne Ramsay has made only three feature films in 15 years. But what a trio of films they are! Ramsay's lack of productivity isn't for want of effort or ambition. She spent several years developing an adaptation of *The Lovely Bones* before it became a bestselling hot property and she was dropped from the project in favour of Peter Jackson. Most recently she mysteriously walked away from a project starring Natalie Portman just as it was about to begin shooting. In interviews Ramsay has spoken out against the hypocrisy and sexism of the film industry on both sides of the Atlantic, which makes her even more worthy of support.

Not difficult to choose three films this time, but each one is true to Ramsay's style:

- *Ratcatcher* **(1999):** Sounds on paper like a typical 'Brit grit' flick, but it goes off into such weird and unexpected directions that Ramsay's unusual talent was evident from the word go. It's a film of few words where the images speak for themselves. Look out for the mouse that flies to the moon in a balloon.

- *Morvern Callar* **(2002):** An abstract and expressionistic film about a young woman living in rural Scotland who finds unexpected financial freedom and squanders it. Samantha Morton is as magnetic as ever, and the film showcases Ramsay's careful attention to soundscapes as well as visual beauty.

✔ *We Need to Talk about Kevin* **(2011):** With an American setting, a bigger budget and well-known character actors, this film seems superficially a more commercial prospect. But in Ramsay's hands it stays true to the pitch blackness of the original source novel. It has amazing performances and touches of the great horror movies of the 1960s and 1970s.

Abbas Kiarostami

Middle Eastern cinema is a particular blind spot on the imaginary world-cinema map. Regional conflicts of previous decades and the negative portrayal of Islamic nations in the West post-9/11 certainly haven't helped. So Iranian Abbas Kiarostami's understated but beautifully constructed films are a wonderful surprise. His work is embedded in a culture unrecognisable from the images of the region that Western news channels show, and all his films are accessible and engaging.

If you don't know where to start with Kiarostami, try these:

✔ *Taste of Cherry* **(Ta'm-e guilass) (1997):** The unexpectedly life-affirming story of a middle-aged man attempting to find someone to help him commit suicide. The film's structure is minimalist but effective, and its cinematography has a low-key beauty. The ending is sure to get you thinking.

✔ *Ten* **(Dah) (2002):** Simply ten sequences featuring exchanges between a driver and the passengers in her car. Through these miniature portraits, the film illuminates the role of women and family in contemporary Iran. Watch for the mother's brilliant reaction to her son's extended outburst.

✔ *Certified Copy* **(Copie conforme) (2010):** Kiarostami's first film set outside Iran is an examination of the relationship between a male writer and a woman, played by French star Juliette Binoche. The exact nature of their relationship is unclear; they may be lovers, former partners or just strangers engaging in elaborate role-play. Either way, what unfolds is intriguing.

John Waters

John Waters is a true auteur of the underground. In his early career, he was inspired by the American avant-garde films of Kenneth Anger (see Chapter 7) and Russ Meyer's exploitation movies. His trashy aesthetic of bad taste reached its zenith in his films of the 1970s, which attracted cult audiences on the 'midnight movie' circuit in the US.

As an openly gay film-maker, his films predate the 'New Queer Cinema' of the 1990s by some 20 years (see Chapter 15 for more on queer film theory). In his later career he found some commercial success and looked to have mellowed. But his recent choices indicate that he continues to do his own thing whether it brings him to wider attention or not.

- ✔ *Pink Flamingos* (1972): Perhaps the perfect example of a cult film in its mode of production, style and reception. It became infamous for a scene in which his provocative drag-queen star Divine appears to eat dog excrement. If you're not shocked, you may need some therapy.

- ✔ *Hairspray* (1988): Began to bring Waters to a wider audience, and later became a hit Broadway musical and film remake. Here Divine plays the mother of Ricki Lake's Tracy, a plump teenager who wants to dance on TV. *Hairspray* is the John Waters movie you can watch with your mother.

- ✔ *Cecil B. Demented* (2000): Proved that the media-friendly Waters could still split critics right down the middle. Although this satire of independent film-making didn't perform well on cinema screens, its 'failure' only endears it to Waters. He describes all his movies as like his children – and this one is arguably his most mentally challenged.

Christine Vachon

I include Christine Vachon, a producer rather than a director, on this list of underrated film-makers because her role as a creative producer challenges the auteurist assumption that the director is the only voice worth listening to (see Chapter 14). Her list of credits contains many of the most significant films of the industry sector known as 'Indie-wood', that blurry zone between independent and mainstream film-making.

Although the number of female film directors is still too small, Vachon serves as a reminder of the many other vital roles that have to be filled in this highly collaborative industry.

- ✔ *Go Fish* (1994): As a 'lesbian rom-com', this film signalled an important shift for queer film-makers towards more mainstream projects. Director and writer Rose Troche later became a force behind the hit TV drama *The L Word* (2004–9).

- ✔ *Boys Don't Cry* (1999): The harrowing tale of a transgender teenager with a show-stopping (and Oscar-winning) performance from Hilary Swank. Vachon was crucial in financing and finding distribution for this extremely risky project.

- ✔ *Far From Heaven* (2002): A glossy melodrama set in the 1950s and shot in the style of Douglas Sirk. Vachon has produced all Todd Haynes's films as well as his TV adaptation of *Mildred Pierce* (2011), demonstrating that partnerships are key in independent film-making.

Andrei Tarkovsky

Cinema has an important place in the history of Soviet culture during the 20th century (see Chapter 13). In its earliest years, Soviet film-makers such as Sergei Eisenstein helped to define the cinematic avant-garde.

Andrei Tarkovsky's position, poised between Soviet and European cinema, makes him the major film-maker of the Cold War era. With his elliptical, enigmatic narratives and steady pacing, he's a key influence upon the so-called slow cinema movement of contemporary art film. But he also plays with film genre, particularly sci-fi, in ways that bring him closer to cult film status than many of his peers.

✔ *Solaris (Solyaris)* **(1972):** This film takes science fiction seriously. Many scholars see it as a Soviet mirror image of Kubrick's *2001: A Space Odyssey* (1968), although its central idea – of a planet that creates hallucinations of mental desires – has striking similarities to an old episode of *Star Trek* (1966–9). Steven Soderbergh remade *Solaris* in 2002.

✔ *Stalker* **(1979):** Another sci-fi film with such an odd visual experience that it veers towards the territory occupied by David Lynch and Jean-Pierre Jeunet. The story, about a future dystopia and a mythical redemptive space, is impossible to unravel, but it looks and sounds so interesting that you don't care.

✔ *The Sacrifice (Offret)* **(1986):** Tarkovsky's last film, made in Sweden, is long, slow and meditative. If you're an impatient viewer, probably best to stay away. But why rush around all the time?

Wong Kar-wai

Wong Kar-wai's films look gorgeous. You perhaps expect that from contemporary art cinema, but you may not also expect a rollicking pace, eye-popping colours and exquisite costume design. Wong began his career in the hectic, productive genre films of the Hong Kong film industry. His early films have a reckless, improvised energy, whereas his more recent work has gone in the opposite direction, towards painstakingly choreography and careful composition. He directed one film in America (*My Blueberry Nights* (2007)) but has since returned to work in Hong Kong.

Here are three Wong films to get you started:

✔ *As Tears Go By (Wong gok ka moon)* **(1988):** Wong's directorial debut is a gangster film displaying his genre film training. But it also contains moments of visual experimentation that signal his artistic ambitions.

- ✔ *Chungking Express (Chung Hing sam lam)* (1994): Brought Wong to the attention of Western festival and art-house audiences – somewhat ironically because he made it quickly and cheaply. It contains a visual device where characters stand frozen in time as crowds rush past them, which many independent films have imitated.

- ✔ *In the Mood for Love (Fa yeung nin wa)* (2000): Cemented Wong's international reputation with a delicate story of impossible love between two married neighbours. Wong uses bold colours, slow motion and lush orchestral music to reach a romantic intensity that rivals Hollywood melodrama.

Chapter 20

Ten Tips for Becoming a Film Student

In This Chapter

▶ Digging deeper into film

▶ Developing good viewing and thinking habits

▶ Being passionate – but also open-minded and critical – about film

*I*f this book achieves anything, I hope it whets your appetite for film studies and leaves you wanting more. Perhaps you may decide to take the plunge and attend a one-off film education event at a film festival or sign up for an evening class in film appreciation, or even pursue a university degree in the subject. In that case, you will want to know how to behave, what to talk about and (most importantly) how to impress your fellow students and tutors.

This chapter gives you some handy suggestions on ways to increase your film knowledge and engage more deeply with the films you love, as well as how to fit in and how to stand out from the cinema crowd.

Going to the Pictures Often

This recommendation may sound blindingly obvious, but you can easily get out of the habit of going to the cinema, particularly when money and time are too tight to mention. Plus, these days you have a range of different ways in which you can consume films (see Chapter 16 for examples).

But I strongly encourage you to make the effort to get out and visit the cinema for a host of reasons. For example, many films simply demand the biggest screen and best sound system in order to make the most of their pleasures. Watching a movie such as *Transformers* (2007) anywhere other than the multiplex severely diminishes the experience. 3D may have its critics, but word of mouth drove the box-office success of Alfonso Cuarón's *Gravity* (2013), with viewers insisting that this film worked stunningly well with the extra depth only possible in a state-of-the-art viewing room.

The biggest, loudest and most spectacular movies aren't the only ones to benefit from the cinema experience. Emotional responses define many genres of film (see Chapter 5), including horror (fear, disgust), comedy (laughter) and tragic romances (weepies). A crowd often magnifies and amplifies these emotions. Of course, the effects of a group emotional experience can work both ways – just as a cinema full of people laughing together is a joyful experience, a comedy met with absolute silence can be excruciating.

Regular cinema-going also allows you to plug into the current trends and keep up with the latest releases, something that's essential for the serious film student. Viewing films in the cinema is still the best way to see them as soon as possible, which enhances your contributions to discussions. You can be the one who's dazzlingly incisive and current.

Yes, cinema-going nowadays has a certain retro pleasure, but a bit of nostalgia is no bad thing. Many independent cinemas capitalise on the power of the experience, providing lovingly restored environments that aim to transport you back to the golden age of cinema. This approach provides an emotional and physical connection to cinema history that you can't get from reading books or watching a digital recording on a television screen or other device. Sit back and enjoy.

Making Sure You See the Classics

What makes one film better than another and what makes a classic? Why is one movie remembered and revered while another is dismissed and forgotten? As a film student you're going to start answering profound questions such as these – and continue to answer them throughout your life.

To be taken seriously, an art form must offer up a core body of works that are untouchably and unarguably great. Classic films form part of the film studies *canon,* a set of *texts* (see Chapter 13) that in some way define the entire field. Certain gatekeepers (critics, artists, scholars) formed the film studies canon over a period of time and often for positive reasons, such as to assist the argument over whether film is an art form at all, and whether directors can be considered artists (see Chapter 14). Unfortunately, this approach grants too much power to a self-selecting group of people who dictate their definition of quality to everyone else. It creates a self-fulfilling prophecy: only those films that the group designates as worthy are archived and restored and therefore continue to be available. Many films from cinema's early years are lost forever because nobody thought they were worth preserving.

You're right to be critical about the canon-forming process, but don't throw the baby out with the bath water. Sharing a canon of films can be a useful starting point, because these films provide instant common ground between students and scholars. After all, you're likely to meet interesting people from different regions, cultures or parts of the world when you begin to study film.

You may also struggle to follow critical discussions if you've not seen the most commonly referenced canonic films. When a debate goes off-topic and someone starts rhapsodising about Orson Welles's use of deep focus in *Citizen Kane* (1941), how Hitchcock creates the jangling suspense in *Psycho* (1960) or De Sica's heart-breaking depiction of poverty in *Bicycle Thieves* (1948), do *you* want to have to admit that you've not seen it? Also, at some point in your studies, you're almost certain to encounter patronising film buffs. ('What? You haven't seen *Rashomon* – what are they teaching you?') Don't give them a way in.

Watching and Re-watching

When you first set out to study cinema, the sheer number of films waiting for you can be daunting. Try really hard to resist the impulse to watch (or even skip through) many films very quickly in order to say that you've seen them. If you're going to really understand how a particular film works, you have to be ready to absorb it, and you can't do that after just one viewing.

Don't worry that re-viewing kills your enjoyment of a film. If you use a sensible strategy, quite the opposite is true. For your first viewing of a film you want to study, give yourself up to the immediately accessible pleasures of story, tension and performance. Just enjoy it! You can concentrate on elements such as sound or visual style on second and subsequent viewings.

Consciously choosing what you want to take from a particular viewing is much more productive than trying to take in everything from one sitting. Focusing on a specific aspect or two also means that boredom due to plot familiarity isn't a problem. If you're busy noting the precise use of camera angles and framing, you probably aren't even noticing the plot any longer.

Going back to a film that meant something to you at a younger age after a few years can be highly rewarding. When you watch your favourite childhood films as an adult, you often find that their meanings are completely different to how you remember them. Clearly you – not the film – have changed. But this realisation is a profound reminder of just how personal and changeable the film-viewing experience is, even for each individual film fan.

Reading about Film in Your Free Time

If you take a film studies course, you'll have some fairly heavy film-criticism and film-theory set texts to read. In this case you may appreciate the chance to chill out with some lighter reading, such as biographies and memoirs of legendary film-makers and stars.

When you take a book on holiday to read by the pool, you're probably not going to pack, say, Marxist philosopher Slavoj Žižek's latest page-turner. You're more likely to speed through a gossipy memoir or well-illustrated 'making of' your favourite movie. Although less challenging than textbooks, these tomes at least put your reading time to some film-related use and you probably find that family members buy you them for Christmas anyway.

Film-related biographies and memoirs can be more than just entertaining. By following the course of a person's life, you can uncover much more, because humans are hard-wired to understand people, not lists of dates. With big personalities and supersized egos finding a natural home in the entertainment industry, the people in question tend to be pretty interesting too.

You need to try and maintain your critical perspective as you read this lighter material. Memory features whims, fancies and plain old mistakes, and people tend to embellish stories until they end up connecting only loosely to actual events. But these human truths can make such books all the more interesting, because the lies people choose to tell are often more revealing than the truth.

Some great examples of entertaining film memoirs include:

- ✔ **Julia Phillips, *You'll Never Eat Lunch in this Town Again* (Random House, 1991):** A notorious exposé of Hollywood's bad behaviour in the 1970s and 80s, written by one of its worst-behaved female producers.

- ✔ **David Lynch, *Catching the Big Fish* (Tarcher, 2007):** A gloriously strange combination of meditation self-help book and film-making memoir that is also available as a fantastic audiobook read by Lynch himself.

- ✔ **Farley Granger, *Include Me Out* (St Martin's Griffin, 2008):** A fascinating insight into behind-closed-doors Hollywood bisexuality by the seriously handsome Granger.

Thinking about What Films Mean to You

When you're passionate about film, you're likely to have one or two movies that genuinely changed the way you think or feel about something really important, such as the horrors of war in *The Deer Hunter* (1978), or the trappings of consumer culture in *Fight Club* (1999). Turning your critical faculties towards the films that mean the most to you is sometimes difficult, but doing so can provide invaluable insights into how cinema works.

For example, you probably have at least one film that's practically guaranteed to make you cry. This movie isn't necessarily a melodramatic tear-jerker such as *Beaches* (1988) or *Terms of Endearment* (1983). It can just as easily be a small moment in a family film, such as *E.T. the Extra Terrestrial* (1982) or Pixar's *Up* (2009). Okay, I admit it; these two are my particular weaknesses.

Ask yourself the tricky question: why does this film really get to me on a deep emotional level? The killer moments are often about death or loss or loneliness – all fundamental human experiences that everyone struggles with from time to time. In this light, theoretical claims about cinema's connection with death (such as those made by Andre Bazin or Laura Mulvey) suddenly seem less pretentious and more reasonable. (See Chapter 1 for more on breaking through your emotions to a critical position.)

Attempting to understand your primal, subconscious reactions to film is only one part of the picture. Cinematic narrative exposes you to ways of thinking about and behaving in the world that can make a lasting impression. Some Marxist critics argue that this influence is dangerous ideological control on behalf of the capitalist elite (see Chapter 13 for more Marx). Do try and understand such critiques of cinema's seductive power, but don't let them ruin your enjoyment of films made by people with different kinds of viewpoints.

Joining a Film Studies Tribe

One of the best things about becoming a film student is that you can try on different identities until you find one that suits you. When you start officially studying film, you may think that all film students are the same, but you quickly realise that various sub-cultures form and flourish under these conditions. The following are just a few of the types I've come to know and love as a film studies tutor:

- ✔ **Cinéastes:** Model themselves on 1960s-style intellectuals. Beyond the black turtleneck sweaters, endless cigarettes and retro geek glasses, they tend to overemphasise the pronunciation of French words such as *homage* and *auteur*. However, cinéastes are often the students who get the highest grades for theoretical essays, so they have the last chuckle.

- ✔ **Movie geeks:** Revere heroes such as Steven Spielberg and Peter Jackson and wear fan T-shirts and baseball caps. They may have beards (if male). They almost certainly spend way too much time ploughing through DVD box sets of American TV shows. However, if you need a world-beating quiz team, just ask the movie geeks. Also, be nice to them, because they often end up wielding power by going into blogging or print journalism.

✔ **Film-makers:** Generally consider themselves too cool to hang out with movie geeks, although they often start out as geeks themselves. They spend all their time discussing lenses, lighting rigs and how 4K is the new HD (basically, sharper and sharper images). They have to work closely in teams (see Chapter 2), which means they develop invaluable social skills such as crisis management and conflict resolution.

If you fancy joining one of these tribes, or creating your own, now's the perfect time to develop your interests into obsessions: write blogs, make documentaries or go to midnight screenings of *The Rocky Horror Picture Show* in fishnet stockings. Get stuck in, whatever your style.

Not Taking Awards Too Seriously

Awards ceremonies are great fun (or at least they can be if they don't go on for too long). The veneer of authority, the exciting competition between films and film-makers, and the glamorous visual appeal can seduce film fans. But after you become a sophisticated film student, do you admit to loving the Oscars – or feign cool indifference?

Well, you can do both. By all means enjoy awards, just don't for a minute take them too seriously. In theory they're democratic endeavours with experts or audiences voting and promises to celebrate excellence over mediocrity. In practice, awards are open to manipulation by the biggest companies or the best marketers. Otherwise why would Hollywood spend millions of dollars every year promoting films 'For your consideration' just before the Oscars?

Yet awards can be a fantastic help to up-and-coming film-makers, actors and technical wizards, because they provide a stamp of approval from the wider industry and a large amount of cheap publicity. In recent decades, Oscars have kick-started the careers of animator Nick Park (*Wallace and Gromit*), actor Anna Paquin (*The Piano*) and director Andrea Arnold (*Wasp*). At the same time, the major awards exclude the vast majority of films and film-makers from outside the Anglophone countries.

And oh, the acceptance speeches – those moments when stars are made or careers blighted. Actors are at their most apparently vulnerable during these ceremonies and so have to let the mask slip just enough to show that they're human after all. Movie history is littered with atrocious gaffs, from Sally Field screaming 'You like me!' to James Cameron's 'I'm the king of the world!' No, you can't take this stuff seriously, but it's certainly entertaining.

Attending Film Festivals and Events

You can attend a huge number and variety of film festivals these days – from the large industry-focused Cannes, Berlin and Sundance, to the smaller specialised events for particular types of film (such as shorts) or passionate fan cultures (for example, horror film festivals). *Film exhibitors* (that is, anyone who screens films in public) are also getting more creative with ways to make cinema-going into special events, with screenings in special locations or with accompanying activities.

Festivals are great opportunities for film students, and so get along to as many as possible. Some aim to provide a feast of the best new commercial and independent cinema to audiences, such as the London or Toronto Film Festivals. Here you can see a diverse range of films, from features to shorts to artists' film, which open your eyes to the incredible variety of film-making practice around the world.

Even more interesting are the *industry-focused festivals* such as Cannes, which aren't just showcases for great films – they're also a marketplace where distributors and film-makers strike deals. Obviously getting into this type of event is a bit harder, but if you're creative you can sometimes peek behind the curtain. Try offering your services as a volunteer, because the festival economy runs on a mixture of goodwill and cheap champagne.

In general, festivals and special film events are great spaces to recharge your passion for cinema. Nothing quite compares to the thrill of finding yourself in *that* screening where the hidden gem of the festival is discovered and the audience applauds rapturously as the credits roll. Or looking over your shoulder and realising that you're sitting a few seats away from one of your favourite directors, who's enjoying the film just like you. Both these memorable moments have happened to me, and they can happen to you too.

Developing a Love for Subtitles

Some people *hate* subtitles: 'If I wanted to read,' they moan, 'I'd pick up a book.' (For some segments of the audience with visual or specific learning difficulties, subtitles can be a nightmare.) But if your reading level is around normal, you can get used to subtitles . . . if you want to. If you just don't want to engage with foreign-language films, however, that's a different matter.

As a film student, you have to open your mind to opportunities outside English-speaking cinema. Therefore the only alternative to subtitling is dubbing, which does happen with commercial cinema in many parts of the world. To British and American ears, however, dubbing sounds ridiculous. Unless the person dubbed is Bruce Lee, and then for some reason it feels fine.

You can train your brain to handle subtitles more effectively: to start, try switching on the titles for English-language films and TV. This experience is likely to be immensely irritating at first, but then suddenly something quite strange happens and everything clicks. Your brain gets so good at scanning the words while watching the images that you forget you're reading while watching. You even sort of remember the film in your own language.

Subtitles are also a great way of introducing yourself to new languages: for example, try watching English-language films with French subtitles on, and vice versa. Some evidence even suggests that subtitled TV helps children learn to read more quickly in their own language. See, Dad, I told you watching TV was good for me!

Being Proud of Your Knowledge

Despite film studies being well established as an academic discipline in most of the world's top universities, film students still tend to get some bad press. People wheel out the old 'Mickey Mouse studies' gibes, along with disparaging jokes about apparently poor job prospects. But increasing evidence (and my own personal experience of staying in touch with students after graduation) shows that this prejudice is simply untrue. Film and media graduates are doing as well as, if not better than, the average at securing work quickly after graduation, and a good proportion end up in careers that are related to their degree in one way or another.

As a film student you have at least as good a chance as other graduates at going into creative, interesting careers. Even if you don't directly use your film knowledge, the skills you gain in research, group work and communication, especially writing, are much prized by employers. If you discover how to shoot, edit and upload a simple digital video, you're likely to be even more in demand, because many non-media jobs now involve video production for corporate communications and websites.

But perhaps even more important than all these practical skills is the critical attitude that film studies enhances. With a constantly enquiring, questioning mind, you can take on anything that the information age throws at you. So be proud of your film studies training. You're getting ready for the rest of your life by doing something that you love, and that's a great place to start.

Index

best boy, 42
Beverly Hills Cop (film), 194
Bicycle Thieves (film), 233
Bienvenue chez le Ch'tis (film), 227
Big Brother (TV programme), 65
Bigelow, Kathryn (film-maker), 303–304
binary oppositions, 84, 277–278
Binoche, Juliette (actress), 60
The Birth, the Life, and the Death of Christ (film), 364
Black Girl (film), 365
Blackton, J. Stuart (author), 128
Blade Runner (film), 358–359
blockbusters, 191–193
blocking, 36
Blood Simple (film), 198
Bollywood, 61–62, 249–251, 252–254
Bond, James (film character), 217–218
Bonnie and Clyde (film), 15, 190
Bordwell, David (author), 17, 79, 156, 320–321, 323
Bourdieu, Pierre (sociologist), 212
Bowles, Simon (art director), 41
Box, John (art director), 41
Boys Don't Cry (film), 368
Brakhage, Stan (film-maker), 37, 141, 150
Brando, Marlon (actor), 58–59
Brazil, cinema from, 254–256
Breathless (film), 357

Britain
about, 201
adapting great works, 212–215
animation from, 138
Brit-grit, 202–207
connections between TV and film, 207–211
film stars in, 60
Harry Potter franchise, 218–220
James Bond franchise, 217–218
producing local films, 215–217
British Film Institute (BFI), 202–203
Brokeback Mountain (film), 38, 39
bromance, 120–121
Brookside (TV programme), 206
Brosnan, Pierce (actor), 218
buddy films, 120
Buñuel, Luis (director), 237
Butch Cassidy and the Sundance Kid (film), 27
Butler, Judith (gender theorist), 318–319

• C •

The Cabbage Fairy (film), 364
The Cabinet of Dr. Caligari (film), 153
Cagney, James (actor), 51
Cahiers du Cinéma (film journal), 16
camera movement, 20
camp, 319
Campbell, Joseph (author), 29
Cannes Film Festival, 227–228
Cannon, 194

Cardiff, Jack (cinematographer), 36, 37, 167
Carolco Pictures, 194
Carroll, Noël (philosopher), 323
cartoons, 126, 145–146
Casablanca (film), 76, 354–355
Catching the Big Fish (Lynch), 374
Catholicism, 237–238
Catmull, Ed (computer scientist), 135
causality, 81–82
Cecil B. Demented (film), 368
Cecilia (film), 257
cel animation, 124
celebrity, 63–65
celluloid strips, 328–329
censorship, 238
Centre National de la Cinématographie (CNC), 226
Certified Copy (film), 367
Chakravorty, Gayatri (critic), 312
Chanan, Michael (historian), 257
Chang Suk-ping, William (editor), 43
Changing Express (film), 370
Channel 4, 209–210
Chaplin, Charlie (film-maker), 26, 49, 77, 286
characters, roles of in narrative, 81–84
Chariots of Fire (film), 214
Cheat Sheet (website), 4, 17
chiaroscuro lighting techniques, 109
chick flicks, 120
Chion, Michael (sound theorist), 86, 349

Poem Field (film), 146
poetic documentaries, 161
poetic realism, 225
poetry, 205–207
politics, film and, 21–22
Ponting, Herbert (film-maker), 202
post-colonialism, 311–312
post-feminism, 316–318
The Postman Always Rings Twice (film), 117
postmodernism, 312–319
post-production, 43–46
post-structuralism, 308–312
post-theory, 319–323
Post-Theory: Reconstructing Film Studies (Bordwell), 320–321
Potter, Sally (director), 155
Powell, Michael (director), 293–294
Pressburger, Emeric (director), 293–294
Pretty Woman (film), 119
primacy effect, 323
Prince, Stephen (theorist), 266
principal photography, 36
private lives, living, 63–64
The Private Life of Henry VIII (film), 214
producers
   importance of, 31–32
   independent, 34–35
   independent producers, 34–35
   studio work, 32–33
producers, as component of Hollywood studio system, 180
production, 40–42, 92
production cycles, 92
pro-filmic event, 160
propaganda film, 21, 167
Psycho (film), 155

psychoanalysis, in sci-fi, 112
psychoanalytic film theory, 117, 278–282
Pulp Fiction (film), 30, 359
puns, 126

● *Q* ●

qualitative data, 10
quantitative data, 10
queer theory, 56, 318–319

● *R* ●

race, 22–23, 134
Rai, Aishwarya (actress), 62
Ramsay, Lynne (director), 207, 366–367
Rank Organisation, 33, 60
rasa, 251
Ratcatcher (film), 366
ratings system, 190
real life, comparing documentary film to, 158–160
realism, 158, 265–267
reality TV stars, 65
rear projection, 71
Rear Window (film), 356
reception theory, 267–268
redrafts, 28
Reeves, Keanu (actor), 57–58
reflexive documentaries, 161
Reisz, Karel (critic), 203
relatability, as film-star quality, 49
release window, 334–335
Remember icon, 4
repetition, 94–95
representation, 22–23, 112
reviews, writing, 14–15
Reville, Alma (screenwriter), 26

Richardson, Tony (critic), 203, 204, 205
RKO, 182
The Road (film), 233
romantic comedy, 118–121
Romantic movement, 284
Rombes, Nicholas (theorist), 330, 350–351
Rome Open City (film), 233
Rosenman, Leonard (composer), 45
rotoscoping, 124
Rowling, JK (author), 218–220
Rozsa, Miklos (composer), 45
Rushmore (film), 198
Russo, Vito (film-maker), 56

● *S* ●

The Sacrifice (film), 369
Said, Edward (literary theorist), 311
Santos, Nelson Pereira dos (Cinema Novo movement leader), 243
Sarris, Andrew (critic), 286, 288
Saturday Night and Sunday Morning (film), 204
Saussure, Ferdinand de (linguist), 274–275
scenes, 68–69, 73–74
Schatz, Thomas (scholar), 94
Schoonmaker, Thelma (editor), 43
Schwarzenegger, Arnold (actor), 48
sci-fi, 110–114
scopophilia, 281
Scorsese, Martin (producer), 197, 296–297, 340
Screenplay (Field), 29

About the Author

Dr James Cateridge is Senior Lecturer in Film Studies at Oxford Brookes University. He had such a good time studying film as an undergraduate at Warwick University that he went back to do an MA and a PhD at the University of East Anglia. In between he worked for Columbia Tristar and the Arts Council of England. Now as a very lucky film scholar he gets to research and write about the films that he loves, as well as subjecting unfortunate students to his personal taste in movies. These are mostly British, but he doesn't discriminate. His film geek obsessions include but are no means limited to: 90s Brit flicks, Hammer horrors (especially those starring Oliver Reed), and trying to figure out why film tourists visit Oxford.

Dedication

This book is dedicated to all the film studies scholars and teachers who have inspired me over the years, to my peers and colleagues, and to my students.

Thanks to my amazing friends and family for keeping me writing, and to the editors at Wiley for their expert advice.

To Stuart and Riley: there's no place like home.

Publisher's Acknowledgements

We're proud of this book; please send us your comments at `http://dummies.custhelp.com`. For other comments, please contact our Customer Care Department within the U.S. at 877-762-2974, outside the U.S. at (001) 317-572-3993, or fax 317-572-4002.

Some of the people who helped bring this book to market include the following:

Acquisitions, Editorial and Vertical Websites

Project Editor: Steve Edwards

Commissioning Editor: Ben Kemble

Development Editor: Brian Kramer

Copy Editor: Andy Finch

Technical Reviewer: Hannah Hamad

Proofreader: James Harrison

Publisher: Miles Kendall

Front Cover Photos: © iStock.com/Sashkinw

Composition Services

Project Coordinator: Melissa Cossell

Take Dummies with you everywhere you go!

Whether you're excited about e-books, want more from the web, must have your mobile apps, or swept up in social media, Dummies makes everything easier.

FOR DUMMIES
A Wiley Brand

BUSINESS

978-1-118-73077-5

978-1-118-44349-1

978-1-119-97527-4

MUSIC

978-1-119-94276-4

978-0-470-97799-6

978-0-470-49644-2

DIGITAL PHOTOGRAPHY

978-1-118-09203-3

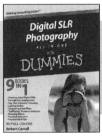

978-0-470-76878-5

978-1-118-00472-2

Algebra I For Dummies
978-0-470-55964-2

Anatomy & Physiology For Dummies, 2nd Edition
978-0-470-92326-9

Asperger's Syndrome For Dummies
978-0-470-66087-4

Basic Maths For Dummies
978-1-119-97452-9

Body Language For Dummies, 2nd Edition
978-1-119-95351-7

Bookkeeping For Dummies, 3rd Edition
978-1-118-34689-1

British Sign Language For Dummies
978-0-470-69477-0

Cricket for Dummies, 2nd Edition
978-1-118-48032-8

Currency Trading For Dummies, 2nd Edition
978-1-118-01851-4

Cycling For Dummies
978-1-118-36435-2

Diabetes For Dummies, 3rd Edition
978-0-470-97711-8

eBay For Dummies, 3rd Edition
978-1-119-94122-4

Electronics For Dummies All-in-One For Dummies
978-1-118-58973-1

English Grammar For Dummies
978-0-470-05752-0

French For Dummies, 2nd Edition
978-1-118-00464-7

Guitar For Dummies, 3rd Edition
978-1-118-11554-1

IBS For Dummies
978-0-470-51737-6

Keeping Chickens For Dummies
978-1-119-99417-6

Knitting For Dummies, 3rd Edition
978-1-118-66151-2

FOR DUMMIES

A Wiley Brand

SELF-HELP

978-0-470-66541-1

978-1-119-99264-6

978-0-470-66086-7

LANGUAGES

978-0-470-68815-1

978-1-119-97959-3

978-0-470-69477-0

HISTORY

978-0-470-68792-5

978-0-470-74783-4

978-0-470-97819-1

Laptops For Dummies 5th Edition
978-1-118-11533-6

**Management For Dummies,
2nd Edition**
978-0-470-97769-9

Nutrition For Dummies, 2nd Edition
978-0-470-97276-2

Office 2013 For Dummies
978-1-118-49715-9

Organic Gardening For Dummies
978-1-119-97706-3

Origami Kit For Dummies
978-0-470-75857-1

Overcoming Depression For Dummies
978-0-470-69430-5

Physics I For Dummies
978-0-470-90324-7

Project Management For Dummies
978-0-470-71119-4

Psychology Statistics For Dummies
978-1-119-95287-9

**Renting Out Your Property For Dummies,
3rd Edition**
978-1-119-97640-0

Rugby Union For Dummies, 3rd Edition
978-1-119-99092-5

Stargazing For Dummies
978-1-118-41156-8

**Teaching English as a Foreign Language
For Dummies**
978-0-470-74576-2

Time Management For Dummies
978-0-470-77765-7

Training Your Brain For Dummies
978-0-470-97449-0

Voice and Speaking Skills For Dummies
978-1-119-94512-3

Wedding Planning For Dummies
978-1-118-69951-5

WordPress For Dummies, 5th Edition
978-1-118-38318-6

Think you can't learn it in a day? Think again!

The *In a Day* e-book series from *For Dummies* gives you quick and easy access to learn a new skill, brush up on a hobby, or enhance your personal or professional life — all in a day. Easy!

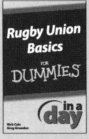